Phonics and Word Recognition

Grade **3**

MW00388216

TABLE OF CONTENTS

About Benchmark Advance Intervention

Benchmark Advance Intervention is intended for students who need extra support to master grade-level standards. It offers reteaching and additional practice to reinforce instruction in the core program. Benchmark Advance Intervention provides direct instruction of the Reading Standards for Foundational Skills, Kindergarten – Grade 5, as outlined in the Common Core Standards. The standards are addressed as shown below.

Kindergarten	Grade 1	Grade 2	Grade 3	Grades 4-6
Print Concepts	Print Concepts	Print Concepts	Print Concepts	Phonics and Word Recognition
Phonological Awareness	Phonological Awareness	Phonological Awareness	Phonological Awareness	Fluency
Phonics and Word Recognition	Phonics and Word Recognition	Phonics and Word Recognition	Phonics and Word Recognition	
Fluency	Fluency	Fluency	Fluency	

At Kindergarten through Grade 3, individual grade-level packages of lessons and blackline masters address all of the reading foundation (RF) standards. An additional package for Grades 4 through 6 addresses the Phonics and Word Recognition and Fluency standards for Grades 2 through 5. In addition, each of the packages at K-3 includes lessons and blackline masters to address the RF standards presented in previous grades. In this way, teachers can address the needs of students at each student's instructional level—whether at/near grade level or below.

The program offers skill-focused sequential and systematic instruction that is parallel to instruction in the core program. Each lesson is designed to target a specific skill that needs bolstering as revealed through program assessments.

It can be implemented flexibly in small groups or to individual students. Each lesson is designed to be completed in 15 minutes.

Lesson Structure

All of the phonics and word recognition lessons in *Benchmark Advance Intervention* follow a consistent instructional design that offers explicit skills instruction and a gradual release model to scaffold student learning.

- The side column at the start of every lesson furnishes the information teachers need to manage student learning.
- The target standard or standards appear at the beginning of each lesson.
- The specific lesson objective states what students will be able to do after completing the lesson.
- The metacognitive strategy increases awareness of the strategies students use as they learn.
- The essential academic language and materials that students will use in the lesson is listed.
- Every lesson offers a reminder of the pre-requisite skills that students need to fully understand the lesson.

The instructional lessons offer consistent and explicit instruction that helps students focus on the specific lesson objectives.

- The Introduce section and State Learning Goal set the learning goal for the lesson.
- The Teach and Model sections of the lesson feature direct instruction and teacher modeling including phonemic awareness and sound/spelling correspondence.
- The Practice and Apply sections offer guided and independent practice of the focus skill. In most lessons, these sections also include practice writing spelling words.
- The Conclusion gives students an opportunity to restate what they've learned in the lesson.
- The Home Connection links the lesson to at-home practice within the family setting.

Every lesson ends with a point-of-use formative assessment so teachers can evaluate whether students have mastered the target skills. Intervention 2 suggestions provide alternative teaching ideas for working with students who need further support.

The blackline masters that accompany the lessons provide practice and application opportunities to promote standards mastery.

Corrective Feedback

Inherent in the teaching profession is the need to make corrections. In both structural and communicative approaches to language teaching and learning, feedback is viewed as a means of fostering learner motivation and ensuring linguistic accuracy (Ellis, 2009). The purpose of the feedback is to close the gap between the student's current learning status and the lesson goals (Sadler, 1989). Students can receive feedback in three ways: from their teachers, from peers, and through their own self-assessment.

Formative assessment is a process that teachers and students use during instruction. It provides feedback to inform ongoing teaching and learning approaches. Corrective feedback is also an essential feature of language development instruction. Teachers provide students with judiciously selected corrective feedback on language usage in ways that are transparent and meaningful to students. Overcorrection or arbitrary corrective feedback is avoided.

Corrective feedback is information given to learners regarding a linguistic error they have made (Loewen, 2012; Sheen, 2007). The feedback information can consist of any one or all of the following:

(a) **an indication that an error has been committed,**

    (b) **provision of the correct target language form, or**

    (c) **metalinguistic information about the nature of the error.**

Corrective feedback can be:
Explicit Corrective feedback overtly draws the learner's attention to the error made. **Implicit** Corrective feedback focuses the learner's attention without overtly informing the learner that he/she has made an error or interrupting the flow of interaction.

Corrective feedback in the form of negotiating for meaning can help learners notice their errors and create meaningful connections, thus aiding acquisition (2003). It is important to emphasize that language learners can only self-correct if they possess the necessary linguistic knowledge (Ellis, 2009).

One solution sometimes advocated to this problem is to conduct corrective feedback as a two-stage process: first encourage self- correction and then, if that fails, provide the correction (Doughty and Varela, 1998).

Corrective Feedback Strategies

	IMPLICIT Attracts learner's attention without overtly informing the learner that he/she has made an error or interrupting the flow of interaction.	EXPLICIT Tries to overtly draw the learner's attention to the error made.
INPUT PROVIDING: **Correct form is given to students.**	**RECAST** The corrector incorporates the content words of the immediately preceding incorrect utterance and changes and corrects the utterance in some way (e.g., phonological, syntactic, morphological or lexical). L: I went school. T: You went to school?	**EXPLICIT CORRECTION** The corrector indicates an error has been committed, identifies the error and provides the correction. L: We will go on May. T: Not on May, in May. T: We will go in May.
OUTPUT PROMPTING: **The student is prompted to self-correct**	**REPETITION** The corrector repeats the learner utterance highlighting the error by means of emphatic stress. L: I will showed you. T: I will *show* you. L: I will show you.	**METALINGUISTIC EXPLANATION** Corrector provides explanation for the errors that have been made. L: two duck T: Do you remember how to show more than one duck? L: ducks T: Yes, you remember that we need to add "s" at the end of a noun to show the plural form.
	CLARIFICATION REQUEST The corrector indicates that he/she has not understood what the learner said. L: on the it go T: Can you please tell me again? T: Do you mean "it goes in your desk?"	**ELICITATION** The corrector repeats part of the learner utterance but not the erroneous part and uses rising intonation to signal the learner should complete it. L: I don't think won't rain. T: I don't think it …… (will) rain.
		PARALINGUISTIC SIGNAL The corrector uses a gesture or facial expression to indicate that the learner has made an error. L: Yesterday I go to the movies. T: (gestures with right forefinger over left shoulder to indicate past).

Adapted from: Ellis, Rod. "Corrective Feedback and Teacher Development." L2 Journal, volume 1, (2009).

Recommendations for English Learners

	Student Language and Literacy Characteristics	Considerations for Instruction
Oral Skills	**No or little spoken English proficiency**	**Students will need instruction in recognizing and distinguishing the sounds of English as compared or contrasted with sounds in their native language.** • Use visuals and gestures to convey that in English, letters are symbols that represent sounds and that words are a sequence of letters that make up a word that conveys meaning.

	Oral skills: Spoken English proficiency	**Students will need instruction in applying their knowledge of the English sound system to foundational literacy learning.**
		
		• Take an inventory of student's oral vocabulary. Draw upon student's known and familiar oral vocabulary to:
		   o Clap syllables in known words.
		   o Segment and blend syllables of known words.
		   o Listen to the sequence of sounds in known words.
		   o Use visuals to support comprehension.

Print Skills	**No or little native language literacy**	**Students will need instruction in print concepts.**
		
		• As students develop an understanding of the organization and basic features of print, they learn that spoken words in English are composed of smaller elements of speech and that letters represent these sounds (alphabetical principle).
		
		• Instruction systematically includes:
		   1 Following words from left to right, top to bottom, and page by page.
		   2. Recognizing that spoken words are represented in written language by specific sequences of letters.
		   3. Understanding that words are separated by spaces in print.
		   4. Recognizing and name all upper- and lowercase letters of the alphabet.
		   5. Recognize the distinguishing features of a sentence (e.g., first word, capitalization, ending punctuation).

	Some foundational literacy proficiency in a language not using the Latin alphabet
	
	(e.g., Arabic, Chinese, Korean, Russian)
		Students will be familiar with print concepts, and will need instruction in learning the Latin alphabet for English, as compared or contrasted with their native language writing system (e.g., direction of print, symbols representing whole words, syllables or phonemes).
		
		• For students who have been taught to use a logographic system, an introduction to the alphabet is necessary and the instruction needs to include sound-symbol relationships. (Chinese languages, Korean)
		
		• For students who use an alphabetic language that does not use the Latin alphabet, an introduction to the alphabet is necessary and the instruction needs to include sound-symbol relationships. (Greek, Arabic, Russian)
		
		  • Compare and contrast directionality and print orientation:
		   o Left to right, top to bottom: Greek, Russian, Barhmic, Thai
		   o Right to left orientation, top to bottom: Arabic, Hebrew, Persian, Syriac, Urdu

	Some foundational literacy proficiency in a language using the Latin alphabet (e.g., Spanish)	**Students will need instruction in applying their knowledge of print concepts, phonics and word recognition to the English writing system, as compared or contrasted with their native language alphabet (e.g., letters that are the same or different, or represent the same or different sounds) and native language vocabulary (e.g., cognates) and sentence structure (e.g., subject verb object vs. subject object verb word order).** • Most languages that use the Latin alphabet have the same line direction (left to right) bottom) and same block direction (top to bottom). (English, Spanish, French, Portuguese)

Please see the Contrastive Analysis Charts provided in the Teacher's Resource System.

Recognize Long Vowel Teams and Single Letters with the Sound /ā/ RF.1.3b, RF.1.3c, RF.1.3g

CCSS RF.1.3.
Know and apply grade-level phonics and word analysis skills in decoding words both in isolation and in text
b. Decode regularly spelled one-syllable words.
c. Know final -e and common vowel team conventions for representing long vowel sounds.
g. Recognize and read grade-appropriate irregularly spelled words.

Lesson Objectives

- Produce the sound /ā/.
- Relate the sound /ā/ to the single letter a.
- Relate the sound /ā/ to vowel teams a, ai, ay.
- Recognize long vowel sound /ā/ in words and pictures.
- Write vowel teams that make the sound /ā/.

METACOGNITIVE STRATEGY
- Selective auditory attention, imagery, auditory representation

ACADEMIC LANGUAGE
- vowel, long vowel sound, vowel team

Additional Materials
Sound Spelling Cards for **a, ai, ay**
Blackline Master 1

Pre-Assess
Student's ability to recognize the **long vowel sound** represented by the corresponding letters and vowel teams.

Student's ability to pronounce the **long vowel sound a.**

Introduce

As students participate in this lesson, they identify the name and sound of the target letter, and identify the letter when the sound and name are given orally. Students will apply their knowledge by recognizing the sound of the target letter using pictures.

State Learning Goal

Say: *Today we will learn to read words with the long a sound. We are going to learn that the sound /ā/ can be formed by two vowels together, called vowel teams.*

Teach

Letters represent sounds. We remember the sounds each letter makes. We use letters to write words we say. We use letters to read and write words. The sound /ā/ is formed by the letter a and teams of vowels such as **a, ai,** and **ay**. We are going to learn words that have the long sound of vowel a.

Phonemic Awareness

Pair sound/spelling cards to review the long sound of a using **a, ai,** and **ay**

Say: *Listen to this sound /ā/. Say it with me: /ā/. Say it on your own: /ā/.*

Sound-Spelling Correspondence

Write and display the letter a and the vowel teams **a, ai,** and **ay**.

Say: *There are different ways to form this sound. Sometimes /ā/ is formed by the letter a on its own. Say the sound with me: /ā/.*

Say: *Sometimes /ā/ is formed by the combination of the letter a and the letter i. Say the sound with me: /ā/.*

Say: *Sometimes /ā/ is formed by the combination of the letter a and the letter y. Say the sound with me: /ā/.*

Model

Use BLM 1, row 1.

Say: *We will look at each picture. We will say its name. Listen for the long sound /ā/. If we hear the long sound of /ā/, we will circle the picture. If we do not hear the long sound /ā/, we will cross out the picture.*

Say: *What do you see in the first picture?* **day.** *Do you hear the long sound /ā/ in the word day? Circle the picture. If you do not hear the sound /ā/, then cross out the picture.*

Practice

Use BLM 1, row 2.

Say: Look *at the first picture.* **Say** *its name.* **Listen** *for the long sound /ā/.*

Say: *What do you see in the picture?* **rail.** *Do you hear the long sound /ā/ in the word rail?*

Say: *What letter or letters make the long sound /ā/? Write the letter or letters that make the long sound /a/ on the line under each picture.*

Apply
Blend Words

Use BLM 1, row 3.

Say: *Look at the third picture. Look at each letter and listen to the long sound /ā/ as I read. /h/a/y/. Your turn: /h/a/y/.*

Say: *Now we are going to blend the sounds together by stretching them out as we read them.*

Point to each letter in a sweeping motion left to right **/hhh/aaa/yyy/**. *What is the word?* **hay.**

Spelling

Use BLM 1, row 4.

Say: *Now we can practice writing the sounds we hear in each long* **a** *word. Say one word at a time, stretching each sound.*

Say: *Say the word slowly; write a letter for each sound you hear.*

Conclusion

Ask: *What did we learn today?* We learned that the sound /a/ can be formed by the vowel **a**, the vowel team **ai**, or the vowel team **ay**. What pictures/words will help you remember the long sound /a/ and the letters that make that sound?

Home Connection

Ask students to practice identifying the vowel sound /ā/ and writing the letters **a, ai,** and **ay** with a family member. Have students identify other words that include the sound /ā/ with their family.

Formative Assessment	
If the student completes each task correctly, precede to the next skill in the sequence. If not, refer to suggested intervention 2.	

Did the student…?	Intervention 2
Identify the names of the letters?	• Use physical rhythmic movements as the letter name is repeated. March while chanting the letter name. Move arms up and down. Sway from side to side.
Identify the sounds of the vowel teams?	• Use rhyming chants that repeat the sound several times and then use words that contain the sound. Example: /ā/ **day, hay**
Produce the vowel sounds?	• Use mirrors to show movement of mouth, tongue, teeth as the sound is produced. Use hand over mouth to explore movement of air as the sound is produced.
Recognize the vowel teams?	• Arrange a list of vowel teams that make the /ā/ sound.
Know the name of pictures?	• Tell students the name of pictures. Have student repeat it aloud. • Discuss meaning of the word. Use the word in context.

Recognize Long Vowel Teams and Single Letters with the Sound /ō/ RF.1.3b, RF.1.3c, RF.1.3g

CCSS RF.1.3.
Know and apply grade-level phonics and word analysis skills in decoding words both in isolation and in text
b. Decode regularly spelled one-syllable words.
c. Know final -e and common vowel team conventions for representing long vowel sounds.
g. Recognize and read grade-appropriate irregularly spelled words.

Lesson Objectives

- Produce the sound /ō/.
- Relate the sound /ō/ to the single letter o.
- Relate the sound /ō/ to vowel teams **oa, ow, oe**.
- Recognize long vowel sound /ō/ in words and pictures.
- Write vowel teams that make the sound /ō/.

METACOGNITIVE STRATEGY
- Selective auditory attention, imagery, auditory representation

ACADEMIC LANGUAGE
- vowel, long vowel sound, vowel team

Additional Materials
- Sound Spelling Card for **o, oa, ow, oe**
- Blackline Master 2

Pre-Assess
Student's ability to recognize the **long vowel sound** represented by the corresponding letters and vowel teams.

Student's ability to pronounce the **long vowel sound**.

Introduce

As students participate in this lesson, they identify the name and sound of the target letter, and identify the letter when the sound and name are given orally. Students will apply their knowledge by recognizing the sound of the target letter using pictures.

State Learning Goal

Today we will learn to read words with the long sound of vowel /o/. We are going to learn that the sound /ō/ can be formed by two vowels together, called vowel teams.

Teach

Letters represent sounds. We remember the sounds each letter makes. We use letters to write words we say. We use letters to read and write words. The sound /ō/ is formed by the letter o and teams of vowels such as **oa, ow,** and **oe**. We are going to learn words that have the long sound produced by the vowel /ō/.

Phonemic Awareness

Pair sound/spelling cards to review the long sound of /ō/ using **o, oa, ow, oe**.

Say: *Listen to this sound /ō/. Say it with me: /ō/. Say it on your own: /ō/.*

Sound-Spelling Correspondence

Write and display the letter **o** and the vowel teams **oa, ow, oe**.

Say: *There are different ways to form this sound. Sometimes /ō/ is formed by the letter o on its own. Say the sound with me: /ō/.*

Say: *Sometimes /ō/ is formed by the combination of the letter **o** and the letter **a**. Say the sound with me: /ō/.*

Say: *Sometimes /ō/ is formed by the combination of the letter **o** and the letter **w**. Say the sound with me: /ō/.*

Say: *Sometimes /ō/ is formed by the combination of the letter **o** and the letter **w**. Say the sound with me: /ō/.*

Model

Use BLM 2, Row 1.

Say: *We will look at each picture. We will say its name. Listen for the long sound /ō/. If we hear the long sound /ō/, we will circle the picture. If we do not hear the long sound /ō/, we will cross out the picture.*

Say: *What do you see in the first picture?* **toe.** *Do you hear the long sound /ō/ in the word* **toe?** *Circle the picture. If you do not hear the sound /ō/, then cross out the picture.*

Practice

Use BLM 2, Row 2.

Say: Look *at the first picture.* **Say** *its name. Listen for the long sound /ō/.*

Say: *What do you see in the picture?* **row.** *Do you hear the long sound /ō/ in the word row?*

Say: *What letter or letters make the long sound /ō/? Write the letter or letters that make the long sound /ō/ on the line under each picture.*

Apply Words

Blend Words

Use BLM 2, Row 3.

Say: *Look at the first picture. Look at each letter and listen to the long sound /ō/ as I read.* **/b/ō/t/** *Your turn:* **/b/ō/t/.**

Say: *Now we are going to blend the sounds together by stretching them out as we read them.*

Point to each letter in a sweeping motion left to right **/b/ōōō/t/.** What is the word? **boat.**

Spelling

Use BLM 2, Row 4.

Say: *Now we can practice writing the sounds we hear in each word. Call one* **long o** *word at a time, stretching each sound.*

Say: *Say the word slowly; write a letter for each sound you hear.*

Conclusion

Ask: *What did we learn today?*

We learned that the sound /ō/ can be formed by the vowel o, the vowel team **oa**, the vowel team **ow**, or the vowel team **oe**. What pictures/words will help you remember the long sound /ō/ and the letters that make that sound?

©2017 Benchmark Education Company, LLC

Home Connection

Ask students to practice identifying vowel sound **/ō/** and writing the letters o, oa, ow, and oe, with a family member. Have students identify other words that include the sound **/ō/** with their family.

✔ **Formative Assessment**

If the student completes each task correctly, proceed to the next skill in the sequence. If not, refer to suggested Intervention 2.

Did the student…?	Intervention 2
Identify the names of the letters?	• Use physical rhythmic movements as the letter name is repeated. March while chanting the letter name. Move arms up and down. Sway from side to side.
Identify the sounds of the vowel teams?	• Use rhyming chants that repeat the sound several times and then use words that contain the sound. Example: /ō/ /ō/ **go, row**
Produce the vowel sounds?	• Use mirrors to show movement of mouth, tongue, teeth as the sound is produced. Use hand over mouth to explore movement of air as the sound is produced.
Recognize the vowel teams?	• Arrange a list of vowel teams that make the /ō/ sound.
Know the name of pictures?	• Know the name of pictures? Tell students the name of pictures, have student repeat it aloud. • Discuss meaning of word. Use word in context.

Recognize Long u Vowel Teams and Syllable Patterns (u, ew, ue)

CCSS RF 2.3.
Know and apply grade-level phonics and word analysis skills in decoding words **both in isolation and in text.**
a. Distinguish long and short vowels when reading regularly spelled one-syllable words.
b. Know spelling-sound correspondences for additional common vowel teams.

Lesson Objectives

- Identify and name long **u** vowel teams syllable patterns **u, ew, ue.**
- Produce the sound of long u vowel teams syllable patterns **u, ew, ue.**
- Relate the long sound /**u**/ to the syllable patterns **u, ew, ue.**
- Recognize long vowel sound /**ū**/ in words/pictures.
- Recognize long vowel team of syllable patterns with long **u.**

METACOGNITIVE STRATEGY
- Selective auditory attention, imagery, auditory representation

ACADEMIC LANGUAGE
- letter name, letter sound, vowel, long vowel sound, syllable, vowel team, pattern

Additional Materials
- Sound Spelling Card **Uu**
- Blackline Master 3

Pre-Assess
Student's ability to recognize the **long vowel sound** represented by the target letter of the alphabet and to identify the letter used to represent the corresponding sound. Student's ability to pronounce the **long vowel sound.**

RF.2.3a, RF.2.3b

Introduce

As students participate in this lesson, they identify the name and sound of the target vowel patterns, and identify the letter or letters when the sound and name are given orally. Students will apply their knowledge by recognizing the **medial** sound of target sounds using pictures.

State Learning Goal

Today we will learn to read words with the long sound of vowel u using vowel teams. Vowel teams are when one or two vowels are put together to form one sound. We are going to read words with the vowel teams **u, ew, ue.**

Teach

Letters represent sounds. We remember the sounds each letter makes. We use letters to write words we say. We use letters to read and write words. The letter u is a vowel. It has a long sound /**ū**/ and a short sound /**u**/. We are going to learn words that have the long sound of vowel u using the vowel teams u, ew, and ue.

Phonemic Awareness

Show picture of sound/spelling card to review long sound of **u.**

Say: *Listen to this sound /**ūūū**/. Say it with me: /**ūūū**/. Say it on your own: /**ūūū**/.*

Say: *This is the long sound of vowel **u**. It sounds like it is saying its name: /**ūūū**/, say it again /**ūūū**/.*

Sound-Spelling Correspondence

Write the word flute on the board. Point out the vowel **u** in the middle of the word.

Say: *The word **flute** has the long u sound in the middle and is spelled using the letter **u**.*

Write the word duel on the board. Point out the vowel u in the middle of the word.

Say: *Look at the word **duel**. The word **duel** has the long **u** sound in the middle and is spelled using the vowel team **ue**. Repeat with **dew**.*

Model

Use BLM 3, Row 1.

Say: *Look at each picture. Say its name. Listen for the long sound of **u**.*

Say: *What do you see in the second picture? **jug**. Do you hear the long sound of **u** in the word **jug**? Circle the picture. If you do not hear the long sound **u**, then cross out the picture.*

PRACTICE
Use BLM 3, Row 2

Say: **Look** at the first picture. **Say** its name. **Listen** for the long sound of **u.**

Say: What do you see in the picture? **duel.** Do you hear the long sound /**ū**/ in the word **duel**?

Say: What letter or letters make the long sound **u**? Write the letter or letters that make the long make the long sound **u** on the line under each picture.

Apply
Blend Words
Use BLM 3, Row 3.

Say: Look at the first picture. Look at each letter and listen to the long sound of vowel **u** as I read /**ch**/**ū**/. Your turn: /**ch**//**ū**/.

Say: Now we are going to blend the sounds together by stretching them out as we read them.

Point to each letter in a sweeping motion left to right /**ccc/hhh/eee/www/.** What is the word? **chew.** Repeat with **suit** and **fuse.**

Spelling

Use BLM 3, Row 4.

Say: Now we can practice writing the sounds we hear in each word. Call one **long u** word at a time, stretching each sound.

Say: Say the word slowly; write a letter for each sound you hear.

Conclusion
Ask: What did we learn today? We learned that the vowel u makes the long sound /**ū**/. We also learned that the vowel teams **ue** and **ew** make the long sound /**u**/. What pictures/words will help you remember the long sound /**ū**/?

Home Connection
Ask students to practice identifying vowel sound /**ū**/ and writing the letters **u, ew,** and **ue**, with a family member. Have students identify other words that include the sound /**ū**/ with their family.

✔ Formative Assessment	
If the student completes each task correctly, precede to the next skill in the sequence. If not, refer to the suggestion under Intervention 2.	
Did the student...?	**Intervention 2**
Identify the names of the letters?	• Use physical rhythmic movements as the letter name is repeated. March while chanting the letter name. Move arms up and down. Sway from side to side.
Identify the sounds of the vowel teams?	• Use exaggeration of forming the /**ū**/ by opening the mouth wide and bringing the lips together in a pucker.
Produce the vowel sounds?	• Use mirrors to show movement of mouth, tongue, teeth as the sound is produced. Use hand over mouth to explore movement of air as the sound is produced.
Recognize the vowel teams?	• Arrange a list of vowel teams that make the /**ū**/ sound.
Know the name of pictures?	• Tell students the name of pictures, have student repeat it aloud. Discuss meaning of word. Use word in context.

CCSS RF 1.3
Know and apply grade-level phonics and word analysis skills in decoding words both in isolation and in text.
b. Decode regularly spelled one-syllable words.
c. Know final -e and common vowel team conventions for representing long vowel sounds.
g. Recognize and read grade-appropriate irregularly spelled words.

Lesson Objectives

- Produce the sound /ē/.
- Relate the sound /ē/ to the single letter e.
- Relate the sound /ē/ to vowel teams **e, ee, ea, ie.**
- Recognize long vowel sound /ē/ in words and pictures.
- Write vowel teams that make the sound /ē/.

METACOGNITIVE STRATEGY

- Selective auditory attention, imagery, auditory representation

ACADEMIC LANGUAGE

- vowel, long vowel sound, vowel team

Additional Materials

- Sound Spelling Cards for e, ee, ea, ie
- Blackline Master 4

Pre-Assess

Student's ability to recognize the **long vowel sound** represented by the corresponding letters and vowel teams.

Student's ability to pronounce the **long vowel sound.**

Recognize Long Vowel Teams and Single Letters with the sound /ē/ RF.1.3b, RF.1.3c, RF.1.3g

Introduce

As students participate in this lesson, they identify the name and sound of sound of the target letter, and identify the letter when the sound and name are given orally. Students will apply their knowledge by recognizing the sound of target letter using pictures.

State Learning Goal

Today we will learn to read words with the long sound of vowel /ē/. We are going to learn that the sound /ē/ can be formed by two vowels together, called vowel teams.

Teach

Letters represent sounds. We remember the sounds each letter makes. We use letters to write words we say. We use letters to read and write words. The sound /ē/ is formed by the letter e and teams of vowels such as ee, ea, and ie. We are going to learn words that have the long sound of vowel /ē/.

Phonemic Awareness

Pair sound/spelling cards to review the long sound of /ē/ using ee, ea, ie

Say: *Listen to this sound: /ē/. Say it with me: /ē/. Say it on your own: /ē/.*

Sound-Spelling Correspondence

Write and display the letter e and the vowel teams ee, ea, ie.

Say: *There are different ways to form this sound. Sometimes /ē/ is formed by the letter ea on its own. Say the sound with me: /ē/.*

Say: *Sometimes /ē/ is formed by the combination of the letter* **e** *and another letter e. Say the sound with me: /ē/.*

Say: *Sometimes /ē/ is formed by the combination of the letter* **e** *and the letter* **a.** *Say the sound with me: /ē/.*

Say: *Sometimes /ē/ is formed by the combination of the letter* **e** *and the letter* **i.** *Say the sound with me: /ē/.*

Model

Use BLM 4, Row 1.

Say: *We will look at each picture. We will say its name. Listen for the long sound /ē/. If we hear the long sound of /ē/, we will circle the picture. If we do not hear the long sound /ē/, we will cross out the picture.*

Say: *What do you see in the first picture?* **dream.** *Do you hear the long sound /ē/ in the word* **dream**? *Circle the picture. If you do not hear the sound /ē/, then cross out the picture.*

Practice

Use BLM 4, Row 2.

Say: **Look** at the middle picture. **Say** its name. Listen for the long sound /ē/.

Say: What do you see in the picture? **feet.** Do you hear the long sound /ē/ in the word **feet?**

Say: What letter or letters make the long sound /ē/? Write the letter or letters that make the long sound /ē/ on the line under each picture.

Apply
Blend Words

Use BLM 4, Row 3.

Say: Look at the first picture. Look at each letter in the last word and listen to the long sound /ē/ as I read. /y/ē/l/d/ Your turn: **/y/ē/l/d/.**

Say: Now we are going to blend the sounds together by stretching them out as we read them. Point to each letter in a sweeping motion left to right **/yyy/ēēē/lll/ddd/. What is the word? yield.**

Spelling

Use BLM 4, Row 4.

Say: Now we can practice writing the sounds we hear in each word. Call one **long e** word at a time, stretching each sound.

Say: Say the word slowly. Write a letter for each sound you hear.

Conclusion

Ask: What did we learn today? We learned that the sound /ē/ can be formed by the vowel **e**, or the vowel team **ee**, or the vowel team ea, or the vowel team **ei**. What pictures/words will help you remember the long sound /ē/ and the letters that make that sound?

Home Connection

Encourage students to practice identifying long vowel sound ē in words with a family member.

Formative Assessment

If the student completes each task correctly, precede to the next skill in the sequence. If not, refer to the suggestion under Intervention 2.

Did the student...?	Intervention 2
Identify the name of the letter?	• Use physical rhythmic movements as the letter name is repeated. March while chanting the letter name. Move arms up and down. Sway from side to side.
Identify the sounds of the letter?	• Use rhyming chants that repeat the sound several times and then use words that contain the sound. Example: /ē/ /ē/ **yield field**
Produce the sounds of the letter?	• Use mirrors to show movement of mouth, tongue, teeth as the sound is produced. Use hand over mouth to explore movement of air as the sound is produced.
Recognize the CVC or CVCe pattern?	• Arrange a list of vowel teams that make the /ē/ sound.
Know the name of pictures?	• Tell students the name of pictures, have student repeat it aloud. • Discuss meaning of word. Use word in context.

Recognize Long Vowel Teams and Single Letters with the sound /ī/ RF.1.3b, RF.1.3c, RF.1.3g

CCSS RF 1.3
Know and apply grade-level phonics and word analysis skills in decoding words both in isolation and in text.
b. Decode regularly spelled one-syllable words.
c. Know final -e and common vowel team conventions for representing long vowel sounds.
g. Recognize and read grade-appropriate irregularly spelled words.

Lesson Objectives

- Produce the sound /ī/
- Relate the sound /ī/ to the single letter **i**
- Relate the sound /ī/ to spellings **y, igh**
- Recognize long vowel sound /ī/ in words and pictures
- Write vowel teams that make the sound /ī/

METACOGNITIVE STRATEGY
- Selective auditory attention, imagery, auditory representation

ACADEMIC LANGUAGE
- vowel, long vowel sound, letter combination

Additional Materials
- Sound Spelling Cards for **i, y, igh**
- Blackline Master 5

Pre-Assess
Student's ability to recognize the long vowel sound represented by the corresponding letters and alternate spellings.

Student's ability to pronounce the long vowel sound.

Introduce

As students participate in this lesson, they identify the name and sound of the target letter, and identify the letter when the sound and name are given orally. Students will apply their knowledge by recognizing the sound of the target letter using pictures.

State Learning Goal

Today we will learn to read words with the long sound of vowel /ī/. We are going to learn that the sound /ī/ can be formed in several different ways.

Teach

Letters represent sounds. We remember the sounds each letter makes. We use letters to write words we say. We use letters to read and write words. The sound /ī/ is formed by the letter i sometimes by the letter y or the letter combination **igh**. We are going to learn words that have the long sound of vowel /ē/.

Phonemic Awareness

Pair sound/spelling cards to review the long sound of /ī/ using **i, y, igh**

Say: *Listen to this sound: /ī/. Say it with me: /ī/. Say it on your own: /ī/.*

Sound-Spelling Correspondence

Write and display the letter **e** and the vowel teams **y, igh.**

Say: *There are different ways to form this sound. Sometimes /ē/ is formed by the letter i on its own. Say the sound with me: /ī/*

Say: *Sometimes /ī/ is formed by the the letter y. Say the sound with me: /ī/.*

Say: *Sometimes /ī/ is formed by the letter combination igh. Say the sound with me: /ī/.*

Model

Use BLM 5, Row 1.

Say: *We will look at each picture. We will say its name. Listen for the long sound /ī/. If we hear the long sound of /ī/, we will circle the picture. If we do not hear the long sound /ī/, we will cross out the picture.*

Say: *What do you see in the first picture?* **cry.** *Do you hear the long sound /ī/ in the word cry? Circle the picture. If you do not hear the sound /ī/, then cross out the picture.*

Practice

Use BLM 5, Row 2.

Say: Look *at the second picture.* **Say** *its name.* **Listen** *for the long sound* /ī/.

Say: *What do you see in the picture?* **high**. *Do you hear the long sound* /ī/ *in the word* **high**?

Say: *What letter or letters make the long sound* /ī/? *Write the letter or letters that make the long sound* /ī/ *on the line under each picture.*

Apply
Blend Words

Use BLM 5, Row 3.

Say: *Look at the third picture. Look at each letter and listen to the long sound* /ī/ *as I read.* /b/ī/c/y/c/l/e/. *Your turn:* /b/ī/c/y/c/l/e/.

Say: *Now we are going to blend the sounds together by stretching them out as we read them.* Point to each letter in a sweeping motion left to right: **/bb//īīī// ccyyy//ccccl/. What is the word? bicycle.**

Spelling

Use BLM 5, Row 4.

Say: *Now we can practice writing the sounds we hear in each word. Call one long* **i** *word at a time, stretching each sound.*

Say: *Say the word slowly. Write a letter for each sound you hear.*

Conclusion

Ask: *What did we learn today?* We learned that the sound /i/ can be formed by the vowel **i**, or the letter **y**, or the letter combination **igh**. What pictures/words will help you remember the long sound /i/ and the letters that make that sound?

Home Connection

Ask students to practice identifying vowel sound /ī/ and writing the letters **i, y,** and **igh**, with a family member. Have students identify other words that include the sound /ī/ with their family.

✔ Formative Assessment

If the student completes each task correctly, precede to the next skill in the sequence. If not, refer to the suggestion under Intervention 2.

Did the student…?	Intervention 2
Identify the names of the letters?	• Use physical rhythmic movements as the letter name is repeated. March while chanting the letter name. Move arms up and down. Sway from side to side.
Identify the sound of the letters that produced the sound?	• Use rhyming chants that repeat the sound several times and then use words that contain the sound. Example: /ī/ /ī/ **find mind**
Produce the vowel sounds?	• Use mirrors to show movement of mouth, tongue, teeth as the sound is produced. Use hand over mouth to explore movement of air as the sound is produced.
Recognize the letters that produced the sound?	• Arrange a list of letter combinations that make the /ī/ sound.
Know the name of pictures?	• Tell students the name of pictures, have student repeat it aloud. • Discuss meaning of word. Use word in context.

Identify and Name Variant Vowel /är/ RF.1.3b

CCSS RF.K.3
Know and apply grade-level phonics and word analysis skills in decoding words both in isolation and in text.
b. Decode regularly spelled one-syllable words.

Lesson Objectives

- Identify and name the letters a and r
- Produce the sound of letters **är**
- Relate the sound /är/ to the letters **ar**
- Recognize **the variant vowel sound** /är/ in words/pictures

METACOGNITIVE STRATEGY
- Selective auditory attention, imagery, auditory representation

ACADEMIC LANGUAGE
- letter name, letter sound, variant vowel

Additional Materials
- Sound Spelling Card **ar**
- Blackline Master 6

Pre-Assess
Student's ability to recognize the sound represented by the target letters of the alphabet and to identify the letters used to represent the corresponding sound.

Introduce

As students participate in this lesson, they identify the name and sound of the target letters, and identify the letters when the sound and name are given orally. Students will apply their knowledge by recognizing the sound of the target letter using pictures.

State Learning Goal

The letter **a** is a vowel. But when a vowel is followed by the letter **r** the vowel is neither long or short. It is a different vowel sound. Today we will listen to the variant vowel **är.**

Teach

Letters represent sounds. We remember the sounds each letter makes. We use letters to write words we say. We use letters to read and write words. The letter a is a vowel. When it is followed by the letter **r** the **a** makes the vowel sound **/ är /.**

Phonemic Awareness

Show picture of sound/spelling cards **a** and **r to review the variant vowel är.**
Say: *Listen to this sound /är/. Say it with me: /är/. Say it on your own: /är/.*

Sound-Spelling Correspondence

Show the sound/spelling card

Say: *The way we write the sound /är/ is with the letters* **ar.**

Say: *The letter r that follows the vowel a makes the vowel sound* **är.**

Say: *What are the names of the letters?* **a** *and* **r** *What is the sound the letter* **a** *makes when it is followed by the letter* **r** *?* /är/

Model

Use BLM 6, Row 1.

Say: *Look at each picture. Say its name. Listen for the vowel sound /är/ in the middle. Say: Do you hear the sound /är/ in the* **middle** *of the word* **park***? If we hear the sound /är/ in the middle of the word, we will circle the picture. If we do not hear the sound /är/ in the middle, we cross out the picture.*

Practice

Use BLM 6, Row 2.

Say: Look at the picture. **Say** its name. **Trace/write** the letters.

Say: What is the picture? **barn**. Do you hear the sound /är/ in the word **barn**? Then **trace/write** the letters **barn.**

Apply
Blend Words
Use BLM 6, Row 3.

Say: Look at each letter of the third word and listen to the sound as I read. /y/ /är/ /n/. Your turn: /y/ /är/ /n/.

Say: Now we are going to blend the sounds together by stretching them out as we read them. Point to each letter in a sweeping motion left to right: /y/aaa/rrr/ /nnn/. What is the word? **yarn.**

Spelling

Use BLM 6, Row 4.

Say: Now we can practice writing the sounds we hear in each word. Call one /är/ word at a time, stretching each sound.

Say: Say the word slowly; write a letter for each sound you hear.

Conclusion

Ask: What did we learn today? We learned that the letters **ar** makes the sound /är/ in some words. What pictures/words will help you remember the sound /är/ and the letters **ar**?

Home Connection
Encourage students to practice identifying the variant **är** vowel sound and writing the letters **ar** with a family member. Encourage students to identify other words that have a variant vowel sound /är/ with their family.

✔ Formative Assessment

If the student completes each task correctly, precede to the next skill in the sequence. If not, refer to the suggestion under Intervention 2.

Did the student…?	Intervention 2
Identify the name of the letter?	• Use physical rhythmic movements as the letter name is repeated. March while chanting the letter name. Move arms up and down. Sway from side to side.
Identify the sound of the letter?	• Have students chant rhyming words with variant vowel sound / är /: **bar, star, bar.**
Produce the sound of the letter?	• Use mirrors to show movement of mouth, tongue, teeth as the sound is produced. • Use hand over mouth to explore movement of air as the sound is produced.
Recognize the beginning sound?	• Use Elkonin boxes – student moves a token into first box as the beginning sound of the word is said.
Write the letter?	• Write the letter, have students trace it. Create letter with clay. • Discuss letter features (lines, shape). Trace over letter with multiple colors.
Know the name of pictures?	• Tell students the name of pictures, have student repeat it aloud. • Discuss meaning of word. Use word in context.

Identify and Name Variant Vowel /ûr/ RF.1.3b

CCSS RF.K.3
Know and apply grade-level phonics and word analysis skills in decoding words both in isolation and in text.
b. Decode regularly spelled one-syllable words

Lesson Objectives

- Identify and name the letters **e, i, u,** and r
- Produce the sound of letters **ûr**.
- Relate the sound / **ûr** / to the letters **er, ir,** and **ur**
- Recognize **the variant vowel sound** /ûr/ in words/pictures

METACOGNITIVE STRATEGY

- Selective auditory attention, imagery, auditory representation

ACADEMIC LANGUAGE

- letter name, letter sound, variant vowel

Additional Materials

- Sound Spelling Cards **ûr**
- Blackline Master 7

Pre-Assess

Student's ability to recognize the sound represented by the target letters of the alphabet and to identify the letters used to represent the corresponding sound.

Introduce

As students participate in this lesson, they identify the name and sound of the target letters, and identify the letters when the sound and name are given orally. Students will apply their knowledge by recognizing the sound of the target letters using pictures.

State Learning Goal

The letters **e, i,** and **u** are vowels. But when these vowels are followed by the letter r, the vowels are neither long nor short. They have a different vowel sound. Today we will listen to the vowel sound /ûr/.

Teach

Letters represent sounds. We remember the sounds each letter makes. We use letters to write words we say. We use letters to read and write words. The letters **e, i,** and **u** are vowels. When they are followed by the letter **r** the vowels make the sound /**ûr**/.

Phonemic Awareness

Show picture of sound/spelling card **ûr to review the variant vowel ûr.**

Say: *Listen to this sound /ûr/. Say it with me: /ûr/. Say it on your own: /ûr/.*

Sound-Spelling Correspondence

Show the sound/spelling card

Say: *The way we write the sound /ûr/ is with the letters* **er, ir,** *and* **ur.**

Say: *The letter r that follows the vowels* **e, i,** *or* **u** *give them a sound that is neither long or short. It gives them a different sound.*

Say: *What are the names of the letters?* **i, e, u,** *and* **r** *What is the sound the vowels* **i, e,** *and* **u** *make when they are followed by the letter* **r?** */ûr/*

Model

Use BLM 7, Row 1.

Say: *Look at the first picture. Say its name. Listen for the vowel sound /ûr/ in the middle.*

Say: *Look at the first word. Do you hear the sound /ûr/ in the* **middle** *of the word* **dirt?** *If we hear the sound of /ûr/ in the middle of the word, we will circle the picture. If we do not hear the sound /ûr/ in the middle, we cross out the picture.*

Practice

Use BLM 7, Row 2.

Say: Look *at the first picture.* **Say** *its name.* **Trace/write** *the letters.*

Say: *What is the picture?* **herd** *Do you hear the sound* /ûr/ *in the word* **herd**? *Then* **trace/write** *the letters* **herd.**

Apply
Blend Words
Use BLM 7, Row 3.

Say: *Look at the first picture. Look at each letter and listen to the sound as I read.* /t/ /ûr/ /n/. *Your turn:*

Say: /t/ /ûr/ /n/. *Now we are going to blend the sounds together by stretching them out as we read them. Point to each letter in a sweeping motion left to right /* **t/uuu/rrr/nnn/.** *What is the word?* **turn**

Spelling

Use BLM 7, Row 4.

Say: *Now we can practice writing the sounds we hear in each word. Call one* /ûr/ *word at a time, stretching each sound.*

Say: *Say the word slowly; write a letter for each sound you hear.*

Conclusion

Ask: *What did we learn today?* We learned that when the vowels **e, i**, and **u** are followed by the letter r they make the sound /ûr/. What pictures/words will help you remember the sound /ûr/ and the letters **er, ir,** and **ur?**

Home Connection
Encourage students to practice identifying the variant vowel sound /ûr/ and writing the letters **er, ir,** and **ur** with a family member. Encourage students to identify other words that have the variant vowel sound /ûr/ with their family.

✔ Formative Assessment

If the student completes each task correctly, precede to the next skill in the sequence. If not, refer to the suggestion under Intervention 2.

Did the student…?	Intervention 2
Identify the name of the letter?	• Use physical rhythmic movements as the letter name is repeated. March while chanting the letter name. Move arms up and down. Sway from side to side.
Identify the sound of the letter?	• Have students chant rhyming words with variant vowel sound • /ûr/: **fern, bird, fur**
Produce the sound of the letter?	• Use mirrors to show movement of mouth, tongue, teeth as the sound is produced. • Use hand over mouth to explore movement of air as the sound is produced.
Recognize the beginning sound?	• Use Elkonin boxes – student moves a token into first box as the beginning sound of the word is said.
Write the letter?	• Write the letter, have students trace it. Create letter with clay. • Discuss letter features (lines, shape). Trace over letter with multiple colors.
Know the name of pictures?	• Tell students the name of pictures, have student repeat it aloud. • Discuss meaning of word. Use word in context.

Identify and Name Closed Syllables RF.K.3d, RF.K.3g

CCSS RF.K.3
Know and apply grade-level phonics and word analysis skills in decoding words both in isolation and in text.
d. Decode two-syllable words following basic patterns by breaking the words into syllables.
g. Recognize and read grade-appropriate irregularly spelled words.

Lesson Objectives

- Identify closed syllables.
- Produce the sound of closed syllables.
- Recognize closed syllables in words/pictures.

METACOGNITIVE STRATEGY
- Selective auditory attention, imagery, auditory representation

ACADEMIC LANGUAGE
- vowel, closed syllable

Additional Materials
- Blackline Master 8

Pre-Assess
Student's ability to recognize the sound represented by a syllable and to identify the letters used to represent the corresponding sound

Introduce

As students participate in this lesson, they identify closed syllables in two-syllable words, and identify syllables when the sound and name are given orally. Students will apply their knowledge by recognizing the sound of closed syllables using pictures.

State Learning Goal

Words are made up of syllables. Each vowel sound makes a syllable. In **closed syllables**, the vowel is followed by a consonant.

Teach

Letters represent sounds. We remember the sounds each letter makes. Letters are divided into vowels and consonants. Every syllable contains a vowel sound. A closed syllable starts with a vowel and ends with a consonant. The vowel in a closed syllable has a short sound. It does not say its name.

Phonemic Awareness

Say: *Listen to this word:* **win**. *Say it with me:* **win**. *Say it on your own:* **win**.

Sound-Spelling Correspondence

Show the letters.

Say: *The word* **win** *is one syllable.*

Say: *The word* **win** *is a closed syllable.*

Say: *How many syllables?* **one** *What kind of syllable?* **closed**

Model

Use BLM 8, Row 1.

Say: *Look at each picture. Say its name. Listen for the closed syllables.*

Say: *Do you hear the closed syllable in the first word,* **trumpet**? *If we hear the closed syllables, we will circle the picture with the trumpet. If we do not hear a closed syllable, we cross out the picture.*

Practice

Use BLM 8, Row 2.

Say: Look at the first picture. **Say** its name. **Write** the letters.

Say: What is the picture? **pencil**. Do you hear the two closed syllables in the word **pencil**? **Circle** the two syllables: **pen/cil**. Write the word on the line below.

Apply
Blend Words
Use BLM 8, Row 3.

Say: Look at the first picture. Look at each letter and listen to the sound as I read. **/b/ /u/ /t/ /t/ /e/ /r/**. Your turn: **/b/ /u/ /t/ /t/ /e/ /r/**.

Say: Now we are going to blend the sounds together by stretching them out as we read them. Point to each letter in a sweeping motion left to right **/b//uuu/ /ttt//ttt//eee//rrr/**. What is the word? **butter**.

Spelling

Use BLM 8, Row 4

Say: Now we can practice writing the sounds we hear in each word. Call one closed syllable word at a time, stretching each sound.

Say: Say the word slowly; write a letter for each sound you hear.

Conclusion

Ask: What did we learn today? We learned that words are made of syllables. Closed syllables have a vowel followed by a consonant. What pictures/words will help you remember closed two-syllable words?

Home Connection

Encourage students to practice identifying closed two-syllable words with a family member. Encourage students to identify other words that have closed syllables with their family.

✔ Formative Assessment

If the student completes each task correctly, precede to the next skill in the sequence. If not, refer to the suggestion under Intervention 2.

Did the student…?	Intervention 2
Identify the name of the letters?	• Use physical rhythmic movements as the letter name is repeated. March while chanting the letter name. Move arms up and down. Sway from side to side.
Identify the sound of the letters?	• Use alliteration, chants that repeat the sound several times then a word that begins with the sound.
Produce the sound of the letters?	• Use mirrors to show movement of mouth, tongue, teeth as the sound is produced. • Use hand over mouth to explore movement of air as the sound is produced.
Recognize the syllables?	• Use Elkonin boxes – student moves a token into the box as each syllable in the word is said.
Write the letters?	• Write the letter, have students trace it. Create letter with clay. • Discuss letter features (lines, shape). Trace over letter with multiple colors.
Know the name of pictures?	• Tell students the name of pictures, have student repeat it aloud. • Discuss meaning of word. Use word in context.

Decode Words with Common Suffixes: -ar, -er, -ir RF.2.3d

CCSS RF.2.3
Know and apply grade-level phonics and word analysis skills in decoding words both in isolation and in text.
d. Decode words with common prefixes and suffixes.

Lesson Objectives

- Recognize and decode common **suffixes.**
- Recognize that suffixes placed at the **end** of a root/base word change the meaning of the word.

METACOGNITIVE STRATEGY
- Selective auditory attention
- Use deductive thinking – generalize a rule

ACADEMIC LANGUAGE
- word ending, different meaning, suffix, base word, root word
- Note: When using Latin-based suffixes, the base word is called a root word.

Additional Materials
- Blackline Master 9

Pre-Assess

Student's ability to recognize **the end of a word** as a clue to word meaning
Student's ability to recognize a base or root word as the part of the word that contains meaning and can stand alone.

Introduce

As students participate in this lesson, they understand that suffixes are a group of letters added at the end of a root word to create a new word with a new meaning. Students recognize and generalize the understanding that that suffixes **–ar, -er** and **-or** mean "one who."

State Learning Goal

Today we will practice adding the suffix **–ar, -er** and **-or** to the end of a word to recognize how they change its meaning. We can use the suffix **–ar**, the suffix **–er** and the suffix **-or** as clues to figure out the meaning of a word.

Teach

Say: *A* **suffix** *is a group of letters that can be* **added to the end** *of a word.*

Ask: *To what part of a word is the suffix added? A suffix is added to the end of a word.*

Write the word teach on the board. Write the suffix **–er** on the board.

Say: *This is the word teach. Read it with me: teach. This is the suffix* **-er**. *Read it with me* **-er**. *I will add the suffix* **–er** *at the end of the word teach to make the word teacher.*

Say: *Read it with me: teacher. Teacher means "one who teaches." The meaning of the word teach changed.*

Write the word sail on the board. Write the suffix **–or** on the board.

Say: *This is the word sail. Read it with me: sail. This is the suffix* **-or**. *Read it with me:* **–or**. *I will add the suffix* **–or** *at the end of the word sail to make the word sailor.*

Say: *Read it with me: sailor. Sailor means "one who sails." The meaning of the word sail changed.*

Say: *When you add a suffix to the end of a word, it changes the meaning of the word.*

Ask: *What happens when you add a suffix to the end of a word? The meaning of the word changes.*

Say: *By adding* **–er** *to the word teach, we created a new word, teacher, which means "one who teaches." By adding* **–or** *to the word sail, we created a new word, sailor, which means "one who sails."*

Ask: *What does teacher mean? It means "one who teaches." What does sailor mean? It means "one who sails".*

Model

Use BLM 9, Row 1.

Say: *I read the word sing. I add –er. It reads: singer. It means "one who sings."*

You can use the suffix **–er**, the suffix **–or** and the suffix **–ar** to understand the meaning of a word.

Practice

Use BLM 9, Row 2

Say: *Let's read the word* **collect.**. *Let's add –or. It reads: collector. It means "one who collects." Let's read the word* **paint**. *Let's add –er. It reads: painter. It means "one who paints." You can use the suffix –er, the suffix –or and the suffix –ar to understand the meaning of a word.*

Apply

Use BLM 9, Row 3.

Say: *You read the word act. You add –or. It reads: actor. What does it mean? You can use the suffix –er or suffix –or to understand the meaning of a word.*

Conclusion

Ask: *What did we learn today?* We learned that when we add the suffix **–er**, the suffix **–or** or the suffix **–ar** to the end of a word, it changes the meaning of the word. The suffixes **–er, -or** and **-ar** all mean "one who."

Home Connection

Ask students to practice adding **-er, -ar** and **-or** to the end of words and to understand the meaning of the new word created. Have students to identify other words that have the suffix **–er, -or** or **–ar** with a family member.

✔ **Formative Assessment**

If the student completes each task correctly, precede to the next skill in the sequence. If not, refer to the suggestion under Intervention 2.

Did the student…?	Intervention 2
Recognize and identify the end of a word?	• Point directly to end of the word. Say this is the end of the word____ or the last part of the word____. Point to the beginning and say, this is the beginning or the first part of the word
Repeat words and phrases when asked?	• Point to the word and have students echo read, then read it on their own while pointing to the word

Identify and Name LE Syllables
RF.2.3c

Introduce

As students participate in this lesson, they identify the name and sound of the targeted letters, and identify the letters when the sounds and names are given orally. Students will apply their knowledge by recognizing the sounds of target endings using pictures.

State Learning Goal

Today we will practice listening to the sound /le/ that the letters **le** make to form the final syllable in two-syllable words.

Teach

Letters represent sounds. We remember the sounds each letter makes. We use letters to write words we say. We use letters to read and write words. Letters are made up of vowels and consonants. Each vowel sound in a word is a syllable.

Phonemic Awareness

Show letter cards **l** and **e** to review the sound.

Say: *Listen to this sound /l/. Say it with me: /l/. Say it on your own: /l/.*

Sound-Spelling Correspondence

Show the letters.

Say: *The way we write the sound /le/ is with the letters **le.***

Say: *The letters le makes the sound /le/.*

Say: *The letters le make a syllable when /le/ is the final sound in a word.*

Say: *What is the name of the letters?* **le** *What sound does the letters make?* /le/

Model

Use BLM 10, Row 1.

Say: *We will look at each picture. Say its name. If we hear the sound of the syllable **le** at the end of the word, we will circle the picture. If we do not hear the sound of the syllable /le/ at the end of the word, we cross out the picture.*

Say: *What do you see in the first picture?* **circle.** *Do you hear the sound of the syllable /le/ at the end of the word circle? Circle the picture. If you do not hear the sound of the syllable /le/ at the end of the word, then cross out the picture.*

CCSS RF.2.3
RF.2.3 Know and apply grade-level phonics and word analysis skills in decoding words both in isolation and in text.
c. Decode regularly spelled two-syllable words with long vowels.

Lesson Objectives

- Identify and name the letters le.
- Produce the sound of word ending le.
- Relate the sound /le/ to the letters le
- Recognize the sound le in words/ pictures.

METACOGNITIVE STRATEGY
- Selective auditory attention, imagery, auditory representation

ACADEMIC LANGUAGE
- letter name, letter sound, final sound, ending sound

Additional Materials
- Letter Cards **l, e**
- Blackline Master 10

Pre-Assess
Student's ability to recognize the sounds represented by the targeted letters of the alphabet and to identify the letters used to represent the corresponding sounds.

Practice

Use BLM 10, Row 2

Say: *Look at the first picture. Say its name. Write the letters.*

Say: *What is the picture?* **cattle.** *Do you hear the sound of the syllable* /**le**/ *at the end of the word* **cattle? Write** *the letters* **le.**

Apply
Blend Words

Use BLM 10, Row 3.

Say: *Look at the first picture. Look at each letter and listen to the sound as I read.* /**t**/ /**u**/ /**r**/ /**t**/ /**l**/. *Your turn:* /**t**/ /**u**/ /**r**/ /**t**/ /**l**/.

Say: *Now we are going to blend the sounds together by stretching them out as we read them. Point to each letter in a sweeping motion left to right* /**t/uuu/rrr/ttt/ lll/**. *What is the word?* **turtle**

Spelling

Use BLM 10, Row 4.

Say: *Now we can practice writing the sounds we hear in each word. Call one word with le at a time, stretching each sound.*

Say: *Say the word slowly; write a letter for each sound you hear.*

Conclusion

Ask: *What did we learn today?* We learned that the letters **le** makes the sound /**le**/. We learned to listen for the sound of this syllable at the end of words. We wrote words using the letters **le** at the end of words. What pictures/words will help you remember the sound /**le**/ and the letters **le** at the end of a word?

Home Connection

Encourage students to practice identifying sound **le** at the end of words and writing the letters **le** with a family member. Encourage students to identify other words with the sound of syllable **le** at the end of words with their family.

✔ Formative Assessment

If the student completes each task correctly, precede to the next skill in the sequence. If not, refer to the suggestion under Intervention 2.

Did the student...?	Intervention 2
Identify the names of the letters?	• Use physical rhythmic movements as the letter name is repeated. March while chanting the letter name. Move arms up and down. Sway from side to side.
Identify the sound of the letters?	• Say words with the target sounds by clearly separating the syllables in the words. Examples: **tur/ tle, cir/cle, mar/ble.**
Produce the sound of the letters?	• Use mirrors to show movement of mouth, tongue, teeth as the sound is produced. Use hand over mouth to explore movement of air as the sound is produced.
Recognize the sounds of the consonant digraphs?	• Use Elkonin boxes – student moves a token into the box as the sound of the consonant digraph is said in the word.
Write the letters?	• Write the letters, have students trace them. Create the letters with clay. Discuss letter features (lines, shape). Trace over the letters with multiple colors.
Know the name of pictures?	• Tell students the name of pictures, have students repeat them aloud. Discuss word and use each word in context.

Read Verbs with Inflectional Endings: –ed, –ing RF.1.3f

CCSS RF 1.3.
Know and apply grade-level phonics and word analysis skills in decoding words both in isolation and in text.
f. Read words with inflectional endings

Lesson Objectives

- Recognize inflectional endings.
- Recognize that inflectional endings. change the meaning of a word.

METACOGNITIVE STRATEGY

- Selective auditory attention; Use deductive thinking – generalize a rule

ACADEMIC LANGUAGE

- word ending, different meaning, inflectional ending

Additional Materials

- Blackline Master 11

Pre-Assess

Student's ability to recognize beginning of a word and end of a word

Introduce

As students participate in this lesson, they understand that inflectional endings are a group of letters at the end of a base word that changes it's meaning.

Students recognize inflectional ending **–ing** and **–ed**.

Students generalize the understanding that inflectional **–ing** and **–ed** change the time an action takes place.

State Learning Goal

Today we will practice adding **-ing** at the end of verbs to change their meaning from present to past.

Teach

Say: *Verbs are words that tell about an action. Present means that the action is happening now. Past means that the action already happened.*

Ask: *What does present mean? Have students echo or repeat: The action is happening now. Ask: What does past mean? Have students echo or repeat. The action already happened.*

Say: *This is the word* **play***. It is a verb. It tells about an action. When I add* **–ing** *at the end of the word* **play***, it reads: playing. I am playing now. When I add* **–ed** *at the end of the word* **play***, it reads: played. I already played.*

Model

Use BLM 11, Row 1.

Say: *I see the picture. It looks like a kid is getting ready to play. I read the word play. Repeat with other words such as walk or cook.*

Practice

Use BLM 11, Row 2.

Say: *In the next picture I see kids playing basketball. Let's add **–ing**. It reads: playing. They are playing now. Let's read the word playing. Repeat with other words.*

Say: *Look at the next picture. I see that the kids are putting the ball away. Let's add **–ed**. It reads played. They already played. Repeat with other words.*

Apply

Use BLM 11, Row 3.

Say: *Look at all three pictures and read the words below each picture to show how to refer to two actions. Repeat with other words.*

Conclusion

Ask: *What did we learn today?* We learned that when we add **–ing** to the end of a verb we mean that the action is happening now, in the present. When we add **–ed** to the end of a verb, we mean that the action already happened, it is in the past.

Home Connection

Ask students to practice adding **–ing** and **–ed** to the end of verbs to show present and past actions with a family member. Have students identify other words that can be changed from present to past by adding **–ed** and **–ing** with a family member.

✔ Formative Assessment

If the student completes each task correctly, precede to the next skill in the sequence. If not, refer to the suggestion under Intervention 2.

Did the student…?	Intervention 2
Understand the academic term present?	• Use movements to show a simple action happening in the present. Call out the action by stating I am ____–ing now. See me ____–ing now.
Understand the academic term past?	• Use movements to show action and stop (walk in place then stop). • Then say, what did I already do? I walked. It already happened. It is in the past.
Read the words?	• Read the words to the student. Point to the word and have students echo read, then read it on their own while pointing to the word. Discuss meaning of word. Act it out.

Identify and Decode Irregular Plural Nouns RF.2.3f

CCSS RF.2.3
Know and apply grade-level phonics and word analysis skills in decoding word both in isolation and in text
f. Recognize and spell grade appropriate irregular plural nouns

Lesson Objectives

- Identify and name plural nouns.
- Learn rules for spelling irregular plural nouns.

METACOGNITIVE STRATEGY
- Selective auditory attention, imagery, auditory representation

ACADEMIC LANGUAGE
- ending sound, irregular, plural, noun

Additional Materials
- Blackline Master 12

Pre-Assess
Student's ability to recognize the rules for forming irregular plural nouns and know that plural nouns mean more than one

Introduce

As students participate in this lesson, they identify and spell irregular plural nouns.

State Learning Goal

Today we will practice identifying and spelling plural nouns that do not end in s.

Teach

Most of the time we form plural nouns by adding **s, es,** or **ies** to the end of words (**vines, pouches, ponies**). But other times plural nouns have irregular spellings. They do not have an s at the end. We change letters in the word to make them plural.

Say: *What is the plural of* **foot**? **feet**

Say: *Sometimes they do not change at all. What is the plural of* **sheep**? **sheep**

Phonemic Awareness.

Display the irregular singular/plural pair **woman/women.**

Say: *Listen to the vowel sound in woman.* /w/o/m/a/n/.

Say: *Now listen to the vowel sound in women.* /w/i/m/e/n/ .

Sound-Spelling Correspondence

Display the irregular plurals child/children.

Say: *The singular form of this noun is* /c/ /h/ / ī / / l/ /d/, *but the plural form is* /c//h/ /i /l/ /d/ /r//e//n/. *Notice that the plural has /r/e/n/ at the end.*

Model

Use BLM 12, Row 1.

Say: *We will look at each picture. What do you see in the picture?* **a hoof**

Say: *We make the singular noun* **hoof** *plural by changing the* **f** *to a* **v** *and adding* **-es**. *Write the plural noun* **hooves** *on the line. Let's do that with the other words (goose, mouse).*

Practice

Use BLM 12, Row 2.

Say: *Look at the words. Read each one.*

Say: *The first word is* **men**. *It is the plural form of the noun* **man**. *Write* **man** *on the line. Let's do that with the other words.*

Apply-Blend Words

Use BLM 12, Row 3.

Say: *Look at each letter and listen to the sound as I read.* **/t//ee//th/**. *Your turn:* **/t//ee//th/**.

Say: *Now we are going to blend the sounds together by stretching them out as we read them. Point to each letter in a sweeping motion left to right* **/t/eeee/th/**. *What is the word? teeth. What is this the plural form of?* **tooth**.

Spelling

Use BLM 12, Row 4.

Say: *Now we can practice writing the sounds we hear in each word. Call one word at a time, stretching each sound.*

Say: *Say the word slowly; write a letter for each sound you hear.*

Conclusion

Ask: *What did we learn today?* We learned that many plural nouns have irregular spellings and that there are some basic rules to help us know how to spell them.

Home Connection

Encourage students to practice identifying **irregularly spelled plural nouns**. Encourage students to identify with their families other **irregularly spelled plural nouns**.

✔ Formative Assessment

If the student completes each task correctly, precede to the next skill in the sequence. If not, refer to the suggestion under Intervention 2.

Did the student...?	Intervention 2
Identify the name of the letter?	• Use physical rhythmic movements as the letter name is repeated. March while chanting the letter name. Move arms up and down. Sway from side to side.
Identify the sound of the letter?	• Say irregular singular/ plural noun pairs: **fish/ fish, mouse/mice, tooth/ teeth**
Produce the sound of the letter?	• Use mirrors to show movement of mouth, tongue, teeth as the sound is produced. Use hand over mouth to explore movement of air as the sound is produced.
Recognize the **final** sound?	• Use Elkonin boxes – student moves a token into the **last** box as the **final** sound of the word is said.
Write the letter?	• Write the letter, have students trace it. Create the letter with clay. • Discuss letter features (lines, shape). Trace over the letter with multiple colors.
Know the name of pictures?	• Tell students the name of pictures, have students repeat them aloud. Discuss word and use each word in context.

Identify and Name Vowel Teams
/ōō/ and /ŏŏ/ RF.1.3b, RF.1.3d, RF.1.3g

CCSS RF 1.3.
Know and apply grade-level phonics and word analysis skills in decoding words both in isolation and in text.
b. Decode regularly spelled one-syllable words.
d. Use knowledge that every syllable must have a vowel sound to determine the number of syllables in a printed word.
g. Recognize and read grade-appropriate irregularly spelled words.

Lesson Objectives

- Identify and name the letters o.
- Produce the sound of letters oo.
- Relate the sound /ōō/ and /ŏŏ/ to the letters oo.
- Recognize vowel team sound ōō and ŏŏ in words/pictures.

METACOGNITIVE STRATEGY
- Selective auditory attention, imagery, auditory representation

ACADEMIC LANGUAGE
- letter name, letter sound, vowel, short sound, **vowel team, middle**

Additional Materials
- Sound Spelling Card **oo**
- Blackline Master 13

Pre-Assess
Student's ability to recognize the sound represented by the target letter of the alphabet and to identify the letter used to represent the corresponding sound.

Introduce

As students participate in this lesson, they identify the name and sound of the target letter, and identify the letter when the sound and name is given orally. Students will apply their knowledge by recognizing the sound of target letters using pictures.

State Learning Goal

The letter o is a vowel. When we double letter **o**, we can form two sounds. The /ōō/ and /ŏŏ/ sound. Today we will listen to the vowel team sound in the middle of words.

Teach

Letters represent sounds. We remember the sounds each letter makes. We use letters to write words we say. We use letters to read and write words. The letter o is a vowel. When doubled, the letter forms two sounds: /ōō/ and /ŏŏ/.

Phonemic Awareness.

Show picture of sound/spelling card to review the sound of /ōō/ and /ŏŏ/.

Say: *Listen to this sound /ōō/. Say it with me: /ōō/. Say it on your own: /ōō/. Repeat for the sound of /ŏŏ/.*

Sound-Spelling Correspondence

Show the letter.

Say: *The way we write the sounds /ōō/ and /ŏŏ/ is with the letters oo.*

Say: *The letters oo make the sound /ōō/ and /ŏŏ/.*

Say: *What is the name of the letters? oo What are the sounds the letters oo make? /ōō/ and /ŏŏ/.*

Model

Use BLM 13, Row 1.

Say: *Look at each picture. Say its name. Listen for the sound of /ōō/ in the middle.*

Say: *Do you hear the sound /ōō/ in the middle of the word* **hook**? *If we hear the sound of ōō in the middle of the word, we will circle the picture* **hook***. If we do not hear the sound /ōō/ in the middle, we cross out the picture. Repeat for the sound ŏŏ in the middle of the word* **broom***.*

Practice

Use BLM 13, Row 2.

Say: *Look at the picture. Say its name.*

Say: *What is the picture? look Do you hear the sound /o͞o/ in the middle of the word look? Then write the letters oo. Repeat for /o͝o/ with the word* **noon.** *Write the letters oo on the lines.*

Apply
Blend Words

Use BLM 13, Row 3.

Say: *Look at each letter and listen to the sound as I read. /b/ /oo/ /k/. Your turn: /b/ /oo/ /k/.*

Say: *Now we are going to blend the sounds together by stretching them out as we read them. Point to each letter in a sweeping motion left to right /b/ooo/kkk/. What is the word?* **book.** *Repeat for* **tools** *and* **noon.**

Spelling

Use BLM 13, Row 4

Say: *Now we can practice writing the sounds we hear in each word. Call one word at a time, stretching each sound.*

Say: *Say the word slowly; write a letter for each sound you hear.*

Conclusion

Ask: *What did we learn today?* We learned that the letters **oo** make the sounds /o͞o/ and /o͝o/ in the middle of some words. What pictures/words will help you remember the sounds /o͞o/ and /o͝o/ and the letters **oo**?

Home Connection

Encourage students to practice identifying the medial vowel team sound and writing the letters **oo** with a family member. Encourage students to identify other words that have either a medial o͞o or o͝o vowel sound with their family.

✔ Formative Assessment

If the student completes each task correctly, precede to the next skill in the sequence. If not, refer to the suggestion under Intervention 2.

Did the student...?	Intervention 2
Identify the name of the letters?	• Use physical rhythmic movements as the letter name is repeated. March while chanting the letter name. Move arms up and down. Sway from side to side.
Identify the sound of the letters?	• Use exaggeration of forming the letters oo by bringing the lips together in a pucker.
Produce the sound of the letters?	• Use mirrors to show movement of mouth, tongue, teeth as the sound is produced. • Use hand over mouth to explore movement of air as the sound is produced.
Recognize the middle sound?	• Use Elkonin boxes – student moves a token into the middle boxes as the middle sound of the word is said.
Write the letters?	• Write the letters, have students trace them. Create letters with clay. Discuss letter features (lines, shape). Trace over letters with multiple colors.
Know the name of pictures?	• Tell students the name of pictures, have student repeat it aloud. • Discuss meaning of word. Use word in context.

Identify and Name Vowel Team

ou   RF.1.3b, RF.1.3d, RF.1.3g

CCSS RF.1.3 Know and apply grade-level phonics and word analysis skills in decoding words both in isolation and in text.
b. Decode regularly spelled one-syllable words.
d. Use knowledge that every syllable must have a vowel sound to determine the number of syllables in a printed word.
g. Recognize and read grade-appropriate irregularly spelled words.

Introduce

As students participate in this lesson, they identify the name and sound of the target letter, and identify the letter when the sound and name is given orally. Students will apply their knowledge by recognizing the sound of target letters using pictures.

State Learning Goal

The letters **o and u** are vowels. The letter **w** is a consonant. They form one sound: the /**ou**/ sound. Today we will listen to the vowel team sound in the middle of words.

Teach

Letters represent sounds. We remember the sounds each letter makes. We use letters to write words we say. We use letters to read and write words. The letters **o** and **u** are vowels. The two vowels form one sound: /**ou**/. The letter **w** is a consonant. The letters o and w also form the /**ou**/ sound.

Phonemic Awareness.

Show picture of sound/spelling card to review the sound of **ou**.

Say: *Listen to this sound* /**ou**/. *Say it with me:* /**ou**/. *Say it on your own*: /**ou**/.

Sound-Spelling Correspondence

Show the letter.

Say: *The way we write the sound* /**ou**/ *is with the letters* **ou** *or* **ow.**

Say: *The letters* **ou** *and* **ow** *make the* **sound** /**ou**/.

Say: *What is the name of the letters?* **ou** *and* **ow.** *What is the sound the letters* **ou** *or* **ow** *make?* /**ou**/

Model

Use BLM 14, Row 1.

Say: *Look at each picture. Say its name. Listen for the sound of* /**ou**/ *in the middle.*

Say: *Do you hear the sound* /**ou**/ *in the middle of the word* **pout**? *If we hear the sound of* **ou** *in the middle of the word, we will circle the picture. If we do not hear the sound* /**ou**/ *in the middle, we cross out the picture. Repeat for the word* **clown.**

Lesson Objectives

- Identify and name the letters **ou** **and ow**
- Produce the sound of letters **ou and ow**

Relate the sound /**ou**/ to the letters **ou** and **ow**

- Recognize **vowel team** sound **ou** in words/pictures

METACOGNITIVE STRATEGY
- Selective auditory attention, imagery, auditory representation

ACADEMIC LANGUAGE
- letter name, letter sound, vowel, short sound, vowel team, middle

Additional Materials
- Sound Spelling Card **ou**
- Blackline Master 14

Pre-Assess

Student's ability to recognize the sound represented by the target letter of the alphabet and to identify the letter used to represent the corresponding sound.

Practice

Use BLM 14, Row 2.

Say: Look *at the picture.* **Say** *its name.* **Write** *the letter.*

Say: *What is the picture?* **mouse** *Do you hear the sound /ou/ in the* **middle** *of the word* **mouse**? *Then write the letters* **ou**. *Repeat for the words* **frown** *and* **town**.

Apply
Blend Words

Use BLM 14, Row 3.

Say: *Look at each letter and listen to the sound as I read.* **/m/ /ou/ /s/.** *Your turn:* **/m/ /ou/ /s/.**

Say: *Now we are going to blend the sounds together by stretching them out as we read them.* **/m/ooouuu/sss/.** *What is the word?* **mouse.** *Repeat for the word* **town**.

Spelling

Use BLM 14, Row 4

Say: *Now we can practice writing the sounds we hear in each word. Call one word at a time, stretching each sound.*

Say: Say the word slowly; write a letter for each sound you hear.

Conclusion

Ask: *What did we learn today?* We learned that the letters **ou** and **ow** make the sound **/ou/** in the middle of some words. What pictures/words will help you remember the sound **/ou/** and the letters **ou** and **ow**?

Home Connection
Encourage students to practice identifying the medial vowel team sound and writing the letters **ou** and **ow** with a family member. Encourage students to identify other words that have a medial **ou** vowel sound with their family. .

✔ Formative Assessment

If the student completes each task correctly, precede to the next skill in the sequence. If not, refer to the suggestion under Intervention 2.

Did the student...?	Intervention 2
Identify the name of the letters?	• Use physical rhythmic movements as the letter name is repeated. March while chanting the letter name. Move arms up and down. Sway from side to side.
Identify the sound of the letters?	• Use exaggeration of forming the /ou/ by opening the mouth wide and bringing the lips together in a pucker.
Produce the sound of the letters?	• Use mirrors to show movement of mouth, tongue, teeth as the sound is produced. • Use hand over mouth to explore movement of air as the sound is produced.
Recognize the middle sound?	• Use Elkonin boxes – student moves a token into the middle boxes as the middle sound of the word is said.
Write the letters?	• Write the letters, have students trace them. Create letters with clay. Discuss letter features (lines, shape). Trace over letters with multiple colors.
Know the name of pictures?	• Tell students the name of pictures, have student repeat it aloud. • Discuss meaning of word. Use word in context.

Identify and Name Variant Vowel /ôr/ RF.1.3b

CCSS RF.K.3
Know and apply grade-level phonics and word analysis skills in decoding words both in isolation and in text.
b. Decode regularly spelled one-syllable words.

Lesson Objectives

- Identify and name the letters **o** and **r.**
- Produce the sound of letters **ôr.**
- Relate the sound **/ôr/** to the letters **or, ore,** and **oar.**
- Recognize **the variant vowel sound /ôr/** in words/pictures.

METACOGNITIVE STRATEGY
- Selective auditory attention, imagery, auditory representation

ACADEMIC LANGUAGE
- letter name, letter sound, variant vowel

Additional Materials
Sound Spelling Cards **ôr**

Blackline Master 15

Pre-Assess
Student's ability to recognize the sound represented by the target letters of the alphabet and to identify the letters used to represent the corresponding sound.

Introduce

As students participate in this lesson, they identify the name and sound of the target letters, and identify the letters when the sound and name is given orally. Students will apply their knowledge by recognizing the sound of the target letters using pictures.

State Learning Goal

The letter **o** is a vowel. But when a vowel is followed by the letter **r**, letters **re** and **ar**, the vowel is neither long or short. It is a different vowel sound. Today we will listen to the vowel sound **/ôr/**.

Teach

Letters represent sounds. We remember the sounds each letter makes. We use letters to write words we say. We use letters to read and write words. The letter **o** is a vowel. When it is followed by the letter r or letters **ar** and **re** it makes the vowel sound **/ôr/**.

Phonemic Awareness.

Show picture of sound/spelling card **ôr** to review the **variant vowel ôr.**

Say: *Listen to this sound /ôr/. Say it with me: /ôr/. Say it on your own: /ôr/.*

Sound-Spelling Correspondence

Show the sound/spelling card

Say: *The way we write the sound /ôr/is with the letters **or, ore,** and **oar.***

Say: *The letter **r** or letters **re** and **ar** that follow(s) the vowel **o** give the **o** a vowel sound that is neither long nor short. It gives it a different sound.*

Say: *What is the sound made by **or, ore**, and **oar**? /ôr/*

Model

Use BLM 15, Row 1.

Say: *Look at each picture. Say its name. Listen for the vowel sound /ôr/ in the middle.*

Say: *Do you hear the sound /ôr/ in the **middle** of the word **storm**? If we hear the sound of /ôr/ in the middle of the word, we will circle the picture. If we do not hear the sound /ôr/ in the middle, we cross out the picture.*

Practice

Use BLM 15, Row 2.

Say: Look at the picture. **Say** its name. **Write** the letters.

Say: What is the picture? **skateboard.** Do you hear the sound **/ôr/** in the word **skateboard**? Then write the letters that make the sound **/ôr/** in **skateboard.**

Apply
Blend Words

Use BLM 15, Row 3.

Say: Look at each letter and listen to the sound as I read. **/h/ /o/ /r/ /s/.** Your turn:

Say: **/h/ /o/ /r/ /s/.** Now we are going to blend the sounds together by stretching them out as we read them. Point to each letter in a sweeping motion left to right **/h/ooo/rrr/sss/.** What is the word? **horse**

Spelling

Use BLM 15, Row 4.

Say: Now we can practice writing the sounds we hear in each word. Call one word at a time, stretching each sound.

Say: Say the word slowly; write a letter for each sound you hear.

Conclusion

Ask: What did we learn today? We learned that the letters r, re, and ar make the sound **/ôr/** in some words. What pictures/words will help you remember the sound **/ôr/** and the letters **r, re,** and **oa?**

Home Connection

Encourage students to practice identifying the variant vowel sound **/ôr/** and writing the letters **or, ore,** or **oar** with a family member. Encourage students to identify other words that have a variant vowel sound **/ôr/** with their family.

✔ Formative Assessment

If the student completes each task correctly, precede to the next skill in the sequence. If not, refer to the suggestion under Intervention 2.

Did the student…?	Intervention 2
Identify the name of the letter?	• Use physical rhythmic movements as the letter name is repeated. March while chanting the letter name. Move arms up and down. Sway from side to side.
Identify the sound of the letter?	• Have students chant rhyming words with variant vowel sound • **/ôr/ oar, store, roar.**
Produce the sound of the letter?	• Use mirrors to show movement of mouth, tongue, teeth as the sound is produced. • Use hand over mouth to explore movement of air as the sound is produced.
Recognize the beginning sound?	• Use Elkonin boxes – student moves a token into first box as the beginning sound of the word is said.
Write the letter?	• Write the letter, have students trace it. Create letter with clay. • Discuss letter features (lines, shape). Trace over letter with multiple colors.
Know the name of pictures?	• Tell students the name of pictures, have student repeat it aloud. • Discuss meaning of word. Use word in context.

Identify and Name Soft g, c
RF.1.3b, RF.1.3g

CCSS RF.1.3
Know and apply grade-level phonics and word analysis skills in decoding words **both in isolation and in text.**
b. Decode regularly spelled one-syllable words.
g. Recognize and read grade-appropriate irregularly spelled words.

Lesson Objectives

- Identify and name the letters **g, c.**
- Produce the **soft** sounds of the letters **g, c.**
- Relate the sounds /j/ /s/ to the letters **g, c.**
- Recognize **soft** sounds of **g, c** in words/pictures.

METACOGNITIVE STRATEGY

- Selective auditory attention, imagery, auditory representation

ACADEMIC LANGUAGE

- letter name, letter sound, initial sound, final sound, ending sound

Additional Materials
- Sound Spelling Cards **Jj, Ss**
- Blackline Master 16

Pre-Assess
Student's ability to recognize the sounds represented by the targeted letters of the alphabet and to identify the letters used to represent the corresponding sounds.

Introduce

As students participate in this lesson, they identify the name and sound of the targeted letters, and identify the letters when the sounds and names are given orally. Students will apply their knowledge by recognizing the sounds of target letters using pictures.

State Learning Goal

Today we will practice listening to the sounds /j/ and /s/ that the letters g, c make.

Teach

Letters represent sounds. We remember the sounds each letter makes. We use letters to write words we say. We use letters to read and write words. Some letters combine to make new sounds.

Phonemic Awareness.

Show the picture of sound/spelling cards **Gg** to review the sound.

Say: *Listen to this sound /j/. Say it with me: /j/. Say it on your own: /j/.*

Sound-Spelling Correspondence

Show the letter.

Say: *One way we write the sound /j/ is with the letter g.*

Say: *The letter g makes the sound /j/ when it is followed by the letters e or i.*

Say: *What is the name of the letter? g What sound does the letter make after the letters e or i? /j/*

Phonemic Awareness.

Show the picture of sound/spelling cards Ss to review the sound. **Say:** Listen to this sound /s/. Say it with me: /s/. Say it on your own: /s/.

Sound-Spelling Correspondence

Show the letter.

Say: *One way we write the sound /s/ is with the letter c.*

Say: *The letter c makes the sound /s/ when it is followed by the letters e or i.*

Say: *What is the name of the letter? c What sound does the letter make after the letters e or i? /s/*

Model

Use BLM 16, Row 1.

Say: *We will look at each picture. Say its name. If we hear the sound /j/ at the beginning of the word, we will circle the picture. If we do not hear the sound /j/, we cross out the picture.*

Say: *What do you see in the picture? gem. Do you hear the sound /j/ in the word gem? If you do not hear the sound /j/ in the word, then cross out the picture. Repeat this with the words **ball,** and **magic trick.***

Model

Use BLM 16, Row 2.

Say: *We will look at each picture. Say its name. If we hear the sound /s/ in the word, we will circle the picture. If we do not hear the sound /s/, we cross out the picture.*

Say: *What do you see in the picture?* **cell.** *Do you hear the sound /s/ in the word* **cell**? *If you do not hear the sound /s/ in the word, then cross out the picture.*

Practice

Use BLM 16, Row 3.

Say: *Look at the picture. Say its name. Write the letters.*

Say: *What is the picture?* **gym.** *Do you hear the sound /j/ in the word* **gym**?

Use BLM 16, Row 4.

Say: *Look at the picture. Say its name. Write the letters.*

Say: *What is the picture?* **face.** *Do you hear the sound /s/ in the word* **face**?

Apply-Blend Words

Use BLM 16, Row 5.

Say: *Look at each letter and listen to the sound as I read. /g/ /e/ /m/. Your turn: /g/ /e/ /m/.*

Say: *Now we are going to blend the sounds together by stretching them out as we read them.* Point to each letter in a sweeping motion left to right: /g/eeee/ mmmm/. What is the word? **gem.**

Spelling

Use BLM 16, Row 6.

Say: *Now we can practice writing the sounds we hear in each word. Call one word at a time, stretching each sound.*

Say: *Say the word slowly; write a letter for each sound you hear.*

Conclusion

Ask: *What did we learn today?* We learned that the letter **g** can make the sound /j/ and the letter **c** can make the sound /s/. What pictures/words will help you remember the sounds /j/ and /s/ and the letters **g** and **c** in words?

Home Connection

Encourage students to practice identifying sounds /j/ and /s/ and writing the letters **g** and **c** with a family member. Encourage students to identify other words that have the letters **g** and **c** with their family.

✔ Formative Assessment

If the student completes each task correctly, precede to the next skill in the sequence. If not, refer to the suggestion under Intervention 2.

Did the student…?	Intervention 2
Identify the names of the letters?	• Use physical rhythmic movements as the letter name is repeated. March while chanting the letter name. Move arms up and down. Sway from side to side.
Identify the sound of the letters?	• Say words with the target sounds by repeating the words three times. Examples: **gem gem gem, cell cell cell**
Produce the sound of the letters?	• Use mirrors to show movement of mouth, tongue, teeth as the sound is produced. Use hand over mouth to explore movement of air as the sound is produced.
Recognize the sounds of the consonant digraphs?	• Use Elkonin boxes – student moves a token into the box as the sound of the consonant digraph is said in the word.
Write the letters?	• Write the letters, have students trace them. Create the letters with clay. Discuss letter features (lines, shape). Trace over the letters with multiple colors.
Know the name of pictures?	• Tell students the name of pictures, have students repeat them aloud. Discuss word and use each word in context.

Identify and Name Vowel Team
oi RF.1.3b, RF.1.3d, RF.1.3g

CCSS RF.1.3
Know and apply grade-level phonics and word analysis skills in decoding words both in isolation and in text.
b. Decode regularly spelled one-syllable words.
d. Use knowledge that every syllable must have a vowel sound to determine the number of syllables in a printed word.
g. Recognize and read grade-appropriate irregularly spelled words.

Lesson Objectives

Identify and name the letters **oi** and **oy.**

Produce the sound of letters **oi** and **oy.**

- Relate the sound /oi/ to the letters **oi** or **oy.**
- Recognize **vowel team** sound **oi** in words/pictures

METACOGNITIVE STRATEGY
- Selective auditory attention, imagery, auditory representation

ACADEMIC LANGUAGE
- letter name, letter sound, vowel, short sound, **vowel team, middle**

Additional Materials
- Sound Spelling Card **oi oy**
- Blackline Master 17

Pre-Assess
Student's ability to recognize the sound represented by the target letter of the alphabet and to identify the letter used to represent the corresponding sound.

Introduce

As students participate in this lesson, they identify the name and sound of the target letter, and identify the letter when the sound and name is given orally. Students will apply their knowledge by recognizing the sound of target letters using pictures.

State Learning Goal

The letters **o, i,** and **y** are vowels. The letters **oi** and **oy** each form one sound. The /oi/ sound. Today we will listen to the vowel team sound in the middle of words.

Teach

Letters represent sounds. We remember the sounds each letter makes. We use letters to read and write words. We know the sounds **o** can make and the sounds i can make, but together, they make the sound /oi/. We also know the sound **y** can make, and together, **o** and **y** also make the sound **/oi/.**

Phonemic Awareness.

Show picture of sound/spelling card **to review the sound of oi.**

Say: *Listen to this sound /oi/. Say it with me: /oi/. Say it on your own: /oi/.*

Sound-Spelling Correspondence

Show the letter.

Say: *The way we write the sound /**oi**/ is with the letters **oi** or **oy**.*

Say: *The letters **oi** and **oy** make the **sound** /**oi**/.*

Say: *What is the name of the letters? **oi** or **oy**. What is the sound the letters **oi** or **oy** make? /**oi**/*

Model

Use BLM 17 Row 1.

Say: *Look at each picture. Say its name. Listen for the sound of /**oi**/ in the middle.*

Say: *Do you hear the sound /**oi**/ in the middle of the word **soil**? If we hear the sound of **oi** in the middle of the word, we will circle the picture **soil.** If we do not hear the sound /**oi**/ in the middle, we cross out the picture. Repeat with the word **boy.***

Practice

Use BLM17, Row 2.

Say: *Look at the picture. Say its name. Trace the letter.*

Say: *What is the picture?* **coil.** *Do you hear the sound* **/oi/** *in the* **middle** *of the word* **coil***? Then* **trace** *the letters* **oi***. Repeat with the word* **toy.**

Apply

Blend Words

Use BLM 17, Row 3.

Say: *Look at each letter and listen to the sound as I read.* **/oi/** **/l/.** *Your turn:* **/oi/** **/l/.**

Say: *Now we are going to blend the sounds together by stretching them out as we read them.* Point to each letter in a sweeping motion left to right: **oooiii/lll/.** *What is the word?* **oil.** *Repeat for the word* **joy.**

Spelling

Use BLM 17, Row 4.

Say: *Now we can practice writing the sounds we hear in each word. Call one word at a time, stretching each sound.*

Say: *Say the word slowly; write a letter for each sound you hear.*

Conclusion

Ask: *What did we learn today?* We learned that the letters **oi** and **oy** make the sound **/oi/** in the middle of some words. What pictures/words will help you remember the sound **/oi/** and the letters **oi** and **oy**?

Home Connection

Encourage students to practice identifying the medial vowel team sound and writing the letters **oi** and **oy** with a family member. Encourage students to identify other words that have a medial **oi** vowel sound with their family.

✔ Formative Assessment

If the student completes each task correctly, precede to the next skill in the sequence. If not, refer to the suggestion under Intervention 2.

Did the student…?	Intervention 2
Identify the name of the letters?	• Use physical rhythmic movements as the letter name is repeated. March while chanting the letter name. Move arms up and down. Sway from side to side.
Identify the sound of the letters?	• Use exaggeration of forming the letters **oi** and **oy** by bringing the lips together in a pucker.
Produce the sound of the letters?	• Use mirrors to show movement of mouth, tongue, teeth as the sound is produced. • Use hand over mouth to explore movement of air as the sound is produced.
Recognize the middle sound?	• Use Elkonin boxes – student moves a token into the middle boxes as the middle sound of the word is said.
Write the letters?	• Write the letters, have students trace them. Create letters with clay. Discuss letter features (lines, shape). Trace over letters with multiple colors.
Know the name of pictures?	• Tell students the name of pictures, have student repeat it aloud. • Discuss meaning of word. Use word in context.

Decode Words with Common Suffixes: -ful, -less RF.3.3a

CCSS RF.3.3
Know and apply grade-level phonics and word analysis skills in decoding words both in isolation and in text.
a. Identify and know the meaning of the most common prefixes and derivational suffixes.

Lesson Objectives

- Recognize and decode common **suffixes.**
- Recognize that suffixes placed at the **end** of a root/base word change the meaning of the word.

METACOGNITIVE STRATEGY

- Selective auditory attention
- Use deductive thinking – generalize a rule

ACADEMIC LANGUAGE

- word ending, different meaning, suffix, base word, root word
- Note: When using Latin-based suffixes, the base word is called a root word.

Additional Materials
Blackline Master 18

Pre-Assess
Student's ability to recognize **the end of a word** as a clue to word meaning Student's ability to recognize a base or root word as the part of the word that contains meaning and can stand alone.

Introduce

As students participate in this lesson, they understand that suffixes are a group of letters added at the **end** of a root word to create a new word with a new meaning. Students recognize and generalize the understanding that that suffix **-ful** means "full of, being, having." Students generalize and generalize the understanding that the suffix **–less** means "not having, without."

State Learning Goal

Today we will practice adding the suffix **–ful** and the suffix **–less** to the end of a word to recognize how they change its meaning. We can use the suffix **–ful** and the suffix **–less** as clues to figure out the meaning of a word.

Teach

Say: *A suffix is a group of letters that can be* **added to the end** *of a word.*

Ask: *To what part of a word is the suffix added? A suffix is added to the end of a word.*

Write the word color on the board. Write the suffix –ful on the board.

Say: *This is the word color. Read it with me: color. This is the suffix -ful. Read it with me*

-ful. I will add the suffix –ful at the end of the word color to make the word colorful.

Say: *Read it with me: colorful. Colorful means "full of color." The meaning of the word color changed. For instance, we say, All the clowns colorful costumes. The suffix -ful changed the meaning of the word, and created a new word colorful that means "full of color."*

Write the word color on the board again. Write the suffix –less on the board.

Say: *This is the word color. Read it with me: color. This is the suffix -less. Read it with me: –less. I will add the suffix –less at the end of the word color to make the word colorless.*

Say: *Read it with me: colorless. Colorless means "not having color, without color." The meaning of the word color changed.*

Say: *When you add a suffix to the end of a word, it changes the meaning of the word.*

Ask: *What happens when you add a suffix to the end of a word? The meaning of the word changes.*

Say: *By adding –ful to the word color, we created a new word, colorful, which means "full of color." By adding –less to the word color, we created a new word, colorless, which means "without color."*

Ask: *What does colorful mean? It means "full of color." What does colorless mean? It means "without color".*

Model

Use BLM 18, Row 1.

Say: *I read the word care. I add –**ful**. It reads: careful. It means "full of care." I read the word care. I add –**less**. It reads: careless. It means "not having any care." You can use the suffix –**ful** and suffix –**less** to understand the meaning of a word.*

Practice

Use BLM 18, Row 2.

Say: *Let's read the word fright. Let's add –**ful**. It reads: graceful. It means "full of grace." Let's read the word hope. Let's add –**less**. It reads hopeess. It means "not having hope." You can use the suffix –**ful** and suffix –**less** to understand the meaning of a word.*

Apply

Use BLM 18, Row 3.

Say: *You read the word sorrow. You add –**ful**. It reads: hopeful. What does it mean? It means full of hopeful. You read the word mercy. You add –**less**. It reads: merciless. What does it mean? It means without any mercy. You can use the suffix –**ful** or suffix –**less** to understand the meaning of a word.*

Conclusion

Ask: *What did we learn today?* We learned that when we add the suffix –**ful** or the suffix –**less** to the end of a word, it changes the meaning of the word. The suffix –**ful** means "full." The suffix –**less** means "not having" or "without."

Home Connection

Ask students to practice adding -**ful** and –**less** to the end of words and to understand the meaning of the new word created. Have students to identify other words that have the suffix –**ful** or –**less** with a family member.

✔ **Formative Assessment**

If the student completes each task correctly, precede to the next skill in the sequence. If not, refer to the suggestion under Intervention 2.

Did the student…?	Intervention 2
Recognize and identify the end of a word?	• Point directly to end of the word. Say this is the end of the word___ or the last part of the word___. Point to the beginning and say, this is the beginning or the first part of the word
Understand the meaning of -ful and -less?	• Show –**ful** and –**less** as opposite categories. Have students sort words under –**ful** and –**less** as the meaning of each pair of opposites are discussed: (**colorful-colorless; joyful-joyless; careful-careless; restful-restless; hopeful-hopeless, flavorful-flavorless**).
Repeat words and phrases when asked?	• Point to the word and have students echo read, then read it on their own while pointing to the word

Decode Words with Common Prefixes: un- RF.3.3a, RF.3.3c

CCSS RF.3.3
Know and apply grade-level phonics and word analysis skills in decoding words both in isolation and in text.
a. Identify and know the meaning of the most common prefixes and derivational suffixes.
c. Decode multisyllable words.

Lesson Objectives

- Recognize and decode common **prefixes.**
- Recognize that prefixes are placed at the **beginning** of a root/base word change the meaning of the word.

METACOGNITIVE STRATEGY
- Selective auditory attention
- Use deductive thinking – generalize a rule

ACADEMIC LANGUAGE
- word ending, different meaning, prefix, base word, root word.
- Note: When using Latin-based suffixes the base word is called a root word.

Additional Materials
Blackline Master 19

Pre-Assess
Student's ability to recognize the beginning of a word as a clue to word meaning. Student's ability to recognize a base or root word as the part of the word that contains meaning and can stand alone.

Introduce

As students participate in this lesson, they understand that prefixes are a group of letters added at the **beginning** of a word to create a new word with a new meaning. Students recognize and generalize the understanding that the prefixes **un-** and **non-** mean "not."

State Learning Goal

Today we will practice adding the prefix un- or non- to the beginning of a word to recognize how it changes its meaning. We will learn we can use the prefixes **un-** and **non-** as a clue to figure out the meaning of a word.

Teach

Say: *A **prefix** is a group of letters that can be **added to the beginning** of a word.*

Ask: *To what part of a word is the **prefix** added? A prefix is added to the beginning of a word.*

Write the word able on the board. Write the prefix un- on the board.

Say: *This is the word **able**. Read it with me: **able.** This is the prefix **un-**. Read it with me un-. I will add the prefix **un-** at the beginning of the word able to make the word unable. Unable means "not able." For instance, we say, "We are unable to go swimming." The prefix **un-** changed the meaning of the word and created a new word **unable** that means "not able."*

Write the word fat on the board. Write the prefix non- on the board.

Say: *This is the word fat. Read it with me: fat. This is the prefix **non-**. Read it with me: **non-**. I will add the prefix **non-** at the beginning of the word **fat** to make the word **nonfat**. Nonfat means "not fat." For example, we say, "The milk is nonfat" The prefix non- changed the meaning of the word fat, and created a new word nonfat, which means "not fat."*

Model

Use BLM 19, Row 1.

Say: *I read the word lock. I add **un-**. It reads: **unlock**. It means "not lock." You can use the prefix **un-** to understand the meaning of a word because the prefix **un-** means "not".*

Practice

Use BLM 19, Row 2.

Say: *Let's read the word able. Let's add* **un-**. *It reads: unable. It means to "not able." Remember, you can use the prefix* **un-** *to understand the meaning of a word because the prefix* **un-** *means to "not."*

Repeat the procedure with aware.

Apply

Use BLM 19, Row 3.

Say: *You read the word tie. Add* **un-** *at the beginning of the word. It reads:* **untie**. *What does it mean? It means "not tie." You can use the prefix* **un-** *to understand the meaning word because the prefix* **un-** *means to "not."*

Spelling

Use BLM 17, Row 4.

Say: *Now we can practice writing the sounds we hear in each word. Call one word at a time, stretching each sound.*

Say: *Say the word slowly; write a letter for each sound you hear.*

Conclusion

Ask: *What did we learn today?* We learned that when we add the prefixes **un–** or **non-** at the beginning of a word, it creates a new word that means not.

Home Connection

Ask students to practice adding the prefixes **un-** and **non-** to the beginning of words to understand the meaning of the new word created. Have students identify words to which the prefixes, **un-** or non-, can be added to create a new word with a family member.

Formative Assessment

If the student completes each task correctly, precede to the next skill in the sequence. If not, refer to the suggestion under Intervention 2.

Did the student…?	Intervention 2
Recognize and identify the beginning or end of a word?	• Point directly to the beginning and say, this is the beginning or the first part of the word ___. Point directly to the end of the word and say this is the end of the word___ or the last part of the word___. Say and point: Show me beginning of word. Show me end of word.
Read words?	• Point to each word and have students repeat, echo, then read it on their own while pointing to the word. Use the word in short sentences and explain its meaning to ensure student understanding.

Decode Words with Common Prefixes: de-, dis- _{RF.3.3a, RF.3.3c}

CCSS RF.3.3
Know and apply grade-level phonics and word analysis skills in decoding words both in isolation and in text.
a. Identify and know the meaning of the most common prefixes and derivational suffixes.
c. Decode multisyllable words.

Lesson Objectives

- Recognize and decode common **prefixes.**
- Recognize that prefixes that are placed at the **beginning** of a root/base word change the meaning of the word.

METACOGNITIVE STRATEGY
- Selective auditory attention
- Use deductive thinking – generalize a rule

ACADEMIC LANGUAGE
- word ending, different meaning, prefix, base word, root word

Additional Materials
Blackline Master 20

Pre-Assess
Student's ability to recognize **the beginning of a word** as a clue to word meaning. Student's ability to recognize a base or root word as the part of the word that contains meaning and can stand alone.

Introduce

As students participate in this lesson, they understand that **prefixes** are a group of letters added at the **beginning** of a word to create a new word with a new meaning. Students recognize and generalize the understanding that the prefix **de-** and the prefix **dis-** mean "not, opposite of."

State Learning Goal

Today we will practice adding the prefix **de-** and the prefix **dis-** to the beginning of a verb or action word to recognize how it changes its meaning. We will learn we can use the prefix **de-** and the prefix **dis-** *as* a clue to figure out the meaning of a word.

Teach

Say: *A prefix is a group of letters that can be added to the beginning of a word.*

Ask: *To what part of a word is the prefix added? A prefix is added to the beginning of a word.*

Write the word on the board. Write the prefix **de-** on the board.

Say: *This is the word forest. Read it with me: forest. This is the prefix* **de-**. *Read it with me* **de-**. *I will add the prefix* **de-** *at the beginning of the word do to make the word deforest.*

Say: *Read it with me: deforest.* **Deforest** *means "not forested or cleared of trees." For instance, we say, "Cutting down all the trees will deforest the area." The prefix* **de-** *changed the meaning of the word, and created a new word deforest that means "not, opposite of."*

Write the word ability on the board. Write the prefix dis- on the board.

Say: *This is the word ability. Read it with me:* **ability**. *This is the prefix* **dis-**. *Read it with me:* **dis-**. *I will add the prefix* **dis-** *at the beginning of the word ability to make the word disability.*

Say: *Read it with me:* **disability**. *Disability means "no ability, or the opposite of able or having ability." For example, we say, "She has a physical disability." The prefix* **dis-** *changed the meaning of the word ability and created a new word disability, which means "no ability, or the opposite of able or having ability."*

Say: *When you add the prefix to the beginning of a word, it creates a new word and changes its meaning.*

Ask: *What happens when you put a prefix at the beginning of a word? The meaning of the word changes.*

Model

Use BLM 20, Row 1.

Say: *I read the word belief. I add* **dis-**. *It reads:* **disbelief.** *It means "not believe." You can use the prefix* **dis-** *to understand the meaning of a word, because the prefix* **dis-** *means to "not, opposite of." The write the root word and its prefix on the line.*

Practice

Use BLM 20, Rows 2-4.

Say: *Let's read the word ice. Let's add* **de-**. *It reads: deice. It means "the opposite if ice, to make not icey." Remember, you can use the prefix* **de-** *to understand the meaning of an action word or verb, because the prefix* **de-** *means to "not, opposite of." Repeat with form and code.*

Apply

Use BLM 20, Rows 5-7.

Say: *You read the word like. Add* **dis-** *at the beginning of the word. It reads: dislike. What does it mean? It means "not like, the opposite of like." You can use the prefix* **dis-** *to understand the meaning of an action or verb because the prefix* **dis-** *means to "not, the opposite of." Repeat with own and connect.*

Conclusion

Ask: *What did we learn today?* We learned that when we add the prefix **dis-** and the prefix **de-** at the beginning of a word or verb, it creates a new word that means "not, opposite of."

Home Connection

Ask students to practice adding the prefixes **de-** and **dis-** to the beginning of words to understand the meaning of the new word created. Have students identify words to which the prefixes, **de-** or **dis-**, can be added to create a new word with a family member.

✔ **Formative Assessment**

If the student completes each task correctly, precede to the next skill in the sequence. If not, refer to the suggestion under Intervention 2.

Did the student...?	Intervention 2
Recognize and identify the beginning or end of a word?	• Point directly to the beginning and say, this is the beginning or the first part of the word **de-**. Point directly to the end of the word and say this is the end of the word place or the last part of the word **defame**. Say and point: Show me the beginning of the word. Show me end of the word.
Understand the meaning of dis- and de-is "not, the opposite of?"	• Say that to **disbelieve** something means 'not to believe it." Then say that **disability** means "not having ability." Have students use these words in sentences to show they understand their meanings.
Read words?	• Point to each word and have students repeat, echo, then read it on their own while pointing to the word. Use the word in short sentences and explain its meaning to ensure student understanding.

Decode Words with Common Suffixes: -able, -ible, -al, -ial
RF.3.3a, RF.3.3b

CCSS RF.3.3
Know and apply grade-level phonics and word analysis skills in decoding words both in isolation and in text.
a. Identify and know the meaning of the most common prefixes and derivational suffixes.
b. Decode words with common Latin suffixes.

Lesson Objectives

- Recognize and decode common **suffixes.**
- Recognize that suffixes placed at the **end** of a root/base word change the meaning of the word.

METACOGNITIVE STRATEGY
- Selective auditory attention
- Use deductive thinking – generalize a rule

ACADEMIC LANGUAGE
- word ending, different meaning, suffix, base word, root word
- Note: When using Latin-based suffixes, the base word is called a root word.

Additional Materials
Blackline Master 21

Pre-Assess
Student's ability to recognize **the end of a word** as a clue to word meaning Student's ability to recognize a base or root word as the part of the word that contains meaning and can stand alone.

Introduce

As students participate in this lesson, they understand that suffixes are a group of letters added at the **end** of a root word to create a new word with a new meaning. Students recognize and generalize the understanding that the suffixes **–able** and -ible mean "able to" or "can be." Students recognize and generalize the understanding that the suffixes **-able** and **-ible** mean "able to" or "can be." Students will also recognize and generalize the understanding that the suffixes **–al** and **–ial** mean "having characteristic of."

State Learning Goal

Today we will practice adding the suffix **–able** and the suffix **-ible** to the end of a word to recognize how they change its meaning. We can use the suffix **–able** and the suffix **-ible** as clues to figure out the meaning of a word. Repeat for **–al** and **–ial**.

Teach

Say: *A* **suffix** *is a group of letters that can be* **added to the end of a word.**

Ask: *To what part of a word is the suffix added? A suffix is added to the end of a word.*

Write the word capable on the board. Underline **–able**.

Say: *This is the word capable. Read it with me: capable. This is the suffix* **–able***. Read it with me* **-able***. The suffix* **–able** *is a word part in the word capable.*

Say: *Read it with me: capable. Capable means "one who is able to."*

Write the word responsible on the board. Underline **–ible**.

Say: *This is the word responsible. Read it with me: responsible. This is the suffix –* **ible***. Read it with me:* **-ible***. The suffix* **–ible** *is a word part in the word responsible.*

Say: *Read it with me: responsible. responsible means "one who is able to make decisions."*

Say: *When you add a suffix to the end of a word, it changes the meaning of the word.*

Ask: *What happens when you add a suffix to the end of a word? The meaning of the word changes.*

Ask: *What does capable mean? It means "one who is able." What does responsible mean? It means "one who is able to make decisions." Repeat the procedure with final and partial.*

Model

Use BLM 21, Row 1.

Say: *I read the word sensible. It has the word part –ible included at the end. It means "able to show good sense." I read the word detachable. It means "able to detach." You can use the suffix –ible and suffix –able to understand the meaning of a word.*

Practice

Use BLM 21, Row 2.

Say: *Let's read the word comical. This word is made up of the word comic and the suffix –al. It means "funny." Let's underline the suffix –al. Repeat with remaining words.*

Apply

Use BLM 21, Row 4-5.

Say: *Now, let's read the word accept. We can add -able It reads: acceptable. It means "able to accept." Let's read the word suggest. It means "to share an idea." You can use suffixes to understand the meaning of a word.*

Conclusion

Ask: *What did we learn today?* We learned that when we add the suffix **–able** or the suffix **–ible** to the end of a word, it changes the meaning of the word. The suffixes **–able** and **–ible** both mean "able to." Repeat with **–al** and **–ial**.

Home Connection

Ask students to practice adding **–able** and **–ible** to the end of words and to understand the meaning of the new word. Ask students to identify other words that have the suffix **-able** or **–ible** with a family member.

✔ Formative Assessment

If the student completes each task correctly, precede to the next skill in the sequence. If not, refer to the suggestion under Intervention 2.

Did the student…?	Intervention 2
Recognize and identify the end of a word?	• Point directly to end of the word. Say this is the end of the word___ or the last part of the word___. Point to the beginning and say, this is the beginning or the first part of the word
Understand the meaning of –able and –ible?	• Show **–able** and **–ible** as similar categories. Have students sort words under **–able** and **–ible** as the meanings of each word is discussed.
Repeat words and phrases when asked?	• Point to the word and have students echo read, then read it on their own while pointing to the word

Decode Words with Common Prefixes: re- RF.3.3a, RF.3.3c

CCSS RF.3.3
Know and apply grade-level phonics and word analysis skills in decoding words both in isolation and in text.
a. Identify and know the meaning of the most common prefixes and derivational suffixes.
c. Decode multisyllable words.

Lesson Objectives

- Recognize and decode common **prefixes.**
- Recognize that prefixes are placed at the **beginning** of a root/base word change the meaning of the word.

METACOGNITIVE STRATEGY
- Selective auditory attention
- Use deductive thinking – generalize a rule

ACADEMIC LANGUAGE
- word ending, different meaning, prefix, base word, root word
- Note: When using Latin-based suffixes the base word is called a root word.

Additional Materials
Blackline Master 22

Pre-Assess
Student's ability to recognize **the beginning of a word** as a clue to word meaning. Student's ability to recognize a base or root word as the part of the word that contains meaning and can stand alone.

Introduce

As students participate in this lesson, they understand that prefixes are a group of letters added at the **beginning** of a word to create a new word with a new meaning. Students recognize and generalize the understanding that the prefix **re-** means "again, to do again."

State Learning Goal

Today we will practice adding the prefix re- to the beginning of a **verb or action word** to recognize how it changes its meaning. We will learn we can use the prefix **re-** as a clue to figure out the meaning of a word.

Teach

Say: *A prefix is a group of letters that can be **added to the beginning** of a word.*

Ask: *To what part of a word is the **prefix** added? A prefix is added to the beginning of a word.*

Write the word do on the board. Write the prefix *re-* on the board.

Say: *This is the word **do**. Read it with me: **do**. This is the prefix **re-**. Read it with me **re-**. I will add the prefix **re-** at the beginning of the word do to make the word **redo**.*

Say: *Read it with me: **redo**. **Redo** means "do again." For instance, we say, We need to redo the work we did yesterday. The prefix **re-** changed the meaning of the word, and created a new word redo that means "do again."*

Repeat the procedure with the word count.

Say: *By adding **re-** to a verb or action word, we create a new word, which means to do the action again.*

Ask: *What does **redo** mean? It means "do again." What does recount mean? It means "count again."*

Model

Use BLM 22, Row 1.

Say: *I read the word name. I add **re-**. It reads: rename. It means "name again." You can use the prefix **re-** to understand the meaning of an action word or verb, because the prefix **re-** means to "repeat the action" or to "do the action again." Write the prefix to create the new*

Practice

Use BLM 22, Rows 2–4.

Say: *Let's read the word fresh. Let's add* **re-**. *It reads: refresh. It means to "make fresh again." Remember, you can use the prefix* **re-** *to understand the meaning of an action word or verb, because the prefix re- means to "do again." Write the prefix to create the new word and then write the new word.*

Repeat the procedure with the other words.

Apply

Use BLM 22, Rows 5–7.

Say: *You read the word state. Add* **re-** *at the beginning of the word. It reads: restate. What does it mean? It means "state again." You can use the prefix* **re-** *to understand the meaning of an action or verb because the prefix* **re-** *means to "do again." Write the prefix to create the new word and then write the new word.*

Conclusion

Ask: *What did we learn today?* We learned that when we add the prefix *re–* at the beginning of an action word or verb, it creates a new word that means repeating the action or doing it again.

Home Connection

Ask students to practice adding the prefix re- the beginning of action words or verbs to understand the meaning of the new word created. Have students identify action words or verbs to which the prefix *re-* can be added to create a new word with a family member.

✔ **Formative Assessment**

If the student completes each task correctly, precede to the next skill in the sequence. If not, refer to the suggestion under Intervention 2.

Did the student…?	Intervention 2
Recognize and identify the beginning or end of a word?	• Point directly to the beginning and say, this is the beginning or the first part of the word ___. Point directly to the end of the word and say this is the end of the word___ or the last part of the word___. Say and point: Show me beginning of word. Show me end of word.
Understand the meaning re-is "do something again?"	• Say that to do something again means 'to repeat the action." Then dramatize an action. Say: Write, I write on a piece of paper. Then write again. Say: I rewrite on a piece of paper. • Act out: open/reopen, try/retry, name/rename, arrange/rearrange.
Read words?	• Point to each word and have students repeat, echo, then read it on their own while pointing to the word. Use the word in short sentences and explain its meaning to ensure student understanding.

Decode Words with Common Prefixes: mis- RF.3.3a, RF.3.3c

CCSS RF.3.3
Know and apply grade-level phonics and word analysis skills in decoding words both in isolation and in text.
a. Identify and know the meaning of the most common prefixes and derivational suffixes.
c. Decode multisyllable words.

Lesson Objectives

- Recognize and decode common **prefixes.**
- Recognize that prefixes that are placed at the **beginning** of a root/base word change the meaning of the word.

METACOGNITIVE STRATEGY
- Selective auditory attention
- Use deductive thinking – generalize a rule

ACADEMIC LANGUAGE
- word ending, different meaning, prefix, base word, root word

Additional Materials
Blackline Master 23

Pre-Assess
Student's ability to recognize **the beginning of a word** as a clue to word meaning. Student's ability to recognize a base or root word as the part of the word that contains meaning and can stand alone.

Introduce

As students participate in this lesson, they understand that **prefixes** are a group of letters added at the **beginning** of a word to create a new word with a new meaning. Students recognize and generalize the understanding that the prefix mis- means "wrongly."

State Learning Goal

Today we will practice adding the prefix mis- to the beginning of a verb or action word to recognize how it changes its meaning. We will learn we can use the prefix **mis-** as a clue to figure out the meaning of a word.

Teach

Say: *A prefix is a group of letters that can be* **added to the beginning** *of a word.*

Ask: *To what part of a word is the* **prefix** *added? A prefix is added to the beginning of a word.*

Write the word behave on the board. Write the prefix mis- on the board.

Say: *This is the word* **behave***. Read it with me:* **behave***. This is the prefix* **mis-***. Read it with me* **mis-***. I will add the prefix* **mis-** *at the beginning of the word do to make the word misbehave.*

Say: *Read it with me:* **misbehave***.* **Misbehave** *means "to do something that is wrong." For instance, we say, "Don't misbehave in class. Listen to your teacher." The prefix* **mis-** *changed the meaning of the word, and created a new word misbehave that means "to do something that is wrong."*

Write the word count on the board. Write the prefix mis on the board.

Say: *This is the word count. Read it with me: count. This is the prefix* **mis-***. Read it with me:* **mis-***. I will add the prefix mis at the beginning of the word count to make the word miscount.*

Say: *Read it with me:* **miscount***.* **Miscount** *means "to count wrongly." For example, we say, "You miscounted the plates. There should be four not five on the table." The prefix* **mis-** *changed the meaning of the word count, and created a new word miscount, which means "to count wrongly."*

Ask: *What does misplace mean? It means "to put in the wrong place." What does miscount mean? It means "to count wrongly."*

Model

Use BLM 23, Row 1.

Say: *I read the word* **treat***. I add* **mis-***. It reads:* **mistreat***. It means "to treat wrongly." You can use the prefix* **mis-** *to understand the meaning of an action word or verb, because the prefix* **mis-** *means to "do something wrongly" or to "do it incorrectly." Then write the root word and its prefix on the line.*

Practice

Use BLM 23, Rows 2–4.

Say: *Let's read the word* **understand**. *Let's add* **mis–**. *It reads:* **misunderstand**. *It means to "understand \wrongly." Remember, you can use the prefix* **mis-** *to understand the meaning of an action word or verb, because the prefix* **mis-** *means to "do wrongly."*

Apply

Use BLM 23, Rows 5–7.

Say: *You read the word* **handle**. *Add* **mis-** *at the beginning of the word. It reads:* **mishandle**. *What does it mean? It means "handle wrongly." You can use the prefix* **mis-** *to understand the meaning of an action or verb because the prefix* **mis-** *means to "do wrongly."*

Conclusion

Ask: *What did we learn today?* We learned that when we add the prefix **mis–** at the beginning of a word or verb, it creates a new word that means doing something wrong.

Home Connection

Ask students to practice adding the prefix **mis-** to he beginning of action words or verbs to understand the meaning of the new word created. Have students identify action words or verbs to which the prefix **mis-** can be added to create a new word with a family member.

✔ Formative Assessment

Ask students to practice adding the prefix mis- to the beginning of action words or verbs to understand the meaning of the new word created. Have students identify action words or verbs to which the prefix **mis-** can be added to create a new word with a family member.

Did the student…?	Intervention 2
Recognize and identify the beginning or end of a word?	• Point directly to the beginning and say, this is the beginning or the first part of the word mis-. Point directly to the end of the word and say this is the end of the word place or the last part of the word misplace. Say and point: Show me the beginning of the word. Show me end of the word.
Understand the meaning re- is "do something again?"	• Say that to mislabel something means 'to label it wrongly." Then dramatize an action. Draw something on the board and label it incorrectly. Say: Look, I mislabeled the picture. Then label it correctly.
Read words?	• Point to each word and have students repeat, echo, then read it on their own while pointing to the word. Use the word in short sentences and explain its meaning to ensure student understanding.

Decode Words with Common Prefixes: trans-, inter- RF.3.3a, RF.3.3c

CCSS RF.3.3
Know and apply grade-level phonics and word analysis skills in decoding words both in isolation and in text.
a. Identify and know the meaning of the most common prefixes and derivational suffixes.
c. Decode multisyllable words.

Lesson Objectives

- Recognize and decode common **prefixes**.
- Recognize that prefixes that are placed at the **beginning** of a root/base word change the meaning of the word.

METACOGNITIVE STRATEGY
- Selective auditory attention
- Use deductive thinking – generalize a rule

ACADEMIC LANGUAGE
- word ending, different meaning, prefix, base word, root word

Additional Materials
Blackline Master 24

Pre-Assess
Student's ability to recognize the beginning of a word as a clue to word meaning. Student's ability to recognize a base or root word as the part of the word that contains meaning and can stand alone.

Introduce

As students participate in this lesson, they will understand that prefixes are a group of letters added at the beginning of a word to create a new word with a new meaning. Students will recognize and generalize the understanding that the prefix **trans-** means "across" and the prefix **inter-** means "between or among."

State Learning Goal

Today we will practice adding the prefix **trans-** to the beginning of a verb or action word to recognize how it changes its meaning. We will learn we can use the prefix **trans-** as a clue to figure out the meaning of a word. We will also practice adding the prefix **inter-** to the beginning of a verb or action word to recognize how it changes its meaning. We will also learn we can use the prefix **inter-** as a clue to figure out the meaning of a word.

Teach

Say: *A* **prefix** *is a group of letters that can be* **added to the beginning** *of a word.*

Ask: *To what part of a word is the prefix added? A* **prefix** *is added to the beginning of a word.*

Write the word Atlantic on the board. Write the prefix trans- on the board.

Say: *This is the word Atlantic. Read it with me: Atlantic. This is the prefix trans-. Read it with me* **trans-**. *I will add the prefix* **trans** *at the beginning of the word atlantic to make the word* **transatlantic**.

Say: *Read it with me:* **transatlantic**. **Transatlantic** *means "to cross the Atlantic Ocean." For instance, we say, "I took a transatlantic trip." The prefix* **trans-** *changed the meaning of the word, and created a new word transatlantic that means "to cross the Atlantic Ocean."*

Write the word school on the board. Write the prefix inter- on the board.

Say: *This is the word school. Read it with me: school. This is the prefix* **inter-**. *Read it with me:* **inter-**. *I will add the prefix* **inter-** *at the beginning of the word school to make the word* **interschool**.

Say: *Read it with me:* **interschool**. **Interschool** *means "between or among schools." For example, we say, "We have an interschool party tomorrow after school. The prefix* **inter-** *changed the meaning of the word school and created a new word* **interschool,** *which means "between or among schools."*

Say: *By adding* **inter-** *to a noun, we create a new word, which means "between or among."*

Ask: *What does* **transatlantic** *mean? It means "to cross the Atlantic Ocean." What does interschool mean? It means "between or among schools."*

Model

Use BLM 24, Row 1.

Say: *I read the word state. I add* **inter-**. *It reads: interstate. It means "between or among states." You can use the prefix* **inter-** *to understand the meaning of a noun, because the prefix* **inter-** *means to "between or among." Write the root word and its prefix on the line.*

Practice

Use BLM 24, Rows 2–4.

Say: *Let's read the word port. Let's add* **trans-**. *It reads:* **transport.** *It means to "carry across something. Remember, you can use the prefix* **trans-** *to understand the meaning of an noun, because the prefix* **trans-** *means "across." Write the root word and its prefix on the line.*

Apply

Use BLM 24, Rows 5–7.

Say: *You read the word* **faith**. *Add* **inter-** *at the beginning of the word. It reads:* **interfaith**. *What does it mean? It means "between or among faiths." You can use the prefix* **inter-** *to understand the meaning of a noun because the prefix* **inter-** *means "between or among." Then write the root word and its prefix on the line.*

Conclusion

Ask: *What did we learn today?* We learned that when we add the prefixes **trans-** and **inter-** at the beginning of nouns, they create new words that mean "across" or "between or among."

Home Connection

Ask students to practice adding the prefixes *trans-* and *inter-* to the beginning of nouns to understand the meaning of the new words created. Have students identify nouns to which the prefix *trans-* and *inter-* can be added to create new words with a family member.

✔ Formative Assessment

If the student completes each task correctly, precede to the next skill in the sequence. If not, refer to the suggestion under Intervention 2.

Did the student…?	Intervention 2
Recognize and identify the beginning or end of a word?	• Point directly to the beginning and say, this is the beginning or the first part of the word inter-. Point directly to the end of the word and say this is the end of the word place or the last part of the word interoffice. Say and point: Show me the beginning of the word. Show me end of the word.
Understand the meaning re-is "do something again?"	• Say that **transcontinental** means "across continents." Have students repeat the word **transcontinental** with you and volunteers use a world map to show what the word means.
Read words?	• Point to each word and have students repeat, echo, then read it on their own while pointing to the word. Use the word in short sentences and explain its meaning to ensure student understanding.

CCSS RF.3.3
Know and apply grade-level phonics and word analysis skills in decoding words both in isolation and in text.
a. Identify and know the meaning of the most common prefixes and derivational suffixes.
b. Decode words with common Latin suffixes.

Lesson Objectives

- Recognize and decode common **suffixes.**
- Recognize that **suffixes** that are placed at the **end** of a root/base word change the meaning of the word.

METACOGNITIVE STRATEGY
- Selective auditory attention
- Use deductive thinking – generalize a rule

ACADEMIC LANGUAGE
- word ending, different meaning, suffix, base word, root word

Additional Materials
Blackline Master 25

Pre-Assess
Student's ability to recognize **the end of a word** as a clue to word meaning. Student's ability to recognize a base or root word as the part of the word that contains meaning and can stand alone.

Decode Words with Common Suffixes: -ment, -tion RF.3.3a, RF.3.3b

Introduce

As students participate in this lesson, they understand that **suffixes** are a group of letters added at the **end** of a word to create a new word with a new meaning. Students recognize and generalize the understanding that the suffix **-ment** means "having the quality of" and the suffix *-tion* means "the act or process of."

State Learning Goal

Today we will practice adding the suffix **-ment** to the end of a of a verb to recognize how it changes its part of speech to a noun and also changes its meaning. We will learn we can use the suffix **-ment** as a clue to figure out the meaning of a word. We will also practice adding the suffix **-tion** to the end of a verb to recognize how it changes its part of speech to a noun and also changes its meaning. We will also learn we can use the suffix **-tion** as a clue to figure out the meaning of a word.

Teach

Say: *A* **suffix** *is a group of letters that can be* **added to the end** *of a word.*

Ask: *To what part of a word is the* **suffix** *added? A suffix is added to the end of a word.*

Write the word govern on the board. Write the suffix *-ment* on the board.

Say: *This is the word government. Read it with me: government. This is the suffix* **-ment**. *Read it with me:* **-ment** *I will add the suffix* **-ment** *at the end of the word govern to make the word government.*

Say: *Read it with me: government. Government means "the act of ruling a country, state, etc." For instance, we say, "We have a democratic government." The suffix -ment changed the meaning of the verb govern, and created a noun government that means "the act of ruling a country, state, etc."*

Write the word direct on the board. Write the suffix **-tion** on the board.

Say: *This is the word direct. Read it with me: direct. This is the suffix* **-tion**. *Read it with me:* **-tion**. *I will add the suffix* **-tion** *at the end of the word direct to make the word direction.*

Say: *Read it with me: direction. Direction means "the act of directing or guiding." For example, we say, "We were given lots of direction to do the project. The suffix* **-tion** *changed the meaning of the verb direct, and created a noun direction which means "the act of directing or guiding."*

Say: *When you add the* **suffix** *to the ending of a word, it creates a new word and changes its meaning.*

Say: *By adding* **-ment** *to the verb govern, we create a new word, a noun, which means "the act of ruling a country, state, etc." By adding* **–tion** *to the verb direct, we create a new word, a noun, which means "the act of directing or guiding."*

Ask: *What does government mean? It means "the act of ruling a country, state, etc." What does direction mean? It means "the act of directing or guiding."*

Model

Use BLM 25, Row 1.

Say: *I read the word* **adopt.** *I add* **-ion.** *It reads:* **adoption.** *It means "having the quality of adopting or taking and using as one's own." You can use the suffix* **-ion** *to understand the meaning of a word, because the suffix* **-ion** *means "having the quality of." Now write the root word and its suffix on the line.*

Practice

Use BLM 25, Rows 2–4.

Say: *Let's read the word* **develop.** *Let's add* **-ment.** *It reads:* **development.** *It means to "the act or process of developing or bring something into being." Remember, you can use the suffix* **-ment** *to understand the meaning of a word, because the suffix* **-ment** *means "the act or process of." Now write the root word and its suffix on the line.*

Apply

Use BLM 25, Rows 5–7.

Say: *You read the word* **announce.** *Add* **-ment** *at the end of the word. It reads:* **announcement.** *What does it mean? It means "having the quality of announcing." You can use the prefix* **-ment** *to understand the meaning of a word because the suffix* **-ment** *means to "having the quality of." Now write the root word and its suffix on the line.*

Conclusion

Ask: *What did we learn today?* We learned that when we add the suffixes **-ment** and **-ion** at the end of verbs, they create new words, nouns, that mean "the act or process of" or "having the quality of."

Home Connection

Ask students to practice adding the suffixes **ment-** and **-ion** to the end of words to understand the meaning of the new words created. Have students identify verbs to which the suffixes **-men**t and **-ion** can be added to create new words that become nouns, with a family member.

✔ Formative Assessment

If the student completes each task correctly, precede to the next skill in the sequence. If not, refer to the suggestion under Intervention 2.

Did the student…?	Intervention 2
Recognize and identify the beginning or end of a word?	• Point directly to the end of the word. Say this is the end of the word • **-ment** or the last part of the word **payment**. Point to the beginning and say, this is the beginning or the first part of the word
Understand the meaning re-is "do something again?"	• Say that **eruption** means "the act or process of **erupting**." Have students repeat the word eruption with you and dramatize an eruption.
Read words?	• Point to each word and have students repeat, echo, then read it on their own while pointing to the word. Use the word in short sentences and explain its meaning to ensure student understanding.

CCSS RF.3.3
Know and apply grade-level phonics and word analysis skills in decoding words both in isolation and in text.
a. Identify and know the meaning of the most common prefixes and derivational suffixes.
b. Decode words with common Latin suffixes.

Lesson Objectives

- Recognize and decode common **suffixes.**
- Recognize that **suffixes** that are placed at the **end** of a root/base word change the meaning of the word.

METACOGNITIVE STRATEGY
- Selective auditory attention
- Use deductive thinking – generalize a rule

ACADEMIC LANGUAGE
- word ending, different meaning, suffix, base word, root word

Additional Materials
Blackline Master 26

Pre-Assess
Student's ability to recognize **the end of a word** as a clue to word meaning. Student's ability to recognize a base or root word as the part of the word that contains meaning and can stand alone.

Decode Words with Common Suffixes: -ous , -eous, and -ious
RF.3.3a, RF.3.3b

Introduce

As students participate in this lesson, they understand that **suffixes** are a group of letters added at the **end** of a word to create a new word with a new meaning. Students recognize and generalize the understanding that the suffixes **-ous , -eous,** and **-ious** mean "having the quality of."

State Learning Goal

Today we will practice adding the suffixes **-ous , -eous,** and **-ious** to the end of a word to recognize how it changes its part of speech to an adjective and also changes its meaning. We will learn we can use the suffixes **-ous , -eous,** and **-ious** as a clue to figure out the meanings of words.

Teach

Say: *A* **suffix** *is a group of letters that can be* **added to the end of a word.**

Ask: *To what part of a word is the* **suffix** *added? A suffix is added to the end of a word.*

Write the word **danger** on the board. Write the suffix *-ous* on the board.

Say: *This is the word* **dangerous***. Read it with me:* **dangerous***. This is the suffix* **-ous***. Read it with me* **-ous***. I will add the suffix* **-ous** *at the end of the word* **danger** *to make the word dangerous. For instance, we say, "Riding a bike without a helmet is a dangerous thing to do." The suffix* **-ous** *changed the meaning of the noun* **danger***, and created an adjective dangerous that means "having the quality of danger."*

Write the word **fury** on the board. Write the suffix *-ious* on the board.

Say: *This is the word fury. Read it with me: fury. This is the suffix* **-ious***. Read it with me:* **-ious***. I will add the suffix* **-ious** *at the end of the word fury to make the word furious.*

Say: *Read it with me:* **furious***. Furious means "having the quality of fury or anger." The suffix* **-ious** *changed the meaning of the noun fury, and created an adjective* **furious** *which means "having the quality of fury or anger."*

Repeat the procedure with the words danger and courage and the suffix –ous and –eous.

Model

Use BLM 26, Row 1.

Say: *I read the word* **joy.** *I add* **-ous.** *It reads:* **joyous.** *It means "having the quality of joy or happiness." You can use the suffix* **-ous** *to understand the meaning of a word, because the suffix* **-ous** *means "having the quality of." Now write the root word and its suffix on the line.*

Practice

Use BLM 26, Rows 2–4.

Say: *Let's read the word* **mystery.** *Let's add* **-ious.** *It reads:* **mysterious.** *It means "having the quality of mystery." Remember, you can use the suffix* **-ious** *to understand the meaning of a word, because the suffix* **-ious** *means "having the quality of." Now write the root word and its suffix on the line. Repeat with* **ceremony** *and* **glory.**

Apply

Use BLM 26, Rows 5–7.

Say: *You read the word* **advantage.** *Add* **-eous** *at the end of the word. It reads:* **advantageous.** *What does it mean? It means "having the quality of an advantage." You can use the suffix* **-eous** *to understand the meaning of a word because the suffix* **-eous** *means to "having the quality of." Now write the root word and its suffix on the line. Repeat with* **gas** *and* **courtesy.**

Conclusion

Ask: *What did we learn today?* We learned that when we add the suffixes **-ous**, **-ious** and **-eous** at the end of nouns, they create new words, adjectives, that mean "having the quality of."

Home Connection

Ask students to practice adding the suffixes **-ous, -ious,** and **-eous** to the end of words to understand the meaning of the new words created. Have students identify nouns to which the suffixes **-ous, -ious,** and **-eous** can be added to create new words that become adjectives, with a family member.

✔ Formative Assessment

If the student completes each task correctly, precede to the next skill in the sequence. If not, refer to the suggestion under Intervention 2.

Did the student...?	Intervention 2
Recognize and identify the beginning or end of a word?	• Point directly to the end of the word. Say this is the end of the word • **-ous** or the last part of the word **poisonous.** Point to the beginning and say, this is the beginning or the first part of the word
Understand the meaning -ous, --ious, and -eous mean "having the quality of?"	• Say that **luxurious** means "have the quality of luxury or comfort." Have students repeat the word **luxurious** with you and name some things they think are luxurious.
Read words?	• Point to each word and have students repeat, echo, then read it on their own while pointing to the word. Use the word in short sentences and explain its meaning to ensure student understanding.

Decode Words with Common Suffixes: -ive , -ative, and -itive
RF.3.3a, RF.3.3b

CCSS RF.3.3
Know and apply grade-level phonics and word analysis skills in decoding words both in isolation and in text.
a. Identify and know the meaning of the most common prefixes and derivational suffixes.
b. Decode words with common Latin suffixes.

Lesson Objectives

- Recognize and decode common **suffixes.**
- Recognize that **suffixes** that are placed at the **end** of a root/base word change the meaning of the word.

METACOGNITIVE STRATEGY
- Selective auditory attention
- Use deductive thinking – generalize a rule

ACADEMIC LANGUAGE
- word ending, different meaning, suffix, base word, root word

Additional Materials
Blackline Master 27

Pre-Assess
Student's ability to recognize **the end of a word** as a clue to word meaning. Student's ability to recognize a base or root word as the part of the word that contains meaning and can stand alone.

Introduce

As students participate in this lesson, they understand that **suffixes** are a group of letters added at the **end** of a word to create a new word with a new meaning. Students recognize and generalize the understanding that the suffixes **-ive , -ative,** and **-itive** mean "having the quality of."

State Learning Goal

Today we will practice adding the suffixes **-ive , -ative,** and **-itive** to the end of a word to recognize how it changes its part of speech to an adjective and also changes its meaning. We will learn we can use the suffixes **-ive , -ative,** and **–itive** as a clue to figure out the meanings of words.

Teach

Say: *A* **suffix** *is a group of letters that can be* **added to the end** *of a word.*

Ask: *To what part of a word is the* **suffix** *added? A suffix is added to the end of a word.*

Write the word adopt on the board. Write the suffix -ive on the board.

Say: *This is the word* **adoptive***. Read it with me:* **adoptive***. This is the suffix* **-ive***. Read it with me* **--ive***. I will add the suffix* **-ive** *at the end of the word adopt to make the word* **adoptive***.*

Say: *Read it with me:* **adoptive***.* **Adoptive** *means "having the quality of being adopted." For instance, we say, "Tim loves his adoptive parents." The suffix* **-ive** *changed the meaning of the verb adopt and created an adjective adoptive that means "having the quality of being adopted."*

Write the word talk on the board. Write the suffix –ative on the board.

Say: *This is the word talk. Read it with me: talk. This is the suffix* **-ative***. Read it with me:* **-ative***. I will add the suffix* **-ative** *at the end of the word talk to make the word talkative.*

Say: *Read it with me: talkative. Talkative means "having the quality of talking a lot." For example, we say, "The talkative student raised his hand a lot in class." The suffix* **-ative** *changed the meaning of the verb talk and created an adjective talkative which means "having the quality of talking a lot."*

Repeat the procedure with the word sense and the suffix –itive. on the board.

Say: *When you add the* **suffix** *to the ending of a word, it creates a new word and changes its meaning.*

Ask: *What happens when you put a* **suffix** *at the end of a word? The meaning of the word changes.*

Model

Use BLM 27, Row 1.

Say: *I read the word protect. I add* **-ive**. *It reads: protective. It means "having the quality of wanting to protect someone or something." You can use the suffix* **-ive** *to understand the meaning of a word, because the suffix* **–ive** *means "having the quality of." Now write the root word and its suffix on the line.*

Practice

Use BLM 27, Rows 2–4.

Say: *Let's read the word* **add**. *Let's add* **-itive**. *It reads:* **additive**. *It means "having the quality of being added." Remember, you can use the suffix* **–itive** *to understand the meaning of a word, because the suffix* **–itive** *means "having the quality of being added." Now write the root word and its suffix on the line. Repeat with define and compete.*

Apply

Use BLM 27, Rows 5–7.

Say: *You read the word imagine. Add* **–ative** *at the end of the word. It reads: imaginative. What does it mean? It means "having the quality of imagination." You can use the suffix -ative to understand the meaning of a word because the suffix* **-ative** *means to "having the quality of." Now write the root word and its suffix on the line. Repeat with compare and cure.*

Conclusion

Ask: *What did we learn today?* We learned that when we add the suffixes **–ive**, **-ative** and **-itive** at the end of nouns, they create new words, adjectives, that mean "having the quality of."

Home Connection

Ask students to practice adding the suffixes **–ive**, **-ative**, and **-itive** to the end of words to understand the meaning of the new words created. Have students identify nouns to which the suffixes **–ive**, **-ative**, and **-itive** can be added to create new words that become adjectives, with a family member.

✔ Formative Assessment

If the student completes each task correctly, precede to the next skill in the sequence. If not, refer to the suggestion under Intervention 2.

Did the student…?	Intervention 2
Recognize and identify the beginning or end of a word?	• Point directly to the end of the word. Say this is the end of the word • **-ive, ative, itive** or the last part of the word **creative, imaginative,** and **competitive.** Point to the beginning and say, this is the beginning or the first part of the word
Understand the meaning –ives, -ative, and -itive mean "having the quality of"	• Say that *–ives, -ative,* and *-itive* all mean "have the quality of." Have students name a word with each suffix and say what the words mean.
Read words?	• Point to each word and have students repeat, echo, then read it on their own while pointing to the word. Use the word in short sentences and explain its meaning to ensure student understanding.

CCSS RF.3.3
Know and apply grade level phonics and word analysis skills in decoding words both in isolation and in text.
a. Identify and know the meaning of the most common prefixes and derivational suffixes.

Lesson Objectives

- Recognize and decode Greek **suffixes.**
- Recognize that **suffixes** that are placed at the **end** of a root/base word change the meaning of the word.

METACOGNITIVE STRATEGY
- Selective auditory attention
- Use deductive thinking – generalize a rule

ACADEMIC LANGUAGE
- word ending, different meaning, suffix, Greek, base word, root word

Additional Materials
Blackline Master 28

Pre-Assess
Student's ability to recognize **the end of a word** as a clue to word meaning. Student's ability to recognize a base or root word as the part of the word that contains meaning and can stand alone.

Decode Words with Common Suffixes: –ology, -graphic, and -graphy RF.3.3a

Introduce

As students participate in this lesson, they understand that **suffixes** are a group of letters added at the end of a word to create a new word with a new meaning. Students recognize and generalize the understanding that the Greek suffix **-ology**, means "the study of," and the Greek suffixes **-graphy** means "letter, writing."

State Learning Goal

Today we will practice adding the Greek suffixes **–ology, -graphic,** and **-graphy** to the end of words to recognize how they change their meanings. We will learn we can use the Greek suffixes **–ology, -graphic,** and **-graphy** as clues to figure out the meaning of words.

Teach

Say: *A* **suffix** *is a group of letters that can be* **added to the end** *of a word.*

Ask: *To what part of a word is the* **suffix** *added? A suffix is added to the end of a word.*

Write the word *bio* on the board. Write the suffix *-ology* on the board.

Say: *This is the word* **bio**. *Read it with me:* **bio**. *Bio is a Greek root meaning "life." This is the suffix* **-ology**. *Read it with me* **-ology**. *I will add the suffix* **–ology** *at the end of the word bio to make the word* **biology.**

Say: *Read it with me:* **biology.** *Biology means "the study of life." For instance, we say, "We studied animals in biology. The suffix* **–ology** *changed the meaning of* **bio** *to mean "the study of life."*

Write the word *ortho* on the board. Write the suffix *–graphic* on the board.

Say: *This is the word* **ortho**. *Read it with me: ortho.* **Ortho** *means "correct." This is the suffix* **-graphic**. *Read it with me: -graphic. I will add the suffix* **-graphic** *at the end of the word* **ortho** *to make the word* **orthographic.**

Say: *Read it with me:* **orthographic.** *Orthographic means "correct writing." For example, we say, "Orthographic sentences have correct spelling and grammar. The suffix* **–graphic** *changed the meaning of the word ortho, and created a new word orthographic, an adjective, which means "correct writing."*

Say: *By adding* **-ology** *to the word bio we create a new word biology which means "the study of life."* **Ask:** *What does* **biology** *mean? It means "the study of life." What does orthographic mean? It means "correct writing." What does orthography mean? It means "the act of correct writing."*

Model

Use BLM 28, Row 1.

Say: *Let's read the word* **geo**. *It's a Greek root that means "earth." Let's add* **-ology**. *It reads:* **geology**. *It means "the study of earth." Remember, you can use the suffix* **–ology** *to understand the meaning of a word, because the suffix* **–ology** *means "the study of."*

Practice

Use BLM 28, Rows 2–4.

Say: *You read the word* **bio**. *Add* **–graphic** *at the end of the word. It reads:* **biographic**. *What does it mean? It means "a type of writing about oneself." You can use the suffix* **–graphic** *to understand the meaning of a word because the suffix* **–graphic** *means "writing." Now write the root word and its suffix on the line.*

Apply

Use BLM 28, Rows 5–7.

Say: *Let's read the word* **planet**. *Let's add* **-ology**. *It reads:* **planetology**. *It means "the study of the planets." Remember, you can use the suffix* **–ology** *to understand the meaning of a word, because the suffix* **–ology** *means "the study of." Repeat with ocean and criminal.*

Conclusion

Ask: *What did we learn today?* What did we learn today? We learned that when we add the suffix **–ology** to a word it changes its meaning to "the study of." And we learned that when we add the suffixes **–graphic** and **-graphy** it changes its meaning to "writing."

✔ Formative Assessment

If the student completes each task correctly, precede to the next skill in the sequence. If not, refer to the suggestion under Intervention 2.

Did the student…?	Intervention 2
Recognize and identify the beginning or end of a word?	• Point directly to the end of the word. Say this is the end of the word • **-ology** and **–graphic**, and **graphy** or the last part of the word biology, and **orthographic** and orthography. Point to the beginning and say, this is the beginning or the first part of the word.
Understand the meanings of the ending –ology means "the study of" and –graphic and -graphy mean "writing?"	• Have students name a word with each suffix and say what the words mean.
Read words?	• Point to each word and have students repeat, echo, then read it on their own while pointing to the word. Use the word in short sentences and explain its meaning to ensure student understanding.

CCSS RF.3.3
Know and apply grade level phonics and word analysis skills in decoding words both in isolation and in text.
a. Identify and know the meaning of the most common prefixes and derivational suffixes.
c. Decode multisyllable words.

Lesson Objectives

- Recognize and decode Greek **suffixes.**
- Recognize that **suffixes** that are placed at the **end** of a root/base word change the meaning of the word.

METACOGNITIVE STRATEGY
- Selective auditory attention
- Use deductive thinking – generalize a rule

ACADEMIC LANGUAGE
- word ending, different meaning, suffix, Greek, base word, root word

Additional Materials
Blackline Master 29

Pre-Assess
Student's ability to recognize **the end of a word** as a clue to word meaning. Student's ability to recognize a base or root word as the part of the word that contains meaning and can stand alone.

Decode Words with Common Suffixes: –phobia, –scope RF.3.3a, RF.3.3c

Introduce

As students participate in this lesson, they understand that **suffixes** are a group of letters added at the end of a word to create a new word with a new meaning. Students recognize and generalize the understanding that the Greek suffix **-phobia**, means "fear of" and that the Greek suffix **–scope** means "view, examine."

State Learning Goal

Today we will practice adding the Greek suffix **–phobia** and **–scope** to the end of words to recognize how the change their meanings. We will learn we can use the Greek suffixes **–phobia** and **-scope** as clues to figure out the meaning of words.

Teach

Say: *A* **suffix** *is a group of letters that can be added to the* **end of a word.**

Ask: *To what part of a word is the* **suffix** *added? A suffix is added to the end of a word.*

Write the word computer on the board. Write the suffix -*phobia* on the board.

Say: *This is the word computer. Read it with me: computer. This is the suffix* **-phobia***. Read it with me* **-phobia***. I will add the suffix* **-phobia** *at the end of the word computer to make the word* **computerphobia***.*

Say: *Read it with me:* **computerphobia***. Computerphobia means "a fear of computers." For instance, I might say, "My grandparents have computerphobia." The suffix* **-phobia** *changed the word to mean "fear of computers."*

Write the word micro on the board. Write the suffix -*scope* on the board.

Say: *This is the word* **micro***. Read it with me:* **micro***. This is the suffix* **-scope***. Read it with me:* **--scope***. I will add the suffix* **-scope** *at the end of the word* **micro** *to make the word* **microscope***.*

Say: *Read it with me:* **microscope***. Microscope means "something to view or examine very small things." For example, we say, "We studied the cell under the microscope." The suffix* **-scope** *changed the meaning of the word* **micro** *and created a new work microscope, which means "something to view or examine very small things."*

Ask: *What does computerphobia mean? It means "having a fear of computers." What does microscope mean? It means "something to view or examine very small things."*

Model

Use BLM 29, Row 1.

Say: *You read the word* **tele***. Tele is a Greek root meaning "far off or at a distance." Add* **–scope** *at the end of the word. It reads:* **telescope***. What does it mean? It means "something that lets you view or examine something far away (such as stars)." You can use the suffix* **–scope** *to understand the meaning of a word because the suffix* **–scope** *means to "view or examine." Now write the root* *word and its suffix on the line.*

Practice

Use BLM 29, Rows 2–4.

Say: *I read the word **hydro**. **Hydro** is a Greek word that means "water." I add –phobia. It reads: **hydrophobia**. It means "having a fear of water." You can use the suffix **–phobia** to understand the meaning of a word, because the suffix **–phobia** means "having a fear of." Then write the root word and its suffix on the line. Repeat with **claustro–** and **arachno–**.*

Apply

Use BLM 29, Rows 5-7.

Say: *Let's read the word **night**. Let's add **–scope**. It reads: **nightscope**. It means "something that let's us examine or view something at night." Remember, you can use the suffix **–scope** to understand the meaning of a word, because the suffix **–scope** means "view or examine. Repeat with **stetho–** and **peri–**.*

Conclusion

Ask: *What did we learn today?* We learned that when we add the suffix **–phobia** to a word it changes its meaning to "fear of." And we learned that when we add the suffix **–scope** it changes its meaning to "view, examine."

Home Connection

Ask students to practice adding the suffixes **–phobia** and **–scope** to the end of words to understand the meaning of the new words created. Have students identify words to which the suffixes **-phobia** and **-scope** that can be added to create new words with a family member.

✔ Formative Assessment

If the student completes each task correctly, precede to the next skill in the sequence. If not, refer to the suggestion under Intervention 2.

Did the student…?	Intervention 2
recognize and identify the beginning or end of a word?	• Point directly to the end of the word. Say this is the end of the word • **-phobia** and **–scope** or the last part of the word **hydrophobia**, and **microscope**. Point to the beginning and say, this is the beginning or the first part of the word
understand the meanings of the ending –phobia means "fear of" and –scope means "view, examine mean "having the quality of?"	• Have students name a word with each suffix and say what the words mean.
read words?	• Point to each word and have students repeat, echo, then read it on their own while pointing to the word. Use the word in short sentences and explain its meaning to ensure student understanding.

Decode Words with Common Suffixes: –ory, –ist RF.3.3a

CCSS RF.3.3
Know and apply grade-level phonics and word analysis skills in decoding words both in isolation and in text.
a. Identify and know the meaning of the most common prefixes and derivational suffixes.

Lesson Objectives

- Recognize and decode Greek **suffixes.**
- Recognize that **suffixes** that are placed at the **end** of a root/base word change the meaning of the word.

METACOGNITIVE STRATEGY
- Selective auditory attention
- Use deductive thinking – generalize a rule

ACADEMIC LANGUAGE
- word ending, different meaning, suffix, Greek, base word, root word

Additional Materials
Blackline Master 30

Pre-Assess
Student's ability to recognize **the end of a word** as a clue to word meaning. Student's ability to recognize a base or root word as the part of the word that contains meaning and can stand alone.

Introduce

As students participate in this lesson, they understand that **suffixes** are a group of letters added at the **end** of a word to create a new word with a new meaning. Students recognize and generalize the understanding that the Greek suffix **-ory**, means "place for" and that the Greek suffix **-ist** means "one who practices."

State Learning Goal

Today we will practice adding the Greek suffix **–ory** and **–ist** to the end of words to recognize how the change their meanings. We will learn we can use the Greek suffixes –ory and -ist as clues to figure out the meaning of words.

Teach

Say: *A* **suffix** *is a group of letters that can be* **added to the end** *of a word.*

Ask: *To what part of a word is the* **suffix** *added? A suffix is added to the end of a word.*

Write the word observe on the board. Write the suffix -ory on the board.

Say: *This is the word* **observe***. Read it with me:* **observe***. This is the suffix* **-ory***. Read it with me* **-ory***. I will add the suffix* **-ory** *at the end of the word observe to make the word observatory.*

Say: *Read it with me:* **observatory***.* **Observatory** *means "a place where someone observes or watches something." For instance, we say, "We watched sea life at the underwater observatory." The suffix* **–ory** *changed the meaning observe to mean "a place to observe or watch."*

Write the word art on the board. Write the suffix -ist on the board.

Say: *This is the word* **art***. Read it with me:* **art***. This is the suffix* **-ist***. Read it with me:* **-ist***. I will add the suffix* **-ist** *at the end of the word art to make the word artist.*

Say: *Read it with me:* **artist***. Artist means "one who practices art." For example, we say, "The artist painted the lake." The suffix* **-ist** *changed the meaning of the word art, and created a new word artist which means "one who practices art."*

Say: *When you add the* **suffix** *to the ending of a word, it creates a new word and changes its meaning.*

Ask: *What does* **observatory** *mean? It means "a place to observe or watch something." What does artist mean? It means "one who practices art."*

Model

Use BLM 30, Row 1.

Say: *Let's read the word guitar. Let's add -ist. It reads: guitarist. It means "one who practices the guitar." Remember, you can use the suffix* **–ist** *to understand the meaning of a word, because the suffix* **–ist** *means "one who practices."*

Practice

Use BLM 30, Rows 2–4.

Say: *You read the word direct. Add **–ory** at the end of the word. It reads: directory. What does it mean? It means "a place for finding diections." You can use the suffix **–ory** to understand the meaning of a word because the suffix **-ory** means to "a place for." Then write the root word and its suffix on the line. Repeat for **explore** and **labor***.

Apply

Use BLM 30, Rows 5–7.

Say: *Let's read the word **piano**. Let's add **-ist**. It reads: **pianist**. It means "one who practices the piano." Remember, you can use the suffix **–ist** to understand the meaning of a word, because the suffix **–ist** means "one who practices. Repeat for cartoon and style.*

Conclusion

Ask: *What did we learn today?* We learned that when we add the suffix **–ory** to a word it changes its meaning to "a place for." And we learned that when we add the suffix **–ist** it changes its meaning to "one who practices."

Home Connection

Ask students to practice adding the suffixes **–ory** and **–ist** to the end of words to understand the meaning of the new words created. Have students identify words to which the suffixes **–ory** and **-ist** that can be added to create new words with a family member.

✔ Formative Assessment

If the student completes each task correctly, precede to the next skill in the sequence. If not, refer to the suggestion under Intervention 2.

Did the student…?	Intervention 2
Recognize and identify the beginning or end of a word?	• Point directly to the end of the word. Say this is the end of the word • **-ory** and **–ist** or the last part of the word **observatory,** and **artist.** Point to the beginning and say, this is the beginning or the first part of the word
Understand the meanings of the ending –ory means "a place for" and –ist means "one who practices?"	• Have students name a word with each suffix and say what the words mean.
Read words?	• Point to each word and have students repeat, echo, then read it on their own while pointing to the word. Use the word in short sentences and explain its meaning to ensure student understanding.

CCSS RF.3.3
Know and apply grade level phonics and word analysis skills in decoding words both in isolation and in text.
a. Identify and know the meaning of the most common prefixes and derivational suffixes.
c. Decode multisyllable words.

Lesson Objectives

- Recognize and decode Greek **suffixes.**
- Recognize that **suffixes** that are placed at the **end** of a root/base word change the meaning of the word.

METACOGNITIVE STRATEGY
- Selective auditory attention
- Use deductive thinking – generalize a rule

ACADEMIC LANGUAGE
- word ending, different meaning, suffix, Greek, base word, root word

Additional Materials
Blackline Master 31

Pre-Assess
Student's ability to recognize **the end of a word** as a clue to word meaning. Student's ability to recognize a base or root word as the part of the word that contains meaning and can stand alone.

Decode Words with Common Suffixes: –ate, –fy RF.3.3a, RF.3.3c

Introduce

As students participate in this lesson, they understand that **suffixes** are a group of letters added at the **end** of a word to create a new word with a new meaning. Students recognize and generalize the understanding that the Greek suffix **-ate**, means "having the quality of" and that the Greek suffix **-fy** means "to make into."

State Learning Goal

Today we will practice adding the Greek suffix **–ate** and **–fy** to the end of words to recognize how the change their meanings. We will learn we can use the Greek suffixes **–ate** and **-fy** as clues to figure out the meaning of words.

Teach

Say: *A* **suffix** *is a group of letters that can be* **added to the end** *of a word.*

Ask: *To what part of a word is the* **suffix** *added? A suffix is added to the end of a word.*

Write the word design on the board. Write the suffix *-ate* on the board.

Say: *This is the word* **design**. *Read it with me:* **design**. *This is the suffix* **-ate**. *Read it with me* **-ate**. *I will add the suffix -ate at the end of the word design to make the word designate.*

Say: *Read it with me:* **designate**. **Designate** *means "to have marks or designs." For instance, we say, "We designate the rivers on the map with a blue wavy line. The suffix* **–ate** *changed the meaning of design to mean "to have marks or designs."*

Write the word class on the board. Write the suffix *-fy* on the board.

Say: *This is the word class. Read it with me: class. This is the suffix -fy. Read it with me: -fy. I will add the suffix* **-fy** *at the end of the word class to make the word classify.*

Say: *Read it with me:* **classify**. **Classify** *means "to make into a class." For example, we say, "We classify plants and animals in science class The suffix* **–fy** *changed the meaning of the word class, and created a new word classify which means "to make into classes.*

Ask: *What does designate mean? It means "to have marks or designs." What does classify mean? It means "to make into classes."*

Model

Use BLM 31, Row 1.

Say: *Let's read the word beauty. Let's add* **-fy**. *It reads: beautify. It means "to make beautiful." Remember, you can use the suffix* **–fy** *to understand the meaning of a word, because the suffix* **–fy** *means "to make into."*

Practice

Use BLM 31, Rows 2–4.

Say: *You read the word accent. Add* **–ate** *at the end of the word. It reads: accentuate. What does it mean? It means "to have accent." You can use the suffix –ate to understand the meaning of a word because the suffix* **–ate** *means to "give the quality of." Then write the root word and its suffix on the line. Repeat with* **alter** *and* **circle***.*

Apply
Blend Words

Use BLM 31, Rows 5–7.

Say: *Let's read the word* **simple***. Let's add* **-fy***. It reads: simplify. It means "to make simple" Remember, you can use the suffix* **–fy** *to understand the meaning of a word, because the suffix* **–fy** *means "to make into." Repeat with glory and pure.*

Conclusion

Ask: *What did we learn today?* We learned that when we add the suffix *–ate* to a word it changes its meaning to "having the quality of." And we learned that when we add the suffix **–fy** it changes its meaning to "to make into."

Home Connection
Ask students to practice adding the suffixes **–ate** and **–fy** to the end of words to understand the meaning of the new words created. Have students identify words to which the suffixes **–ate** and –fy that can be added to create new words with a family member..

✔ Formative Assessment

If the student completes each task correctly, precede to the next skill in the sequence. If not, refer to the suggestion under Intervention 2.

Did the student…?	Intervention 2
Recognize and identify the beginning or end of a word?	• Point directly to the end of the word. Say this is the end of the word **-ate** and **–fy** or the last part of the word **designate**, and **classify.** Point to the beginning and say, this is the beginning or the first part of the word.
Understand the meanings of the ending –ate means "having the quality of" and –fy means "to make into?"	• Have students name a word with each suffix and say what the words mean.
Read words?	• Point to each word and have students repeat, echo, then read it on their own while pointing to the word. Use the word in short sentences and explain its meaning to ensure student understanding.

Identify and Name Suffixes –s, –es RF.2.3d

CACC RF.2.3
Know and apply grade-level phonics and word analysis skills in decoding words both in isolation and in text
d. Decode words with common prefixes and suffixes

Lesson Objectives

- Identify and name suffixes, –s, –es.
- Recognize suffixes in words/ pictures.

METACOGNITIVE STRATEGY
- Selective auditory attention, imagery, auditory representation

ACADEMIC LANGUAGE
- letter name, letter sound, plural, suffix, suffixes

Additional Materials
Sound Spelling Card –s, –es

Blackline Master 32

Pre-Assess
Student's ability to recognize the difference between a base word and a suffix and to identify the letters and sounds associated with suffixes.

Introduce

As students participate in this lesson, they identify the difference between singular and plural nouns when **–s** and **–es** are added to the end of some singular nouns. Students will apply their knowledge by recognizing the difference between singular and plural nouns using pictures.

State Learning Goal

Say: *Today we will practice adding the letters –s and –es to the **end** of some words to make them mean more than one.*

Teach

A noun is a person, place, or thing. Some nouns are singular. This means one. When you add **–s** to the end of some nouns, it makes the noun **plural**. When you add **–es** to the end of other nouns, it also makes plural.

Phonemic Awareness

Show picture of sound/spelling card to review the sound.

Say: *Listen to the /s/ at the end. Say it with me: /ssss/. Say it on your own: **ssss**. Repeat with the suffix **–es**.*

Sound-Spelling Correspondence

Show the letter.

Say: *The way we write the sound /s/ is with the letter **s**.*

Say: *The letter **s** makes the sound /s/. We add the letter **s** to the end of a noun to make it plural.*

Say: *What is the name of the letter? **s** What sound does the letter make? /s/*

Model

Use BLM 32, row 1.

Say: *We will look at each picture. Say its name. If we hear an –s or –es at the end of the word, we will circle the picture. If we do not hear an –s or –es at the end of the word, we cross out the picture.*

Say: *What do you see in the first picture? **clocks**. Do you hear an –s or –es at the end of the word **clocks**? Circle the picture. If you do not hear an –s or –es at the end of the word, then cross out the picture. Repeat with **watches**.*

Practice

Use BLM 32, row 2.

Say: **Look** *at the picture.* **Say** *its name.*

Say: *What is the picture?* **cats** *Do you hear the* **–s** *at the end of the word* **cats**? **Write** *the word* **cats**. *Repeat with the word* **dishes**.

Apply
Blend Words

Use BLM 32, row 3.

Say: *Look at each letter and listen to the ending sound as I read.* **/k/ /e/ /z/.** *Your turn:* **/k/ /e/ /z/.**

Say: *Now we are going to blend the sounds together by stretching them out as we read them. Point to each letter in a sweeping motion from left to right* **/k/ eeee/zzz/.** *What is the word?* **keys**. *Repeat with the word* **benches**.

Spelling

Use BLM 32, row 4.

Say: *Now we can practice writing the sounds we hear in each word. Call one word at a time, stretching each sound.*

Say: *Say the word slowly; write a letter for each sound you hear.*

Conclusion

Ask: *What did we learn today?* We learned that we can add **–s** or **–es** to certain nouns to make them plural. We wrote words using **–s** and **–es** at the end. What pictures/words will help you remember **–s** and **–es** at the end of a word?

Home Connection

Encourage students to practice identifying words with **suffixes –s** and **–es** with a family member. Encourage students to identify other words that **end** with suffixes **–s** and **–es** with their family.

✔ Formative Assessment

If the student completes each task correctly, precede to the next skill in the sequence. If not, refer to suggested intervention 2.

Did the student...?	Intervention 2
Identify the name of the suffixes?	• Use physical rhythmic movements as the suffix is repeated. March while chanting the suffix. Move arms up and down. Sway from side to side.
Identify the sound of the letter?	• Overemphasize the forming of the **/s/** sound when you reach the end of an example word, such as **chairs**.
Produce the sound of the letter?	• Use mirrors to show movement of mouth, tongue, teeth as the sound is produced. Use hand over mouth to explore movement of air as the sound is produced.
Recognize the **final** sound?	• Use Elkonin boxes – student moves a token into the **last** box as the **final** sound of the word is said.
Write the letters?	• Write the letters, have students trace them. Create the letters with clay. • Discuss letter features (lines, shape). Trace over the letters with multiple colors.
Know the name of pictures?	• Tell students the name of pictures, have students repeat them aloud. Discuss word and use each word in context.
Echo or choral read	• Echo read one phrase or sentence at a time, and check for understanding.
Retell Informational Text	• Use informational text board and sentence frames or sentence starters correlated to each picture.

Recognize Long u vowel teams syllable patterns (u, ew, ue) RF.2.3b

CCSS: RF.2.3
Know and apply grade-level phonics and word analysis skills in decoding words both in isolation and in text.
b. Know spelling-sound correspondences for additional common vowel teams.

Introduce

As students participate in this lesson, they identify the name and sound of the target vowel patterns, and identify the letter or letters when the sound and name are given orally. Students will apply their knowledge by recognizing the medial sound of target sounds using pictures.

State Learning Goal

Today we will learn to read words with the long sound of vowel **u** using vowel teams. Vowel teams are when one or two vowels are put together to form one sound. We are going to read words with the vowel teams **u, ew, ue.**

Teach

Letters represent sounds. We remember the sounds each letter makes. We use letters to write words we say. We use letters to read and write words. The letter **u** is a vowel. It has a long sound /u/ and a short sound /u/. We are going to learn words that have the long sound of vowel **u** using the vowel teams **u, ew,** and **ue.**

Phonemic Awareness

Show picture of sound/spelling card to review long sound of **u.**

Say: *Listen to this sound /***uuu***/. Say it with me:* **uuu.** *Say it on your own:* **uuu.**

Say: *This is the long sound of vowel* **u.** *It sounds like it is saying its name: /***uuu***/, say it again /***uuu***/.*

Sound-Spelling Correspondence

Write the word **unicycle** on the board. Point out the vowel **u** in the word.

Say: *The word* **unicycle** *has the long* **u** *sound in the beginning and is spelled using the letter* **u.**

Write the word **glue** on the board. Point out the vowel **u** in the word.

Say: *Look at the word* **glue.** *The word* **glue** *has the long* **u** *sound and is spelled using the vowel team* **ue.** *Repeat with* **screw.**

Model

Use BLM 33, #1.

Say: *Look at each picture. Say its name. Listen for the long sound of /***u***/. Circle the picture if you hear the long sound of /***u***/. Cross out the picture if you do not hear the long sound of /***u***/.*

Say: *Look at the picture. Say its name.* **unicycle.** *Do you hear the long sound of /***u***/? Circle the picture. Repeat with* **jug.**

Lesson Objectives

- Identify and name long **u** vowel teams syllable patterns **u, ew, ue.**
- Produce the sound of long **u** vowel teams syllable patterns **u, ew, ue.**
- Relate the long sound /**u**/ to the syllable patterns **u, ew, ue.**
- Recognize long vowel sound **u** in words/pictures.
- Recognize long vowel teams syllable patterns with long **u.**

METACOGNITIVE STRATEGY
- Selective auditory attention, imagery, auditory representation

ACADEMIC LANGUAGE
- letter name, letter sound, vowel, long vowel sound, syllable, vowel team, pattern

Additional Materials
- Sound Spelling Card **u**
- Blackline Master 33

Pre-Assess
Student's ability to recognize the long vowel sound represented by the target letter of the alphabet and to identify the letter used to represent the corresponding sound. Ability to pronounce the long vowel sound.

Practice

Use BLM 33, #2.

Say: *Look at the picture. Say its name. Listen for the long sound of /u̅/. Is it spelled with a **u**, **ue**, or **ew**?*

Say: *Do you hear the long sound /u̅/? Write the letters that form the long sound of /u̅/ in each picture.*

Apply
Blend Words

Use BLM 33, #3

Say: *Look at each letter and listen to the long sound of vowel **u** as I read /v/u/w/. Your turn: /v/u/w/.*

Say: *Now we are going to blend the sounds together by stretching them out as we read them.* Point to each letter in a sweeping motion left to right /v/uuu/www/. *What is the word? **view.** Repeat with **future** and **juice.***

Spelling

Use BLM 33, #4.

Say: *Now we can practice writing the sounds we hear in each word.*

Call one word at a time, stretching each sound.

Say: *Say the word slowly; write a letter for each sound you hear.*

Conclusion

Ask: *What did we learn today?* We learned that the vowel **u** makes the long sound /u̅/. We also learned that the vowel teams **ue** and **ew** make the long sound /u̅/. What pictures/words will help you remember the long sound /u̅/?

Home Connection

Encourage students to practice identifying the long vowel sound **u** in words with a family member.

✔ Formative Assessment

If the student completes each task correctly, proceed to the next skill in the sequence. If not, refer to the suggestion under Intervention 2.

Did the student...?	Intervention 2
Identify the name of the letter?	• Use physical rhythmic movements as the letter name is repeated. March while chanting the letter name. Move arms up and down. Sway from side to side.
Identify the sounds of the letter?	• Use exaggeration of forming the /u/ by opening the mouth wide and bringing the lips together in a pucker.
Produce the sounds of the letter?	• Use mirrors to show movement of mouth, tongue, teeth as the sound is produced. Use hand over mouth to explore movement of air as the sound is produced.
Recognize the CVC or CVCe pattern?	• Arrange a list of common same vowel words vertically, point out pattern.
Know the name of pictures?	• Tell students the name of pictures, have student repeat it aloud.

Recognize R-controlled Syllable Patterns with Long E RF.2.3e

CCSS: RF.2.3
Know and apply grade-level phonics and word analysis skills in decoding words both in isolation and in text.
e. Identify words with inconsistent but common spelling-sound correspondences.

Lesson Objectives

- Identify the long vowel sound **e** in r-controlled syllable patterns
- Produce the sound of letter **e** in r-controlled syllable patterns
- Relate the sound /**e**/ to the letters **ear, eer, ere**
- Recognize long vowel sound **e** in words/pictures

METACOGNITIVE STRATEGY
- Selective auditory attention, imagery, auditory representation

ACADEMIC LANGUAGE
- letter name, letter sound, vowel, long vowel sound, silent e, pattern

Additional Materials
- Sound Spelling Card **Ee, Aa, Rr**
- Blackline master 34

Pre-Assess
Student's ability to recognize the **long vowel sound** represented by the target letter of the alphabet and to identify the letters used to represent the corresponding sound. Ability to pronounce the long vowel sound.

Introduce

As students participate in this lesson, they identify the name and sound of the target letter, and identify the letter when the sound and name are given orally. Students will apply their knowledge by recognizing the initial sound of target letter using pictures.

State Learning Goal

Today we will learn to read words with the long sound of vowel **e** in **r**-controlled syllable patterns.

Teach

Letters represent sounds. We remember the sounds each letter makes. We use letters to write words we say. We use letters to read and write words. The letter **e** is a vowel. It has a long sound /**e**/ found in the syllables **ear, eer** and **ere**. We are going to learn words that have the long sound of vowel **e** in the r-controlled syllables of **ear, eer** and **ere**.

Phonemic Awareness

Show picture of sound/spelling card to review long sound of **Ee**.

Say: *Listen to this sound /e/. Say it with me:* **e**. *Say it on your own:* **e**.

Say: *This is the long sound of vowel* **e**. *It sounds like it is saying its name: /e/. Say it again, /e/.*

Say: *We can also hear the long sound of vowel* **e** *in words with the letter patterns of* **ear, eer** *and* **ere**. *Some of these words can be homophones. Homophones are words that sound the same but are spelled differently and have different meanings, like* **hear** *and* **here**.

Sound-Spelling Correspondence

Show the letters.

Say: *We can write the long vowel sound /e/ with the letter patterns of* **ear, eer** *and* **ere**.

Say: *We hear the sound /e/ in the letter patterns of* **ear, eer** *and* **ere**. Write the word *fears* on the board. Point out the vowel **e**.

Say: *When you see the vowel* **e** *in the syllable* **ear** *the vowel* **e** *makes its long sound.* Write the word *cheers* on the board. Point out the vowel **e**.

Say: *When you see the vowel* **e** *in the syllable* **eer** *the vowel* **e** *makes its long sound.*

Write the word *sphere* on the board. Point out the vowel *e*.

Say: *When you see the vowel* **e** *in the syllable* **ere** *the vowel* **e** *makes its long sound.*

Model

Use BLM 34, #1.

Say: **Look** at each picture. **Say** its name. **cheers** Listen for the long sound of /**e**/. Does it have the syllable **ear, eer** or **ere**?

Say: Do you hear the long sound of /**e**/ in the word **cheers**? Does the word **cheers** have the syllable **ear, eer** or **ere**? If it does, circle the picture. If not, cross out the picture.

Practice

Use BLM 34, #2

Say: Look at the picture. Say its name. Listen for the long sound of /**e**/. Does the word **sphere** have the syllable **ear, eer** or **ere**?

Say: Do you hear the long sound /**e**/? Write the word. Repeat with **cheers** and **spear**.

Apply
Blend Words

Use BLM 34, #3

Say: Look at each letter and listen to the long sound of vowel **e** as I read /s/p/ e/r/. Your turn: /s/p/e/r/.

Say: Now we are going to blend the sounds together by stretching them out as we read them.

Point to each letter in a sweeping motion left to right /**ssss/pppp/eeee/rrrr**/. What is the word? **spear**

Spelling

Use BLM 34, #4

Say: Now we can practice writing the sounds we hear in each word. Call one word at a time, stretching each sound.

Say: Say the word slowly; write a letter for each sound you hear.

Conclusion

Ask: What did we learn today? We learned that the vowel **e** makes the long sound /**e**/ in the r-controlled syllables of *ear, eer* and *ere*. What pictures/words will help you remember the long sound /**e**/ with the syllables *ear, eer* and *ere*?

Home Connection

Encourage students to practice identifying long vowel sound **e** in **ear, eer** and **ere** syllable words with a family member.

✔ Formative Assessment	
If the student completes each task correctly, precede to the next skill in the sequence. If not, refer to the suggestion under Intervention 2.	
Did the student...?	**Intervention 2**
Identify the name of the letter?	• Use physical rhythmic movements as the letter name is repeated. March while chanting the letter name. Move arms up and down. Sway from side to side.
Identify the sounds of the letter?	• Say words with the target sounds by repeating the words three times. Examples: **spear spear spear, sphere sphere, sphere, cheers cheers cheers**
Produce the sounds of the letter?	• Use mirrors to show movement of mouth, tongue, teeth as the sound is produced. Use hand over mouth to explore movement of air as the sound is produced.
Recognize the CVCe pattern?	• Arrange a list of common same vowel CVCe words vertically, point out pattern.
Know the name of pictures?	• Tell students the name of pictures, have student repeat it aloud. Discuss meaning of word. Use word in context.

Recognize R-controlled Syllable Patterns with Long A RF.2.3b, RF.2.3e

CCSS: RF.2.3
Know and apply grade-level phonics and word analysis skills in decoding words both in isolation and in text.
b. Know spelling-sound correspondences for additional common vowel teams.
e. Identify words with inconsistent but common spelling-sound correspondences.

Lesson Objectives

- Identify the long vowel sound a in r-controlled syllable patterns.
- Produce the sound of letter a in r-controlled syllable patterns.
- Relate the sound /a/ to the letters air, are.
- Recognize long vowel sound a in words/pictures.

METACOGNITIVE STRATEGY
- Selective auditory attention, imagery, auditory representation

ACADEMIC LANGUAGE
- letter name, letter sound, vowel, long vowel sound, silent e, pattern

Additional Materials
- Sound Spelling Card **Ee, Aa, Ii, Rr**
- Blackline master 35

Pre-Assess
Student's ability to recognize the long vowel sound represented by the target letter of the alphabet and to identify the letters used to represent the corresponding sound. Ability to pronounce the long vowel sound.

Introduce

As students participate in this lesson, they identify the name and sound of the target letter, and identify the letter when the sound and name are given orally. Students will apply their knowledge by recognizing the initial sound of target letter using pictures.

State Learning Goal

Today we will learn to read words with the long sound of vowel a in r-controlled syllable patterns.

Teach

Letters represent sounds. We remember the sounds each letter makes. We use letters to write words we say. We use letters to read and write words. The letter a is a vowel. It has a long sound /a/ found in the syllables **air** and **are**. We are going to learn words that have the long sound of vowel a in the **r**-controlled syllables of **air** and **are**.

Phonemic Awareness

Show picture of sound/spelling card to review long sound of **Aa**.

Say: *Listen to this sound /a/. Say it with me: a. Say it on your own: a.*

Say: *This is the long sound of vowel a. It sounds like it is saying its name: /a/. Say it again, /a/.*

Say: *We can also hear the long sound of vowel a in words with the letter patterns of air and are. Some of these words can be homophones. Homophones are words that sound the same but are spelled differently and have different meanings, like fair and fare.*

Sound-Spelling Correspondence

Show the letters.

Say: *We can write the long vowel sound /a/ with the letter patterns of air and are.*

Say: *We hear the sound /a/ in the letter patterns of air and are.*

Write the word fair on the board. Point out the vowel a. **Say:** *When you see the vowel a in the syllable air the vowel a makes its long sound.*

Write the word mare on the board. Point out the vowel a. **Say:** *When you see the vowel a in the syllable are the vowel a makes its long sound.*

Model

Use BLM 35, #1.

Say: *Look at each picture. Say its name. Listen for the long sound of /a/. Does it have the syllable **air** or **are**?*

Say: *Do you hear the long sound of /a/ in the word hair? If we hear the sound of a with the syllable **air** or **are** we will circle the picture. If we do not hear the sound a in these syllables we cross out the picture.*

Practice

Use BLM 35, #2

Say: *Look at the picture. Say its name. Listen for the long sound of /a/. Does the word share have the syllable air or are?*

Say: *Do you hear the long sound /a/? Write the word.*

Apply
Blend Words

Use BLM 35, #3

Say: *Look at each letter and listen to the long sound of vowel **a** as I read /h/a/r/. Your turn: /h/a/r/.*

Say: *Now we are going to blend the sounds together by stretching them out as we read them.* Point to each letter in a sweeping motion left to right: **/hhhh/aaaa/rrrr/**. *What is the word?* **hair**

Spelling

Use BLM 35, #4

Say: *Now we can practice writing the sounds we hear in each word. Call one word at a time, stretching each sound.*

Say: *Say the word slowly; write a letter for each sound you hear.*

Conclusion

Ask: *What did we learn today?* We learned that the vowel a makes the long sound /a/ in the r-controlled syllables of air and are. What pictures/words will help you remember the long sound /a/ with the syllables **air** and **are**?

Home Connection

Encourage students to practice identifying long vowel sound **a** in air and are syllable words with a family member.

✔ Formative Assessment

If the student completes each task correctly, precede to the next skill in the sequence. If not, refer to the suggestion under Intervention 2.

Did the student...?	Intervention 2
Identify the name of the letter?	• Use physical rhythmic movements as the letter name is repeated. March while chanting the letter name. Move arms up and down. Sway from side to side.
Identify the sounds of the letter?	• Say words with the target sounds by repeating the words three times. Examples: **hair hair hair, square square square**
Produce the sounds of the letter?	• Use mirrors to show movement of mouth, tongue, teeth as the sound is produced. Use hand over mouth to explore movement of air as the sound is produced.
Recognize the CVCe pattern?	• Arrange a list of common same vowel CVCe words vertically, point out pattern.
Know the name of pictures?	• Tell students the name of pictures, have student repeat it aloud. Discuss meaning of word. Use word in context.

CCSS: RF.2.3
Know and apply grade-level phonics and word analysis skills in decoding words both in isolation and in text.
b. Know spelling-sound correspondences for additional common vowel team.
e. Identify words with inconsistent but common spelling-sound correspondences.

Lesson Objectives

- Identify and name the letters **oo, ui, ew.**
- Produce the sound of vowel teams **oo, ui** and letters **ew.**
- Relate the sound /**oo**/ to vowel teams **oo, ui,** and letters **ew.**
- Recognize vowel sound /**oo**/ in words.
- Recognize vowel sound /**oo**/ in words with different vowel teams and letters.

METACOGNITIVE STRATEGY
- Selective auditory attention, imagery, auditory representation

ACADEMIC LANGUAGE
- letter name, letter sound, vowel, vowel team

Additional Materials
- Sound Spelling Cards **OO, UI, EW, U**
- Blackline master 36

Pre-Assess
Student's ability to recognize the **vowel sound** represented by the target letters of the alphabet and to identify the vowel teams used to represent the corresponding sound. Ability to **pronounce the vowel sound.**

Recognize Vowel Teams /oo/ with Syllable Patterns oo, ui, ew

RF.2.3b, RF.2.3e

Introduce

As students participate in this lesson, they identify the name and sound of the target vowel teams, and identify the letters when the sound and name are given orally. Students will apply their knowledge by recognizing the sound of target letters.

State Learning Goal

Today we will learn to read words with vowel teams that make the sound /**oo**/. We are going to learn that there are several ways to make the sound /**oo**/. The vowel teams **oo** and **ui** and the letters **ew** can all make the sound /**oo**/.

Teach

Letters represent sounds. We remember the sounds each letter makes. We use letters to write words we   say. We use letters to read and write words. Remember the sound of long vowel **u**. It makes the sound /**oo**/. There are other ways to make the sound /**oo**/. The vowel team **oo** makes the sound /**oo**/. The vowel team **ui** makes the sound /**oo**/. The letters **ew** make the sound /**oo**/. We are going to learn words that use different vowel teams and letters to make the sound /**oo**/.

Sound-Spelling Correspondence

Write the word **scoop** on the board. Point out the vowel team **oo** in the word.

Say: *The vowel team* **oo** *makes the sound* /**oo**/.

Say: *Look at the word* **scoop**. *Does it have a vowel team* **oo**? *Point: The vowel team* **oo** *sounds like* /**oo**/.

Say: *Read it with me* **scoop**. *Repeat with words* **spoon** *and* **stoop**.

Sound-Spelling Correspondence

Write the word **bruise** on the board. Point out the vowel team **ui** in the word.

Say: *The vowel team* **ui** *makes the sound* /**oo**/.

Say: *Look at the word* **bruise**. *Does it have a vowel team* **ui**? *Point: The vowel team* **ui** *sounds like* /**oo**/.

Say: *Read it with me* **bruise**. *Repeat with the word* **cruise**.

Sound-Spelling Correspondence

Write the word **screw** on the board. Point out the letters **ew** in the word.

Say: *The letters* **ew** *make the sound* /**oo**/.

Say: *Look at the word* **screw**. *Does it have the letters* **ew**? *Point: The letters* **ew** *sounds like* /**oo**/.

Say: *Read it with me* **screw**. *Repeat with word* **newt**.

Model

Use BLM 36, #1.

Say: *Look at each word. Say it aloud. Listen for the sound of /oo/. Does it have vowel team* **oo, ui,** *or the letters* **ew**?

Say: *Do you hear the sound /oo/? If we hear the sound /oo/ we will circle the word and put a line under the letters that make the sound. If we do not hear the sound /oo/ we will cross out the word.*

Practice

Use BLM 36, #2.

Say: *Look at each word. Say it aloud. Listen for the sound of /oo/. Does it have vowel team* **oo, ui,** *or the letters* **ew**?

Say: *Do you hear the sound /oo/? Put a line under the letters that make the sound /oo/.*

Apply
Blend Words

Use BLM 36, #3

Say: *Look at each letter and listen to the sound /oo/ as I read:* **/s//t//oo//p/**. *Your turn:* **/s//t//oo//p/**.

Say: *Now we are going to blend the sounds together by stretching them out as we read them.*

Point to each letter in a sweeping motion left to right **/s/ttt/oooo/ppp/**. *What is the word?* **stoop**.

Spelling

Use BLM 36, #4.

Say: *Now we can practice writing the sounds we hear in each word.*

Call one word at a time, stretching each sound.

Say: *Say the word slowly; write a letter for each sound you hear.*

Conclusion

Ask: *What did we learn today?* We learned that different letters make the sound /**oo**/. The vowel teams **oo** and **ui** and the letters **ew** make the sound /**oo**/. This sound is like the sound of long vowel **u**. What words will help you remember the sound /**oo**/ made by the letters **oo, ui,** and **ew**?

Home Connection

Encourage students to practice identifying the sound /oo/ in words with the letters **oo, ui,** and **ew** with a family member.

✔ Formative Assessment

If the student completes each task correctly, proceed to the next skill in the sequence. If not, refer to the suggestion under Intervention 2.

Did the student...?	Intervention 2
Identify the name of the letter?	• Use physical rhythmic movements as the letter name is repeated. March while chanting the letter name. Move arms up and down. Sway from side to side.
Identify the sounds of the letter?	• Use chants that repeat the sound several times then a word that includes with the sound. Example: /oo/ /oo/ /oo/ **bloom**.
Produce the sounds of the letter?	• Use mirrors to show movement of mouth, tongue, teeth as the sound is produced. Use hand over mouth to explore movement of air as the sound is produced.
Pronounce the words correctly?	• Tell students the word, have student repeat it aloud. • Discuss meaning of word. Use word in context.

Identify and Name Inflectional Endings with Spelling Changes
RF.1.3f

CCSS: RF.1.3
Know and apply grade-level phonics and word analysis skills in decoding words both in isolation and in text.
f. Read words with inflectional endings..

Introduce
As students participate in this lesson, they identify the name and sound of the targeted letter, and identify the letters when the sound and name are given orally. Students will apply their knowledge by recognizing the sounds of inflected endings in words with spelling changes.

State Learning Goal
Today we will practice listening to the sounds /ed/ and /ing/ that the letters **ed** and **ing** make when added to the end of words. We will practice the spelling changes that happen when **ed** and **ing** are added to words that end in **e** or a vowel followed by a consonant.

Teach
Letters represent sounds. We remember the sounds each letter makes. We use letters to write words we say. We use letters to read and write words. Some letters combine to make new sounds. We add the sounds to the end of words. Sometimes we change the spelling of words when we add new endings.

Sound-Spelling Correspondence
Show the letters.

Say: *The way we write the sound /ed/ is with the letters* **ed**.

Say: *The letters* **ed** *make the sound /ed/.*

Say: *What is the name of the letters that combine?* **ed** *What sound do the letters make?* /ed/

Sound-Spelling Correspondence
Show the letters.

Say: *The way we write the sound /ing/ is with the letters* **ing**.

Say: *The letters* **ing** *make the sound /ing/.*

Say: *What is the name of the letters that combine?* **ing** *What sound do the letters make?* /ing/

Model
Use BLM 37, #1.

Say: *What is the word?* **grab** *Say: Now we add* **ed** *to the end of the word* **grab**. *Say: What is the word?* **grabbed**. *Do you hear the sound /ed/ at the end of the word* **grabbed**? *Circle the letters* **ed**. *Notice how we double the letter* **b** *when we add* **ed** *to make the word* **grabbed**. *Underline the letters* **bb**.

Say: *Now we add* **ing** *to the end of the word* **grab**. *Say: What is the word?* **grabbing**. *Do you hear the sound /ing/ at the end of the word* **grabbing**? *Circle the letters* **ing**. *Notice how we double the letter* **b** *when we add* **ing** *to make the word* **grabbing**. *Underline the letters* **bb**.

Lesson Objectives
- Identify and name the letters **ed** and **ing**
- Produce the sound of inflectional endings **ed** and **ing**
- Relate the sounds /ed/ and /ing/ to the letters **ed** and **ing**
- Recognize final sounds **ed** and **ing** in words with spelling changes

METACOGNITIVE STRATEGY
- Selective auditory attention, imagery, auditory representation

ACADEMIC LANGUAGE
- letter name, letter sound, final sound, ending sound

Additional Materials
- Letter Cards **e, d, i, n, g**
- Blackline Master 37

Pre-Assess
Student's ability to recognize the sound represented by the targeted letters of the alphabet and to identify the letters used to represent the corresponding sound in inflectional endings.

Use BLM 37, #2.

Say: *What is the word?* **change** Say: *Now we add* **ed** *to the end of the word* **change**. Say: *What is the word?* **changed**. *Do you hear the sound* /**ed**/ *at the end of the word* **changed**? *Circle the letters* **ed**. *Notice how we double the letter* **b** *when we add* **ed** *to make the word* **changed**. *Underline the spelling change* **-ged**.

Say: *Now we add* **ing** *to the end of the word* **change**.

Say: *What is the word?* **changing**. *Do you hear the sound* /**ing**/ *at the end of the word* **changing**? *Circle the letters* **ing**. *Notice how we double the letter* **e** *when we add* **ing** *to make the word* **changing**. *Underline the spelling change* **-gi**.

Practice

Use BLM 37, #3.

Say: **Look** *at the word.* **Say** *its name.* **Write** *the letters.*

Say: *What is the word?* **grabbed** *Do you hear the sound* /**ed**/ *or* /**ing**/ *at the end of the word* **grabbed**? **Circle** *the letters* **ed**. **Underline** *the spelling change* **bb**.

Apply
Blend Words

Use BLM 37, #4.

Say: *Look at each letter and listen to the sound as I read.* /g/r/a/b/i/n/g/. *Your turn:* /g/r/a/b/i/n/g/

Say: *Now we are going to blend the sounds together by stretching them out as we read them.*

Point to each letter in a sweeping motion left to right /ggg/rrr/aaa/bbb/iii/nnn/ggg/. *What is the word?* **grabbing**.

Spelling

Use BLM 37, #5.

Say: *Now we can practice writing the sounds we hear in each word.*

Call one word at a time, stretching each sound.

Say: *Say the word slowly; write a letter for each sound you hear.*

Conclusion

Ask: *What did we learn today?* We learned that the letters **ed** make the sound /ed/. We learned that the letters **ing** make the sound /ing/. We wrote words adding the letters **ed** and **ing** at the end. We learned about spelling changes when we add **ed** and **ing** to the end of words. We learned that if the word ends in a vowel followed by a consonant, we double the consonant. We learned that if the word ends in the letter **e**, we drop the letter **e** before we add the ending. What words will help you remember the sounds /**ed**/ and /**ing**/, the letters **ed** and **ing**, and the spelling changes when we add these letters to the end of words?

Home Connection

Encourage students to practice identifying sounds **ed** and **ing** at the end of words and writing the letters **ed** and **ing** with a family member. Encourage students to identify spelling changes when they add these endings to words with their family.

✔ Formative Assessment

If the student completes each task correctly, precede to the next skill in the sequence. If not, refer to suggested intervention 2.

Did the student...?	Intervention 2
Identify the name of the letters?	• Use physical rhythmic movements as the letter name is repeated. March while chanting the letter name. Move arms up and down. Sway from side to side.
Identify the sound of the letters?	• Say words with the target sounds by emphasizing the sounds, then write the words for students to see the spelling changes. Examples: **tug, tugged, tugging**.
Produce the sound of the letters?	• Use mirrors to show movement of mouth, tongue, teeth as the sound is produced. Use hand over mouth to explore movement of air as the sound is produced.
Recognize the sounds of the inflectional endings?	• Use Elkonin boxes – student moves a token into the **last** box as the ending of the word is said.
Recognize the spelling changes when adding inflectional endings?	• Make a three-column chart with VC and VCe words, the words with the ending **ed**, and the words with the ending **ing**. Have students look for the patterns in the spelling changes.
Write the letters?	• Write the letter, have students trace it. Create the letter with clay. • Discuss letter features (lines, shape). Trace over the letter with multiple colors.

Identify and Decode Suffixes: -y, -ly RF.2.3c, RF.2.3d

CCSS: RF.2.3
Know and apply grade-level phonics and word analysis skills in decoding words both in isolation and in text.
c. Decode regularly spelled two-syllable words with long vowels
d. Decode words with common prefixes and suffixes.

Lesson Objectives

- Identify and name the **y** and **ly** suffixes.
- Understand that adding **y** and **ly** to words changes their meaning.
- Understand the spelling rules for adding the suffixes **y** and **ly** to root words.

METACOGNITIVE STRATEGY
- Selective auditory attention, imagery, auditory representation

ACADEMIC LANGUAGE
- final sound, ending sound, suffix, adjective, adverb

Additional Materials
- Sound/Spelling Cards: -y and -ly endings
- Blackline Master 38

Pre-Assess
Student's ability to recognize root words and suffixes

Introduce

As students participate in this lesson, they identify **-y** and **-ly** suffixes and understand how they change the meaning of words. Students will apply their knowledge by recognizing target suffixes and adding them to root words using the correct spelling rules.

State Learning Goal

Say: *Today we will practice identifying and writing words that end in* **y** *and* **ly** *and understand how they change the meanings of words.*

Teach

Most of the time we can add a **-y** to a noun to form an adjective or describing word. For example, we add **-y** to the noun **mist** to get the adjective **misty**. It is a **misty** day.

And most of the time we can add an **-ly** to turn adjectives into adverbs, words that tell how something is done. For example the adjective **quiet** becomes the adverb **quietly**. He spoke **quietly**.

Sound-Spelling Correspondence

Show the letter.

Say: *We can write the sound /ē/ at the end of a word with the letter* **y***.*

Say: *The letter* **y** *makes the sound /ē/. We add the letter* **y** *to the end of a noun to make an adjective.*

Say: *What is the name of the letter?* **y** *What sound does the letter make?* /ē/

Say: *We can write the sound /l/ /y/ at the end of a word with the letters* **ly***.*

Say: *The letters* **ly** *makes the sound /l/. We add the letters* **ly** *to the end of a noun to make an adverb.*

Say: *What are the names of the letters?* **l** *and* **y** *What sounds do the letters make?* /l/

Model

Use BLM 38, row 1.

Say: *Look at the words.*

Say: *What is the first word?* **scare** *Write the adjective under the picture. Remember we drop the* **e** *and add* **y** *to form the adjective:* **scary***.*

Practice

Use BLM 38, row 2.

Say: Look *at the words. Add the suffix* **ly** *to change the words into adverbs. Say the first word* **busy**.

Ask: *What do I need to do to the word* **busy** *before I add* **-ly**? *Change the* **y** *to* **i—busily***. Write the word.*

Apply
Blend Words

Use BLM 38, row 3.

Say: *Look at each letter and listen to the sound as I read.* /g/r/e/d/i/l/e/. *Your turn:* /g/r/e/d/i/l/e/.

Say: *Now we are going to blend the sounds together by stretching them out as we read them.* Point to each letter in a sweeping motion left to right. /g/rrr/eee/ddd/iii/lll/eee/ *What is the word?* **greedily**.

Spelling

Use BLM 38, row 4.

Say: *Now we can practice writing the sounds we hear in each word.*

Call one word at a time, stretching each sound.

Say: *Say the word slowly; write a letter for each sound you hear.*

Conclusion

What did we learn today? We learned the suffix **y** changes a noun to an adjective and the suffix **ly** changes a word to an adverb. We also learned the special spelling rules for adding these suffixes correctly.

Home Connection

Encourage students to practice identifying adjectives and adverbs with a family member. Encourage students to identify other words that **end** with y and ly with their family and to explain the rules for their spelling.

✓ Formative Assessment

If the student completes each task correctly, precede to the next skill in the sequence. If not, refer to suggested intervention 2.

Did the student…?	Intervention 2
Identify the name of the letter?	• Use physical rhythmic movements as the letter name is repeated. March while chanting the letter name. Move arms up and down.
Identify the sound of the letter?	• Say words with the target suffixes **y** and **ly**, emphasizing the sound **eee/ leee bad lee bump eee**
Produce the sound of the letter?	• Use mirrors to show movement of mouth, tongue, teeth as the sound is produced. Use hand over mouth to explore movement of air as the sound is produced.
Recognize the **final** sound?	• Use Elkonin boxes – student moves a token into the **last** box as the **final** sound of the word is said.
Write the letter?	• Write the letter, have students trace it. Create the letter with clay. • Discuss letter features (lines, shape). Trace over the letter with multiple colors.
Know name of pictures?	• Tell students the name of pictures, have students repeat them aloud. Discuss word and use each word in context.

Identify and Decode Irregular Plural Nouns RF.2.3f

CCSS: RF.2.3
Know and apply grade-level phonics and word analysis skills in decoding words both in isolation and in text.
f. Recognize and read grade-appropriate irregularly spelled words.

Lesson Objectives

- Identify and name plural nouns
- Learn rules for spelling irregular plural nouns

METACOGNITIVE STRATEGY
- Selective auditory attention, imagery, auditory representation

ACADEMIC LANGUAGE
- ending sound, irregular, plural, noun

Additional Materials
- Blackline Master 39

Pre-Assess
Student's ability to recognize the rules for forming irregular plural nouns and know that plural nouns mean more than one

Introduce

As students participate in this lesson, they identify and spell irregular plural nouns

State Learning Goal

Say: *Today we will practice identifying and spelling plural nouns that do not end in s.*

Teach

Say: *Most of the time we form plural nouns by adding* **s, es,** *or* **ies** *to the end of words (***vines, pouches, ponies***). But other times plural nouns have irregular spellings. They do not have an* **s** *at the end. We change letters in the word to make them plural.*

Say: *What is the plural of* **foot**? **feet**

Say: *Sometimes they do not change at all. What is the plural of* **sheep**? **sheep**

Phonemic Awareness

Display the irregular singular/plural pair **woman/women**.

Say: *Listen to the vowel sound in* **man**. /w//o//m//a//n/.

Say: *Now listen to the vowel sound in* **men**. /w//o//m//e//n/.

Sound-Spelling Correspondence

Display the irregular singular/plural pair **child/children**.

Say: *The singular form of this noun is* /c/ /h/ / i / / l/ /d/, *but the plural form is* /c//h/ /ĭ /l/ /d/ /r//e//n/. *Notice that the plural has* /r/e/n/ *at the end.*

Model

Use BLM 39, row 1.

Say: *We will look at each word. Read the words. Say: What is the first word?* **elf**

Say: *We make the singular noun* **elf** *plural by changing the* **f** *to a* **v** *and adding* **es***. Write the plural noun* **elves** *on the line. Repeat the procedure with* **moose** *and* **leaf**.

Practice

Use BLM 39, row 2.

Say: **Look** *at the words. Read each one.*

Say: *The first word is* **women**. *It is the plural form of the noun* **woman**. *Write* **woman** *on the line. Explain to students that if the noun is plural they are to write its singular form on the line. If it is singular they are to write its plural form on the line. Remind students that some words have the same singular/plural form.*

Apply
Blend Words

Use BLM 39, row 3.

Say: *Look at each letter and listen to the sound as I read.* **/l/i /v/z/**. *Your turn:* **/l/ i/v/z/**.

Say: *Now we are going to blend the sounds together by stretching them out as we read them. Point to each letter in a sweeping motion left to right* **/l/iii/vvv/ zzz/**. *What is the word?* **lives**

Spelling

Use BLM 39, row 4.

Say: *Now we can practice writing the sounds we hear in each word.*

Call one word at a time, stretching each sound.

Say: *Say the word slowly; write a letter for each sound you hear.*

Conclusion

Ask: *What did we learn today?* We learned that many plural nouns have irregular spellings and that there are some basic rules to help us know how to spell them.

Home Connection

Encourage students to practice identifying **irregularly spelled plural nouns**. Encourage students to identify other **irregularly spelled plural nouns** with their family.

✔ Formative Assessment

If the student completes each task correctly, precede to the next skill in the sequence. If not, refer to suggested intervention 2.

Did the student…?	Intervention 2
Identify the name of the letter?	• Use physical rhythmic movements as the letter name is repeated. March while chanting the letter name. Move arms up and down. Sway from side to side.
Identify the sound of the letter?	• Say irregular singular/plural noun pairs: **fish/fish, mouse/mice, tooth/teeth**
Produce the sound of the letter?	• Use mirrors to show movement of mouth, tongue, teeth as the sound is produced. Use hand over mouth to explore movement of air as the sound is produced.
Recognize the **final** sound?	• Use Elkonin boxes – student moves a token into the **last** box as the **final** sound of the word is said.
Write the letter?	• Write the letter, have students trace it. Create the letter with clay. • Discuss letter features (lines, shape). Trace over the letter with multiple colors.
Know name of pictures?	• Tell students the name of pictures, have students repeat them aloud. Discuss word and use each word in context.

Identify and Name Double Final Consonants RF.1.3b, RF.1.3g

CCSS: RF.1.3
Know and apply grade-level phonics and word analysis skills in decoding words both in isolation and in text
b. Decode regularly spelled one-syllable words.
g. Recognize and read grade-appropriate irregularly spelled words.

Lesson Objectives

- Identify and name double final consonants.
- Produce the sound of double final consonants.
- Relate the sounds /**ll**/, /**ff**/, /**ss**/ to the letters **l, f, s.**
- Recognize final sounds in words/ pictures.

METACOGNITIVE STRATEGY
- Selective auditory attention, imagery, auditory representation

ACADEMIC LANGUAGE
- letter name, letter sound, initial sound, final sound, ending sound, high frequency word

Additional Materials
- Sound Spelling Card **Ll, Ff, Ss**
- Blackline Master 40

Pre-Assess
Student's ability to recognize the sound represented by the targeted letter of the alphabet and to identify the letter used to represent the corresponding sound in final position.

Introduce

students participate in this lesson, they identify the name and sound of sound of the targeted letter, and identify the letter when the sound and name is given orally. Students will apply their knowledge by recognizing the **final**, or **ending**, sound of target letter using pictures. Students apply skill in context by reading decodable simple sentences that include high frequency words.

State Learning Goal
Today we will practice listening to the sound that double letters make at the **end** of words.

Teach

Letters represent sounds. We remember the sounds each letter makes. Sometimes words end with a double consonant. We use letters to write words we say. We use letters to read and write words.

Phonemic Awareness
Show pictures of sound/spelling cards to review the sounds.
Say: Listen to this sound /ll/. Say it with me: **ll**. *Say it on your own:* **ll**. *Say: Listen to this sound /ff/. Say it with me:* **ff**. *Say it on your own:* **ff**.
Say: Listen to this sound /ss/. Say it with me: **ss**. *Say it on your own:* **ss**.

Sound-Spelling Correspondence
Show the letter cards.

Say: *What is the name of the letter?* **l** *What sound does the letter make?* /l/

Say: *What is the name of the letter?* **f** *What sound does the letter make?* /f/

Say: *What is the name of the letter?* **s** *What sound does the letter make?* /s/

Say: *The way we write the sound /l/ at the end of a word is with the letter* **l** *or* **ll**.

Say: *The way we write the sound /f/ at the end of a word is with the letter* **f** *or* **ff**.

Say: *The way we write the sound /s/ at the end of a word is with the letter* **s** *or* **ss**.

Say: *The letters ll make the sound /l/, the letters ff make the sound /f/, the letters ss make the sound /s/.*

Model

Use BLM 40, #1.

Say: *We will look at each picture.* **Say** *its name.* If we hear one sound made by two letters at the end of the word, we will circle the letters. If we do not hear one sound made by two letters at the end, we cross out the picture.

Say: *What do you see in the picture?* **shell** *Do you hear the sound /l/ at the end of the word* **shell**? *Circle the letters* **ll**. *If you do not hear the sound /l/ at the end of the word, then cross out the picture.*

Practice

Use BLM 40, #2.

Say: *Look at the picture.* **Say** *its name.* **Write** *the letters.*

Say: *What is the picture?* **grass** *Do you hear one sound made by two letters at the end of the word* **grass**? *Write the letter* **s**.

Apply

Blend Wordsl

Use BLM 40, # 3.

Say: *Look at each letter and listen to the sound as I read:* /k̆/ /l̆/ /ĭ/ /f̆/. *Your turn:* /k̆/ /l̆/ /ĭ/ /f̆/

Say: *Now we are going to blend the sounds together by stretching them out as we read them.* Point to each letter in a sweeping motion left to right /**cccc**/**llll**/**iiii**/**ffff**/. What is the word? **cliff**.

Spelling

Use BLM 40, # 4.

Say: *Now we can practice writing the sounds we hear in each word.* Call one word at a time, stretching each sound.

Say: *Say the word slowly; write a letter for each sound you hear.*

Conclusion

Ask: *What did we learn today?* We learned that double letters at the end of a word make the same sound as the letter. We wrote words with double letters at the end.

Home Connection

Encourage students to practice identifying **final** double letter sounds and writing the letters with a family member. Encourage students to identify other words that end with double letters with their family..

✔ Formative Assessment

If the student completes each task correctly, precede to the next skill in the sequence. If not, refer to suggested Intervention 2.

Did the student…?	Intervention 2
Identify the name of the letter?	• Use physical rhythmic movements as the letter name is repeated. March while chanting the letter name. Move arms up and down. Sway from side to side..
Identify the sound of the letter?	• Say words with the target sound in final position, emphasizing the sound. Example: shellllllllll. .
Produce the sound of the letter?	Use mirrors to show movement of mouth, tongue, teeth as the sound is produced. Use hand over mouth to explore movement of air as the sound is produced.
Recognize the **final** sound?	Use Elkonin boxes – student moves a token into the last box as the **final** sound of the word is said.
Write the letter?	Write the letter, have students trace it. Create the letter with clay. Discuss letter features (lines, shape). Trace over the letter with multiple colors.
Know name of pictures?	Tell students the name of pictures, have students repeat them aloud. Discuss word and use each word in context.

Identify and Name L Blends
RF.1.3b, RF.1.3g

CCSS: RF.1.3
Know and apply grade-level phonics and word analysis skills in decoding words both in isolation and in text.
b. Decode regularly spelled one-syllable words.
g. Recognize and read grade-appropriate irregularly spelled words.

Introduce

As students participate in this lesson, they identify the names and sounds of the targeted letters, and identify the letters when the sound and name is given orally. They will apply their knowledge by recognizing the sound the blend using pictures. They will also apply the skill in context by reading decodable simple sentences that include high frequency words.

State Learning Goal

Today we will practice listening to the sound that letters make when we blend them with the letter **l**.

Lesson Objectives

- Identify and name **l** blends.
- Produce the sound of **l** blends
- Relate the sound /l/ to **l** blends.
- Recognize the sound of **l** blends in words/pictures.
-

METACOGNITIVE STRATEGY
- Selective auditory attention

ACADEMIC LANGUAGE
- letter name, letter sound, initial sound, high frequency word

Teach

Letters represent sounds. We remember the sounds each letter makes. We use letters to write words we say. We use letters to read and write words.

Phonemic Awareness

Show pictures of sound/spelling card to review the sound.

Say: *This is the* **bl** *card.*

Say: *Listen to this sound /***bl***/. Say it with me: bl. Now say it on your own:* **bl** *. Let's try another.*

Say: *This is the* **pl** *card.*

Say:: *Listen to this sound /***pl***/. Say it with me:* **pl***. Now say it on your own:* **pl***.*

Sound-Spelling Correspondence

Show the letter cards.

Say: *Show the letters.*

Say: *The way we write the blend /***bl***/ is with the letters* **b** *and* **l***.*

Say: *The letters* **b** *and* **l** *make the sound /***bl***/.*

Say: *What is the name of the blend?* **bl** *What sound does the blend make? /***bl***/.*

Model

Use BLM 41, # 1.

Say: *We will look at each picture.* **Say** *its name.* If we hear the sound of an **l** blend at the beginning of the word, we will circle the picture. If we do not hear the sound of an **l** blend at the beginning, we cross out the picture.

Say: *What do you see in the picture?* **black** Do you hear the sound /**bl**/ at the beginning of the word **black**? Circle the letters **bl**. If you do not hear the sound of an **l** blend at the beginning of the word, then cross out the picture.

Additional Materials
- Sound Spelling Card **Cl, Gl, Bl, Pl, Sl**
- Blackline Master 41
-

Pre-Assess
Student's ability to recognize the sound represented by the targeted letter of the alphabet and to identify the letter used to represent the corresponding sound.
.

Practice

Use BLM 41, # 2..

Say: *Look at the picture.* **Say** *its name.* **Write** *the letter.*

Say: *What do you see in the picture?* **plant** Do you hear the sound of an I blend at the beginning of the word **plant**? **Write** the letters.

Apply
Blend Words

Use BLM 41, #3.

Say: *Look at each letter and listen to the sound as I read: /s/ /l/ /i/ /p/. Your turn: /s/ /l/ /i/ /p/.*

Say: *Now we are going to blend the sounds together by stretching them out as we read them.* Point to each letter in a sweeping motion left to right /**ssss**/**llll**/**iiii**/ **pppp**/. What is the word? **slip**

Spelling

Use BLM 41, #4.

Say: *Now we can practice writing the sounds we hear in each word. Call one word at a time, stretching each sound.*

Say: *Say the word slowly; write a letter for each sound you hear.*

Conclusion

Ask: *What did we learn today?* We learned that some letters can blend with the letter I. What pictures/words will help you remember the sounds and letters in **I** blends?.

Home Connection
Ask students to practice identifying I blends and writing them with a family member. Have students to identify other words that begin with I blends with their family.

✔ Formative Assessment

If the student completes each task correctly, precede to the next skill in the sequence. If not, refer to suggested Intervention 2.

Did the student...?	Intervention 2
Identify the name of the letter?	• Use physical rhythmic movements as the letter name is repeated. March while chanting the letter name. Move arms up and down. Sway from side to side..
Identify the sound of the letter?	• Use alliteration, chants that repeat the sound several times then a word that begins with the sound. Example: /**bl**/ /**bl**/ /**bl**/ **black**
Produce the sound of the letter?	Use mirrors to show movement of mouth, tongue, and teeth as the sound is produced. Use hand over mouth to explore movement of air as the sound is produced.
Recognize the beginning sound?	Use Elkonin boxes – student moves a token into first box as the beginning sound of the word is said. .
Write the letter?	Write the letter, have students trace it. Create letter with clay. Discuss letter features (lines, shape). Trace over letter with multiple colors.
Know name of pictures?	Tell students the name of pictures, have students repeat them aloud. Discuss word and use each word in context.

Identify and Name R Blends
RF.1.3b, RF.1.3g

CCSS: RF.1.3
Know and apply grade-level phonics and word analysis skills in decoding words both in isolation and in text.
b. Decode regularly spelled one-syllable words.
g. Recognize and read grade-appropriate irregularly spelled words.

Lesson Objectives

- Identify and name **r** blends.
- Produce the sound of **r** blends.
- Relate the sound /**r**/ to **r** blends.
- Recognize the sound of r blends in words/pictures.

METACOGNITIVE STRATEGY
- Selective auditory attention

ACADEMIC LANGUAGE
- letter name, letter sound, initial sound, high frequency word

Additional Materials
- Sound Spelling Card **Dr, Gr, Br, Cr, Fr, Pr**
- Blackline Master 42

Pre-Assess
Student's ability to recognize the sound represented by the targeted letter of the alphabet and to identify the letter used to represent the corresponding sound
.

Introduce

As students participate in this lesson, they identify the names and sounds of the targeted letters, and identify the letters when the sound and name is given orally. They will apply their knowledge by recognizing the sound of the blend using pictures. They will also apply the skill in context by reading decodable simple sentences that include high frequency words.

State Learning Goal
Today we will practice listening to the sound that letters make when we blend them with the letter **r**.

Teach

Letters represent sounds. We remember the sounds each letter makes. We use letters to write words we say. We use letters to read and write words.

Phonemic Awareness
Show pictures of sound/spelling card to review the sound.

Say: *This is the* **gr** *card. Listen to this sound /***gr***/.* **Say** *it with me:* **gr***. Now say it on your own:* **gr***. Let's try another. This is the* **pr** *card. Listen to this sound /***pr***/.* **Say** *it with me:* **pr***. Now say it on your own:* **pr***. Now one more. This is the* **cr** *card. Listen to this sound /***cr***/. Say it with me:* **cr***. Now say it on your own:* **cr***.*

Sound-Spelling Correspondence
Show the letters

Say: *The way we write the blend /***dr***/ is with the letters* **d** *and* **r***.*

Say: *The letters* **d** *and* **r** *make the sound /***dr***/.*

Say: *What is the name of the blend?* **dr** *What sound does the blend make? /***dr***/*

Model

Use BLM 42, # 1.

Say: *We will look at each picture.* **Say** *its name. If we hear the sound of an r blend at the beginning of the word, we will circle the picture. If we do not hear the sound of an r blend at the beginning, we cross out the picture.*

Say: *What do you see in the picture?* **bright** *Do you hear the sound /***br***/ at the beginning of the word bright? Circle the letters* **br***. If you do not hear the sound of an* **r** *blend at the beginning of the word, then cross out the picture.*

Practice

Use BLM 42, #2

Say: *Look at the picture.* **Say** *its name.* **Write** *the letter.*

Say: *What do you see in the picture?* **frown** *Do you hear the sound of an* **r** *blend at the beginning of the word frown?* **Write** *the letters.*

Apply
Blend Words

Use BLM 42, #3

Say: *Look at each letter and listen to the sound as I read:* /k/ /r/ /o/ /w/ /n/*Your turn:* /k/ /r/ /o/ /w/ /n/.

Say: *Now we are going to blend the sounds together by stretching them out as we read them.* Point to each letter in a sweeping motion left to right: **/k/rrrr/oooo/ wwww/nnnn/**. *What is the word?* **crown**

Spelling

Use BLM 41, #4.

Say: *Now we can practice writing the sounds we hear in each word. Call one word at a time, stretching each sound.*

Say: *Say the word slowly; write a letter for each sound you hear.*

Conclusion

Ask: *What did we learn today?* We learned that some letters can blend with the letter r. What pictures/words will help you remember the sounds and letter in **r**-blends?

Home Connection
Ask students to practice identifying **r** blends and writing them with a family member. Have students to identify other words that begin with **r** blends with their family.

✔ Formative Assessment

If the student completes each task correctly, precede to the next skill in the sequence. If not, refer to suggested Intervention 2.

Did the student...?	Intervention 2
Identify the name of the letter?	• Use physical rhythmic movements as the letter name is repeated. March while chanting the letter name. Move arms up and down. Sway from side to side..
Identify the sound of the letter?	• Use alliteration, chants that repeat the sound several times then a word that begins with the sound. Example: **/br/ /br/ /br/ brown**
Produce the sound of the letter?	Use mirrors to show movement of mouth, tongue, and teeth as the sound is produced. Use hand over mouth to explore movement of air as the sound is produced.
Recognize the beginning sound?	Use Elkonin boxes – student moves a token into first box as the beginning sound of the word is said.
Write the letter?	Write the letter, have students trace it. Create letter with clay. Discuss letter features (lines, shape). Trace over letter with multiple colors.
Know name of pictures?	Tell students the name of pictures, have students repeat them aloud. Discuss word and use each word in context.

Identify and Name S Blends

RF.1.3b, RF.1.3g

CCSS: RF.1.3
Know and apply grade-level phonics and word analysis skills in decoding words **both in isolation and in text.**
b. Decode regularly spelled one-syllable words.
g. Recognize and read grade-appropriate irregularly spelled words.

Lesson Objectives

- Identify and name **s blends.**
- Produce the sound **s blends.**
- Relate the sound **/s/** to s **blends.**
- Recognize **s blends** in words/ pictures.
-

METACOGNITIVE STRATEGY
- Selective auditory attention

ACADEMIC LANGUAGE
- letter name, letter sound, initial sound, final sound, ending sound, high frequency word

Additional Materials
- Sound Spelling Cards **St, Sn, Sl, Sw, Sp, Sm**
- Blackline Master 43

Pre-Assess
Student's ability to recognize the sounds represented by the targeted letters of the alphabet and to identify the letters used to represent the corresponding sounds.

.

Introduce

As students participate in this lesson, they identify the name and sound of the targeted blends, and identify the letters when the sounds and names are given orally. Students will apply their knowledge by recognizing the sounds of target blends using pictures. Students apply skill in context by reading decodable simple sentences that include high frequency words.

State Learning Goal
Today we will practice listening to the sounds of **s blends**.

Teach

Letters represent sounds. We remember the sounds each letter makes. We use letters to write words we say. We use letters to read and write words. Some letters combine to make new sounds.

Phonemic Awareness
Show pictures of sound/spelling card to review the sound.

Say: *This is the* **st** *card.*

Say: *Listen to this sound /st/. Say it with me:* **st***. Now say it on your own:* **st**

Say: *This is the* **sn** *card.*

Say: *Listen to this sound /sn/. Say it with me:* **sn***. Now say it on your own:* **sn**

Sound-Spelling Correspondence
Show the letters

Say: *The way we write the blend* /**st**/ *is with the letters* **s** *and* **t**.

Say: *The letters* **s** *and* **t** *make the sound* /**st**/.

Say: *What is the name of the blend?* **st** *What sound does the blend make?* /**st**/

Say: *The way we write the blend* /**sn**/ *is with the letters* **s** *and* **n**.

Say:: *The letters* **s** *and* **n** *make the sound* /**sn**/.

Say: *What is the name of the blend?* **sn** *What sound does the blend make?* /**sn**/

Model

Use BLM 43, # 1

Say: *We will look at each picture.* **Say** *its name.* If we hear the sound of an **s** blend in the word, we will circle the picture. If we do not hear the sound of an **s** blend, we cross out the picture..

Say: *What do you see in the picture*? **stump** Do you hear the sound /**st**/ in the word **stump**? Circle the picture. If you do not hear the sound of an **s** blend, then cross out the picture.

Practice

Use BLM 43, # 2

Say: **Look** at the picture. **Say** its name. If we hear the sound of an s blend in the word, we will circle the picture. If we do not hear the sound of an s blend, we cross out the picture.

Say: What do you see in the picture? **snail** Do you hear the sound /sn/ in the word **snail**? Circle the picture. If you do not hear the sound of an **s** blend, then cross out the picture.

Apply
Blend Words

Use BLM 43, #3.

Say: Look at each letter and listen to the sound as I read. /b/ /l/ /a/ /s/ /t/. Your turn: /b/ /l/ /a/ /s/ /t/.

Say: Now we are going to blend the sounds together by stretching them out as we read them. Point to each letter in a sweeping motion left to right: /b/llll/aaaa/ssss/tttt /. What is the word? **bast**

Spelling

Use BLM 43, #6.

Say: Now we can practice writing the sounds we hear in each word. Call one word at a time, stretching each sound.

Say: Say the word slowly; write a letter for each sound you hear.

Say: Say the word slowly; write a letter for each sound you hear.

Conclusion

Ask: What did we learn today? We learned that some letters can blend with the letter **s**. What pictures/words will help you remember the sounds and letter in **s** blends?.

Home Connection
Ask students to practice identifying **s** blends and writing them with a family member. Have students to identify other words that begin with s blends with their family..

✔ Formative Assessment

If the student completes each task correctly, precede to the next skill in the sequence. If not, refer to suggested Intervention 2.

Did the student…?	Intervention 2
Identify the name of the letter?	• Use physical rhythmic movements as the letter name is repeated. March while chanting the letter name. Move arms up and down. Sway from side to side..
Identify the sound of the letter?	• Say words with the target sounds by repeating the words three times. Examples: stump **stump stump, snail snail snail, last last last**. .
Produce the sound of the letter?	Use mirrors to show movement of mouth, tongue, teeth as the sound is produced. Use hand over mouth to explore movement of air as the sound is produced.
Recognize the sounds of the consonant digraphs?	Use Elkonin boxes – student moves a token into the box as the sound of the consonant digraph is said in the word.
Write the letter?	Write the letters. Have students trace them. Create the letters with clay. Discuss letter features (lines, shape). Trace over the letters with multiple colors..
Know name of pictures?	Tell students the name of pictures, have students repeat them aloud. Discuss word and use each word in context..

Identify and Name Final Blends
RF.1.3b, RF.1.3g
Introduce

As students participate in this lesson, they will identify the name and sound of the targeted blends, and identify the letters when the sounds and names are given orally. Students will apply their knowledge by recognizing the sounds of target blends using pictures. Students will also apply the skill in context by reading decodable simple sentences that include high frequency words..

State Learning Goal
Today we will practice listening to the sounds of **final blends**.

Teach

Letters represent sounds. We remember the sounds each letter makes. We use letters to write words we say. We use letters to read and write words. Some letters combine to make new sounds.

Sound-Spelling Correspondence
Show the letters.
Say: *We write the blend* /**nt**/ *with the letters* **n** *and* **t**. *What is the name of the blend?* **nt** *What sound does the blend make?* /**nt**/. *The way we write the blend* /**nd**/ *is with the letters* **n** *and* **d**. *What is the name of the blend?* **nd** *What sound does the blend make?* /**nd**/

Model

Use BLM 44, # 1
Say: *We will look at each picture.* **Say** *its name. If we hear the sound of a final blend in the word, we will circle the picture. If we do not hear the sound of a final blend, we cross out the picture. What do you see in the picture?* **peppermint** *Do you hear the sound* /**nt**/ *in the word peppermint? Circle the picture. If you do not hear the sound of a final blend, then cross out the picture.*
Use BLM 44, # 2
Say: *We will look at each picture Say its name. If we hear the sound of a* **final blend** *in the word, we will circle the picture. If we do not hear the sound of a* **final blend**, we cross out the picture.
Say: *What do you see in the picture?* **round** *Do you hear the sound* /**nd**/ *in the word round? Circle the picture. If you do not hear the sound of final blend, then cross out the picture.*
Use BLM 44, #3
Say: *We will look at each picture. Say its name. If we hear the sound of a* **final blend** *in the word, we will circle the picture. If we do not hear the sound of a* **final blend**, *we cross out the picture.*
Say: *What do you see in the picture?* **stamp** *Do you hear the sound* /**mp**/ *in the word* **stamp**? *Circle the picture. If you do not hear the sound of a* **final blend**, *then cross out the picture.*

CCSS:RF.1.3
Know and apply grade-level phonics and word analysis skills in decoding words **both in isolation and in text.**
b. Decode regularly spelled one-syllable words.
g. Recognize and read grade-appropriate irregularly spelled words.

Lesson Objectives

- Identify and name **final blends.**
- Produce the sound **final blends.**
- Relate sounds to **final blends.**
- Recognize **final blends** in words/ pictures.

METACOGNITIVE STRATEGY
- Selective auditory attention

ACADEMIC LANGUAGE
- letter name, letter sound, initial sound, final sound, ending sound, high frequency word

Materials
- Sound Spelling Cards **Nt, Nd, Mp, St, Nk**
- Blackline Master 44

Pre-Assess
Student's ability to recognize the sounds represented by the targeted letters of the alphabet and to identify the letters used to represent the corresponding sounds.

Practice

Use BLM 44, #4

Say: **Look** at the picture. **Say** *its name.* **Write** the letters.

Say *What is the picture?* **peppermint** Do you hear a **final blend** in the word **peppermint**? **Write** the letters.

Say: *What do you see in the picture?* **snail** Do you hear the sound /sn/ in the word **snail**? Circle the picture. If you do not hear the sound of an s blend, then cross out the picture.

Apply

Blend Words

Use BLM 44, #5.

Say: *Look at each letter and listen to the sound as I read.* /s/ /t/ /a/ /m/ /p/. *Your turn:* /s/ /t/ /a/ /m/ /p/.

Say: *Now we are going to blend the sounds together by stretching them out as we read them.* Point to each letter in a sweeping motion left to right: /ssss/tttt/aaaa/mmmm/pppp/. *What is the word?* **stamp**

Spelling

Use BLM 43, #4.

Say:*Now we can practice writing the sounds we hear in each word. Call one word at a time, stretching each sound.*

Say: *Say the word slowly; write a letter for each sound you hear.*

Say: *Say the word slowly; write a letter for each sound you hear.*

Conclusion

Ask: *What did we learn today?* We learned that some words end in a **final blend**. What pictures/words will help you remember the sounds and letters in **final blend**?

Home Connection

Ask students to practice identifying **s** blends and writing them with a family member. Have students to identify other words that begin with s blends with their family.

✔ Formative Assessment

If the student completes each task correctly, precede to the next skill in the sequence. If not, refer to suggested Intervention 2.

Did the student…?	Intervention 2
Identify the name of the letter?	• Use physical rhythmic movements as the letter name is repeated. March while chanting the letter name. Move arms up and down. Sway from side to side..
Identify the sound of the letter?	• Say words with the target sounds by repeating the words three times. Examples: **mint mint mint, round round round, stamp, stamp, stamp .**
Produce the sound of the letter?	Use mirrors to show movement of mouth, tongue, teeth as the sound is produced. Use hand over mouth to explore movement of air as the sound is produced.
Recognize the sounds of the consonant digraphs?	Use Elkonin boxes – student moves a token into the box as the sound of the consonant digraph is said in the word.
Write the letter?	Write the letters, have students trace them. Create the letters with clay. Discuss letter features (lines, shape). Trace over the letters with multiple colors.
Know name of pictures?	Tell students the name of pictures, have students repeat them aloud. Discuss word and use each word in context.

CCSS: RF.1.3
Know and apply grade-level phonics and word analysis skills in decoding words **both in isolation and in text**.
a. Know the spelling-sound correspondences for common consonant digraphs.
b. Decode regularly spelled one-syllable words.

Lesson Objectives

- Identify and name the letters **ck, ch, and tch.**
- Produce the sounds of consonants **ck, ch, and tch.**
- Relate the sounds **/ck/, /ch/,** and **/tch/** to the letters **ck, ch, and tch.**
- Recognize sounds **ck, ch,** and **tch** in words/pictures.

METACOGNITIVE STRATEGY

- Selective auditory attention, imagery, auditory representation

ACADEMIC LANGUAGE

- letter name, letter sound, initial sound, final sound, ending sound, high frequency word

Materials

- Sound Spelling Cards **ck, ch, tch**
- Blackline Master 45

Pre-Assess

Student's ability to recognize the sounds represented by the targeted letters of the alphabet and to identify the letters used to represent the corresponding sounds..

Identify and Name Digraphs ck, ch, tch RF.1.3a, RF.1.3b

Introduce

As students participate in this lesson, they identify the name and sound of the targeted letters, and identify the letters when the sounds and names are given orally. Students will apply their knowledge by recognizing the sounds of target consonant digraphs using pictures. Students apply skill in context by reading decodable simple sentences that include high frequency words.

State Learning Goal

Today we will practice listening to the sounds **/ck/, /ch/ and /tch/** that the letters **ck, ch, and tch** make.

Teach

Letters represent sounds. We remember the sounds each letter makes. We use letters to write words we say. We use letters to read and write words. Some letters combine to make new sounds.

Sound-Spelling Correspondence

Say: *The way we write the sound /ck/ is with the letters ck. The letters ck make the sound /ck/. What is the name of the letters that combine?* **ck** *What sound does the letters make?* **/ck/**

Model

Use BLM 45, # 1.

Say: *We will look at each picture.* **Say** *its name. If we hear the sound of* **ck** *at the end of the word, we will circle the letters ck. If we do not hear the sound /ck/, we cross out the picture. What do you see in the picture?* **clock** *Do you hear the sound /ck/ at the end of the word clock? Circle the letters* **ck**. *If you do not hear the sound /ck/ at the end of the word, then cross out the picture.*

Sound-Spelling Correspondence

Show the letters.

Say: *The way we write the sound /ch/ is with the letters* **ch**. *The letters* **ch** *make the sound /ch/. What is the name of the letters that combine? ch What sound does the letters make?* **/ch/**

Use BLM 45, # 2

Say: *We will look at each picture. Say its name. If we hear the sound of* **ch** *at the beginning of the word, we will circle the letters* **ch**. *If we do not hear the sound /ch/, we cross out the picture. What do you see in the picture?* **chips** *Do you hear the sound /ch/ at the beginning of the word* **chips**? *Circle the letters* **ch**. *If you do not hear the sound /ch/ at the beginning of the word, then cross out the picture.*

Sound-Spelling Correspondence

Show the letters.

Say: *The way we write the sound /tch/ is with the letters **tch**. The letters tch make the sound /tch/. What is the name of the letters that combine? **tch** What sound does the letters make? /tch/*

Use BLM 45, # 3.

Say: *We will look at each picture. Say its name. If we hear the sound of tch at the end of the word, we will circle the letters tch. If we do not hear the sound /tch/, we cross out the picture.*

Say: *What do you see in the picture? stretch Do you hear the sound /tch/ at the beginning of the word stretch? Circle the letters tch. If you do not hear the sound /tch/ at the end of the word, then cross out the picture.*

Practice

Use BLM 45, # 4.

Say: Look *at the picture.* **Say** *its name.* **Write** *the letters.*

Say: *What is the picture? **cherry**. Do you hear the sounds /ck/, /ch/, or /tch/ in the word **child**? Write the letters **ch**.*

Apply

Blend Words

Use BLM 45, # 5.

Say: *Look at each letter and listen to the sound as I read. /t/ /r/ /a/ /k/. Your turn: /t/ /r/ /a/ /k/.*

Say: *Now we are going to blend the sounds together by stretching them out as we read them. Point to each letter in a sweeping motion left to right /t/rrr/aaa/kkk/.. What is the word? **track**.*

Spelling

Use BLM 45, # 6

Say: *Now we can practice writing the sounds we hear in each word. Call one word at a time, stretching each sound.*

Say: *Say the word slowly; write a letter for each sound you hear.*

Conclusion

Ask: *What did we learn today?* We learned the that the letters **ck** make the sound /**ck**/. The letters **ch** make the sound /**ch**/. The letters **tch** make the sound /**tch**/.. We wrote words using the combined letters **ck, ch,** and **tch**. What pictures/words will help you remember the sounds /**ck**/, /**ch**/, and /**tch**/ and the letters **ck, ch, and tch** at the beginning or end of a word?

✔ Formative Assessment

If the student completes each task correctly, precede to the next skill in the sequence. If not, refer to suggested Intervention 2.

Did the student...?	Intervention 2
Identify the name of the letter?	• Use physical rhythmic movements as the letter name is repeated. March while chanting the letter name. Move arms up and down. Sway from side to side.
Identify the sound of the letter?	• Say words with the target sounds by repeating the words three times. Examples: **cheap cheap cheap, black black black, sketch sketch sketch**..
Produce the sound of the letter?	Use mirrors to show movement of mouth, tongue, teeth as the sound is produced. Use hand over mouth to explore movement of air as the sound is produced.
Recognize the sounds of the consonant digraphs?	Use Elkonin boxes – student moves a token into the box as the sound of the consonant digraph is said in the word.
Write the letter?	Write the letters, have students trace them. Create the letters with clay. Discuss letter features (lines, shape). Trace over the letters with multiple colors.
Know name of pictures?	Tell students the name of pictures, have students repeat them aloud. Discuss word and use each word in context.

Identify and Name Digraph sh
RF.1.3a, RF.1.3b

Introduce

As students participate in this lesson, they identify the name and sound of the targeted letters, and identify the letters when the sounds and names are given orally. Students will apply their knowledge by recognizing the sounds of target consonant digraphs using pictures. Students apply skill in context by reading decodable simple sentences that include high frequency words.

State Learning Goal

Today we will practice listening to the sound /sh/ that the letters **sh** make.

Teach

Letters represent sounds. We remember the sounds each letter makes. We use letters to write words we say. We use letters to read and write words. Some letters combine to make new sounds.

Phonemic Awareness

Show picture of sound/spelling card **SH** to review the sound.
Say: *Listen to this sound /sh/. Say it with me:* **sh.** *Say it on your own:* **sh.**

Sound-Spelling Correspondence

Show the letters
Say: *The way we write the sound /sh/ is with the letters* **sh.**
Say: *The letters* **sh** *make the sound /sh/.*
Say: *What is the name of the letters that combine? sh What sound does the letters make? /sh/*

Model

Use BLM 46, # 1.
Say: *We will look at each picture.* **Say** *its name.* If we hear the sound of **sh** at the beginning or end of the word, we will circle the letters **sh**. If we do not hear the sound /sh/, we cross out the picture.

CCSS: RF.1.3
Know and apply grade-level phonics and word analysis skills in decoding words both in isolation and in text.
a. Know the spelling-sound correspondences for common consonant digraphs.
b. Decode regularly spelled one-syllable words.

Lesson Objectives

- Identify and name the letters **sh**
- Produce the sounds of consonants **sh**
- Relate the sound /**sh**/ to the letters **sh**
- Recognize sound **sh** in words/ pictures

METACOGNITIVE STRATEGY
- Selective auditory attention, imagery, auditory representation

ACADEMIC LANGUAGE
- letter name, letter sound, initial sound, final sound, ending sound, high frequency word

Materials
- Sound Spelling Card **SH**
- Blackline Master 46

Pre-Assess
Student's ability to recognize the sounds represented by the targeted letters of the alphabet and to identify the letters used to represent the corresponding sounds.

Practice

Use BLM 46, # 2.

Say: Look *at the picture.* **Say** *its name.* **Write** *the letters.*

Say: What is the picture? **sheep**. *Do you hear the sound* /**sh**/ *in the word* **sheep***?* **Write** *the letters* **sh***.*

Apply

Blend Words

Use BLM 46, #3.

Say: *Look at each letter and listen to the sound as I read.* /**b**/ /**r**/ /**u**/ /**sh**/. *Your turn:* /**b**/ /**r**/ /**u**/ /**sh**/.

Say: *Now we are going to blend the sounds together by stretching them out as we read them. Point to each letter in a sweeping motion left to right* /**b**/ /**rrr**/ /**uuu**/ /**sh**/. *What is the word?* brush.

Spelling

Use BLM 46, # 4.

Say: *Now we can practice writing the sounds we hear in each word. Call one word at a time, stretching each sound.*

Say: *Say the word slowly; write a letter for each sound you hear.*

Conclusion

Ask: *What did we learn today?* We learned that the letters **sh** make the sound /**sh**/. We wrote words using the combined letters **sh**. What pictures/words will help you remember the sound /sh/ and the letters **sh** at the beginning or end of a word?

Home Connection

Use BLM 46. Encourage students to practice identifying sound sh and writing the letters **sh** with a family member. Encourage students to identify other words with the sound **sh** with their family..

✔ Formative Assessment

If the student completes each task correctly, precede to the next skill in the sequence. If not, refer to suggested Intervention 2.

Did the student...?	Intervention 2
Identify the name of the letter?	• Use physical rhythmic movements as the letter name is repeated. March while chanting the letter name. Move arms up and down. Sway from side to side..
Identify the sound of the letter?	• Say words with the target sound, emphasizing the sound. Examples: **shhhhine, flashhhh...**
Produce the sound of the letter?	Use mirrors to show movement of mouth, tongue, teeth as the sound is produced. Use hand over mouth to explore movement of air as the sound is produced.
Recognize the sounds of the consonant digraphs?	Use Elkonin boxes – student moves a token into the box as the sound of the consonant digraph is said in the word.
Write the letter?	Write the letters, have students trace them. Create the letters with clay. Discuss letter features (lines, shape). Trace over the letters with multiple colors..
Know name of pictures?	Tell students the name of pictures, have students repeat them aloud. Discuss word and use each word in context.

Identify and Name Digraph wh
RF.1.3a, RF.1.3b

Introduce

As students participate in this lesson, they identify the name and sound of the targeted letters, and identify the letters when the sounds and names are given orally. Students will apply their knowledge by recognizing the sounds of target consonant digraphs using pictures. Students apply skill in context by reading decodable simple sentences that include high frequency words.

State Learning Goal

Today we will practice listening to the sound /**th**/ that the letters **th** make and the sound /**wh**/ that the letters **wh** make.

Teach

Letters represent sounds. We remember the sounds each letter makes. We use letters to write words we say. We use letters to read and write words. Some letters combine to make new sounds.

Phonemic Awareness

Show picture of sound/spelling card **TH** to review the sound.

Say: *Listen to this sound /**th**/. Say it with me: th. Say it on your own: **th**.*

Sound-Spelling Correspondence

Show the letters

Say: *The way we write the sound /**th**/ is with the letters **th**. The letters **th** make the sound /**th**/. What is the name of the letters that combine? **th** What sound does the letters make? /**th**/*

Model

Use BLM 47, # 1

Say: *We will look at each picture. **Say** its name. If we hear the sound of **th** at the beginning or end of the word, we will circle the letters **th**. If we do not hear the sound /**th**/, we cross out the picture. What do you see in the picture? thorn. Do you hear the sound /**th**/ at the beginning or end of the word **thorn**? Circle the letters th. If you do not hear the sound /**th**/ at the beginning or end of the word, then cross out the picture.*

Phonemic Awareness

Show picture of sound/spelling card **WH** to review the sound.

Say: *Listen to this sound /**wh**/. Say it with me: wh. Say it on your own: **wh**.*

Sound-Spelling Correspondence

Show the letters.

Say: *The way we write the sound /**wh**/ is with the letters **wh**. The letters wh make the sound /**wh**/. What is the name of the letters that combine? wh What sound does the letters make? /**wh**/*

CCSS: RF.1.3
Know and apply grade-level phonics and word analysis skills in decoding words **both in isolation and in text**.
a. Know the spelling-sound correspondences for common consonant digraphs.
b. Decode regularly spelled one-syllable words.

Lesson Objectives

- Identify and name the letters **th and wh**
- Produce the sounds of consonants **th and wh**
- Relate the sounds /**th**/ and /**wh**/ to the letters **th** and **wh**
- Recognize sounds **th** and **wh** in words/pictures

METACOGNITIVE STRATEGY
- Selective auditory attention, imagery, auditory representation

ACADEMIC LANGUAGE
- letter name, letter sound, initial sound, final sound, ending sound, high frequency word

Materials
- Sound Spelling Cards **TH, WH**
- Blackline Master 47

Pre-Assess
Student's ability to recognize the sounds represented by the targeted letters of the alphabet and to identify the letters used to represent the corresponding sounds.

Use BLM 47, #2.

Say: *We will look at each picture. Say its name.* If we hear the sound of **wh** at the beginning of the word, we will circle the letters wh. If we do not hear the sound /**wh**/, we cross out the picture.

Say: *What do you see in the picture?* **whale**. Do you hear the sound /**wh**/ at the beginning of the word whale? Circle the letters **wh**. If you do not hear the sound /**wh**/ at the beginning of the word, then cross out the picture.

Practice

Use BLM 47, # 3.

Say: Look *at the picture.* **Say** *its name.* **Write** *the letters.*

Say: *What is the picture?* **thumb**. *Do you hear the sound /th/ in the word thumb?* **Write** *the letters* **th**.

Apply

Blend Words

Use BLM 47, # 4.

Say: *Look at each letter and listen to the sound as I read.* /**m**/ /**o**/ /**n**/ /**th**/. *Your turn:* /**m**/ /**o**/ /**n**/ /**th**/. *Now we are going to blend the sounds together by stretching them out as we read them. Point to each letter in a sweeping motion left to right* /**m/ooo/nnn/th**/. *What is the word?* **month**.

Spelling

Use BLM 47, #5.

Say: *Now we can practice writing the sounds we hear in each word. Call one word at a time, stretching each sound. Say: Say the word slowly; write a letter for each sound you hear.*

Conclusion

Ask: *What did we learn today?* We learned that the letters th make the sound /**th**/. We learned that the letters wh make the sound /**wh**/. We wrote words using the combined letters th and **wh**. What pictures/words will help you remember the sounds /**th**/ and /**wh**/ and the letters **th** and **wh** at the beginning or end of a word?

Home Connection

Use BLM 47. Encourage students to practice identifying sounds **th** and **wh** and writing the letters **th** and **wh** with a family member. Encourage students to identify other words with the sounds **th** and **wh** with their family..

✓ **Formative Assessment**

If the student completes each task correctly, precede to the next skill in the sequence. If not, refer to suggested Intervention 2.

Did the student...?	Intervention 2
Identify the name of the letter?	• Use physical rhythmic movements as the letter name is repeated. March while chanting the letter name. Move arms up and down. Sway from side to side..
Identify the sound of the letter?	• Say words with the target sound, emphasizing the sound. Examples: **thhhhing, whhhhile**..
Produce the sound of the letter?	Use mirrors to show movement of mouth, tongue, teeth as the sound is produced. Use hand over mouth to explore movement of air as the sound is produced.
Recognize the sounds of the consonant digraphs?	Use Elkonin boxes – student moves a token into the box as the sound of the consonant digraph is said in the word.
Write the letter?	Write the letters, have students trace them. Create the letters with clay. Discuss letter features (lines, shape). Trace over the letters with multiple colors.
Know name of pictures?	Tell students the name of pictures, have students repeat them aloud. Discuss word and use each word in context.

Identify and Name Inflectional Endings -s, -ed, -ing RF.1.3a, RF.1.3b, RF.1.3f

Introduce

As students participate in this lesson, they identify the name and sound of the targeted letters, and identify the letters when the sounds and names are given orally. Students will apply their knowledge by recognizing the sounds of target inflected endings using pictures. Students apply skill in context by reading decodable simple sentences that include high frequency words.

State Learning Goal

Today we will practice listening to the sounds /s/, /ed/, and /ing/ that the letters s, **ed**, and **ing** make when added to the end of words.

Teach

Letters represent sounds. We remember the sounds each letter makes. We use letters to write words we say. We use letters to read and write words. Some letters combine to make new sounds. We add the sounds to the end of words.

Phonemic Awareness

Show picture of sound/spelling card **S** to review the sound.

Say: *Listen to this sound /s/.* **Say** *it with me:* **s.** *Say it on your own:* **s.**

Sound-Spelling Correspondence

Show the letters

Say: *The way we write the sound /s/ is with the letter* **s.** *The letter* **s** *makes the sound /s/. What is the name of the letter?* **s** *What sound does the letter make? /s/*

Model

Use BLM 48, #1.

Say: *We will look at each picture.* **Say** *its name.* If we hear the sound of s at the end of the word, we will circle the letter **s**. If we do not hear the sound /s/, we cross out the picture. What do you see in the picture? climbs. Do you hear the sound /s/ at the end of the word **climbs**? Circle the letter **s**. If you do not hear the sound /s/ at the end of the word, then cross out the picture.

Sound-Spelling Correspondence

Show the letters.

Say: *The way we write the sound /ing/ is with the letters* **ing**. *The letters* **ing** *make the sound /ing/. What is the name of the letters that combine?* **ing** *What sound does the letters make? /ing/*

Use BLM 48, # 2.

Say: *We will look at each picture.* **Say** *its name.* If we hear the sound of ing at the end of the word, we will circle the letters **ing**. If we do not hear the sound /ing/, we cross out the picture. What do you see in the picture? climbing. Do you hear the sound /ing/ at the end of the word climbing? Circle the letters **ing**. If you do not hear the sound /ing/ at the end of the word, then cross out the picture.

Sound-Spelling Correspondence

Show the letters

Say: *The way we write the sound /ed/ is with the letters* **ed**. *The letters* **ed** *make the sound /ed/. What is the name of the letters that combine?* **ed** *What sound does the letters make? /ed*

CCSS: RF.1.3
Know and apply grade-level phonics and word analysis skills in decoding words both in isolation and in text.
a. Know the spelling-sound correspondences for common consonant digraphs.
b. Decode regularly spelled one-syllable words.
f. Read words with inflectional endings.

Lesson Objectives

- Identify and name the letters s, **ed**, and **ing**.
- Produce the sounds of inflectional endings s, **ed** and **ing**.
- Relate the sounds /s/, /**ed**/, and /**ing**/ to the letters s, **ed** and **ing**.
- Recognize sounds s, **ed** and **ing** in words/pictures.

METACOGNITIVE STRATEGY

- Selective auditory attention, imagery, auditory representation

ACADEMIC LANGUAGE

- letter name, letter sound, initial sound, final sound, ending sound, high frequency word

Materials

- Sound Spelling Cards **S, ED, ING**
- Blackline Master 48

Pre-Assess

Student's ability to recognize the sounds represented by the targeted letters of the alphabet and to identify the letters used to represent the corresponding sounds.

Use BLM 48, #3.

Say: *We will look at each picture. Say its name. If we hear the sound of* **ed** *at the end of the word, we will circle the letters* **ed**. *If we do not hear the sound* /**ed**/, *we cross out the picture. What do you see in the picture?* **climbed**. *Do you hear the sound* /**ed**/ *at the end of the word* **climbed**? *Circle the letters ed. If you do not hear the sound* /**ed**/ *at the end of the word, then cross out the picture.*

Practice

Use BLM 48, # 4

Say: *Look at the picture. Say its name.* **Write** *the letters. What is the picture?* **climbs**. *Do you hear the sounds* /**s**/, /**ing**/, **or** /**ed**/ *at the end of the word* **climbs**?

Apply

Blend Words

Use BLM 48, # 5

Say: *Look at each letter and listen to the sound as I read.* /**k**/ /**l**/ /**i**/ /**m**/ /**i**/ /**n**/ /**g**/. *Your turn:* /**k**/ /**l**/ /**i**/ /**m**/ /**i**/ /**n**/ /**g**/.

Say: *Now we are going to blend the sounds together by stretching them out as we read them. Point to each letter in a sweeping motion left to right* /**k**/**lll**/**iii**/**mmm**/ **iii**/**nnn**/**ggg**/. *What is the word?* **climbing**.

Spelling

Use BLM 48, #6.

Say: *Now we can practice writing the sounds we hear in each word. Call one word at a time, stretching each sound.*

Say: *Say the word slowly; write a letter for each sound you hear.*

Conclusion

Ask: *What did we learn today?* We learned that the letter s makes the sound /s/. We learned that the letters **ing** make the sound /**ing**/. We learned that the letters ed make the sound /**ed**/. We learned to listen for these sounds at the end of words. We wrote words using the letters s, ing, and ed at the end of words. What pictures/words will help you remember the sounds /**s**/, /**ing**/, and /**ed**/ and the letters **s**, **ing**, and **ed** at the end of a word?

Home Connection

Use BLM 48. Encourage students to practice identifying sounds **s, ed**, and **ing** at the end of words and writing the letters **s, ed**, and **ing** with a family member. Encourage students to identify other words with the sounds **s, ed**, and **ing** at the end of words with their family.

✔ **Formative Assessment**

If the student completes each task correctly, precede to the next skill in the sequence. If not, refer to suggested Intervention 2..

Did the student...?	Intervention 2
Identify the name of the letter?	• Use physical rhythmic movements as the letter name is repeated. March while chanting the letter name. Move arms up and down. Sway from side to side.
Identify the sound of the letter?	• Say words with the target sounds by emphasizing the sounds. Examples: **dances, dancing, danced..**
Produce the sound of the letter?	Use mirrors to show movement of mouth, tongue, teeth as the sound is produced. Use hand over mouth to explore movement of air as the sound is produced.
Recognize the sounds of the consonant digraphs?	Use Elkonin boxes – student moves a token into the box as the sound of the consonant digraph is said in the word.
Write the letter?	Write the letters, have students trace them. Create the letters with clay. Discuss letter features (lines, shape). Trace over the letters with multiple colors..
Know name of pictures?	Tell students the name of pictures, have students repeat them aloud. Discuss word and use each word in context.

Identify and Name Inflectional Endings -er, -est RF.1.3e, RF.1.3f, RF.1.3g

CCSS:RF.1.3
Know and apply grade-level phonics and word analysis skills in decoding words **both in isolation and in text.**
e. Decode two-syllable words following basic patterns by breaking the words into syllables.
f. Read words with inflectional endings.
g. Recognize and read grade-appropriate irregularly spelled words.

Lesson Objectives

- Identify and name the letters er and **est**
- Produce the sounds of inflectional endings er and **est**
- Relate the sounds /**er**/, and /**est**/ to the letters er and **est**
- Recognize sounds **er** and **est** in words/pictures

METACOGNITIVE STRATEGY
- Selective auditory attention, imagery, auditory representation

ACADEMIC LANGUAGE
- letter name, letter sound, initial sound, final sound, ending sound, high frequency word

Materials
- Letter Cards **e, r, s, t**
- Blackline Master 49

Pre-Assess
Student's ability to recognize the sounds represented by the targeted letters of the alphabet and to identify the letters used to represent the corresponding sounds.

Introduce

As students participate in this lesson, they identify the name and sound of the targeted letters, and identify the letters when the sounds and names are given orally. Students will apply their knowledge by recognizing the sounds of target inflected endings using pictures. Students apply skill in context by reading decodable simple sentences that include high frequency words.

State Learning Goal
Today we will practice listening to the sounds that the letters **er** and **est** make when added to the end of words.

Teach
Letters represent sounds. We remember the sounds each letter makes. We use letters to write words we say. We use letters to read and write words. Some letters combine to make new sounds. We add the sounds to the end of words.

Phonemic Awareness
Show letter cards **e** and **r** to review the sound. Say: Listen to this sound /**er**/. Say it with me: **er**. Say it on your own: **er**.

Sound-Spelling Correspondence
Show the letters
Say: *The way we write the sound /**er**/ is with the letters er.*
Say: *The letters er makes the sound /**er**/.*
Say: *What is the name of the letters?* **er** *What sound does the letters make?* /**er**/

Model

Use BLM 49, # 1.
Say: *We will look at each picture.* **Say** *its name.* If we hear the sound of **er** at the end of the word, we will circle the letter **er**. If we do not hear the sound /**er**/, we cross out the picture.
Say: *What do you see in the picture?* **darker**. Do you hear the sound /**er**/ at the end of the word **darker**? Circle the letters **er**. If you do not hear the sound /**er**/ at the end of the word, then cross out the picture.

Phonemic Awareness
Show letter cards **e, s** and **t** to review the sound.
Say: *Listen to this sound /**est**/. Say it with me:* **est**. *Say it on your own:* **est**.

Sound-Spelling Correspondence
Show the letters.
Say: *The way we write the sound /**est**/ is with the letters* **est**.

Use BLM 49, # 2.

Say: *We will look at each picture.* Say *its name. If we hear the sound of* est *at the end of the word, we will circle the letters* est. *If we do not hear the sound* /est/, *we cross out the picture. What do you see in the picture?* darkest. *Do you hear the sound* /est/ *at the end of the word* darkest? *Circle the letters* est. *If you do not hear the sound* /est/ *at the end of the word, then cross out the picture.*

Practice

Use BLM 49, # 3.

Say: **Look** *at the picture.* **Say** *its name.* **Write** *the letters. What is the picture?* darker. *Do you hear the sounds* /er/ *or* /est/ *at the end of the word* darker? *Write the letters* er.

Apply
Blend Words

Use BLM 49, # 4.

Say: *Look at each letter and listen to the sound as I read.* /d/ /a/ /r/ /k/ /e/ /s/ /t/. *Your turn:* /d/ /a/ /r/ /k/ /e/ /s/ /t. Now we are going to blend the sounds together by stretching them out as we read them. Point to each letter in a sweeping motion left to right* /d/aaa/rrr/kkk/eee/sss/ttt/. *What is the word?* darkest.

Spelling

Use BLM 49, # 5.

Say: *Now we can practice writing the sounds we hear in each word. Call one word at a time, stretching each sound. Say the word slowly; write a letter for each sound you hear.*

Conclusion

Ask: *What did we learn today?* We learned that the letters er makes the sound /er/. We learned that the letters est make the sound /est/. We learned to listen for these sounds at the end of words. We wrote words using the letters er and est at the end of words. What pictures/words will help you remember the sounds /er/ and /est/ and the letters er and est at the end of a word?

Home Connection
Use BLM 49. Encourage students to practice identifying sounds er and est at the end of words and writing the letters er and est with a family member. Encourage students to identify other words with the sounds er and est at the end of words with their family.the end of words with their family.

✔ Formative Assessment

If the student completes each task correctly, precede to the next skill in the sequence. If not, refer to suggested Intervention 2..

Did the student...?	Intervention 2
Identify the name of the letter?	• Use physical rhythmic movements as the letter name is repeated. March while chanting the letter name. Move arms up and down. Sway from side to side..
Identify the sound of the letter?	• Say words with the target sounds by repeating the words three times. Examples: **faster, fastest, longer, longest**..
Produce the sound of the letter?	Use mirrors to show movement of mouth, tongue, teeth as the sound is produced. Use hand over mouth to explore movement of air as the sound is produced.
Recognize the sounds of the consonant digraphs?	Use Elkonin boxes – student moves a token into the box as the sound of the consonant digraph is said in the word.
Write the letter?	Write the letters, have students trace them. Create the letters with clay. Discuss letter features (lines, shape). Trace over the letters with multiple colors..
Know name of pictures?	Tell students the name of pictures, have students repeat them aloud. Discuss word and use each word in context..

Identify and Name Closed Syllables RF.1.3e, RF.1.3g

CCSS: RF.1.3
Know and apply grade-level phonics and word analysis skills in decoding words both in isolation and in text.

e. Decode two-syllable words following basic patterns by breaking the words into syllables.
g. Recognize and read grade-appropriate irregularly spelled words.

Lesson Objectives

- Identify closed syllables.
- Produce the sound of closed syllables.
- Recognize closed syllables in words/pictures.

METACOGNITIVE STRATEGY
- Selective auditory attention, imagery, auditory representation

ACADEMIC LANGUAGE
- vowel, closed syllable

Materials
- Letter Cards **w, i, n**
- Blackline Master 50

Pre-Assess
Student's ability to recognize the sound represented by a syllable and to identify the letters used to represent the corresponding sound.

Introduce
As students participate in this lesson, they identify closed syllables in two-syllable words, and identify syllables when the sound and name is given orally. Students will apply their knowledge by recognizing the sound of closed syllables using pictures. Students apply the skill in context by reading simple decodable sentences that include high frequency words.

State Learning Goal
Words are made up of syllables. Each vowel sound makes a syllable. In **closed syllables**, the vowel is followed by a consonant. .

Teach

Letters represent sounds. We remember the sounds each letter makes. Letters are divided into vowels and consonants. Every syllable contains a vowel sound. A closed syllable starts with a vowel and ends with a consonant. The vowel in a closed syllable has a short sound. It does not say its name.

Phonemic Awareness
Show letter cards to spell **win**. Say: Listen to this word: **win**. Say it with me: **win**. Say it on your own: **win**.

Sound-Spelling Correspondence
Show the letters
Say: *The word* **win** *is one syllable. The word* **win** *is a closed syllable. How many syllables?* **one** *What kind of syllable?* **closed**

Model

Use BLM 50, # 1.
Say: *We will look at each picture.* **Say** *its name.* **Listen for the closed syllables.**
Say: *Do you hear the closed syllables in the word* **pumpkin***? It has two closed syllables:* **pump/kin***. If we hear two closed syllables, we will circle the picture* **pumpkin***. If we do not hear two closed syllables, we cross out the picture.*

Practice

Use BLM 50, #2.

Say: *Look at the picture.* **Say** *its name.* **Write** *the letters.*

Say: *What is the picture?* **dentist** *Do you hear the two closed syllables in the word* **dentist**? **Circle** *the two syllables:* **den/tist**.

Apply

Blend Words

Use BLM 50, #3.

Say: *Look at each letter and listen to the sound as I read.* /n/ /a/ /p/ /k/ /i/ /n/. *Your turn:* /n/ /a/ /p/ /k/ /i/ /n/.

Say: *Now we are going to blend the sounds together by stretching them out as we read them. Point to each letter in a sweeping motion left to right* /n/aaa/ppp/ kkk/iii/nnn/. *What is the word?* **napkin**.

Spelling

Use BLM 50, #4.

Say: *Now we can practice writing the sounds we hear in each word. Call one word at a time, stretching each sound.*

Say: *Say the word slowly; write a letter for each sound you hear.*

Conclusion

Ask: *What did we learn today?* We learned that words are made of syllables. Closed syllables have a vowel followed by a consonant. What pictures/words will help you remember closed two-syllable words?

Home Connection

Use BLM 50. Encourage students to practice identifying closed two-syllable words with a family member. Encourage students to identify other words that have closed syllables with their family.

✔ Formative Assessment

If the student completes each task correctly, precede to the next skill in the sequence. If not, refer suggested Intervention 2.

Did the student…?	Intervention 2
Identify the name of the letter?	• Use physical rhythmic movements as the letter name is repeated. March while chanting the letter name. Move arms up and down. Sway from side to side.
Identify the sound of the letter?	• Use alliteration, chants that repeat the sound several times then a word that begins with the sound.
Produce the sound of the letter?	Use mirrors to show movement of mouth, tongue, teeth as the sound is produced. Use hand over mouth to explore movement of air as the sound is produced.
Recognize the syllables?	Use Elkonin boxes – student moves a token into the box as each syllable in the word is said.
Write the letter?	Write the letter, have students trace it. Create letter with clay. Discuss letter features (lines, shape). Trace over letter with multiple colors.
Know name of pictures?	Tell students the name of pictures, have student repeat it aloud. Discuss meaning of word. Use word in context.

Identify and Name 3-Letter Blends scr, spr, spl, str RF.1.3b, RF.1.3g

Introduce

As students participate in this lesson, they identify the name and sound of the targeted letters, and identify the letters when the sounds and names are given orally. Students will apply their knowledge by recognizing the sounds of target consonant digraphs using pictures. Students apply skill in context by reading decodable simple sentences that include high frequency words.

State Learning Goal

Today we will practice listening to the sounds /scr/, /spr/, /spl/ and /str/ that the letters **scr, spr, spl** and **str** make.

Teach

Letters represent sounds. We remember the sounds each letter makes. We use letters to write words we say. We use letters to read and write words. Some letters combine to make new sounds.

Sound-Spelling Correspondence

Say: *The way we write the sound /scr/ is with the letters* **scr***. The letters* **scr** *make the sound /scr/. What is the name of the letters that combine?* **scr** *What sound do the letters make? /scr/*

Model

Use BLM 51, # 1A

Say: *We will look at each picture. Say its name. If we hear the sound /scr/ at the beginning of the word, we will circle the letters* **scr***. If we do not hear the sound /scr/, we cross out the picture. What do you see in the picture?* **screw** *Do you hear the sound /scr/ at the beginning of the word* **screw***? Circle the letters* **scr***. If you do not hear the sound /scr/ at the beginning of the word, then cross out the picture.*

Sound-Spelling Correspondence

Show the letters.

Say: *The way we write the sound /***spr***/ is with the letters* spr*. The letters* **spr** *make the sound /***spr***/. What is the name of the letters that combine? spr What sound do the letters make? /***spr***/*

Use BLM 51, # 1B

Say: *We will look at each picture.* **Say** *its name. If we hear the sound /***spr***/ at the beginning of the word, we will circle the letters* **spr***. If we do not hear the sound /***spr***/, we cross out the picture. What do you see in the picture?* **sprout** *Do you hear the sound /***spr***/ at the beginning of the word* **sprout***? Circle the letters* **spr***. If you do not hear the sound /***spr***/ at the beginning of the word, then cross out the picture.*

Sound-Spelling Correspondence

Show the letters.

Say: *The way we write the sound /spl/ is with the letters* **spl***. The letters* **spl** *make the sound /spl/. What is the name of the letters that combine?* **spl** *What sound do the letters make? /spl/*

CCSS: RF.1.3
Know and apply grade-level phonics and word analysis skills in decoding words both in isolation and in text.
b. Decode regularly spelled one-syllable words.
g. Recognize and read grade-appropriate irregularly spelled words.

Lesson Objectives

- Identify and name the letters **scr, spr, spl** and **str.**
- Produce the sounds of consonants **scr, spr, spl** and **str.**
- Relate the sounds **/scr/, /spr/, /spl/** and **/str/** to the letters **scr, spr, spl** and **str.**
- Recognize sounds **scr, spr, spl** and **str** in words/pictures.

METACOGNITIVE STRATEGY
- Selective auditory attention, imagery, auditory representation

ACADEMIC LANGUAGE
- letter name, letter sound, initial sound, final sound, ending sound, high frequency word

Materials
- Letter Cards **s, c, r, p, l, t**
- Blackline Master 51

Pre-Assess
Student's ability to recognize the sounds represented by the targeted letters of the alphabet and to identify the letters used to represent the corresponding sounds.

Use BLM 51, # 1C

Say: *We will look at each picture.* **Say** *its name. If we hear the sound /spl/ at the beginning of the word, we will circle the letters* **spl***. If we do not hear the sound /spl/, we cross out the picture.*

Say: *What do you see in the picture?* **splits** *Do you hear the sound /spl/ at the beginning of the word* **splits***? Circle the letters* **spl***. If you do not hear the sound /spl/ at the beginning of the word, then cross out the picture.*

Practice
Use BLM 51, # 2
Sound-Spelling Correspondence
Show the letters.

Say: *The way we write the sound /str/ is with the letters* **str***. The letters* **str** *make the sound /str/. What is the name of the letters that combine?* str *What sound do the letters make? /str/*

Say: *We will look at each picture.* **Say** *its name. If we hear the sound /str/ at the beginning of the word, we will circle the letters* **str***. If we do not hear the sound /str/, we cross out the picture.*

Say: *What do you see in the picture?* **street** *Do you hear the sound /str/ at the beginning of the word* **street***? Circle the letters* **str***. If you do not hear the sound /str/ at the beginning of the word, then cross out the picture.*

Apply
Blend Words
Use BLM 51, # 3
Say: *Look at each letter and listen to the sound as I read. /s/ /t/ /r/ /a/ /n/. Your turn: /s/ /t/ /r/ /a/ /n/. Now we are going to blend the sounds together by stretching them out as we read them. Point to each letter in a sweeping motion left to right /s/ttt/rrr/aaa/nnn/. What is the word?* **strain***.*

Spelling
Use BLM 51, #4
Say: *Now we can practice writing the sounds we hear in each word. Call one word at a time, stretching each sound.*
Say: *Say the word slowly; write a letter for each sound you hear.*

Conclusion
Ask: What did we learn today? We learned that the letters **scr** make the sound /scr/. The letters spr make the sound /spr/. The letters **spl** make the sound /spl/. The letters **str** make the sound /str/. We wrote words using the combined letters **scr, spr, spl and str**. What pictures/words will help you remember these sounds and the letters at the beginning of a word?

Home Connection
Use BLM 51. Encourage students to practice identifying sounds **scr, spr, spl and str** and writing the letters **scr, spr, spl and str** with a family member. Encourage students to identify other words that combine letters **scr, spr, spl and str** with their family.

✔ Formative Assessment

If the student completes each task correctly, precede to the next skill in the sequence. If not, refer to suggested Intervention 2..

Did the student...?	Intervention 2
Identify the name of the letter?	• Use physical rhythmic movements as the letter name is repeated. March while chanting the letter name. Move arms up and down. Sway from side to side..
Identify the sound of the letter?	• Say words with the target sounds by repeating the words three times. Examples: **script script script, sprout sprout sprout, splits splits splits, street street street.**
Produce the sound of the letter?	Use mirrors to show movement of mouth, tongue, teeth as the sound is produced. Use hand over mouth to explore movement of air as the sound is produced.
Recognize the sounds of the consonant digraphs?	Use Elkonin boxes – student moves a token into the box as the sound of the consonant digraph is said in the word.
Write the letter?	Write the letters, have students trace them. Create the letters with clay. Discuss letter features (lines, shape). Trace over the letters with multiple colors..
Know name of pictures?	Tell students the name of pictures, have students repeat them aloud. Discuss word and use each word in context.

CCSS: RF.1.3
Know and apply grade-level phonics and word analysis skills in decoding words **both in isolation and in text.**
b. Decode regularly spelled one-syllable words.
g. Recognize and read grade-appropriate irregularly spelled words.

Lesson Objectives

- Identify and name the letters **g, c**
- Produce the soft sounds of the letters **g, c**
- Relate the sounds /j/ /s/ to the letters **g, c**
- Recognize soft sounds of **g, c** in words/pictures

METACOGNITIVE STRATEGY
- Selective auditory attention, imagery, auditory representation

ACADEMIC LANGUAGE
- letter name, letter sound, initial sound, final sound, ending sound, high frequency word

Materials
- Sound Spelling Cards **Gg, Cc**
- Blackline Master 52

Pre-Assess
Student's ability to recognize the sounds represented by the targeted letters of the alphabet and to identify the letters used to represent the corresponding sounds.

Identify and Name Soft G, C
RF.1.3b, RF.1.3g

Introduce

As students participate in this lesson, they identify the name and sound of the targeted letters, and identify the letters when the sounds and names are given orally. Students will apply their knowledge by recognizing the sounds of target letters using pictures. Students apply skill in context by reading decodable simple sentences that include high frequency words.

State Learning Goal

Today we will practice listening to the sounds **/j/ and /s/** that the letters **g, c** make.

Teach

Letters represent sounds. We remember the sounds each letter makes. We use letters to write words we say. We use letters to read and write words. Some letters combine to make new sounds.

Phonemic Awareness

Show the picture of sound/spelling cards **Gg** to review the sound. Say: Listen to this sound **/j/**. Say it with me: **/j/**. Say it on your own: **/j/**.

Sound-Spelling Correspondence

Show the letters
Say: *One way we write the sound /j/ is with the letter* **g**.
Say: *The letter* **g** *makes the sound /j/.*
Say: *What is the name of the letter?* **g** *What sound does the letter make? /j/*

Model

Use BLM 52, # 1A
Say: *We will look at each picture.* **Say** *its name. If we hear the sound /j/ at the beginning of the word, we will circle the picture. If we do not hear the sound /j/, we cross out the picture.*
Say: *What do you see in the picture?* **gem** *Do you hear the sound /j/ in the word* **genie**? *If you do not hear the sound /j/ in the word, then cross out the picture.*

Phonemic Awareness

Show the picture of sound/spelling cards **Cc** to review the sound. Say: Listen to this sound **/s/**. Say it with me: **/s/**. Say it on your own: **/s/**.

Sound-Spelling Correspondence

Show the letter.
Say: *One way we write the sound /s/ is with the letter c. The letter* **c** *makes the sound /s/. What is the name of the letter?* **c** *What sound does the letter make? /s/*

Use BLM 52, # 1B
Say: *We will look at each picture. Say its name. If we hear the sound /s/ in the word, we will circle the picture. If we do not hear the sound /s/, we cross out the picture. What do you see in the picture?* **center** *Do you hear the sound /s/ in the word* **center**? *If you do not hear the sound /s/ in the word, then cross out the picture.*

Practice

Use BLM 52, # 2A

Say: Look *at the picture.* **Say** *its name.* **Write** *the letters.*
Say: *What is the picture?* **giant***. Do you hear the sound* /j/ *in the word* **giant***?*

Use BLM 52, # 2B
Say: Look *at the picture.* **Say** *its name.* **Write** *the letters.*
Say: *What is the picture?* **ace***. Do you hear the sound* /s/ *in the word* **face***?*

Apply
Blend Words

Use BLM 52, # 3
Say: *Look at each letter and listen to the sound as I read.* /**h**/ /**i**/ /**n**/ /**g**/ *. Your turn:* /**h**/ /**i**/ /**n**/ /**g**/.
Say: *Now we are going to blend the sounds together by stretching them out as we read them. Point to each letter in a sweeping motion left to right* /**hhhh/iiii/nnnn/ gggg**/*. What is the word?* **hinge***.*

Spelling

Use BLM 52, # 4
Say: *Now we can practice writing the sounds we hear in each word. Call one word at a time, stretching each sound.*
Say: *Say the word slowly; write a letter for each sound you hear.*

Conclusion

Ask: *What did we learn today?* We learned that the letter **g** can make the sound /**j**/ and the letter **c** can make the sound /**s**/. What pictures/words will help you remember the sounds /**j**/ and /**s** / and the letters **g** and **c** in words?

Home Connection
Use BLM 52. Encourage students to practice identifying sounds /**j**/ and /**s**/ and writing the letters **g** and **c** with a family member. Encourage students to identify other words that have the letters **g** and **c** with their family.

✔ Formative Assessment

If the student completes each task correctly, precede to the next skill in the sequence. If not, refer to suggested Intervention 2.

Did the student...?	Intervention 2
Identify the name of the letter?	• Use physical rhythmic movements as the letter name is repeated. March while chanting the letter name. Move arms up and down. Sway from side to side..
Identify the sound of the letter?	• Say words with the target sounds by repeating the words three times. Examples: **genie genie genie, dice dice dice**
Produce the sound of the letter?	Use mirrors to show movement of mouth, tongue, teeth as the sound is produced. Use hand over mouth to explore movement of air as the sound is produced.
Recognize the sounds of the consonant digraphs	Use Elkonin boxes – student moves a token into the box as the sound of the consonant digraph is said in the word.
Write the letter?	Write the letters, have students trace them. Create the letters with clay. Discuss letter features (lines, shape). Trace over the letters with multiple colors.
Know name of pictures?	Tell students the name of pictures, have students repeat them aloud. Discuss word and use each word in context.

Recognize Long Vowel Sound (CVCe) Pattern with Long a
RF.1.3b, RF.1.3c

CCSS: RF.1.3
Know and apply grade-level phonics and word analysis skills in decoding words both in isolation and in text.
b. Decode regularly spelled one-syllable words.
c. Know final –e and common vowel team conventions for representing long vowel sounds.

Lesson Objectives

- Identify and name the letter **a**
- Produce the sound of letter **a**
- Relate the sound /a/ to the letter **a**
- Recognize long vowel sound **a** in words/pictures
- Recognize long vowel sound (CVCe) pattern with long **a**

METACOGNITIVE STRATEGY
- Selective auditory attention, imagery, auditory representation

ACADEMIC LANGUAGE
- letter name, letter sound, vowel, long vowel sound, silent e, pattern

Materials
- Sound Spelling Card **a**
- Blackline master 53

Pre-Assess
Student's ability to recognize the **short vowel sound** represented by the target letter of the alphabet and to identify the letter used to represent the corresponding sound. Ability to **pronounce the long vowel** sound.

Introduce
As students participate in this lesson, they identify the name and sound of sound of the target letter, and identify the letter when the sound and name is given orally. Students will apply their knowledge by recognizing the initial sound of target letter using pictures. Students apply skill in context by reading decodable simple sentences that include high frequency words.

State Learning Goal
Today we will learn to read words with the long sound of vowel **a**. We are going to learn that when we put the **vowel e** at the **end** of some words, the **first vowel** in the word **make its long sound** and the **vowel e** remains silent.

Teach

Letters represent sounds. We remember the sounds each letter makes. We use letters to write words we say. We use letters to read and write words. The letter a is a vowel. It has a long sound /a/ and **a** short sound /a/. We are going to learn words that have the long sound of vowel **a**.

Phonemic Awareness
Show picture of sound/spelling card to **review long sound of a**.
Say: *Listen to this sound /aaa/.* **Say** *it with me:* **aaa**. *Say it on your own:* **aaa**.
Say:: *This is the long sound of vowel* **a**. *It sounds like it is saying its name:* /**aaa**/, *say it again* /**aaa**/.

Sound-Spelling Correspondence
Write the word **same** on the board. Point out the vowel **a** at the beginning of the word and the vowel **e** at the end.
Say: *Say when you see vowel* **e** *at the end of a 4 letter word, the* **e** *is silent and the first vowel makes its long sound.*
Say: *Look at the word* **cane**. *Point: Does it have a vowel* **e** *at the end? Point: Then vowel* **aaa** *says its name.*
Say: *Read it with me* **same**. *Repeat with words* **stale, tale**, *and* **gave**.

Model

Use BLM 53, #1.
Say: *Look at each picture.* **Say** *its name. Listen for the long sound of /a/. Does it have vowel e at the end? Do you hear the long sound of /a/? Put a line long line over vowel* **a**, *cross out vowel* **e**. *It is silent.*

Practice

Use BLM 53, #2.

Say: *Look at the picture. Say its name. Listen for the long sound of /a/. Does it have vowel e at the end? Do you hear the long sound /a/? Put a line long line over vowel **a** and cross out vowel **e**. It is silent.*

Apply

Blend Words

Use BLM 53, # 3.

Say: *Look at each letter and listen to the long sound of vowel a as I read /s/k/ a/l/. Your turn: /s/k/a/l/. Now we are going to blend the sounds together by stretching them out as we read them. Point to each letter in a sweeping motion left to right /s/kkk/aaa/lll/. What is the word?* **scale**.

Spelling

Use BLM 53, #4.

Say: *Now we can practice writing the sounds we hear in each word. Call one word at a time, stretching each sound.*

Say: *Say the word slowly; write a letter for each sound you hear.*

Conclusion

Ask: *What did we learn today?* We learned that the vowel a makes the long sound /**aaa**/, when vowel **e** is at the end. What pictures/words will help you remember the long sound /a/ with the silent e at the end?

Home Connection

Use BLM #53. Encourage students to practice identifying long vowel sound a in CVCe words with a family member.

.

✔ Formative Assessment

If the student completes each task correctly, precede to the next skill in the sequence. If not, refer to suggested Intervention 2. .

Did the student…?	Intervention 2
Identify the name of the letter?	• Use physical rhythmic movements as the letter name is repeated. March while chanting the letter name. Move arms up and down. Sway from side to side..
Identify the sound of the letter?	• Use chants that repeat the sound several times then a word that includes the sound. Example: /a/ /a/ /a/ **cage**
Produce the sound of the letter?	Use mirrors to show movement of mouth, tongue, teeth as the sound is produced. Use hand over mouth to explore movement of air as the sound is produced.
Recognize the CVCe pattern?	Arrange a list of common same vowel CVCe words vertically, point out pattern.
Know name of pictures?	Tell students the name of pictures, have student repeat it aloud. Discuss meaning of word. Use word in context.

Recognize Long Vowel Sound (CVCe) Pattern with Long o RF 1.3b, RF.1.3c

Introduce

As students participate in this lesson, they identify the name and sound of sound of the target letter, and identify the letter when the sound and name is given orally. Students will apply their knowledge by recognizing the initial sound of target letter using pictures. Students apply skill in context by reading decodable simple sentences that include high frequency words.

State Learning Goal

Today we will learn to read words with the long sound of vowel **o**. We are going to learn that when we put the **vowel e** at the **end** of some words, the **first vowel** in the word **make its long sound** and the **vowel e** remains silent.

Teach

Letters represent sounds. We remember the sounds each letter makes. We use letters to write words we say. We use letters to read and write words. The letter **o** is a vowel. It has a long sound /**o**/ and a short sound /**o**/. We are going to learn words that have the long sound of vowel **o**.

Phonemic Awareness

Show picture of sound/spelling card to review long sound of **o**.
Say: *Listen to this sound /***ooo***/. Say it with me: ***ooo***. Say it on your own: ***ooo***.*
Say: *This is the long sound of vowel ***o***. It sounds like it is saying its name: /***ooo***/, say it again /***ooo***/.*

Sound-Spelling Correspondence

Write the word **role** on the board. Point out the vowel **o** at the beginning of the word and the vowel **e** at the end
Say: Say *when you see vowel ***e*** at the end of a 4 letter word, the ***e*** is silent and the first vowel makes its long sound.*
Say: *Look at the word ***role***. Point: Does it have a vowel e at the end? Point: Then vowel ***ooo*** says its name.*
Say: *Read it with me ***joke***. Repeat with words ***tone, smoke***.*

Model

Use BLM 54, #1..
Say: *Look at each picture. ***Say*** its name. Listen for the long sound of /***o***/. Does it have vowel e at the end?*
Say: *Do you hear the long sound of /***o***/? Put a line long line over vowel ***o***, cross out vowel ***e***. It is silent.*

CCSS: RF.1.3
Know and apply grade-level phonics and word analysis skills in decoding words both in isolation and in text.
b. Decode regularly spelled one-syllable words.
c. Know final –e and common vowel team conventions for representing long vowel sounds.

Lesson Objectives

- Identify and name the letter **o**
- Produce the sound of letter **o**
- Relate the sound /o/ to the letter **o**
- Recognize long vowel sound **o** in words/pictures
- Recognize long vowel sound (CVCe) pattern with long o

METACOGNITIVE STRATEGY
- Selective auditory attention, imagery, auditory representation

ACADEMIC LANGUAGE
- letter name, letter sound, vowel, long vowel sound, silent e, pattern

Materials
- Sound Spelling Card **Oo**
- Blackline master 54

Pre-Assess
Student's ability to recognize the **short vowel sound** represented by the target letter of the alphabet and to identify the letter used to represent the corresponding sound. Ability to **pronounce the long vowel** sound.

Practice

Use BLM 54, #2.

Say: *Look at the picture. Say its name. Listen for the long sound of /**o**/. Does it have vowel e at the end?*

Say: *Do you hear the long sound /**o**/? Put a line long line over vowel **o** and cross out vowel **e**. It is silent.*

Apply

Blend Words

Use BLM 54, #3..

Say: *Look at each letter and listen to the long sound of vowel **o** as I read /**b**//**o**//**n**/. Your turn: /**b**//**o**//**n**/.*

Say: *Now we are going to blend the sounds together by stretching them out as we read them.*

*Point to each letter in a sweeping motion left to right /**bbb**/**ooo**/**nnn**/. What is the word?* **rode**.

Spelling

Use BLM 54, #4.

Say: *Now we can practice writing the sounds we hear in each word. Call one word at a time, stretching each sound.*

Say: *Say the word slowly; write a letter for each sound you hear.*

Conclusion

Ask: *What did we learn today?* We learned that the vowel **o** makes the long sound /**ooo**/, when vowel **e** is at the end. What pictures/words will help you remember the long sound /**o**/ with the silent e at the end?

Home Connection

Use BLM 54. Encourage students to practice identifying long vowel sound o in CVCe words with a family member.

✔ Formative Assessment

If the student completes each task correctly, precede to the next skill in the sequence. If not, refer to suggested Intervention 2.

Did the student…?	Intervention 2
Identify the name of the letter?	• Use physical rhythmic movements as the letter name is repeated. March while chanting the letter name. Move arms up and down. Sway from side to side..
Identify the sound of the letter?	• Use chants that repeat the sound several times then a word that includes the sound. Example: /o/ /o/ /o/ **hose**
Produce the sound of the letter?	Use mirrors to show movement of mouth, tongue, teeth as the sound is produced. Use hand over mouth to explore movement of air as the sound is produced.
Recognize the CVCe pattern?	Arrange a list of common same vowel CVCe words vertically, point out pattern.
Know name of pictures?	Tell students the name of pictures, have student repeat it aloud. Discuss meaning of word. Use word in context.

Recognize Long Vowel Sound (CVCe) Pattern with Long i..RF 1.3b, RF.1.3c

Introduce

As students participate in this lesson, they identify the name and sound of sound of the target letter, and identify the letter when the sound and name is given orally. Students will apply their knowledge by recognizing the initial sound of target letter using pictures. Students apply skill in context by reading decodable simple sentences that include high frequency words.

State Learning Goal

Today we will learn to read words with the long sound of vowel **i**. We are going to learn that when we put the **vowel e** at the end of some words, the **first vowel** in the word **make its long sound** and the **vowel e** remains silent.

Teach

Letters represent sounds. We remember the sounds each letter makes. We use letters to write words we say. We use letters to read and write words. The letter **i** is a vowel. It has a long sound /i/ and a short sound /i/. We are going to learn words that have the long sound of vowel **i**.

Phonemic Awareness

Show picture of sound/spelling card to review long sound of **i**.
Say: *Listen to this sound /iii/.* **Say** *it with me:* **iii**. **Say** *it on your own:* **iii**.
Say: *This is the long sound of vowel **i**. It sounds like it is saying its name: /iii/, say it again /iii/.*

Sound-Spelling Correspondence

Write the word **tile** on the board. Point out the vowel i at the beginning of the word and the vowel e at the end.
Say: *Say when you see vowel e at the end of a 4 letter word, the e is silent and the first vowel makes its long sound.*
Say: *Look at the word **tile**. Point: Does it have a vowel e at the end? Point: Then vowel **iii** says its name.*
Say: *Read it with me tile. Repeat with words* **slime, smile, dine**

Model

Use BLM 55, #1.
Say: *Look at each picture. Say its name. Listen for the long sound of /i/. Does it have vowel **e** at the end? Say: Do you hear the long sound of /i/? Put a long line over vowel i, cross out vowel e. It is silent..*

CCSS: RF.1.3
Know and apply grade-level phonics and word analysis skills in decoding words both in isolation and in text.
b. Decode regularly spelled one-syllable words.
c. Know final –e and common vowel team conventions for representing long vowel sounds.

Lesson Objectives

- Identify and name the letter **i**
- Produce the sound of letter **i**
- Relate the sound /i/ to the letter **i**
- Recognize long vowel sound **i** in words/pictures
- Recognize long vowel sound (CVCe) pattern with long **i**

METACOGNITIVE STRATEGY
- Selective auditory attention, imagery, auditory representation

ACADEMIC LANGUAGE
- letter name, letter sound, vowel, long vowel sound, silent e, pattern

Materials
- Sound Spelling Card **Ii**
- Blackline Master 55

Pre-Assess
Student's ability to recognize the **short vowel sound** represented by the target letter of the alphabet and to identify the letter used to represent the corresponding sound. Ability to **pronounce the long vowel** sound..

Practice

Use BLM 55, #2.

Say: *Look at the picture. Say its name. Listen for the long sound of /ī/. Does it have vowel e at the end?*

Say: *Do you hear the long sound /ī/? Put a line long line over vowel **i** and cross out vowel **e**. It is silent.*

Apply

Blend Words

Use BLM 55, #3.

Say: *Look at each letter and listen to the long sound of vowel **i** as I read /s/l/i/d/. Your turn: /s/l/i/d/.*

Say: *Now we are going to blend the sounds together by stretching them out as we read them.* Point to each letter in a sweeping motion left to right: /**sss/lll/iii/ ddd**/. *What is the word?* **slide**.

Spelling

Use BLM 55, #4.

Say: *Now we can practice writing the sounds we hear in each word. Call one word at a time, stretching each sound.*

Say: *Say the word slowly; write a letter for each sound you hear.*

Conclusion

Ask: *What did we learn today?* We learned that the vowel **i** makes the long sound /iii/, when vowel **e** is at the end. What pictures/words will help you remember the long sound /i/ with the silent **e** at the end?

Home Connection

Use BLM #55. Encourage students to practice identifying long vowel sound **i** in CVCe words with a family member.

✔ Formative Assessment

If the student completes each task correctly, precede to the next skill in the sequence. If not, refer to suggested Intervention 2. .

Did the student...?	Intervention 2
Identify the name of the letter?	• Use physical rhythmic movements as the letter name is repeated. March while chanting the letter name. Move arms up and down. Sway from side to side..
Identify the sound of the letter?	• Use chants that repeat the sound several times then a word that includes the sound. Example: /i/ /i/ /i/ bike
Produce the sound of the letter?	Use mirrors to show movement of mouth, tongue, teeth as the sound is produced. Use hand over mouth to explore movement of air as the sound is produced.
Recognize the CVCe pattern?	Arrange a list of common same vowel CVCe words vertically, point out pattern.
Know name of pictures?	Tell students the name of pictures, have student repeat it aloud. Discuss meaning of word. Use word in context.

Recognize Long Vowel Sound (CVCe) Pattern with Long u RF 1.3b, RF.1.3c

CCSS: RF.1.3
Know and apply grade-level phonics and word analysis skills in decoding words both in isolation and in text.
b. Decode regularly spelled one-syllable words.
c. Know final –e and common vowel team conventions for representing long vowel sounds.

Lesson Objectives

- Identify and name the letter **u**
- Produce the sound of letter **u**
- Relate the sound /**u**/ to the letter **u**
- Recognize long vowel sound **u** in words/pictures
- Recognize long vowel sound (CVCe) pattern with long **u**

METACOGNITIVE STRATEGY
- Selective auditory attention, imagery, auditory representation

ACADEMIC LANGUAGE
- letter name, letter sound, vowel, long vowel sound, silent e, pattern

Materials
- Sound Spelling Card **Uu**
- Blackline master 56

Pre-Assess
Student's ability to recognize the **short vowel sound** represented by the target letter of the alphabet and to identify the letter used to represent the corresponding sound. Ability to **pronounce the long vowel** sound.

Introduce
As students participate in this lesson, they identify the name and sound of sound of the target letter, and identify the letter when the sound and name is given orally. Students will apply their knowledge by recognizing the initial sound of target letter using pictures. Students apply skill in context by reading decodable simple sentences that include high frequency words.

State Learning Goal
Today we will learn to read words with the long sound of vowel **u**. We are going to learn that when we put the **vowel e** at the end of some words, the **first vowel** in the word
make its long sound and the **vowel e** remains silent.

Teach
Letters represent sounds. We remember the sounds each letter makes. We use letters to write words we say. We use letters to read and write words. The letter **u** is a vowel. It has a long sound /**u**/ and a short sound /**u**/. We are going to learn words that have the long sound of vowel **u**.

Phonemic Awareness
Show picture of sound/spelling card to review long sound of **i**.
Say: *Listen to this sound /iii/.* **Say** *it with me:* **iii**. **Say** *it on your own:* **iii**.
Say: *This is the long sound of vowel* **i**. *It sounds like it is saying its name: /iii/, say it again /iii/.*

Sound-Spelling Correspondence
Write the word **mule** on the board. Point out the vowel **u** at the beginning of the word and the vowel **e** at the end.
Say: *Say when you see vowel* **e** *at the end of a 4 letter word, the* **e** *is silent and the first vowel makes its long sound.*
Say: *Look at the word* **mule**. *Point: Does it have a vowel e at the end? Point: Then vowel* **uuu** *says its name.*
Say: *Read it with me* **mule**. *Repeat with words* **flute, glue**.

Model
Use BLM 17, #1.
Say: *Look at each picture. Say its name. Listen for the long sound of /*u*/. Does it have vowel* **e** *at the end?*
Say: *Do you hear the long sound of /*u*/? Put a line long line over vowel* **u**, *cross out vowel* **e**. *It is silent..*

Practice

Use BLM 56, #2.

Say: *Look at the picture. Say its name. Listen for the long sound of /u/. Does it have vowel **e** at the end?*

Say: *Do you hear the long sound /u/? Put a line long line over vowel **u** and cross out vowel **e**. It is silent.*

Apply

Blend Words

Use BLM 56, #3.

Say: *Look at each letter and listen to the long sound of vowel u as I read **e**.*

Say: */f/l/u/t/ Your turn: /f/l/u/t/.*

Say: *Now we are going to blend the sounds together by stretching them out as we read them.* Point to each letter in a sweeping motion left to right: */f/llll/uuu/ttt/. What is the word?* **flute**.

Spelling

Use BLM 56, #4.

Say: *Now we can practice writing the sounds we hear in each word. Call one word at a time, stretching each sound.*

Say: *Say the word slowly; write a letter for each sound you hear.*

Conclusion

Ask: *What did we learn today?* We learned that the vowel **u** makes the long sound /uuu/, when vowel **e** is at the end. What pictures/words will help you remember the long sound /u/ with the silent **e** at the end?

Home Connection

Use BLM #56. Encourage students to practice identifying long vowel sound u in CVCe words with a family member.

✔ Formative Assessment

If the student completes each task correctly, precede to the next skill in the sequence. If not, refer to suggested Intervention 2.

Did the student…?	Intervention 2
Identify the name of the letter?	• Use physical rhythmic movements as the letter name is repeated. March while chanting the letter name. Move arms up and down. Sway from side to side.
Identify the sound of the letter?	• Use chants that repeat the sound several times then a word that includes the sound. Example: **/u/ /u/ /u/ cube**
Produce the sound of the letter?	Use mirrors to show movement of mouth, tongue, teeth as the sound is produced. Use hand over mouth to explore movement of air as the sound is produced.
Recognize the CVCe pattern?	Arrange a list of common same vowel CVCe words vertically, point out pattern..
Know name of pictures?	Tell students the name of pictures, have student repeat it aloud. Discuss meaning of word. Use word in context.

Recognize Long Vowel Sound (CVCe) Pattern with Long e

RF.1.3b, RF.1.3c, RF.1.3g

CCSS: RF.1.3
Know and apply grade-level phonics and word analysis skills in decoding words both in isolation and in text.
b. Decode regularly spelled one-syllable words.
c. Know final –e and common vowel team conventions for representing long vowel sounds.
g. Recognize and read grade-appropriate irregularly spelled words.

Lesson Objectives

- Identify and name words with the long vowel VCe pattern
- Produce the sound of words with the long vowel VCe pattern
- Relate the long vowel sounds to their letters
- Recognize long vowel sounds in words/pictures with the VCe pattern
- Recognize long vowel sound (VCe) pattern in VCe words

METACOGNITIVE STRATEGY
- Selective auditory attention, imagery, auditory representation

ACADEMIC LANGUAGE
- letter name, letter sound, vowel, long vowel sound, silent e, pattern

Materials
- Sound Spelling Cards **e, a, i, o, u**
- Blackline master 57

Pre-Assess
Student's ability to recognize the **short vowel sound** represented by the target letter of the alphabet and to identify the letter used to represent the corresponding sound. Ability to **pronounce the long vowel** sound.

Introduce

As students participate in this lesson, they identify the name and sound of sound of the target letter, and identify the letter when the sound and name is given orally. Students will apply their knowledge by recognizing the initial sound of target letter using pictures. Students apply skill in context by reading decodable simple sentences that include high frequency words.

State Learning Goal

Today we will learn to read words with long vowel sounds. We are going to learn that when we put the **vowel e** at the **end** of some words, the **first vowel** in the word **make its long sound** and the **vowel e** remains silent.

Teach

Letters represent sounds. We remember the sounds each letter makes. We use letters to write words we say. We use letters to read and write words. The letter **e** is a vowel. It has a long sound /**e**/ and a short sound /**e**/. We are going to learn words that have the long sound of vowel **e**. Repeat with letters **a, i, o, and u**.

Phonemic Awareness

Show picture of sound/spelling card to review long sound of **e**.

Say: *Listen to this sound /**eee**/. Say it with me: eee. Say it on your own: **eee**.*

Say: *This is the long sound of vowel **e**. It sounds like it is saying its name: /**eee**/, say it again /**eee**/. Repeat with the letters **a, i, o, and u**.*

Sound-Spelling Correspondence

Write the word **mole** on the board. Point out the vowel **o** at the beginning of the word and the vowel **e** at the end..

Say: *Say when you see vowel e at the end of a 4 letter word, the e is silent and the first vowel makes its long sound.*

Say: *Look at the word **mole**. Point: Does it have a vowel **e** at the end? Point: Then vowel **eee** says its name.*

Say: *Read it with me **mole**. Repeat with words **base** and **dime**.*

Model

Use BLM 57, #1.

Explain that some two-syllable words have one syllable with the vowel-consonant-e pattern. For example, **escape** has two syllables. Remind students that each syllable has a vowel sound. We divide the word between the two consonants: **es cape**. The first syllable is closed and has a short vowel sound. A syllable with the vowel-consonant-e usually has a long vowel sound. The syllable **c-a-p-e** has the vowel-consonant-e pattern, and so the vowel sound is long **a: cape**.

Practice

Use BLM 57, #2.

Display the words. Have students divide each word into syllables, tell the vowel sound in each syllable, and then blend the syllables to read the word: **concrete, reptile, escape.**

Apply

Blend Words

Use BLM 57, #3.

Say: *Look at each letter and listen to the long sound of vowel e as I read /a/th/l/e/t/. Your turn: /a/th/l/e/t/.*

Say: *Now we are going to blend the sounds together by stretching them out as we read them.*

Point to each letter in a sweeping motion left to right /aaa/th/lll/eee/ttt/. What is the word? **athlete**. *Repeat with words* **cascade, extreme,** *and* **ignore**.

Spelling

Use BLM 57, #4.

Say: *Now we can practice writing the sounds we hear in each word. Call one word at a time, stretching each sound.*

Say: *Say the word slowly; write a letter for each sound you hear.*

Conclusion

Ask: *What did we learn today?* We learned that words with the vowel-consonant-silent e pattern makes long vowel sounds when vowel **e** is at the end. What pictures/words will help you remember long vowel sounds with the silent **e** at the end?

Home Connection

Use BLM #57. Encourage students to practice identifying long vowel sounds in VCe words with a family member.

✔ Formative Assessment

If the student completes each task correctly, precede to the next skill in the sequence. If not, refer to suggested Intervention 2.

Did the student...?	Intervention 2
Identify the name of the letter?	• Use physical rhythmic movements as the letter name is repeated. March while chanting the letter name. Move arms up and down. Sway from side to side..
Identify the sound of the letter?	• Use exaggeration when forming the long vowel sounds with your mouth.
Produce the sound of the letter?	Use mirrors to show movement of mouth, tongue, teeth as the sound is produced. Use hand over mouth to explore movement of air as the sound is produced.
Recognize the VCe pattern?	Arrange a list of common same vowel VCe words vertically, point out pattern..
Know name of pictures?	Tell students the name of pictures, have student repeat it aloud. Discuss meaning of word. Use word in context.

Recognize Long Vowel Teams and Single Letters with the sound /ā/ RF.1.3b, RF.1.3c, RF.1.3g

CCSS: RF.1.3
Know and apply grade-level phonics and word analysis skills in decoding words both in isolation and in text.
b. Decode regularly spelled one-syllable words.
c. Know final -e and common vowel team conventions for representing long vowel sounds.
g. Recognize and read grade-appropriate irregularly spelled words.

Lesson Objectives

- Produce the sound /ā/
- Relate the sound /ā/ to the single letter a
- Relate the sound /ā/ to vowel teams **a, ai, ay**
- Recognize long vowel sound /ā/ in words and pictures
- Write vowel teams that make the sound /ā/

METACOGNITIVE STRATEGY
- Selective auditory attention, imagery, auditory representation

ACADEMIC LANGUAGE
- vowel, long vowel sound, vowel team

Materials
- Sound Spelling Cards for **a, ai, ay**
- Blackline master 58

Pre-Assess
Student's ability to recognize the **long vowel sound** represented by the corresponding letters and vowel teams. Ability to pronounce the **long vowel sound.**

Introduce

As students participate in this lesson, they identify the name and sound of sound of the target letter, and identify the letter when the sound and name is given orally. Students will apply their knowledge by recognizing the initial sound of target letter using pictures. Students apply skill in context by reading decodable simple sentences that include high frequency words.

State Learning Goal

Today we will learn to read words with the long sound of vowel /ā/. We are going to learn that the sound /ā/ can be formed by two vowels together, called vowel teams.

Teach

Letters represent sounds. We remember the sounds each letter makes. We use letters to write words we say. We use letters to read and write words. The sound /ā/ is formed by the letter a and teams of vowels such as **a, ai**, and **ay**. We are going to learn words that have the long sound of vowel /ā/.

Phonemic Awareness

Pair sound/spelling cards to review the long sound of /ā/ using **a, ai**, and **ay**
Say: *Listen to this sound /ā/. Say it with me: /ā/. Say it on your own: /ā/.*

Sound-Spelling Correspondence

Write and display the letter a and the vowel teams **a, ai,** and ay.
Say: *There are different ways to form this sound. Sometimes /ā/ is formed by the letter a on its own. Say the sound with me: /ā/.*
Say: *Sometimes /ā/ is formed by the combination of the letter a and the letter i.* **Say** *the sound with me: /ā/.*
Say: *Sometimes /ā/ is formed by the combination of the letter a and the letter y.* **Say** *the sound with me: /ā/.*

Model

Use BLM 58, #1.
Say: *We will look at each picture. We will say its name. Listen for the long sound /ā/. If we hear the long sound of /ā/, we will circle the picture. If we do not hear the long sound /ā/, we will cross out the picture.*
Say: *What do you see in the picture?* **chain***. Do you hear the long sound /ā/ in the word* **chain***? Circle the picture. If you do not hear the sound /ā/, then cross out the picture.*

Practice

Say: *Look at the second picture. Say its name. Listen for the long sound /ā/.*

Say: *What do you see in the picture?* **braid** *Do you hear the long sound /ā/ in the word* **braid***?*

Say: *What letter or letters make the long sound /ā/? Write the letter or letters that make the long sound /ā/ on the line under each picture.*

Apply

Blend Words

Use BLM 58, #3.

Say: *Look at each letter and listen to the long sound /ā/ as I read.* **/t//r//ā/ /n/.** *Your turn:* **/t/r/ā/n/.**

Say: *Now we are going to blend the sounds together by stretching them out as we read them.* Point to each letter in a sweeping motion left to right: **/ttt/rrr/ ā ā ā/nnn/.** *What is the word?* **train***.*

Spelling

Use BLM 58, #4.

Say: *Now we can practice writing the sounds we hear in each word. Call one word at a time, stretching each sound.*

Say: *Say the word slowly; write a letter for each sound you hear.*

Conclusion

Ask: *What did we learn today?* We learned that the sound /ā/ can be formed by the vowel **a**, or the vowel team **ai**, or the vowel team **ay**. What pictures/words will help you remember the long sound /ā/ and the letters that make that sound?

Home Connection

Use BLM 58. Ask students to practice identifying vowel sound /ā/ and writing the letters **a, ai**, and **ay** with a family member. Have students identify other words that include the sound /ā/ with their family.

✔ Formative Assessment

If the student completes each task correctly, precede to the next skill in the sequence. If not, refer to suggested Intervention 2.

Did the student…?	Intervention 2
Identify the name of the letter?	• Use physical rhythmic movements as the letter name is repeated. March while chanting the letter name. Move arms up and down. Sway from side to side..
Identify the sounds of the vowel teams?	• Use rhyming chants that repeat the sound several times and then use words that contain the sound. Example: /ā/ /ā/ **rain train**
Produce the vowel sounds?	Use mirrors to show movement of mouth, tongue, teeth as the sound is produced. Use hand over mouth to explore movement of air as the sound is produced.
Recognize the vowel teams??	Arrange a list of vowel teams that make the /ā/ sound.
Know name of pictures?	Tell students the name of pictures, have student repeat it aloud. Discuss meaning of word. Use word in context.

Recognize Long Vowel Teams and Single Letters with the Sound /ō/ RF.1.3b, RF.1.3c, RF.1.3g

CCSS: RF.1.3
Know and apply grade-level phonics and word analysis skills in decoding words both in isolation and in text.
b. Decode regularly spelled one-syllable words.
c. Know final -e and common vowel team conventions for representing long vowel sounds.
g. Recognize and read grade-appropriate irregularly spelled words.

Lesson Objectives

- Produce the sound /ō/
- Relate the sound /ō/ to the single letter o
- Relate the sound /ō/ to vowel teams **oa, ow, oe**
- Recognize long vowel sound /ō/ in words and pictures
- Write vowel teams that make the sound /ō/

METACOGNITIVE STRATEGY
- Selective auditory attention, imagery, auditory representation

ACADEMIC LANGUAGE
- vowel, long vowel sound, vowel team

Materials
- Sound Spelling Cards for **o, oa, ow, oe**
- Blackline master 59

Pre-Assess
Student's ability to recognize the **long vowel sound** represented by the corresponding letters and vowel teams. Ability to pronounce the **long vowel sound**.

.

Introduce
As students participate in this lesson, they identify the name and sound of sound of the target letter, and identify the letter when the sound and name is given orally. Students will apply their knowledge by recognizing the initial sound of target letter using pictures. Students apply skill in context by reading decodable simple sentences that include high frequency words.

State Learning Goal
Today we will learn to read words with the long sound of vowel /ō/. We are going to learn that the sound /ō/ can be formed by two vowels together, called vowel teams

Teach
Letters represent sounds. We remember the sounds each letter makes. We use letters to write words we say. We use letters to read and write words. The sound /ō/is formed by the letter **e** and teams of vowels such as **oa, ow**, and **oe**. We are going to learn words that have the long sound of vowel /ō/.

Phonemic Awareness
Pair sound/spelling cards to review the long sound of /ō/ using **o, oa, ow, oe**.
Say: *Listen to this sound /ō/. Say it with me: /ō/. Say it on your own: /ō/.*

Sound-Spelling Correspondence
Write and display the letter a and the vowel teams **a, ai**, and **ay**.
Say: *There are different ways to form this sound. Sometimes /ō/ is formed by the letter o on its own. Say the sound with me: /ō/.*
Say: *Sometimes /ō/ is formed by the combination of the letter o and the letter a. Say the sound with me: /ō/.*
Say: *Sometimes /ō/ is formed by the combination of the letter o and the letter w. Say the sound with me: /ō/.*
Say: *Sometimes /ō/ is formed by the combination of the letter o and the letter w. Say the sound with me: /ō/.*

Model

Use BLM 59, #1.
Say: *We will look at each picture. We will say its name. Listen for the long sound /ō/. If we hear the long sound /ō/, we will circle the picture. If we do not hear the long sound /ō/, we will cross out the picture.*

Say: *What do you see in the picture?* **float** *Do you hear the long sound /ō/ in the word* **float***? Circle the picture. If you do not hear the sound /ō/, then cross out the picture.*

Practice

Use BLM 59, #2.

Say: Look at the picture. **Say** its name. Listen for the long sound /ō/.

Say: What do you see in the picture? **grown** Do you hear the long sound /ō/ in the word **grown**?

Say: What letter or letters make the long sound /ō/? Write the letter or letters that make the long sound /ō/ on the line under each picture.

Apply

Blend Words

Use BLM 59, #3.

Say: Look at each letter and listen to the long sound /o/ as I read. /c//l//ō//k/ Your turn: blend the sounds together by stretching them out as we read them. Point to each letter in a sweeping motion left to right: /c/lllll/ōōō/kkk/. What is the word? cloak.

Spelling

Use BLM 59, #4.

Say: Now we can practice writing the sounds we hear in each word. Call one word at a time, stretching each sound.

Say: Say the word slowly; write a letter for each sound you hear.

Conclusion

Ask: What did we learn today? We learned that the sound /ō/ can be formed by the vowel **o**, or the vowel team oa, or the vowel team **ow**, or the vowel team **oe**. What pictures/words will help you remember the long sound /ō/ and the letters that make that sound?

Home Connection

Use BLM 59. Ask students to practice identifying vowel sound /ō/ and writing the letters **o, oa, ow**, and **oe**, with a family member. Have students identify other words that include the sound /ō/ with their family..

✔ **Formative Assessment**

If the student completes each task correctly, precede to the next skill in the sequence. If not, refer to suggested Intervention 2.

Did the student…?	Intervention 2
Identify the name of the letter?	• Use physical rhythmic movements as the letter name is repeated. March while chanting the letter name. Move arms up and down. Sway from side to side..
Identify the sounds of the vowel teams?	• Use rhyming chants that repeat the sound several times and then use words that contain the sound. Example: /o/ /ō/ **boat float**.
Produce the vowel sounds?	Use mirrors to show movement of mouth, tongue, teeth as the sound is produced. Use hand over mouth to explore movement of air as the sound is produced.
Recognize the vowel teams??	Arrange a list of vowel teams that make the /ō/ sound.
Know name of pictures?	Tell students the name of pictures, have student repeat it aloud. Discuss meaning of word. Use word in context.

Recognize Long Vowel Teams and Single Letters with the sound /ē/ RF.1.3b, RF.1.3c, RF.1.3g

CCSS: RF.1.3
Know and apply grade-level phonics and word analysis skills in decoding words both in isolation and in text.
b. Decode regularly spelled one-syllable words.
c. Know final -e and common vowel team conventions for representing long vowel sounds.
g. Recognize and read grade-appropriate irregularly spelled words.

Lesson Objectives

- Produce the sound /ē/
- Relate the sound /ē/ to the single letter e
- Relate the sound /ē/ to vowel teams **e, ee, ea, ie**
- Recognize long vowel sound /ē/ in words and pictures
- Write vowel teams that make the sound /ē/

METACOGNITIVE STRATEGY
- Selective auditory attention, imagery, auditory representation

ACADEMIC LANGUAGE
- vowel, long vowel sound, vowel team

Materials
- Sound Spelling Cards for **e, ee, ea, ie**
- Blackline master 60

Pre-Assess
Student's ability to recognize the **long vowel sound** represented by the corresponding letters and vowel teams. Ability to pronounce the **long vowel sound**.

Introduce
As students participate in this lesson, they identify the name and sound of sound of the target letter, and identify the letter when the sound and name is given orally. Students will apply their knowledge by recognizing the initial sound of target letter using pictures. Students apply skill in context by reading decodable simple sentences that include high frequency words.

State Learning Goal
Today we will learn to read words with the long sound of vowel /ē/. We are going to learn that the sound /ē/ can be formed by two vowels together, called vowel teams.

Teach
Letters represent sounds. We remember the sounds each letter makes. We use letters to write words we say. We use letters to read and write words. The sound /ē/ is formed by the letter e and teams of vowels such as **ee, ea,** and **ie**. We are going to learn words that have the long sound of vowel /ē/.

Phonemic Awareness
Pair sound/spelling cards to review the long sound of /ē/ using **ee, ea, ie**
Say: *Listen to this sound: /ē/. Say it with me: /ē/. Say it on your own: /ē/.*

Sound-Spelling Correspondence
Write and display the letter **e** and the vowel teams **ee, ea, ie**..
Say: *There are different ways to form this sound. Sometimes /ē/ is formed by the letter ea on its own. Say the sound with me: /ē/.*
Say: *Sometimes /ē/ is formed by the combination of the letter e and another letter e. Say the sound with me: /ē/.*
Say: *Sometimes /ē/ is formed by the combination of the letter e and the letter a. Say the sound with me: /ē/.*
Say: *Sometimes /ē/ is formed by the combination of the letter e and the letter i. Say the sound with me: /ē/.*

Model

Use BLM 60, #1.
Say: *We will look at each picture. We will say its name. Listen for the long sound /ē/. If we hear the long sound of /ē/, we will circle the picture. If we do not hear the long sound /ē/, we will cross out the picture.*
Say: *What do you see in the picture?* **chief**. *Do you hear the long sound /ē/ in the word* **chief**? *Circle the picture. If you do not hear the sound /ē/, then cross out the picture*

Practice

Use BLM 60, #2..

Say: Look *at the picture.* **Say** *its name. Listen for the long sound /ē/.*

Say *What do you see in the picture? feet Do you hear the long sound /ē/ in the word wheel?*

Say *What letter or letters make the long sound /ē/? Write the letter or letters that make the long sound /ē/ on the line under each picture.*

Apply

Blend Words

Use BLM 60, #3.

Say: *Look at each letter and listen to the long sound /ē/ as I read. /b/l/ē/ch/. Your turn: /b/l/ē/ch/.*

Say: *Now we are going to blend the sounds together by stretching them out as we read them. Point to each letter in a sweeping motion left to right: /bbb/lll/ ē ē ē /ch/. What is the word?* **bleach**.

Spelling

Use BLM 60, #4.

Say: *Now we can practice writing the sounds we hear in each word. Call one word at a time, stretching each sound.*

Say: *Say the word slowly; write a letter for each sound you hear.*

Conclusion

Ask: *What did we learn today?* We learned that the sound /ē/ can be formed by the vowel **e**, or the vowel team **ee**, or the vowel team ea, or the vowel team **ei**. What pictures/words will help you remember the long sound /ē/ and the letters that make that sound?

Home Connection

Use BLM 60. Ask students to practice identifying vowel sound /ē/ and writing the letters **e, ee, ea, and ei**, with a family member. Have students identify other words that include the sound /ē/ with their family.

✔ Formative Assessment

If the student completes each task correctly, precede to the next skill in the sequence. If not, refer to suggested Intervention 2.

Did the student…?	Intervention 2
Identify the name of the letter?	• Use physical rhythmic movements as the letter name is repeated. March while chanting the letter name. Move arms up and down. Sway from side to side..
Identify the sounds of the vowel teams?	• Use rhyming chants that repeat the sound several times and then use words that contain the sound. Example: /ē/ /ē/ **wheel steel.**
Produce the vowel sounds?	Use mirrors to show movement of mouth, tongue, teeth as the sound is produced. Use hand over mouth to explore movement of air as the sound is produced.
Recognize the vowel teams??	Arrange a list of vowel teams that make the /ē/ sound.
Know name of pictures?	Tell students the name of pictures, have student repeat it aloud. Discuss meaning of word. Use word in context.

Recognize Long Vowel Teams and Single Letters with the Sound /ī/ RF.1.3b, RF.1.3c, RF.1.3g

CCSS: RF.1.3
Know and apply grade-level phonics and word analysis skills in decoding words both in isolation and in text
b. Decode regularly spelled one-syllable words.
c. Know final -e and common vowel team conventions for representing long vowel sounds.
g. Recognize and read grade-appropriate irregularly spelled words.

Lesson Objectives

- Produce the sound /ī/.
- Relate the sound //ī/ to the single letter i.
- Relate the sound /ī/ to spellings y, **igh.**
- Recognize long vowel sound /ī/ in words and pictures.
- Write vowel teams that make the sound /ī/.

METACOGNITIVE STRATEGY
- Selective auditory attention, imagery, auditory representation

ACADEMIC LANGUAGE
- vowel, long vowel sound, vowel team

Materials
- Sound Spelling Cards for **i, y, igh**
- Blackline master 61

Pre-Assess
Student's ability to recognize the **long vowel sound** represented by the corresponding letters and alternate spellings. Ability to pronounce the **long vowel sound**..

Introduce

As students participate in this lesson, they identify the name and sound of sound of the target letter, and identify the letter when the sound and name is given orally. Students will apply their knowledge by recognizing the initial sound of target letter using pictures. Students apply skill in context by reading decodable simple sentences that include high frequency words.

State Learning Goal

Today we will learn to read words with the long sound of vowel /ī/. We are going to learn that the sound /ī/ can be formed in several different ways...

Teach

Letters represent sounds. We remember the sounds each letter makes. We use letters to write words we say. We use letters to read and write words. The sound /ī/ is formed by the letter **i** sometimes by the letter y or the letter combination **igh**. We are going to learn words that have the long sound of vowel /ē/.

Phonemic Awareness

Pair sound/spelling cards to review the long sound of /ī/ using **i, y, igh**
Say: *Listen to this sound: /ē/. Say it with me: /ē/. Say it on your own: /ē/.*

Sound-Spelling Correspondence

Write and display the letter e and the vowel teams **y, igh**.
Say: *There are different ways to form this sound. Sometimes /ē/ is formed by the letter **i** on its own. Say the sound with me: /ī/*
Say: *Sometimes /ī/is formed by the the letter y. Say the sound with me: /ī/.*
Say: *Sometimes /ī/ is formed by the letter combination igh. Say the sound with me: /ī/.*

Model

Use BLM 61, #1.
Say: *We will look at each picture. We will say its name. Listen for the long sound /ī/. If we hear the long sound of /ī/, we will circle the picture. If we do not hear the long sound /ī/, we will cross out the picture.*
Say: *What do you see in the picture? **light** Do you hear the long sound /ī/ in the word **light**? Circle the picture. If you do not hear the sound /ī/, then cross out the picture.*

Practice

Use BLM 61, #2.

Say: Look at the picture. **Say** its name. Listen for the long sound /ī/.

Say: What do you see in the picture? **light** Do you hear the long sound /ī/ in the word **light**?

Say: What letter or letters make the long sound /ī/? Write the letter or letters that make the long sound /ī/ on the line under each picture.

Apply

Blend Words

Use BLM 61, #3.

Say: Look at each letter and listen to the long sound /ī/ as I read. /**n**/**ī**/**t**/. Your turn: /**n**/ /**t**/.

Say: Now we are going to blend the sounds together by stretching them out as we read them. Point to each letter in a sweeping motion left to right: /**nnn**/**īī**/**ttt**/. What is the word? night

Spelling

Use BLM 61, #4.

Say: Now we can practice writing the sounds we hear in each word. Call one word at a time, stretching each sound.

Say: Say the word slowly; write a letter for each sound you hear.

Conclusion

Ask: What did we learn today? We learned that the sound /ī/ can be formed by the vowel i, or the letter y, or the letter combination **igh**. What pictures/words will help you remember the long sound /ī/ and the letters that make that sound?

Home Connection

Use BLM 61. Ask students to practice identifying vowel sound /ī/ and writing the letters i, y, and igh, with a family member. Have students identify other words that include the sound /ī/ with their family.

✔ Formative Assessment

If the student completes each task correctly, precede to the next skill in the sequence. If not, refer to suggested Intervention 2.

Did the student…?	Intervention 2
Identify the name of the letter?	• Use physical rhythmic movements as the letter name is repeated. March while chanting the letter name. Move arms up and down. Sway from side to side..
Identify the sounds of the vowel teams?	• Use rhyming chants that repeat the sound several times and then use words that contain the sound. Example: /ī/ī/ī/ night
Produce the vowel sounds?	Use mirrors to show movement of mouth, tongue, teeth as the sound is produced. Use hand over mouth to explore movement of air as the sound is produced.
Recognize the vowel teams??	Arrange a list of vowel teams that make the /ī/ sound.
Know name of pictures?	Tell students the name of pictures, have student repeat it aloud. Discuss meaning of word. Use word in context.

Recognize Open Syllables RF.1.3b, RF.1.3c, RF.1.3g

CCSS: RF 1.3
Know and apply grade-level phonics and word analysis skills in decoding words both in isolation and in text.
b. Decode regularly spelled one-syllable words.
c. Know final -e and common vowel team conventions for representing long vowel sounds.
g. Recognize and read grade-appropriate irregularly spelled words.

Lesson Objectives

- Produce open syllables
- Relate open syllables to the letters that make them
- Recognize open syllables words and pictures
- Write letters and letter combinations that make open syllables

METACOGNITIVE STRATEGY
- Selective auditory attention, imagery, auditory representation

ACADEMIC LANGUAGE
- vowel, long vowel sound, vowel team

Materials
- Sound Spelling Cards for **a, ai, ay, e, y, ey**
- Blackline master 62

Pre-Assess
Student's ability to recognize the open syllables represented by the corresponding letters and vowel teams. Ability to pronounce the long vowel sound /ē/.

Introduce

As students participate in this lesson, they identify open syllables. Students will apply their knowledge by recognizing words containing open syllables using pictures. Students apply skill in context by reading decodable simple sentences that include high frequency words.

State Learning Goal
Today we will learn to read words with that have open syllables.

Teach

An open syllable has a vowel sound as the last sound. To say a syllable that ends in a vowel, we have to end the syllable with our mouths open. Usually, the vowel sound in an open syllable is a long vowel sound: /ā/ē/ī/ō/ū/.

Phonemic Awareness
Say: Listen to this word: he. The last letter in this word is e. The last sound in this word is long /ē/. We finish saying it with our mouths open. He is a word with one syllable. That syllable is an open syllable.

Sound-Spelling Correspondence
Write and display the sound /ā/ and the letters ai and ay, as well as the sound /ē/ and the letters **ee, ie,** and **ea**.

Say: Each long vowel sound has different letters that spell that sound.

Say: For example, the sound /ā/ can be formed by different letter combinations, such as ai and ay. Say the sound with me: /ā/.

Say: The sound /ē/ can be formed by different letter combinations, such as ee, ie, and ea. Say the sound with me: /ē/.

Say: Open syllables end with vowel sounds. These sounds can be formed by different letters.

Model

Use BLM 62, #1.

Say: We will look at each picture. We will say its name. Listen for the open syllable. If we hear the open syllable, we will circle the picture. If we do not hear the open syllable, we will cross out the picture.

*Say: What do you see in the picture? **three**. Do you hear the open syllable in the word **three**? Circle the picture. If you do not hear the open syllable, then cross out the picture.*

Practice

Use BLM 62, #2.

Say: **Look** at the picture. **Say** its name. Listen for the open syllable.

Say: What do you see in the picture? **pie**. Do you hear the open syllable in the word **cry**? What is the vowel sound in the open syllable? /ī/

Say: What letter or letters make the sound /ī/ in the open syllable? Write the letter or letters that make the sound /ī/ in the open syllable on the line under each picture.

Apply

Blend Words

Use BLM 62, #3.

Say: Look at the word and listen for the open syllable as I read. /f/r/o/z/e/n/. Your turn: /f/r/o/z/e/n/.

Say: Now we are going to blend the sounds together by stretching them out as we read them. Point to each letter in a sweeping motion left to right: **/f/rrr/ooo/zzz/eee/nnn/**. What is the word? **frozen**

Spelling

Use BLM 62, #4.

Say: Now we can practice writing the sounds we hear in each word. Call one word at a time, stretching each sound.

Say: Say the word slowly; write a letter for each sound you hear.

Conclusion

Ask: What did we learn today? We learned that open syllables end in a long vowel sound. We learned that long vowel sounds can be formed by different letters.

Home Connection

Use BLM 62. Ask students to practice identifying open syllables a family member. Have students identify other words that include open syllables with their family.

✔ Formative Assessment

If the student completes each task correctly, precede to the next skill in the sequence. If not, refer to suggested Intervention 2.

Did the student…?	Intervention 2
Identify open syllables?	Model saying open and closed syllables while students focus on the position of your mouth. Then have students identify open vowel sounds based on your mouth position. Ask them to repeat the open syllable after you.
Identify the sounds in the open syllables?	Use sound/spelling cards to review each long vowel sound and its different spellings
Produce the vowel sounds?	Use mirrors to show movement of mouth, tongue, and teeth as the sound is produced. Use hand over mouth to explore movement of air as the sound is produced.
Know name of pictures?	Tell students the name of pictures, have student repeat it aloud. Discuss meaning of word. Use word in context.

Identify and Name Variant Vowel är RF.1.3b, RF.1.3c

Introduce

As students participate in this lesson, they identify the name and sound of the target letters, and identify the letters when the sound and name is given orally. Students will apply their knowledge by recognizing the sound of the target letter using pictures. Students apply the skill in context by reading simple decodable sentences that include high frequency words.

State Learning Goal

The letter **a** is a vowel. But when a vowel is followed by the letter **r** the vowel is neither long or short. It is a different vowel sound. Today we will listen to the variant vowel **är**.

Teach

Letters represent sounds. We remember the sounds each letter makes. We use letters to write words we say. We use letters to read and write words. The letter **a** is a vowel. When it is followed by the letter **r** the a makes the vowel sound / **är** /.

Phonemic Awareness

Show picture of sound/spelling cards **a** and **r to review the variant vowel är.**
Say: *Listen to this sound / är /.* **Say** *it with me: är. Say it on your own: är.*

Sound-Spelling Correspondence

Show the sound/spelling card

Say: *The way we write the sound / är / is with the letters **ar**.*

Say: *The letter **r** that follows the vowel **a** makes the vowel sound / är /.*

Say: *What are the names of the letters? a and r What is the sound the letter **a** makes when it is followed by the letter **r** ? / är /*

Model

Use BLM 63, # 1.

Say: *Look at each picture. Say its name. **Listen for the vowel sound / är / in the middle.**

Say: *Do you hear the sound /ar/ in the **middle** of the word shark? If we hear the sound / ar / in the middle of the word, we will circle the picture. If we do not hear the sound / är / in the middle, we cross out the picture.*

CCSS: RF.1.3
Know and apply grade-level phonics and word analysis skills in decoding words both in isolation and in text.
b. Associate the variant vowel sound / är /.
c. Read common high-frequency words by sight.

Lesson Objectives

- Identify and name the letters **a** and **r**
- Produce the sound of letters **är**
- Relate the sound / är / to the letters **ar**
- Recognize **the variant vowel sound** / är / in words/pictures

METACOGNITIVE STRATEGY
- Selective auditory attention, imagery, auditory representation

ACADEMIC LANGUAGE
- letter name, letter sound, variant vowel

Materials
- Sound Spelling Cards AR, ar
- Blackline master 63

Pre-Assess
Student's ability to recognize the sound represented by the target letters of the alphabet and to identify the letters used to represent the corresponding sound.

Practice

Use *BLM 63, #2.*

Say: *Look at the picture. Say its name.* **Trace/write** *the letters.*

Say: *What is the picture? a garden Do you hear the sound / är / in the word star? Then* **trace/write** *the letters garden.*

Apply

Blend Words

Use BLM 63, #3.

Say: *Look at each letter and listen to the sound as I read. /f/ /a/ /r/ /m/ e/ /r /. Your turn: /f/ /a/ /r/ /m/ e/ /r/*

Say: *Now we are going to blend the sounds together by stretching them out as we read them.* Point to each letter in a sweeping motion left to right: **/f/aaa/rrr/ mmm/eee/rrr/**. *What is the word?* **farmer**.

Spelling

Use BLM 63, #4

Say: *Now we can practice writing the sounds we hear in each word. Call one word at a time, stretching each sound.*

Say: *Say the word slowly; write a letter for each sound you hear.*

Conclusion

Ask: *What did we learn today?* We learned that the letters **ar** makes the sound / är / in some words. What pictures/words will help you remember the sound / är / and the letters **ar**?

Home Connection

Use BLM 63. Encourage students to practice identifying the variant vowel sound / **är** / and writing the letters **ar** with a family member. Encourage students to identify other words that have a variant vowel sound / **är** / with their family.

✔ Formative Assessment

If the student completes each task correctly, precede to the next skill in the sequence. If not, refer suggested Intervention 2.

Did the student…?	Intervention 2
Identify the name of the letter?	Use physical rhythmic movements as the letter name is repeated. March while chanting the letter name. Move arms up and down. Sway from side to side.
Identify the sound of the letter?	Have students chant rhyming words with variant vowel sound / är / **bar, star, bar**.
Produce the sound of the letter?	Use mirrors to show movement of mouth, tongue, teeth as the sound is produced. Use hand over mouth to explore movement of air as the sound is produced.
Recognize the beginning sound?	Use elkonin boxes – student moves a token into first box as the beginning sound of the word is said.
Write the letter?	Write the letter, have students trace it. Create letter with clay. Discuss letter features (lines, shape). Trace over letter with multiple colors.
Know name of pictures?	Tell students the name of pictures, have student repeat it aloud. Discuss meaning of word. Use word in context.

Identify and Name Variant Vowel /ôr/ RF.1.3b

CCSS: RF.1.3
Know and apply grade-level phonics and word analysis skills in decoding words both in isolation and in text.
b. Decode regularly spelled one-syllable words.

Lesson Objectives

- Identify and name the letters **o** and **r**
- Produce the sound of letters **ôr**.
- Relate the sound / ôr / to the letters **or, ore,** and **oar**
- Recognize **the variant vowel sound** / ôr / in words/pictures

METACOGNITIVE STRATEGY
- Selective auditory attention, imagery, auditory representation

ACADEMIC LANGUAGE
- letter name, letter sound, variant vowel

Materials
- Sound Spelling Cards **ôr**
- Blackline master 64

Pre-Assess
Student's ability to recognize the sound represented by the target letters of the alphabet and to identify the letters used to represent the corresponding sound.

Introduction
As students participate in this lesson, they identify the name and sound of the target letters, and identify the letters when the sound and name is given orally. Students will apply their knowledge by recognizing the sound of the target letters using pictures. Students apply the skill in context by reading simple decodable sentences that include high frequency words.

State Learning Goal The letter **o** is a vowel. But when a vowel is followed by the letter **r**, letters re and **ar**, the vowel is neither long or short. It is a different vowel sound. Today we will listen to the vowel sound / ôr /.

Teach
Letters represent sounds. We remember the sounds each letter makes. We use letters to write words we say. We use letters to read and write words. The letter **o** is a vowel. When it is followed by the letter **r** or letters **ar** and **re** it makes the vowel sound / ôr /.

Phonemic Awareness
Show picture of sound/spelling card **ôr to review the variant vowel ôr**. Say: Listen to this sound / **ôr** /. Say it with me: **ôr**. Say it on your own: **ôr**.

Sound-Spelling Correspondence
Show the sound/spelling card

Say: *The way we write the sound / ôr / is with the letters* **or, ore,** *and* **oar**.

Say: *The letter r or letters* **re** *and* **ar** *that follow(s) the vowel* **o** *give the* **o** *a vowel sound that is neither long or short. It gives it a different sound.*

Say: *What is the sound made by* **or, ore***, and* **oar***?* / ôr /

Model
Use BLM 64, # 1.

Say*: Look at each picture. Say its name.* **Listen for the vowel sound** / ôr / **in the middle.**

Say*: Do you hear the sound /ôr/ in the* **middle** *of the word* **cord***? If we hear the sound of ôr in the middle of the word, we will circle the picture. If we do not hear the sound / ôr / in the middle, we cross out the picture.*

Practice

Use BLM 64, #2.

Say: *Look at the picture.* **Say** *its name.* **Trace/write** *the letters.*

Say: *What is the picture?* **sword** *Do you hear the sound /* **ôr** */ in the word* **sword**? *Then* **trace/write** *the letters sword.*

Apply

Blend Words

Use BLM 64, #3.

Say: *Look at each letter and listen to the sound as I read.* **/ h / / o / / r / /n/.** *Your turn: Say /* **h / / o / / r / / n** */. Now we are going to blend the sounds together by stretching them out as we read them.* **Point to each letter in a sweeping motion left to right**: **/ hhh / ooo /rrr/ nnn /.** *What is the word?* **horn**.

Spelling

Use BLM 64, #4

Say: *Now we can practice writing the sounds we hear in each word. Call one word at a time, stretching each sound.*

Say: *Say the word slowly; write a letter for each sound you hear.*

Conclusion

Ask: *What did we learn today?* We learned that the letters **r, re**, and **ar** make the sound / **ôr** / in some words. What pictures/words will help you remember the sound / **ôr** / and the letters **r, re, and oa**?

Home Connection

Use BLM 64. Encourage students to practice identifying the variant vowel sound

/ **ôr** /and writing the letters **or, ore**, or **oar** with a family member. Encourage students to identify other words that have a variant vowel sound / **ôr** / with their family.

✔ Formative Assessment

If the student completes each task correctly, precede to the next skill in the sequence. If not, refer suggested Intervention 2.

Did the student…?	Intervention 2
Identify the name of the letter?	Use physical rhythmic movements as the letter name is repeated. March while chanting the letter name. Move arms up and down. Sway from side to side.
Identify the sound of the letter?	Have students chant rhyming words with variant vowel sound / **ôr** /: **oar, store, roar**
Produce the sound of the letter?	Use mirrors to show movement of mouth, tongue, teeth as the sound is produced. Use hand over mouth to explore movement of air as the sound is produced.
Recognize the beginning sound?	Use elkonin boxes – student moves a token into first box as the beginning sound of the word is said.
Write the letter?	Write the letter, have students trace it. Create letter with clay. Discuss letter features (lines, shape). Trace over letter with multiple colors.
Know name of pictures?	Tell students the name of pictures, have student repeat it aloud. Discuss meaning of word. Use word in context.

Identify and Name Variant Vowel ûr RF.1.3b

Introduce

As students participate in this lesson, they identify the name and sound of the target letters, and identify the letters when the sound and name is given orally. Students will apply their knowledge by recognizing the sound of the target letters using pictures. Students apply the skill in context by reading simple decodable sentences that include high frequency words.

State Learning Goal

The letters **e**, **i**, and **u** are vowels. But when these vowels are followed by the letter **r**, the vowels are neither long or short. They have a different vowel sound. Today we will listen to the vowel sound / **ûr** /.

Teach

Letters represent sounds. We remember the sounds each letter makes. We use letters to write words we say. We use letters to read and write words. The letters **e**, **i**, and **u** are vowels. When they are followed by the letter **r** the vowels make the sound / **ûr** /.

Phonemic Awareness

Show picture of sound/spelling card **ûr to review the variant vowel ûr. Say**: *Listen to this sound / ûr /.* **Say** *it with me: ûr. Say it on your own:* **ûr**.

Sound-Spelling Correspondence

Show the sound/spelling card

Say: *The way we write the sound / ûr / is with the letters* **er**, **ir**, *and* **ur**.

Say: *The letter* **r** *that follows the vowels* **e**, **i**, *or* **u** *give them a sound that is neither long or short. It gives them a different sound.*

Say: *What are the names of the letters?* **i**, **e**, **u**, *and* **r** *What is the sound the vowels* **i**, **e**, *and* **u** *make when they are followed by the letter r? / ûr /*

Model

Use BLM 65, # 1.

Say: *Look at each picture. Say its name.* **Listen for the vowel sound** / ûr / **in the middle**. *Say: Do you hear the sound /ûr/ in the* **middle** *of the word* **fern**? *If we hear the sound of ûr in the middle of the word, we will circle the picture. If we do not hear the sound / ûr / in the middle, we cross out the picture.*

CCSS: RF.1.3
Know and apply grade-level phonics and word analysis skills in decoding words both in isolation and in text.
b. Decode regularly spelled one-syllable words..

Lesson Objectives

- Identify and name the letters **e**, **i**, **u**, and **r**
- Produce the sound of letters **ûr**.
- Relate the sound / ûr / to the letters **er**, **ir**, and **ur**
- Recognize **the variant vowel sound** / ûr / in words/pictures

METACOGNITIVE STRATEGY
- Selective auditory attention, imagery, auditory representation

ACADEMIC LANGUAGE
- letter name, letter sound, variant vowel

Materials
- Sound Spelling Cards **ûr**
- Blackline master 65

Pre-Assess
Student's ability to recognize the sound represented by the target letters of the alphabet and to identify the letters used to represent the corresponding sound..

Practice

Use BLM 65, #2.

Say: **Look** at the picture. **Say** its name. **Trace/write** the letters.

Say: What is the picture? surf Do you hear the sound / **ûr** / in the word **surf**? Then **trace/write** the letters **surf**.

Apply

Blend Words

Use BLM 65, #3.

Say: Look at each letter and listen to the sound as I read. / s / / k / /ûr/ / t /. Your turn:

Say: / s / / k / /ûr/ / t t /. Now we are going to blend the sounds together by stretching them out as we read them. Point to each letter in a sweeping motion left to right: / s /kkk/uuu /rrr/ttt/. What is the word? **skirt**.

Spelling

Use BLM 65, #4.

Say: Now we can practice writing the sounds we hear in each word. Call one word at a time, stretching each sound.

Say: Say the word slowly; write a letter for each sound you hear.

Conclusion

Ask: What did we learn today? We learned that when the vowels **e, i**, and **u** are followed by the letter r they make the sound / **ûr** /. What pictures/words will help you remember the sound / **ûr** / and the letters **er, ir**, and **ur**?

Home Connection

Use BLM 65. Encourage students to practice identifying the variant vowel sound /**ûr**/ and writing the letters **er**, **ir**, and **ur** with a family member. Encourage students to identify other words that have the variant vowel sound /**ûr**/ with their family.

✔ Formative Assessment

If the student completes each task correctly, precede to the next skill in the sequence. If not, refer suggested Intervention 2.

Did the student…?	Intervention 2
Identify the name of the letter?	Use physical rhythmic movements as the letter name is repeated. March while chanting the letter name. Move arms up and down. Sway from side to side.
Identify the sound of the letter?	Have students chant rhyming words with variant vowel sound / **ûr** /: **fern, bird, fur**
Produce the sound of the letter?	Use mirrors to show movement of mouth, tongue, teeth as the sound is produced. Use hand over mouth to explore movement of air as the sound is produced.
Recognize the beginning sound?	Use elkonin boxes – student moves a token into first box as the beginning sound of the word is said.
Write the letter?	Write the letter, have students trace it. Create letter with clay. Discuss letter features (lines, shape). Trace over letter with multiple colors.
Know name of pictures?	Tell students the name of pictures, have student repeat it aloud. Discuss meaning of word. Use word in context.

CCSS: RF.1.3
Know and apply grade-level phonics and word analysis skills in decoding words both in isolation and in text.
b. Decode regularly spelled one-syllable words.
d. Use knowledge that every syllable must have a vowel sound to determine the number of syllables in a printed word.
g. Recognize and read grade-appropriate irregularly spelled words.

Lesson Objectives

- Identify and name the letters **ou and ow**
- Produce the sound of letters **ou and ow**
- Relate the sound /**ou**/ to the letters **ou and ow**
- Recognize **vowel team** sound **ou** in words/pictures
-

METACOGNITIVE STRATEGY
- Selective auditory attention, imagery, auditory representation

ACADEMIC LANGUAGE
- letter name, letter sound, vowel, short sound, **vowel team, middle**

Materials
- Sound Spelling Card **ou**
- Blackline Master 66

Pre-Assess
Student's ability to recognize the sound represented by the target letter of the alphabet and to identify the letter used to represent the corresponding sound.

Phonics and Word Recognition
RF.1.3b, RF.1.3d, RF.1.3g

Introduce
As students participate in this lesson, they identify the name and sound of the target letter, and identify the letter when the sound and name is given orally. Students will apply their knowledge by recognizing the sound of target letters using pictures. Students apply the skill in context by reading simple decodable sentences that include high frequency words.

State Learning Goal
The letters **o and u** are vowels. The letter **w** is a consonant. They form one sound. The /ou/ sound. Today we will listen to the vowel team sound in the middle of words.

Teach
Letters represent sounds. We remember the sounds each letter makes. We use letters to write words we say. We use letters to read and write words. The letters **o** and **u** are vowels. The two vowels form one sound: /**ou**/. The letter **w** is a consonant. The letters **o** and **w** also form the /**ou**/ sound.

Phonemic Awareness
Show picture of sound/spelling card **to review the sound of ou**. **Say:** *Listen to this sound /ou/. Say it with me: ou. Say it on your own: ou.*

Sound-Spelling Correspondence
Show the letter.

Say: *The way we write the sound /ou/ is with the letters ou or* **ow.**

Say: *The letters* **ou** *and* **ow** *make the sound /ou/.*

Say: *What is the name of the letters? ou and* **ow.** *What is the sound the letters* **ou** *or ow make? /**ou**/*

Model
BLM 66, # 1.

Say: *Look at each picture. Say its name.* **Listen for the sound of /ou/ in the middle.**

Say: *Do you hear the sound /ou/ in the* **middle** *of the word* **cloud***? If we hear the sound of ou in the middle of the word, we will circle the* **cloud** *item in the picture. If we do not hear the sound /ou/ in the middle, we cross out the picture. Repeat for the word* **cloud.**

Practice

Use BLM 66, #2.

Say: **Look** at the picture. **Say** its name. **Trace** the letter.

Say: What is the picture? **shout** Do you hear the sound /**ou**/ in the **middle** of the word **shout**? Then **trace** the letters **ou**. Repeat for the word **town**.

Apply

Blend Words

Use BLM 66, #3..

Say: Look at each letter and listen to the sound as I read. /**m**/ /**ou**/ /**s**/. Your turn: /**m**/ /**ou**/ /**s**/.

Say: Now we are going to blend the sounds together by stretching them out as we read them. /**m/ooouuu/sss**/. What is the word? **mouse**. Repeat for the word **town**.

Spelling

Use BLM 66, #4.

Say: Now we can practice writing the sounds we hear in each word. Call one word at a time, stretching each sound. Say the word slowly; write a letter for each sound you hear.

Conclusion

Ask: What did we learn today? We learned that the letters ou and ow make the sound /**ou**/ in the middle of some words. What pictures/words will help you remember the sound /**ou**/ and the letters ou and ow?

Home Connection

Use BLM 66. Encourage students to practice identifying the medial vowel team sound and writing the letters **ou** and **ow** with a family member. Encourage students to identify other words that have a medial ou vowel sound with their family.

✔ Formative Assessment

If the student completes each task correctly, proceed to the next skill in the sequence. If not, refer suggested Intervention 2.

Did the student...?	Intervention 2
Identify the name of the letter?	Use physical rhythmic movements as the letter name is repeated. March while chanting the letter name. Move arms up and down. Sway from side to side.
Identify the sound of the letter?	Use exaggeration of forming the /**ou**/ by opening the mouth wide and bringing the lips together in a pucker.
Produce the sound of the letter?	Use mirrors to show movement of mouth, tongue, teeth as the sound is produced. Use hand over mouth to explore movement of air as the sound is produced.
Recognize the middle sound?	Use Elkonin boxes – student moves a token into the middle boxes as the middle sound of the word is said.
Write the letter?	Write the letters, have students trace them. Create letters with clay. Discuss letter features (lines, shape). Trace over letters with multiple colors.
Know name of pictures?	Tell students the name of pictures, have student repeat it aloud. Discuss meaning of word. Use word in context.

CCSS: RF.1.3
Know and apply grade-level phonics and word analysis skills in decoding words both in isolation and in text.
b. Decode regularly spelled one-syllable words.
d. Use knowledge that every syllable must have a vowel sound to determine the number of syllables in a printed word.
g. Recognize and read grade-appropriate irregularly spelled words.

Lesson Objectives

- Identify and name the letters **oi** and **oy**
- Produce the sound of letters **oi** and **oy**
- Relate the sound /**oi**/ to the letters **oi** or **oy**
- Recognize **vowel team** sound **oi** in words/pictures

METACOGNITIVE STRATEGY
- Selective auditory attention, imagery, auditory representation

ACADEMIC LANGUAGE
- letter name, letter sound, vowel, short sound, **vowel team, middle**

Materials
- Sound Spelling Card **oi oy**
- Blackline Master 67

Pre-Assess
Student's ability to recognize the sound represented by the target letter of the alphabet and to identify the letter used to represent the corresponding sound.

Identify and Name Vowel Team
oi RF.1.3b, RF.1.3d, RF.1.3g

Introduce
As students participate in this lesson, they identify the name and sound of the target letter, and identify the letter when the sound and name is given orally. Students will apply their knowledge by recognizing the sound of target letters using pictures. Students apply the skill in context by reading simple decodable sentences that include high frequency words.

State Learning Goal
The letters **o, i, and y** are vowels. The letters oi and oy each form one sound. The /**oi**/ sound. Today we will listen to the vowel team sound in the middle of words.

Teach
Letters represent sounds. We remember the sounds each letter makes. We use letters to read and write words. We know the sounds o can make and the sounds i can make, but together, they make the sound /**oi**/. We also know the sound y can make, and together, **o** and **y** also make the sound /**oi**/.

Phonemic Awareness
Show picture of sound/spelling card **to review the sound of oi** Say: *Listen to this sound /**oi**/. Say it with me: oi. Say it on your own:* **oi**.

Sound-Spelling Correspondence
Show the letter.

Say: *The way we write the sound /**oi**/ is with the letters* **oi** *or* **oy**.

Say: *The letters oi and oy make the* **sound** /**oi**/.

Say: *What is the name of the letters?* **oi** *or* **oy**. *What is the sound the letters* **oi** *or* **oy** *make?* /**oi**/

Model
Use BLM 67, # 1.

Say: *Look at each picture. Say its name.* **Listen for the sound of /oi/ in the middle.**

Say: *Do you hear the sound /**oi**/ in the* **middle** *of the word* **boil***? If we hear the sound of oi in the middle of the word, we will circle the picture* **boil***. If we do not hear the sound /**oi**/ in the middle, we cross out the picture. Repeat with the word* **Roy***.*

Practice

Use BLM 67, #2.

Say: **Look** at the picture. **Say** its name. **Trace** the letter.

Say: What is the picture? **coin**. *Do you hear the sound /oi/ in the* **middle** *of the word* **foil**? *Then trace the letters oi. Repeat with the word* **toy**.

Apply

Blend Words

Use BLM 66, #3..

Say: *Look at each letter and listen to the sound as I read. /oi/ /l/. Your turn: /oi/ /l/.*

Say: *Now we are going to blend the sounds together by stretching them out as we read them. Point to each letter in a sweeping motion left to right oooiii/lll/. What is the word?* **oil**. *Repeat for the word* **joy**.

Spelling

Use BLM 67, #4.

Say: *Now we can practice writing the sounds we hear in each word. Call one word at a time, stretching each sound. Say the word slowly; write a letter for each sound you hear.*

Conclusion

Ask: *What did we learn today?* We learned that the letters **oi** and **oy** make the sound /oi/ in the middle of some words. What pictures/words will help you remember the sound /oi/ and the letters **oi** and **oy**?

Home Connection

Encourage students to practice identifying the medial vowel team sound and writing the letters **oi** and **oy** with a family member. Encourage students to identify other words that have a medial **oi** vowel sound with their family.

✔ Formative Assessment

If the student completes each task correctly, proceed to the next skill in the sequence. If not, refer suggested Intervention 2.

Did the student…?	Intervention 2
Identify the name of the letter?	Use physical rhythmic movements as the letter name is repeated. March while chanting the letter name. Move arms up and down. Sway from side to side.
Identify the sound of the letter?	Use exaggeration of forming the letters **oi** and **oy** by bringing the lips together in a pucker..
Produce the sound of the letter?	Use mirrors to show movement of mouth, tongue, teeth as the sound is produced. Use hand over mouth to explore movement of air as the sound is produced.
Recognize the middle sound?	Use elkonin boxes – student moves a token into the middle boxes as the middle sound of the word is said.
Write the letter?	Write the letters, have students trace them. Create letters with clay. Discuss letter features (lines, shape). Trace over letters with multiple colors.
Know name of pictures?	Tell students the name of pictures, have student repeat it aloud. Discuss meaning of word. Use word in context.

Identify and Name Vowel Teams
/ōō/ and /ŏŏ/ RF.1.3b, RF.1.3d, RF.1.3g

Introduce

As students participate in this lesson, they identify the name and sound of the target letter, and identify the letter when the sound and name is given orally. Students will apply their knowledge by recognizing the sound of target letters using pictures. Students apply the skill in context by reading simple decodable sentences that include high frequency words.

State Learning Goal

The letter **o** is a vowel. When we double letter o, we can form two sounds. The /ōō/ and /ŏŏ/ sound. Today we will listen to the vowel team sound in the middle of words.

Teach

Letters represent sounds. We remember the sounds each letter makes. We use letters to write words we say. We use letters to read and write words. The letter o is a vowel. When doubled, the letter forms two sounds: /ōō/ and /ŏŏ/.

Phonemic Awareness

Show picture of sound/spelling card to review the sound of /ōō/ and /ŏŏ/.
Say: *Listen to this sound /ōō/. Say it with me: /ōō/. Say it on your own: lōō/. Repeat for the sound of /ŏŏ/.*

Sound-Spelling Correspondence

Show the letter.

Say: *The way we write the sounds /ōō/ and /ŏŏ/ is with the letters oo.*
Say: *The letters oo make the sound /ōō/ and /ŏŏ/.*
Say: *What is the name of the letters? oo What are the sounds the letters oo make? /ōō/ and /ŏŏ/.*

Model

Use BLM 68, # 1.

Say: *Look at each picture. Say its name.* **Listen for the sound of /ōō/ in the middle.**

Say: *Do you hear the sound /ōō/ in the **middle** of the word **book**? If we hear the sound of ōō in the middle of the word, we will circle the picture brook. If we do not hear the sound /ōō/ in the middle, we cross out the picture. Repeat for the sound ŏŏ in the middle of the word **broom**.*

CCSS: RF.1.3
Know and apply grade-level phonics and word analysis skills in decoding words both in isolation and in text.
b. Decode regularly spelled one-syllable words.
d. Use knowledge that every syllable must have a vowel sound to determine the number of syllables in a printed word.
g. Recognize and read grade-appropriate irregularly spelled words.

Lesson Objectives

- Identify and name the letters oo
- Produce the sound of letters oo
- Relate the sound /ōō/ and /ŏŏ/ to the letters oo
- Recognize vowel team sound **ōō** and **ŏŏ** in words/pictures

METACOGNITIVE STRATEGY
- Selective auditory attention, imagery, auditory representation

ACADEMIC LANGUAGE
- letter name, letter sound, vowel, short sound, **vowel team, middle**

Materials
- Sound Spelling Card **oo**
- Blackline Master 68

Pre-Assess
Student's ability to recognize the sound represented by the target letter of the alphabet and to identify the letter used to represent the corresponding sound.

Practice

Use BLM 68, #2.

Say: **Look** at the picture. **Say** its name. **Trace** the letter.

Say: What is the picture? **look** Do you hear the sound /o͞o/ in the **middle** of the word **look**? Then **trace** the letters oo. Repeat for /o͝o/ with the word **brook**.

Apply

Blend Words

Use BLM 68, #3.

Say: Look at each letter and listen to the sound as I read. /k/ /oo/ /k/. Your turn: /k/ /oo/ /k/.

Say: Now we are going to blend the sounds together by stretching them out as we read them. Point to each letter in a sweeping motion left to right: /k/ooo/kkk/. What is the word? **cook**. Repeat for **look**.

Spelling

Use BLM 68, #4..

Say: Now we can practice writing the sounds we hear in each word. Call one word at a time, stretching each sound. Say the word slowly; write a letter for each sound you hear..

Conclusion

Ask: What did we learn today? We learned that the letters **oo** make the sounds /o͞o/ and /o͝o/ in the middle of some words. What pictures/words will help you remember the sounds /o͞o/ and /o͝o/ and the letters **oo**??

Home Connection

Use BLM 68. Encourage students to practice identifying the medial vowel team sound and writing the letters oo with a family member. Encourage students to identify other words that have either a medial o͞o or o͝o vowel sound with their family.

✔ Formative Assessment

If the student completes each task correctly, proceed to the next skill in the sequence. If not, refer to suggested Intervention 2..

Did the student...?	Intervention 2
Identify the name of the letter?	Use physical rhythmic movements as the letter name is repeated. March while chanting the letter name. Move arms up and down. Sway from side to side.
Identify the sound of the letter?	Use exaggeration of forming the letters oo by bringing the lips together in a pucker.
Produce the sound of the letter?	Use mirrors to show movement of mouth, tongue, teeth as the sound is produced. Use hand over mouth to explore movement of air as the sound is produced.
Recognize the middle sound?	Use elkonin boxes – student moves a token into the middle boxes as the middle sound of the word is said.
Write the letter?	Write the letters, have students trace them. Create letters with clay. Discuss letter features (lines, shape). Trace over letters with multiple colors.
Know name of pictures?	Tell students the name of pictures, have student repeat it aloud. Discuss meaning of word. Use word in context.

Identify and Name Silent Letters wr, kn, gn RF.1.3a, RF.1.3b, RF.1.3g

Introduce

As students participate in this lesson, they identify the name and sound of the targeted letters, and identify the letters when the sounds and names are given orally. Students will apply their knowledge by recognizing the sounds of target consonant digraphs using pictures. Students apply skill in context by reading decodable simple sentences that include high frequency words.

State Learning Goal

Today we will practice listening to the sounds /r/, /n/ and /n/ that the letters **wr, kn** and **gn** make.

Teach

Letters represent sounds. We remember the sounds each letter makes. We use letters to write words we say. We use letters to read and write words. Some letters combine to make new sounds.

Phonemic Awareness

Show the picture of sound/spelling cards **wr** to review the sound. **Say**: *Listen to this sound /r/.* **Say** *it with me:* **wr**. *Say it on your own:* **wr**.

Sound-Spelling Correspondence

Show the letter.

Say: *One way we write the sound /r/ is with the letters wr. The* **w** *is silent*

Say: *The letters* **wr** *make the sound /r/.*

Say: *What is the name of the letters that combine?* **wr** *What sound do the letters make? /r/*

Model

Use BLM 69, # 1

Say: *We will look at each picture. Say its name. If we hear the sound /r/ at the beginning of the word, we will circle the picture. If we do not hear the sound /r/, we cross out the picture.*

Say: *What do you see in the picture?* **wrinkle** *Do you hear the sound /r/ at the beginning of the word* **wrinkle**? *Circle the picture. If you do not hear the sound /r/ at the beginning of the word, then cross out the picture.*

Phonemic Awareness

Show the picture of sound/spelling cards **kn** to review the sound. **Say**: *Listen to this sound /n/.* **Say** *it with me:* **kn**. **Say** *it on your own:* **kn**.

Sound-Spelling Correspondence

Show the letter.

Say: *One way we write the sound /n/ is with the letters* **kn**. *The* **k** *is silent.*

Say: *The letters kn make the sound /n/.*

Say: **kn** *What sound do the letters make? /n/*

Model

Use BLM 69, # 2

Say: *We will look at each picture. Say its name. If we hear the sound /n/ at the beginning of the word, we will circle the picture. If we do not hear the sound /n/, we cross out the picture.*

Say: *What do you see in the picture?* **knuckle** *Do you hear the sound /n/ at the beginning of the word* **knuckle**? *Circle the picture. If you do not hear the sound /n/ at the beginning of the word, then cross out the picture.*

CCSS: RF.1.3

Know and apply grade-level phonics and word analysis skills in decoding words **both in isolation and in text.**

a. Know the spelling-sound correspondences for common consonant digraphs.

b. Decode regularly spelled one-syllable words.

g. Recognize and read grade-appropriate irregularly spelled words.

Lesson Objectives

- Identify and name the letters **wr, kn** and **gn**
- Produce the sounds of consonants **wr, kn** and **gn**
- Relate the sounds /r/, /n/ and /n/ to the letters **wr, kn** and **gn**
- Recognize sounds /r/, /n/ and /n/ in words/pictures
-

METACOGNITIVE STRATEGY
- Selective auditory attention, imagery, auditory representation

ACADEMIC LANGUAGE
- letter name, letter sound, initial sound, final sound, ending sound, high frequency word

Materials
- Sound Spelling Cards **Wr, Kn and Gn**
- Blackline Master 69

Pre-Assess

Student's ability to recognize the sound represented by the target letter of the alphabet and to identify the letter used to represent the corresponding sound.

Phonemic Awareness

Show the picture of sound/spelling cards **gn** to review the sound. **Say**: *Listen to this sound /n̊/. **Say** it with me: **gn**. Say it on your own: **gn**.*

Sound-Spelling Correspondence

Show the letter.

Say: *One way we write the sound /n̊/ is with the letters **gn**. The g is silent.*

Say: *The letters **gn** make the sound /n̊/.*

Say: *What is the name of the letters that combine? **gn** What sound do the letters make? /n̊/*

Model

Use BLM 69, # 3

Say *We will look at each picture. Say its name. If we hear the sound /n̊/ at the beginning of the word, we will circle the picture. If we do not hear the sound /n̊/, we cross out the picture.*

Say: *What do you see in the picture? **gnomes** Do you hear the sound /n̊/ at the beginning of the word **gnomes**? Circle the picture. If you do not hear the sound /n̊/ at the beginning of the word, then cross out the picture.*

Practice

Use BLM 69, # 4.

Say: ***Look** at the picture. **Say** its name. **Write** the letters. Say: What is the picture? **wreath**. Do you hear the sound /r/ **or** /n̊/ in the word **wreath**? **Write** the letters **wr**.*

Apply

Blend Words

Use BLM 69, # 5

Say: *Look at each letter and listen to the sound as I read. /n/ /o/ /t/ Your turn: /n/ /o/ /t/.*

Say: *Now we are going to blend the sounds together by stretching them out as we read them. Point to each letter in a sweeping motion left to right: /n/ooo/ttt/. What is the word? **knot**.*

Spelling

Use BLM 69, #6

Say: *Now we can practice writing the sounds we hear in each word. Call one word at a time, stretching each sound.*

Say: *Say the word slowly; write a letter for each sound you hear.*

Conclusion

Ask: *What did we learn today?* We learned that the letters **wr** can make the sound /r/. The letters **kn** can make the sound /n̊/ and the letters gn can make the sound /n̊/. We wrote words using the combined letters **wr**, **kn** and **gn**. What pictures/words will help you remember the sounds /r/, /n̊/ and /n̊/ made by the letters **wr**, **kn** and **gn** at the beginning of a word?

Home Connection

Encourage students to practice identifying sounds **wr**, **kn** and **gn** and writing the letters **wr**, **kn** and gn with a family member. Encourage students to identify other words that combine letters **wr**, **kn** and **gn** with their family.

✔ Formative Assessment

If the student completes each task correctly, precede to the next skill in the sequence. If not, refer to suggested Intervention 2..

Did the student…?	Intervention 2
Identify the name of the letter?	Use physical rhythmic movements as the letter name is repeated. March while chanting the letter name. Move arms up and down. Sway from side to side.
Identify the sound of the letter?	Say words with the target sounds by repeating the words three times. Examples: wrench wrench **wrench, kneecap kneecap kneecap, gnomes gnomes gnomes**.
Produce the sound of the letter?	Use mirrors to show movement of mouth, tongue, teeth as the sound is produced. Use hand over mouth to explore movement of air as the sound is produced.
Recognize the middle sound?	Use elkonin boxes – student moves a token into the middle boxes as the middle sound of the word is said.
Write the letter?	Write the letters, have students trace them. Create letters with clay. Discuss letter features (lines, shape). Trace over letters with multiple colors.
Know name of pictures?	Tell students the name of pictures, have student repeat it aloud. Discuss meaning of word. Use word in context.

Identify and Name Vowel Sounds aw, au, al, augh
RF.1.3d, RF.1.3g

Introduce
As students participate in this lesson, they identify the name and sound of sound of the target letters, and identify the letters when the sound and name is given orally. Students will apply their knowledge by recognizing the vowel sound of target letter using pictures. Students apply the skill in context by reading simple decodable sentences that include high frequency words.

State Learning Goal
Vowels make different sounds. One vowel sound is /ô/. This sound is made when the vowel a combines with different vowels and consonants.

Teach
Letters represent sounds. We remember the sounds each letter makes. We use letters to write words we say. We use letters to read and write words. The letter **a** is a vowel. It has a sound /ô/ when it combines with different vowels and consonants.

Phonemic Awareness
Show the sound/spelling card.
Say: *Listen to this sound /ô/. Say it with me: ô. Say it on your own: /ô/.*

Sound-Spelling Correspondence
Show the letter.
Say: *One way we write the sound /ô/ is with the letters **aw**.*
Say: *The letters **aw** make the vowel sound /ô/.*
Say: *What is the vowel sound the letters **aw** make? /ô/*

Model
Use BLM 70, # 1A
Say: *Look at each picture. Say its name.* **Listen for the sound of /ô/.** *Do you hear the sound /ô/ in the word **crawl**? It is made by the letters **aw**. Circle the picture **crawl**. If we do not hear the sound /ô/, we cross out the picture.*

Phonemic Awareness
Show picture of sound/spelling card **AU**. **Say**: *Listen to this sound /ô/. Say it with me: ô. Say it on your own: /ô/.*

Sound-Spelling Correspondence
Show the letters.
Say: *One way we write the sound /ô/ is with the letters **au**.*

Model
Use BLM 70, # 2B
Say: *Look at each picture. Say its name.* **Listen for the sound of /ô/.** *Say: Do you hear the sound /ô/ in the word **saucer**? It is made by the letters **au**. If we hear the letters au making the sound /ô/, we will circle the picture **saucer**. If we do not hear the letters au making the sound /ô/, we cross out the picture.*

Phonemic Awareness
Show picture of sound/spelling card **AL**. **Say**: *Listen to this sound /ô/. Say it with me: ô. Say it on your own: /ô/.*

Sound-Spelling Correspondence
Show the letters.
Say: *One way we write the sound /ô/ is with the letters al.*

CCSS: RF.1.3
Know and apply grade-level phonics and word analysis skills in decoding words both in isolation and in text.
d. Use knowledge that every syllable must have a vowel sound to determine the number of syllables in a printed word.
g. Recognize and read grade-appropriate irregularly spelled words.

Lesson Objectives
- Identify and name the letters **aw**, **au**, **al**, and **augh**
- Produce the sound of letters **aw**, **au**, **al**, and **augh**
- Relate the sound /ô/ to the letters **aw**, **au**, **al**, and **augh**
- Recognize vowel a sound ô in words/pictures

METACOGNITIVE STRATEGY
- Selective auditory attention, imagery, auditory representation

ACADEMIC LANGUAGE
- letter name, letter sound, vowel

Materials
- Sound Spelling Card aw, au, al, augh
- Blackline Master 70

Pre-Assess
Student's ability to recognize the sound represented by the target letters of the alphabet and to identify the letters used to represent the corresponding sound..

Model
Use BLM 70, # 1C

Say: *Look at each picture. Say its name.* **Listen for the sound of** /ô/.

Say: *Do you hear the sound /ô/ in the word* **chalk**? *It is made by the letters* **al**. *If we hear the letters* **al** *making the sound /ô/, we will circle the picture* **chalk**. *If we do not hear the letters al making the sound /ô/, we cross out the picture*

Phonemic Awarenes
Show picture of sound/spelling card **AUGH**. Say: Listen to this sound /ô/. *Say it with me: ô. Say it on your own: /ô/.*

Practice
Use BLM 70, #2

Say: *Look at the picture.* **Say** *its name.* **Write** *the letters.*

Say: *What is the picture?* **stalk** *Do you hear the sound /ô/ from the letters* **aw, au, al,** *or* **augh** *in the word* **stalk**? *Write the letters* **al**.

Apply
Blend Words
Use BLM 70, #3

Say: *Look at each letter and listen to the sound as I read.* /d/ /i/ /s/ /t/ /r/ / ô / /t/. *Your turn:* /d/ /i/ /s/ /t/ /r / ô / /t/.

Say: *Now we are going to blend the sounds together by stretching them out as we read them. Point to each letter in a sweeping motion left to right* /d/iii/sss/ttt/rrr/ ô ô ô /ttt/. *What is the word?* **distraught**.

Spelling
Use BLM 70, #4

Say: *Now we can practice writing the sounds we hear in each word. Call one word at a time, stretching each sound.*

Say: Say the word slowly; write a letter for each sound you hear.

Conclusion
Ask: *What did we learn today?* We learned that the letters **aw, au, al,** and **augh** make the sound /ô/. What pictures/words will help you remember the sound /ô/ and the letters **aw, au, al,** and **augh**?

Home Connection
Encourage students to practice identifying the sound /ô/ and writing the letters aw, au, al, and augh with a family member. Encourage students to identify other words that have a /ô/ vowel sound and the letters **aw, au, al,** and **augh** with their family.

✔ Formative Assessment

If the student completes each task correctly, precede to the next skill in the sequence. If not, refer suggested Intervention 2..

Did the student…?	Intervention 2
Identify the name of the letter?	Use physical rhythmic movements as the letter name is repeated. March while chanting the letter name. Move arms up and down. Sway from side to side.
Identify the sound of the letter?	Use chants that repeat the sound several times then a word that begins with the sound. Example: **/aw/ /aw/ /aw/ draw**
Produce the sound of the letter?	Use mirrors to show movement of mouth, tongue, teeth as the sound is produced. Use hand over mouth to explore movement of air as the sound is produced.
Recognize the vowel sound?	Use Elkonin boxes – student moves a token into the box as the vowel sound of the word is said.
Write the letter?	Write the letter, have students trace it. Create letter with clay. Discuss letter features (lines, shape). Trace over letter with multiple colors.
Know name of pictures?	Tell students the name of pictures, have student repeat it aloud. Discuss meaning of word. Use word in context.

Recognize Long Vowel Teams and Single Letters with the sound /ē/ RF.1.3b, RF.1.3c, RF.1.3g

CCSS:RF 1.3.
Know and apply grade-level phonics and word analysis skills in decoding words both in isolation and in text.
b. Decode regularly spelled one-syllable words.
c. Know final -e and common vowel team conventions for representing long vowel sounds.
g. Recognize and read grade-appropriate irregularly spelled words.

Lesson Objectives

- Produce the sound /ē/
- Relate the sound /ē/ to the single letter e
- Relate the sound /ē/ to letters **y, ey**
- Recognize long vowel sound /ē/ in words and pictures
- Write letters and letter combinations that make the sound /ē/

METACOGNITIVE STRATEGY
- Selective auditory attention, imagery, auditory representation

ACADEMIC LANGUAGE
- letter name, letter sound, vowel

Materials
- Sound Spelling Cards for **e, y, ey**
- Blackline Master 71

Pre-Assess
Student's ability to recognize the long vowel sound /ē/ represented by the corresponding letters and vowel teams. Ability to pronounce the long vowel sound ē/.

Introduce

As students participate in this lesson, they identify the name and sound of sound of the target letter, and identify the letter when the sound and name is given orally. Students will apply their knowledge by recognizing the initial sound of target letter using pictures. Students apply skill in context by reading decodable simple sentences that include high frequency words.

State Learning Goal

Today we will learn to read words with the long sound of vowel /ē/. We are going to learn that the sound /ē/ can be formed by different letters, such as **y** and **ey**.

Teach

Letters represent sounds. We remember the sounds each letter makes. We use letters to write words we say. We use letters to read and write words. The sound /ē/ is formed by the letter e and other letters, such as y and the combined letters ey. We are going to learn words that have the long sound of vowel /ē/.

Phonemic Awareness

Pair sound/spelling cards to review the long sound of /ē/ using e, y, and ey   **Say**: *Listen to this sound /ē/. Say it with me: /ē/. Say it on your own: /ē/.*

Sound-Spelling Correspondence

Write and display the sound /ē/ and the letters **y** and **ey**.

Say: *There are different ways to form this sound. Sometimes /ē/ is formed by the letter y. Say the sound with me: /ē/.*

Say: Sometimes /ē/ is formed by the combination of the letter e and the letter y. Say the sound with me: /ē/.

Model

Use BLM 71, #1.

Say: *We will look at each picture. We will say its name. Listen for the long sound /ē/. If we hear the long sound of /ē/, we will circle the picture. If we do not hear the long sound /ē/, we will cross out the picture.*

Say: What do you see in the picture? **family**. *Do you hear the long sound /ē/ in the word* **family**? *Circle the picture. If you do not hear the sound /ē/, then cross out the picture.*

Practice

Use BLM 71, #2..

Say: **Look** at the picture. **Say** *its name. Listen for the long sound /ē/.*

Say: *What do you see in the picture? tiny Do you hear the long sound /ē/ in the word tiny?*

Say: *What letter or letters make the long sound /ē/? Write the letter or letters that make the long sound /ē/ on the line under each picture.*

Apply

Blend Words

Use BLM 71, #3.

Say: *Look at each letter and listen to the long sound /ē/ as I read. /t/ü/r/k/ē/. Your turn: /t/ü/r/k/ē/.*

Say: *Now we are going to blend the sounds together by stretching them out as we read them.*

Point to each letter in a sweeping motion left to right /t/üüü/rrr/kkk/eee/. What is the word? turkey

Spelling

Use BLM 71, #4.

Say: *Now we can practice writing the sounds we hear in each word. Call one word at a time, stretching each sound. Say: Say the word slowly; write a letter for each sound you hear.*

Conclusion

Ask: *What did we learn today?* We learned that the sound /ē/ can be formed by the letter y or the letter combination ey. What pictures/words will help you remember the long sound /ē/ and the letters that make that sound?

Home Connection

Ask students to practice identifying vowel sound /ē/ and writing the letters y and ey with a family member. Have students identify other words that include the sound /ē/ with their family.

✔ Formative Assessment

If the student completes each task correctly, precede to the next skill in the sequence. If not, refer to suggested Intervention 2.

Did the student…?	Intervention 2
Identify the name of the letter?	Use physical rhythmic movements as the letter name is repeated. March while chanting the letter name. Move arms up and down. Sway from side to side..
Identify the sounds of the vowel teams?	Use rhyming chants that repeat the sound several times and then use words that contain the sound. Example: **pretty/ city/ /ē/ /ē/**
Produce the vowel sounds?	Use mirrors to show movement of mouth, tongue, teeth as the sound is produced. Use hand over mouth to explore movement of air as the sound is produced.
Recognize the vowel teams?	Arrange a list of letter combinations that make the /ē/ sound.
Know name of pictures?	Tell students the name of pictures, have student repeat it aloud. Discuss meaning of word. Use word in context.

Identify and Name le Syllables_{RF.1.3e, RF.1.3g}

CCSS:RF 1.3.
Know and apply grade-level phonics and word analysis skills in decoding words both in isolation and in text.
e. Decode two-syllable words following basic patterns by breaking the words into syllables.
g. Recognize and read grade-appropriate irregularly spelled words.

Lesson Objectives

- Identify and name the letters **le.**
- Produce the sound of word ending le.
- Relate the sound /**le**/ to the letters **le.**
- Recognize the sound **le** in words/pictures.

METACOGNITIVE STRATEGY

- Selective auditory attention, imagery, auditory representation

ACADEMIC LANGUAGE

- letter name, letter sound, vowel

Materials

- Letter Cards **LE**
- Blackline Master 72

Pre-Assess

Student's ability to recognize the sounds represented by the targeted letters of the alphabet and to identify the letters used to represent the corresponding sounds..

Introduce

As students participate in this lesson, they identify the name and sound of the targeted letters, and identify the letters when the sounds and names are given orally. Students will apply their knowledge by recognizing the sounds of target endings using pictures. Students apply skill in context by reading decodable simple sentences that include high frequency words.

State Learning Goal

Today we will practice listening to the sound /**le**/ that the letters **le** make to form the final syllable in two-syllable words.

Teach

Letters represent sounds. We remember the sounds each letter makes. We use letters to write words we say. We use letters to read and write words. Letters are made up of vowels and consonants. Each vowel sound in a word is a syllable.

Phonemic Awareness

Show Letter Cards L and E to review the sounds.
Say: *Listen to this sound /le/.* **Say** *it with me: /le/. Say it on your own: /le/..*

Sound-Spelling Correspondence

Show the letters.
Say: *The way we write the sound /le/ is with the letters* **le**.
Say: *The letters le makes the sound /le/.*
Say: *The letters le make a syllable when /le/ is the final sound in a word.*
Say: *What is the name of the letters?* **le** *What sound does the letters make? /le/*

Model

Use BLM 72, # 1.
Say: *We will look at each picture. Say its name. If we hear the sound of the syllable* **le** *at the end of the word, we will circle the letters* **le**. *If we do not hear the sound of the syllable /le/ at the end of the word, we cross out the picture.*
Say: *What do you see in the picture?* **castle**. *Do you hear the sound of the syllable /le/ at the end of the word* **castle**? *Circle the letters le. If you do not hear the sound of the syllable /le/ at the end of the word, then cross out the picture.*

Practice

Use BLM 72, # 2.

Say: **Look** at the picture. **Say** its name. **Write** the letters.

Say: What is the picture? bubble. Do you hear the sound of the syllable /le/ at the end of the word **bubble**? Write the letters **le**.

Apply

Blend Words

Use BLM 72, # 3.

Say: Look at each letter and listen to the sound as I read. /**n**/ /**e**/ /**d**/ /**l**/. Your turn: /**n**/ /**e**/ /**d**/ /**l**/.

Say: Now we are going to blend the sounds together by stretching them out as we read them. Point to each letter in a sweeping motion left to right /**n**/**eee**/**ddd**/**lll**/. What is the word? **needle**.

Spelling

Use BLM 72, # 4.

Say: Now we can practice writing the sounds we hear in each word. Call one word at a time, stretching each sound.

Say: Say the word slowly; write a letter for each sound you hear.

Conclusion

Ask: What did we learn today? We learned that the letters **le** makes the sound /**le**/. We learned to listen for the sound of this syllable at the end of words. We wrote words using the letters **le** at the end of words. What pictures/words will help you remember the sound /**le**/ and the letters le at the end of a word?

Home Connection

Encourage students to practice identifying sound **le** at the end of words and writing the letters **le** with a family member. Encourage students to identify other words with the sound of syllable le at the end of words with their family.

✔ Formative Assessment

If the student completes each task correctly, precede to the next skill in the sequence. If not, refer to suggested Intervention 2.

Did the student…?	Intervention 2
Identify the name of the letter?	Use physical rhythmic movements as the letter name is repeated. March while chanting the letter name. Move arms up and down. Sway from side to side..
Identify the sounds of the vowel teams?	Say words with the target sounds by clearly separating the syllables in the words. Examples: **can/dle, bub/ble, nee/dle**
Produce the sound of the letters?	Use mirrors to show movement of mouth, tongue, teeth as the sound is produced. Use hand over mouth to explore movement of air as the sound is produced.
Recognize the sounds of the consonant digraphs?	Use Elkonin boxes – student moves a token into the box as the sound of the consonant digraph is said in the word. .
Write the letters?	Write the letters, have students trace them. Create the letters with clay. Discuss letter features (lines, shape). Trace over the letters with multiple colors.
tters? Know name of pictures?	Tell students the name of pictures, have students repeat them aloud. Discuss word and use each word in context.

CCSS RF.K.3
Know and apply grade-level phonics and word analysis skills in decoding words both in isolation and in text
a. Demonstrate basic knowledge of one-to-one letter-sound correspondences by producing the primary sounds or many of the most frequent sounds for each consonant.

Identify and Name Initial Consonant Mm RF.K.3a

Introduce

As students participate in this lesson, they identify the name and sound of the targeted letter, and identify the letter when the sound and name are given orally. They will apply their knowledge by recognizing the **initial** sound of the target letter using pictures.

State Learning Goal

Today we will practice matching the sound and letter **m.** Display letter card m. **Say**: *This is capital **M**. This is lowercase **m**.*

Lesson Objectives

- Identify and name the letter **Mm**
- Produce the sound of letter Mm.
- Relate the sound /**m**/ to the letter **m**.
- Recognize initial sound **m** in words/pictures.

METACOGNITIVE STRATEGY
- Selective auditory attention

ACADEMIC LANGUAGE
- letter name, letter sound, initial sound

Teach

Letters represent sounds. We remember the sounds each letter makes. We use letters to write words we say. We use letters to read and write words.

Phonemic Awareness

Show picture of sound/spelling card to review the sound. This is the **m** card.

Say: *Listen to this sound /**m**/. Say it with me: **m**. Now say it on your own: **m**.*

Additional Materials
Sound Spelling Card Mm
Blackline Master 73

Pre-Assess
Student's ability to recognize the sound represented by the targeted letter of the alphabet and to identify the letter used to represent the corresponding sound.

Sound-Spelling Correspondence

Show the letter.

Say: *The way we write the sound /**m**/ is with the letter **m**.*

Say: *The letter **m** makes the sound /**m**/.*

Say: *What is the name of the letter? **m** What sound does the letter make? /**m**/*

Model

Use BLM 73, row 1.

Say: *We will look at each picture. Say its name. If we hear the sound of **m** at the beginning of the word, we will circle the picture. If we do not hear the sound /**m**/ at the beginning, we will cross out the picture.*

Say: *What do you see in the picture? **math** Do you hear the sound /**m**/ at the beginning of the word **math?** Circle the picture. If you do not hear the sound /**m**/ at the beginning of the word, then cross out the picture.*

Practice

Use BLM 73, row 2.

Say: *Look at the picture. Say its name. Write the letter.* Say: *What do you see in the picture?* **meat** *Do you hear the sound /m/ at the beginning of the word meat?* **Write** *the letter* **m**.

Apply—Blend Words

Use BLM 73, row 3.

Say: *Look at each letter and listen to the sound as I read: /m/ /a/ /sh/. Your turn: /m/ /a/ /sh/.* Say: *Now we are going to blend the sounds together by stretching them out as we read them.* Point to each letter in a sweeping motion left to right: */m/aaa/sh/. What is the word?* **mash.**

Spelling

Use BLM 73, row 4.

Say: *Now we can practice writing the sounds we hear in each word. Call one word at a time, stretching each sound. Say the word slowly; write a letter for each sound you hear.*

Conclusion

Ask: *What did we learn today?* We taught the letter m makes the sound /**m**/. We wrote words using the letter **m**. What pictures/words will help you remember the sound /**m**/ and the letter **m**?

Home Connection

Ask students to practice identifying initial sound m and writing the letter m with a family member. Have students identify other words that begin with letter m with their family.

✔ Formative Assessment

If the student completes each task correctly, proceed to the next skill in the sequence. If not, refer to suggested Intervention 2.

Did the student...?	Intervention 2
Identify the name of the letter?	• Use physical rhythmic movements as the letter name is repeated. March while chanting the letter name. Move arms up and down. Sway from side to side.
Identify the sound of the letter?	• Use alliteration, chants that repeat the sound several times then a word that begins with the sound. Example: /m/ /e/ /a/ /t/ meat
Produce the sound of the letter?	• Use mirrors to show movement of mouth, tongue, and teeth as the sound is produced. Use hand over mouth to explore movement of air as the sound is produced.
Recognize the beginning sound?	• Use Elkonin boxes – student moves a token into first box as the beginning sound of the word is said.
Write the letter?	• Write the letter, have students trace it. Create letter with clay. • Discuss letter features (lines, shape). Trace over letter with multiple colors.
Know the name of pictures?	• Tell students the name of pictures, have students repeat them aloud. • Discuss words and use each word in context.

Identify and Name Initial Consonant Ss RF.K.3a

CCSS: RF.K.3.
Know and apply grade-level phonics and word analysis skills in decoding words both in isolation and in text
a. Demonstrate basic knowledge of one-to-one letter-sound correspondences by producing the primary sounds or many of the most frequent sounds for each consonant.

Lesson Objectives

- Identify and name the letter **Ss**.
- Produce the sound of letter **Ss**
- Relate the sound **/s /** to the letter **s**.
- Recognize initial sound **s** in words/pictures.

METACOGNITIVE STRATEGY
- Selective auditory attention

ACADEMIC LANGUAGE
- letter name, letter sound, initial sound

Additional Materials
Sound Spelling Card Ss
Blackline Master 74

Pre-Assess
Student's ability to recognize the sound represented by the targeted letter of the alphabet and to identify the letter used to represent the corresponding sound.

Introduce

As students participate in this lesson, they identify the name and sound of the targeted letter, and identify the letter when the sound and name are given orally. They will apply their knowledge by recognizing the initial sound of the target letter using pictures.

State Learning Goal
Today we will practice matching the sound and letter **s**. Display letter card **s**.
Say: *This is capital* **S**. *This is lowercase* **s**.

Teach

Letters represent sounds. We remember the sounds each letter makes. We use letters to write words we say. We use letters to read and write words.

Phonemic Awareness
Show picture of sound/spelling card to review the sound. This is the **s** card.

Say: *Listen to this sound /s/. Say it with me:* **s**. *Now say it on your own:* **s**.

Sound-Spelling Correspondence
Show the letter.

Write the word **unicycle** on the board. Point out the vowel **u** in the word.

Say: *The way we write the sound /s/ is with the letter* **s**.

Say: *The letter* **s** *makes the sound /s/.*

Say: *What is the name of the letter?* **s** *What sound does the letter make?* /s/

Model
Use BLM 74, Row 1.

Say: *We will look at each picture. We will say its name. If we hear the sound of* **s** *at the beginning of the word, we will circle the picture. If we do not hear the sound /s/ at the beginning, we will cross out the picture.*

Say: *What do you see in the picture?* **stars** *Do you hear the sound /s/ at the beginning of the word sit? Circle the picture. If you do not hear the sound /s/ at the beginning of the word, then cross out the picture.*

Practice

Use BLM 74, #2.

Say: *Look at the picture. Say its name. Write the letter.* **Say:** *What do you see in the picture?* **store** *Do you hear the sound /s/ at the beginning of the word store?* **Write** *the letter* **s**.

Apply–Blend Words

Use BLM 74, #3

Say: *Look at each letter and listen to the sound as I read: /s//t//a//i//r//s/. Your turn: /s//t//a//i//r//s/.* **Say:** *Now we are going to blend the sounds together by stretching them out as we read them.* **Point to each letter in a sweeping motion left to right:** /s/ /tt/ /aaa//rrr/ /sss/. *What is the word?* **stairs.**

Spelling

Use BLM 74, #4.

Say: *Now we can practice writing the sounds we hear in each word. Call one word at a time, stretching each sound. Say the word slowly; write a letter for each sound you hear.*

Call one word at a time, stretching each sound.

Say: *Say the word slowly; write a letter for each sound you hear.*

Conclusion

Ask: *What did we learn today?* We taught the letter **s** makes the sound /**s**/. We wrote words using the letter **s**. What pictures/words will help you remember the sound /**s**/ and the letter **s**?

Home Connection
Ask students to practice identifying initial sound s and writing the letter s with a family member. Have students identify other words that begin with letter s with their family.

✔ **Formative Assessment**

If the student completes each task correctly, proceed to the next skill in the sequence. If not, refer to suggested Intervention 2.

Did the student...?	Intervention 2
Identify the name of the letter?	• Use physical rhythmic movements as the letter name is repeated. March while chanting the letter name. Move arms up and down. Sway from side to side.
Identify the sound of the letter?	• Use alliteration, chants that repeat the sound several times then a word that begins with the sound. Example: /s/ /t/ /o/ /r/ /e/ store.
Produce the sound of the letter?	• Use mirrors to show movement of mouth, tongue, and teeth as the sound is produced. Use hand over mouth to explore movement of air as the sound is produced.
Recognize the beginning sound?	• Use Elkonin boxes – student moves a token into first box as the beginning sound of the word is said.
Write the letter?	• Write the letter, have students trace it. Create letter with clay. • Discuss letter features (lines, shape). Trace over letter with multiple colors.
Know the name of pictures?	• Tell students the name of pictures, have students repeat them aloud. • Discuss word and use each word in context.

Identify and Name Initial Consonant Tt RF.K.3a

CCSS: RF.K.3.
Know and apply grade-level phonics and word analysis skills in decoding words both in isolation and in text
a. Demonstrate basic knowledge of one-to-one letter-sound correspondences by producing the primary sounds or many of the most frequent sounds for each consonant.

Lesson Objectives

- Identify and name the letter **Tt**.
- Produce the sound of letter **Tt**.
- Relate the sound /**t**/ to the letter **t**.
- Recognize initial sound **t** in words/pictures.

METACOGNITIVE STRATEGY
- Selective auditory attention

ACADEMIC LANGUAGE
- letter name, letter sound, initial sound

Additional Materials
Sound Spelling Card Tt
Blackline Master 75

Pre-Assess
Student's ability to recognize the sound represented by the targeted letter of the alphabet and to identify the letter used to represent the corresponding sound.

Introduce

As students participate in this lesson, they identify the name and sound of the targeted letter, and identify the letter when the sound and name are given orally. They will apply their knowledge by recognizing the **initial** sound of the target letter using pictures.

State Learning Goal

Today we will practice matching the sound and letter **t**. Display letter card **t**.
Say: *This is capital* **T**. *This is lowercase* **t**

Teach

Letters represent sounds. We remember the sounds each letter makes. We use letters to write words we say. We use letters to read and write words.

Phonemic Awareness

Show picture of sound/spelling card to review the sound. This is the **t** card.
Say: Listen to this sound /t/. Say it with me: **t**. Now say it on your own: **t**.
Display the poetry poster and read it aloud.

Sound-Spelling Correspondence

Show the letter.

Say: *The way we write the sound* /t/ *is with the letter* **t**.

Say: *The letter* **t** *makes the sound* /t/.

Say: *What is the name of the letter?* **t** *What sound does the letter make?* /t/

Model

Use BLM 75, Row 1.

Say: *We will look at each picture. Say its name. If we hear the sound of* /t/ *at the beginning of the word, we will circle the picture. If we do not hear the sound* /t/ *at the beginning, we will cross out the picture.*

Say: *What do you see in the picture?* **test** *Do you hear the sound* /t/ *at the beginning of the word* **test**? *Circle the picture. If you do not hear the sound* /t/ *at the beginning of the word, then cross out the picture.*

Practice

Use BLM 75, #2.

Say: Look *at the picture.* **Say** *its name.* **Write** *the letter.* **Say:** *What do you see in the picture?* **turkey** *Do you hear the sound /t/ at the beginning of the word* **turkey**? **Write** *the letter* **t**.

Apply—Blend Words

Use BLM 75, #3

Say: *Look at each letter and listen to the sound as I read: /t/ /i/ /m/ /e/. Your turn: /t/ /i/ /m/ /e/.* **Say:** *Now we are going to blend the sounds together by stretching them out as we read them.* Point to each letter in a sweeping motion left to right: /t/iii/mmm/. *What is the word?* **time**.

Spelling

Use BLM 75, #4.

Say: *Now we can practice writing the sounds we hear in each word. Call one word at a time, stretching each sound. Say the word slowly; write a letter for each sound you hear.*

Conclusion

Ask: *What did we learn today?* We taught the letter **t** makes the sound /t/. We wrote words using the letter **t**. What pictures/words will help you remember the sound /t/ and the letter **t**?

Home Connection

Ask students to practice identifying initial sound **t** and writing the letter **t** with a family member. Have students identify other words that begin with letter **t** with their family.

✔ Formative Assessment

If the student completes each task correctly, proceed to the next skill in the sequence. If not, refer to suggested Intervention 2.

Did the student…?	Intervention 2
Identify the name of the letter?	• Use physical rhythmic movements as the letter name is repeated. March while chanting the letter name. Move arms up and down. Sway from side to side.
Identify the sound of the letter?	• Use alliteration, chants that repeat the sound several times then a word that begins with the sound. **Example:** /t/ /i/ /p/ **tip**
Produce the sound of the letter?	• Use mirrors to show movement of mouth, tongue, and teeth as the sound is produced. Use hand over mouth to explore movement of air as the sound is produced.
Recognize the beginning sound?	• Use Elkonin boxes – student moves a token into first box as the beginning sound of the word is said.
Write the letter?	• Write the letter, have students trace it. Create letter with clay. • Discuss letter features (lines, shape). Trace over letter with multiple colors
Know the name of pictures?	• Tell students the name of pictures, have students repeat them aloud. • Discuss word and use each word in context.

Identify and Name Initial Consonant Nn RF.K.3a

CCSS: RF.K.3.
Know and apply grade-level phonics and word analysis skills in decoding words both in isolation and in text
a. Demonstrate basic knowledge of one-to-one letter-sound correspondences by producing the primary sounds or many of the most frequent sounds for each consonant.

Lesson Objectives

- Identify and name the letter **Nn**
- Produce the sound of letter **Nn**
- Relate the sound /**n**/ to the letter **n**.
- Recognize initial sound n in words/ pictures.

METACOGNITIVE STRATEGY
- Selective auditory attention

ACADEMIC LANGUAGE
- letter name, letter sound, initial sound

Additional Materials
Sound Spelling Card Nn
Blackline master 76

Pre-Assess
Student's ability to recognize the sound represented by the targeted letter of the alphabet and to identify the letter used to represent the corresponding sound.

Introduce

As students participate in this lesson, they identify the name and sound of the targeted letter, and identify the letter when the sound and name are given orally. They will apply their knowledge by recognizing the **initial** sound of the target letter using pictures.

State Learning Goal

Today we will practice matching the sound and letter **n**. Display letter card **n**. **Say:** This is capital **N**. This is lowercase **n**.

Teach

Letters represent sounds. We remember the sounds each letter makes. We use letters to write words we say. We use letters to read and write words.

Phonemic Awareness

Show picture of sound/spelling card to review the sound. This is the **n** card.

Say: Listen to this sound /**n**/. Say it with me: **n**. Now say it on your own: **n**.

Sound-Spelling Correspondence

Show the letters.

Say: *The way we write the sound* /**n**/ **is** *with the letter* **n.**

Say: *The letter* **n** *makes the sound* /**n**/.

Say: *What is the name of the letter?* **N** *What sound does the letter make?* /**n**/

Model

Use BLM 76, Row 1

Say: *We will look at each picture. Say its name. If we hear the sound of* /**n**/ *at the beginning of the word, we will circle the picture. If we do not hear the sound* /**n**/ *at the beginning, we cross out the picture.*

Say: *What do you see in the picture?* **nail** *Do you hear the sound* /**n**/ *at the beginning of the word* **nail**? *Circle the picture* **nail**. *If you do not hear the sound* /**n**/ *at the beginning of the word, then cross out the picture.*

Practice

Use BLM 76, Row 2

Say: Look *at the picture.* **Say** *its name. Write the letter.* **Say:** *What do you see in the picture?* **noon** *Do you hear the sound /**n**/ at the beginning of the word* **noon?** **Write** *the letter* **n.**

Apply
Blend Words
Use BLM 76, Row 3

Say: *Look at each letter and listen to the sound as I read: /**n**/ /e/ /a/ /**t**/. Your turn: /**n**/ /e/ /a/ /**t**/.*

Say: *Now we are going to blend the sounds together by stretching them out as we read them.* Point to each letter in a sweeping motion left to right: /**n**/eee/**ttt**/. *What is the word?* **neat**

Spelling

Use BLM 76, Row 4

Say: *Now we can practice writing the sounds we hear in each word. Call one word at a time, stretching each sound. Say the word slowly; write a letter for each sound you hear.*

Conclusion

Ask: *What did we learn today?* We taught the letter **n** makes the sound /**n**/. We wrote words using the letter n. What pictures/words will help you remember the sound /**n**/ and the letter **n**?

Home Connection

Ask students to practice identifying initial sound **n** and writing the letter **n** with a family member. Have students identify other words that begin with letter **n** with their family.

✔ Formative Assessment

If the student completes each task correctly, proceed to the next skill in the sequence. If not, refer to suggested Intervention 2.

Did the student…?	Intervention 2
Identify the name of the letter??	• Use physical rhythmic movements as the letter name is repeated. March while chanting the letter name. Move arms up and down. Sway from side to side.
Identify the sound of the letter?	• Use alliteration, chants that repeat the sound several times then a word that begins with the sound. Example: /**n**/ /i/ /p/ **nip**
Produce the sound of the letter?	• Use mirrors to show movement of mouth, tongue, and teeth as the sound is produced. Use hand over mouth to explore movement of air as the sound is produced.
Recognize the beginning sound?	• Use Elkonin boxes – student moves a token into first box as the beginning sound of the word is said.
Write the letter?	• Write the letter, have students trace it. Create letter with clay. • Discuss letter features (lines, shape). Trace over letter with multiple colors.
Know the name of pictures?	• Tell students the name of pictures, have students repeat them aloud. • Discuss word and use each word in context.

Identify and Name Initial Consonant Ff RF.K.3a

CCSS: RF.K.3
Know and apply grade-level phonics and word analysis skills in decoding words both in isolation and in text
a. Demonstrate basic knowledge of one-to-one letter-sound correspondences by producing the primary sounds or many of the most frequent sounds for each consonant.

Lesson Objectives

- Identify and name the letter **Ff**
- Produce the sound of letter **Ff**
- Relate the sound /f/ to the letter
- Recognize initial sound **f** in words/pictures.

METACOGNITIVE STRATEGY
- Selective auditory attention

ACADEMIC LANGUAGE
- letter name, letter sound, initial sound

Additional Materials
Sound Spelling Card Ff
Blackline master 77

Pre-Assess
Student's ability to recognize the sound represented by the targeted letter of the alphabet and to identify the letter used to represent the corresponding sound.

Introduce

As students participate in this lesson, they identify the name and sound of the targeted letter, and identify the letter when the sound and name are given orally. They will apply their knowledge by recognizing the **initial** sound of the target letter using pictures.

State Learning Goal

Today we will practice matching the sound and letter **f**. Display letter card **f**. Say: This is capital **F**. This is lowercase **f**.

Teach

Letters represent sounds. We remember the sounds each letter makes. We use letters to write words we say. We use letters to read and write words.

Phonemic Awareness

Show picture of sound/spelling card to review the sound. This is the **Ff** card.

Say: Listen to this sound /f/. Say it with me: **f**. Now say it on your own: **f**.

Sound-Spelling Correspondence

Show the letter.

Say: *The way we write the sound /f/ is with the letter **f**.*

Say: *The letter **f** makes the sound /f/.*

Say: *What is the name of the letter?* **f** *What sound does the letter make?* /f /

Model

Use BLM 77, Row 1.

Say: *We will look at each picture. Say its name. If we hear the sound of /f/ at the beginning of the word, we will circle the picture. If we do not hear the sound /f/ at the beginning, we will cross out the picture.*

Say: *What do you see in the picture?* **feet**. *Do you hear the sound /f/ at the beginning of the word? Circle the picture. If you do not hear the sound /f/ at the beginning of the word, then cross out the picture.*

Practice

Use BLM 77, Row 2

Say: Look *at the picture.* **Say** *its name.* **Write** *the letter.* **Say:** *What do you see in the picture?* **fruit.** *Do you hear the sound* /f/ **at the beginning of the word f?** **Write** *the letter* **f.**

Apply—Blend Words

Use BLM 77, row 3

Say: *Look at each letter and listen to the sound as I read:* /f/ /o/ /o/ /t/. *Your turn:* /f/ /o/ /o/ /t/.

Say: *Now we are going to blend the sounds together by stretching them out as we read them.* Point to each letter in a sweeping motion left to right: /f/oooo/tttt/. *What is the word?* **foot.**

Spelling

Use BLM 77, row 4

Say: *Now we can practice writing the sounds we hear in each word. Call one word at a time, stretching each sound. Say the word slowly; write a letter for each sound you hear.*

Conclusion

Ask: *What did we learn today?* We taught the letter **f** makes the sound / **f** /. We wrote words using the letter **f**. What pictures/words will help you remember the sound / **f** / and the letter **f** ?

Home Connection

Ask students to practice identifying initial sound f and writing the letter **f** with a family member. Have students identify other words that begin with letter **f** with their family.

✔ Formative Assessment

If the student completes each task correctly, proceed to the next skill in the sequence. If not, refer to suggested Intervention 2.

Did the student…?	Intervention 2
Identify the name of the letter?	• Use physical rhythmic movements as the letter name is repeated. March while chanting the letter name. Move arms up and down. Sway from side to side.
Identify the sound of the letter?	• Use alliteration, chants that repeat the sound several times then a word that begins with the sound. Example: /f/ /f/ /f/ **feet.**
Produce the sound of the letter	• Use mirrors to show movement of mouth, tongue, and teeth as the sound is produced. Use hand over mouth to explore movement of air as the sound is produced.
Recognize the beginning sound?	• Use Elkonin boxes – student moves a token into first box as the beginning sound of the word is said.
Write the letter?	• Write the letter, have students trace it. Create letter with clay. • Discuss letter features (lines, shape). Trace over letter with multiple colors.
Know the name of pictures?	• Tell students the name of pictures, have students repeat them aloud. • Discuss word and use each word in context.

Identify and Name Initial Consonant Pp RF.K.3a

CCSS: RF.K.3
Know and apply grade-level phonics and word analysis skills in decoding words both in isolation and in text
a. Demonstrate basic knowledge of one-to-one letter-sound correspondences by producing the primary sounds or many of the most frequent sounds for each consonant.

Lesson Objectives

- Identify and name the letter **Pp.**
- Produce the sound of letter **Pp.**
- Relate the sound /**p**/ to the letter **p.**
- Recognize initial sound **p** in words/pictures.

METACOGNITIVE STRATEGY
- Selective auditory attention

ACADEMIC LANGUAGE
- letter name, letter sound, initial sound

Additional Materials
Sound Spelling Card Pp
Blackline master 78

Pre-Assess
Student's ability to recognize the sound represented by the targeted letter of the alphabet and to identify the letter used to represent the corresponding sound.

Introduce

As students participate in this lesson, they identify the name and sound of the targeted letter, and identify the letter when the sound and name are given orally. They will apply their knowledge by recognizing the **initial** sound of the target letter using pictures.

State Learning Goal
Today we will practice matching the sound and letter **p**. Display letter card **p**.

Say: This is capital **P**. This is lowercase **p**.

Teach

Letters represent sounds. We remember the sounds each letter makes. We use letters to write words we say. We use letters to read and write words.

Phonemic Awareness
Show picture of sound/spelling card to review the sound. This is the **p** card.

Say: Listen to this sound /**p**/. Say it with me: **p** Now say it on your own: **p**.

Sound-Spelling Correspondence
Show the letter.

Say: *The way we write the sound /***p***/ is with the letter p.*

Say: *The letter p makes the sound /***p***/.*

Say: *What is the name of the letter?* **p** *What sound does the letter make?* /**p**/.

Phonemic Awareness
Show picture of sound/spelling card **UI**.

Say: *Listen to this sound /***oo***/. Say it with me:* **oo**. *Say it on your own:* **oo**.

Say: *This is the sound of vowel team* **ui**. *It sounds like long* **u**. *Say it again /***oo***/.*

Sound-Spelling Correspondence
Write the word **bruise** on the board. Point out the vowel team **ui** in the word.

Say: *The vowel team* **ui** *makes the sound /***oo***/.*

Say: *Look at the word* **bruise**. *Does it have a vowel team* **ui**? *Point: The vowel team* **ui** *sounds like /***oo***/.*

Say: *Read it with me* **bruise**. *Repeat with the word* **cruise**.

Model

Use BLM 78, row 1.

Say: *We will look at each picture. Say its name. If we hear the sound of /**p**/ at the beginning of the word, we will circle the picture. If we do not hear the sound /**p**/ at the beginning, we cross out the picture.*

Say: *What do you see in the picture?* **pail** *Do you hear the sound /**p**/ at the beginning of the word? Circle the picture. If you do not hear the sound /**p**/ at the beginning of the word, then cross out the picture.*

Practice

Use BLM 78, Row 2.

Say: Look *at the picture.* **Say** *its name.* **Write** *the letter.* **Say:** *What do you see in the picture?* **plow** *Do you hear the sound /**p**/ at the beginning of the word plow?* **Write** *the letter* **p**.

Apply

Blend Words

Use BLM 78, Row 3

Say: *Look at each letter and listen to the sound as I read:* /**p**/ /**ee**/ /**k**/. *Your turn:* /**p**/ /**ee**/ /**k**/. **Say:** *Now we are going to blend the sounds together by stretching them out as we read them.* Point to each letter in a sweeping motion left to right: /**p/eee/kkk**/. *What is* **the word? peek.**

Spelling

Use BLM 6, Row 4.

Say: *Now we can practice writing the sounds we hear in each word. Call one word at a time, stretching each sound. Say the word slowly; write a letter for each sound you hear.*

Conclusion

Ask: *What did we learn today?* We taught the letter **p** makes the sound / **p** /. We wrote words using the letter **p**. What pictures/words will help you remember the sound / **p** / and the letter **p**?

Home Connection
Ask students to practice identifying initial sound p and writing the letter p with a family member. Have students identify other words that begin with letter p with their family.

Formative Assessment	
If the student completes each task correctly, proceed to the next skill in the sequence. If not, refer to the suggestion under Intervention 2.	

Did the student...?	Intervention 2
Identify the name of the letter?	• Use physical rhythmic movements as the letter name is repeated. March while chanting the letter name. Move arms up and down. Sway from side to side.
Identify the sound of the letter?	• Use alliteration, chants that repeat the sound several times then a word that begins with the sound. Example: /**p**/ /**p**/ /**p**/ **pail.**
Produce the sound of the letter?	• Use mirrors to show movement of mouth, tongue, and teeth as the sound is produced. Use hand over mouth to explore movement of air as the sound is produced.
Recognize the beginning sound?	• Use Elkonin boxes – student moves a token into first box as the beginning sound of the word is said.
Write the letter?	• Write the letter, have students trace it. Create letter with clay. • Discuss letter features (lines, shape). Trace over letter with multiple colors.
Know the name of pictures?	• Tell students the name of pictures, have students repeat them aloud. • Discuss word and use each word in context.

Identify and Name Initial Consonant Cc RF.K.3a

CCSS: RF.K.3.
Know and apply grade-level phonics and word analysis skills in decoding words both in isolation and in text
a. Demonstrate basic knowledge of one-to-one letter-sound correspondences by producing the primary sounds or many of the most frequent sounds for each consonant.

Lesson Objectives

- Identify and name the letter **Cc**.
- Produce the sound of letter **Cc**.
- Relate the sound /**k**/ to the letter **c**.
- Recognize initial sound **k** in words/pictures.

METACOGNITIVE STRATEGY
- Selective auditory attention

ACADEMIC LANGUAGE
- letter name, letter sound, initial sound

Additional Materials
Sound Spelling Card Cc
Blackline Master 79

Pre-Assess
Student's ability to recognize the sound represented by the targeted letter of the alphabet and to identify the letter used to represent the corresponding sound.

Introduce

As students participate in this lesson, they identify the name and sound of the targeted letter, and identify the letter when the sound and name are given orally. They will apply their knowledge by recognizing the **initial** sound of the target letter using pictures.

State Learning Goal

Today we will practice matching the sound and letter **c**. Display letter card **c**. **Say:** This is capital **C**. This is lowercase **c**.

Teach

Letters represent sounds. We remember the sounds each letter makes. We use letters to write words we say. We use letters to read and write words.

Phonemic Awareness

Show picture of sound/spelling card to review the sound. This is the c card.

Say: Listen to this sound /**k**/. Say it with me: /**k**/ Now say it on your own: /**k**/.

Sound-Spelling Correspondence

Show the letter.

Say: The way we write the sound /**k**/ is with the letter **c**.

Say: The letter c makes the sound /**k**/.

Say: What is the name of the letter? **c** What sound does the letter make? /**k**/

Model

Use BLM 79, Row 1

Say: *We will look at each picture. Say its name. If we hear the sound of /**k**/ at the beginning of the word, we will circle the picture. If we do not hear the sound /**k**/ at the beginning, we will cross out the picture.*

Say: *What do you see in the picture?* **coat** *Do you hear the sound /**k**/ at the beginning of the word? Circle the picture. If you do not hear the sound /**k**/ at the beginning of the word, then cross out the picture.*

Practice

Use BLM 79, row 2

Say: Look *at the picture.* **Say** *its name.* **Write** *the letter.*

Say: *What do you see in the picture?* **cloud** *Do you hear the sound* **/k/** *at the beginning of the word cloud?* **Write** *the letter* **c.**

Apply

Blend Words

Use BLM 79, Row 3.

Say: Look at each letter and listen to the sound as I read: **/k/ /o/ /o/ /k/.** Your turn: **/k/ /o/ /o/ /k/. Say:** Now we are going to blend the sounds together by stretching them out as we read them. Point to each letter in a sweeping motion left to right: **/k/oooo/kkk/.** What is the word? **cook**

Spelling

Use BLM 79, Row 4.

Say: *Now we can practice writing the sounds we hear in each word. Call one word at a time, stretching each sound. Say the word slowly; write a letter for each sound you hear.*

Conclusion

Ask: *What did we learn today?* We learned to identify and name the initial consonan the letter **c.** We wrote words usuing the letter **c**. What pictures/words will help you remember the sound **/k/** and the letter **c**?

Home Connection

Ask students to practice identifying initial sound k and writing the letter c with a family member. Have students identify other words that begin with letter c with their family.

✔ **Formative Assessment**

If the student completes each task correctly, proceed to the next skill in the sequence. If not, refer to suggested Intervention 2.

Did the student…?	Intervention 2
Identify the name of the letter?	• Use physical rhythmic movements as the letter name is repeated. March while chanting the letter name. Move arms up and down. Sway from side to side.
Identify the sound of the letter?	• Use alliteration, chants that repeat the sound several times then a word that begins with the sound. Example: **/c/ /c/ /c/coat**
Produce the sound of the letter?	• Use mirrors to show movement of mouth, tongue, and teeth as the sound is produced. Use hand over mouth to explore movement of air as the sound is produced.
Recognize the beginning sound?	• Use Elkonin boxes – student moves a token into first box as the beginning sound of the word is said.
Write the letter?	• Write the letter, have students trace it. Create letter with clay. • Discuss letter features (lines, shape). Trace over letter with multiple colors.
Know the name of pictures?	• Tell students the name of pictures, have students repeat them aloud. • Discuss word and use each word in context.

Identify and Name Initial Consonant Hh RF.K.3a

CCSS: RF.K.3
Know and apply grade-level phonics and word analysis skills in decoding words both in isolation and in text
a. Demonstrate basic knowledge of one-to-one letter-sound correspondences by producing the primary sounds or many of the most frequent sounds for each consonant.

Introduce

As students participate in this lesson, they identify the name and sound of the targeted letter, and identify the letter when the sound and name are given orally. They will apply their knowledge by recognizing the **initial** sound of the target letter using pictures.

State Learning Goal

Today we will practice matching the sound and letter **h**. Display letter card **h**.

Say: This is capital **H**. This is lowercase **h**.

Teach

Letters represent sounds. We remember the sounds each letter makes. We use letters to write words we say. We use letters to read and write words.

Phonemic Awareness

Show picture of sound/spelling card to review the sound. This is the **h** card.

Say: *Listen to this sound /h/. Say it with me: /h/ Now say it on your own: /h/.*

Sound-Spelling Correspondence

Show the letter.

Say: *The way we write the sound /h/ is with the letter **h**.*

Say: *The letter **h** makes the sound /h/.*

Say: *What is the name of the letter? **h** What sound does the letter make? /h/*

Model

Use BLM 80, Row 1.

Say: We will look at each picture. Say its name. If we hear the sound of **h** at the beginning of the word, we will circle the picture. If we do not hear the sound /h/ at the beginning, we cross out the picture.

Say: What do you see in the picture? **heel** Do you hear the sound /h/ at the beginning of the word? Circle the picture. If you do not hear the sound /h/ at the beginning of the word, then cross out the picture.

Lesson Objectives

- Identify and name the letter **Hh**.
- Produce the sound of letter **Hh**.
- Relate the sound / **h** / to the letter **h**.
- Recognize initial sound **h** in words/pictures.

METACOGNITIVE STRATEGY
- Selective auditory attention

ACADEMIC LANGUAGE
- letter name, letter sound, initial sound

Additional Materials
Sound Spelling Card Hh
Blackline Master 80

Pre-Assess
Student's ability to recognize the sound represented by the targeted letter of thealphabet and to identify the letter used to represent the corresponding sound.

Practice

Use BLM 80, Row 2.

Say: Look at the picture. **Say** its name. **Write** the letter. **Say:** *What do you see in the picture? hair Do you hear the sound /h/ at the beginning of the word hair? Write the letter h.*

Apply

Blend Words

Use BLM 38, row 3.

Say: Look at each letter and listen to the sound as I read: **/h/ /ow/ /s/.** Your turn:

/h/ /ow/ /s/ Say: Now we are going to blend the sounds together by stretching them out as we read them. Point to each letter in a sweeping motion left to right: **/h/oowww/sss/.** What is the word? **house.**

Spelling

Use BLM 38, row 4.

Say: *Now we can practice writing the sounds we hear in each word.*

Call one word at a time, stretching each sound.

Say: *Say the word slowly; write a letter for each sound you hear.*

Conclusion

Ask: *What did we learn today?* We taught the letter **h** makes the sound /h/. We wrote words using the letter **h**. What pictures/words will help you remember the sound /h/ and the letter **h**?

Home Connection

Ask students to practice identifying initial sound h and writing the letter h with a family member. Have students identify other words that begin with letter h with their family.

✔ Formative Assessment

If the student completes each task correctly, precede to the next skill in the sequence. If not, refer to suggested intervention 2.

Did the student...?	Intervention 2
Identify the name of the letter?	• Use physical rhythmic movements as the letter name is repeated. March while chanting the letter name. Move arms up and down. Sway from side to side.
Identify the sound of the letter?	• Use alliteration, chants that repeat the sound several times then a word that begins with the sound. Example: **/h/ /h/ /h/heel**
Produce the sound of the letter?	• Use mirrors to show movement of mouth, tongue, and teeth as the sound is produced. Use hand over mouth to explore movement of air as the sound is produced.
Recognize the beginning sound?	• Use Elkonin boxes – student moves a token into first box as the beginning sound of the word is said.
Write the letter?	• Write the letter, have students trace it. Create letter with clay. • Discuss letter features (lines, shape). Trace over letter with multiple colors.
Know name of pictures?	• Tell students the name of pictures, have students repeat them aloud. • Discuss word and use each word in context.

Identify and Name Initial Consonant Bb RF.K.3a

CCSS: RF.K.3
Know and apply grade-level phonics and word analysis skills in decoding words both in isolation and in text
a. Demonstrate basic knowledge of one-to-one letter-sound correspondences by producing the primary sounds or many of the most frequent sounds for each consonant.

Lesson Objectives

- Identify and name the letter **Bb**.
- Produce the sound of letter **Bb**.
- Relate the sound / b / to the letter **b**.
- Recognize initial sound **b** in words/pictures.

METACOGNITIVE STRATEGY
- Selective auditory attention

ACADEMIC LANGUAGE
- letter name, letter sound, initial sound

Additional Materials
Sound Spelling Card Bb
Blackline Master 81

Pre-Assess
Student's ability to recognize the sound represented by the targeted letter of thealphabet and to identify the letter used to represent the corresponding sound.

Introduce

As students participate in this lesson, they identify the name and sound of the targeted letter, and identify the letter when the sound and name are given orally. They will apply their knowledge by recognizing the **initial** sound of the target letter using pictures.

State Learning Goal

Today we will practice matching the sound and letter **b**. Display letter card **b**.

Say: This is capital **B**. This is lowercase **b**.

Teach

Letters represent sounds. We remember the sounds each letter makes. We use letters to write words we say. We use letters to read and write words.

Phonemic Awareness
Show picture of sound/spelling card to review the sound. This is the **b** card.

Say: *Listen to this sound /b /. Say it with me: b Now say it on your own: b.*

Sound-Spelling Correspondence
Show the letter.

Say: The way we write the sound /**b**/ is with the letter c.

Say: The letter c makes the sound /**b**/.

Say: What is the name of the letter? **b** What sound does the letter make? /**b**/

Model
Use BLM 81, Row 1.

Say: *We will look at each picture. Say its name. If we hear the sound of **b** at the beginning of the word, we will circle the picture. If we do not hear the sound /**b**/ at the beginning, we will cross out the picture.*

Say: What do you see in the first picture? **a book** Do you hear the sound /**b**/ at the beginning of the word? Circle the picture. If you do not hear the sound /**b**/ at the beginning of the word, then cross out the picture.

Practice

Use BLM 81, Row 2.

Say: *Look at the first picture.* **Say** *its name.* **Write** *the letter.*

Say: *What do you see in the picture?* **a beetle** *Do you hear the sound* **/b/** *at the beginning of the word* **beetle?** **Write** *the letter* **b.**

Apply
Blend Words

Use BLM 81, Row 3

Say: Look at each letter and listen to the sound as I read: **/b/ /ee/ /v/ /r/.** **Your turn: /b/ /ee/ /v/ /r/.**

Say: Now we are going to blend the sounds together by stretching them out as we read them. Point to each letter in a sweeping motion left to right **/b/eee/vvv/rrr/.** What is the word? **beaver.**

Spelling

Use BLM 81, Row 4.

Say: *Now we can practice writing the sounds we hear in each word. Call one word at a time, stretching each sound. Say the word slowly; write a letter for each sound you hear.*

Conclusion

Ask: *What did we learn today?* We taught the letter **b** makes the sound **/b/.** We wrote words using the letter **b.** What pictures/words will help you remember the sound **/b/** and the letter **b?**

Home Connection

Ask students to practice identifying initial sound **b** and writing the letter **b** with a family member. Have students identify other words that begin with letter **b** with their family.

✔ Formative Assessment

If the student completes each task correctly, proceed to the next skill in the sequence. If not, refer to suggested Intervention 2.

Did the student…?	Intervention 2
Identify the name of the letter?	• Use physical rhythmic movements as the letter name is repeated. March while chanting the letter name. Move arms up and down. Sway from side to side.
Identify the sound of the letter?	• Use alliteration, chants that repeat the sound several times then a word that begins with the sound. Example: /b/ /b/ /b/ book.
Produce the sound of the letter?	• Use mirrors to show movement of mouth, tongue, and teeth as the sound is produced. Use hand over mouth to explore movement of air as the sound is produced.
Recognize the **final** sound?	• Use Elkonin boxes – student moves a token into first box as the beginning sound of the word is said.
Write the letter?	• Write the letter, have students trace it. Create letter with clay. • Discuss letter features (lines, shape). Trace over letter with multiple colors.
Know name of pictures?	• Tell students the name of pictures, have students repeat them aloud. • Discuss word and use each word in context.

Identify and Name Initial Consonant Rr RF.K.3a

CCSS: RF.K.3
Know and apply grade-level phonics and word analysis skills in decoding words both in isolation and in text
a. Demonstrate basic knowledge of one-to-one letter-sound correspondences by producing the primary sounds or many of the most frequent sounds for each consonant.

Lesson Objectives

- Identify and name the letter **Rr**
- Produce the sound of letter **Rr**
- Relate the sound /r/ to the letter **r**
- Recognize initial sound **r** in words/pictures.

METACOGNITIVE STRATEGY
- Selective auditory attention

ACADEMIC LANGUAGE
- letter name, letter sound, initial sound

Additional Materials
Sound Spelling Card Rr
Blackline Master 82

Pre-Assess
Student's ability to recognize the sound represented by the targeted letter of the alphabet and to identify the letter used to represent the corresponding sound.

Introduce

As students participate in this lesson, they identify the name and sound of the targeted letter, and identify the letter when the sound and name are given orally. They will apply their knowledge by recognizing the initial sound of the target letter using pictures.

State Learning Goal

Today we will practice matching the sound and letter **r**. Display letter card **r**.

Say: *This is capital R. This is lowercase r.*

Teach

Letters represent sounds. We remember the sounds each letter makes. We use letters to write words we say. We use letters to read and write words.

Phonemic Awareness
Show picture of sound/spelling card to review the sound. This is the **r** card.

Say: Listen to this sound: /**r**/. Say it with me: /**r**/. Now say it on your own: /**r**/.

Sound-Spelling Correspondence
Show the letter.

Say: *The way we write the sound /r/ is with the letter r.*

Say: *The letter r makes the sound /r/.*

Say: *What is the name of the letter? r What sound does the letter make? /r/*

Model

Use BLM 82, Row 1.

Say: *We will look at each picture. Say its name. If we hear the sound of r at the beginning of the word, we will circle the picture. If we do not hear the sound /r/ at the beginning, we will cross out the picture.*

Say: *What do you see in the first picture? rain. Do you hear the sound /r/ at the beginning of the word rain? Circle the letter r. If you do not hear the sound /r/ at the beginning of the word, then cross out the letter r.*

Practice

Use BLM 82, Row 2.

Say: *Look at the first picture. Say its name. Write the letter.*

Say: *What do you see in the picture? roof. Do you hear the sound /r/ at the beginning of the word roof? Write the letter r.*

Apply
Blend Words

Use BLM 82, Row 3.

Say: *Look at each letter and listen to the sound as I read: /**r**/**a**/**m**/.*

Your turn: */r/a/m/.*

Say: *Now we are going to blend the sounds together by stretching them out as we read them. Point to each letter in a sweeping motion left to right: /rrr/aaa/mmm. What is the word? ram.*

Spelling

Use BLM 82, Row 4.

Say: *Now we can practice writing the sounds we hear in each word. Call one word at a time, stretching each sound. Say the word slowly; write a letter for each sound you hear.*

Conclusion

Ask: *What did we learn today?* We learned that the letter r makes the sound /**r**/. We wrote words using the letter **r**. What pictures/words will help you remember the sound /**r**/ and the letter **r**?

Home Connection

Ask students to practice identifying initial sound **r** and writing the letter **r** with a family member. Have students identify other words that begin with letter **r** with their family.

✔ Formative Assessment

If the student completes each task correctly, proceed to the next skill in the sequence. If not, refer to suggested Intervention 2.

Did the student…?	Intervention 2
Identify the name of the letter?	• Use physical rhythmic movements as the letter name is repeated. March while chanting the letter name. Move arms up and down. Sway from side to side.
Identify the sound of the letter?	• Use alliteration, chants that repeat the sound several times then a word that begins with the sound. Example: /**r**/ /**r**/ /**r**/ **rain**
Produce the sound of the letter?	• Use mirrors to show movement of mouth, tongue, and teeth as the sound is produced. Use hand over mouth to explore movement of air as the sound is produced.
Recognize the **final** sound?	• Use Elkonin boxes – student moves a token into first box as the beginning sound of the word is said.
Write the letter?	• Write the letter, have students trace it. Create letter with clay. • Discuss letter features (lines, shape). Trace over letter with multiple colors.
Know name of pictures?	• Tell students the name of pictures, have students repeat them aloud. • Discuss word and use each word in context.

Identify and Name Initial Consonant Gg RF.K.3a

CCSS: RF.K.3
Know and apply grade-level phonics and word analysis skills in decoding words both in isolation and in text
a. Demonstrate basic knowledge of one-to-one letter-sound correspondences by producing the primary sounds or many of the most frequent sounds for each consonant.

Lesson Objectives

- Identify and name the letter **Gg**
- Produce the sound of letter **Gg**
  Relate the sound /**g**/ to the letter **g**
- Recognize initial sound **g** in words/pictures.

METACOGNITIVE STRATEGY
- Selective auditory attention

ACADEMIC LANGUAGE
- letter name, letter sound, initial sound

Additional Materials
Sound Spelling Card Gg
Blackline Master 83

Pre-Assess
Student's ability to recognize the sound represented by the targeted letter of the alphabet and to identify the letter used to represent the corresponding sound.

Introduce

As students participate in this lesson, they identify the name and sound of the targeted letter, and identify the letter when the sound and name is given orally. They will apply their knowledge by recognizing the initial sound of the target letter using pictures.

State Learning Goal

Today we will practice matching the sound and letter **g**. Display letter card **g**.

Say: This is capital **G**. This is lowercase **g**.

Teach

Letters represent sounds. We remember the sounds each letter makes. We use letters to write words we say. We use letters to read and write words.

Phonemic Awareness
Show picture of sound/spelling card to review the sound. This is the r card.

Say: Listen to this sound: /**g**/. Say it with me: /**g**/. Now say it on your own: /**g**/.

Sound-Spelling Correspondence
Show the letter.

Say: The way we write the sound /**g**/ is with the letter **g**.

Say: The letter **g** makes the sound /**g**/.

Say: What is the name of the letter? **g** What sound does the letter make? /**g**/

Model

Use BLM 83, Row 1.

Say: *We will look at each picture. Say its name. If we hear the sound of **g** at the beginning of the word, we will circle the picture. If we do not hear the sound /**g**/ at the beginning, we will cross out the picture.*

Say: *What do you see in the first picture? golf. Do you hear the sound /g/ at the beginning of the word golf? Circle the letter g. If you do not hear the sound /g/ at the beginning of the word, then cross out the letter g.*

Practice

Use BLM 83, Row 2.

Say: Look at the picture. **Say** its name. **Write** the letter.

Say: What do you see in the picture? **goat.** Do you hear the sound /g/ at the beginning of the word goat? **Write** the letter **g.**

Apply
Blend Words

Use BLM 83, Row 3.

Say: Look at each letter and listen to the sound as I read: **/gr/a/ss/.** Your turn: / gr/ /ss/.

Say: Now we are going to blend the sounds together by stretching them out as we read them. Point to each letter in a sweeping motion left to right. **/ggg/rrr/aaa/sss/sss/.** What is the word? **grass.**

Spelling

Use BLM 83, Row 4.

Say: *Now we can practice writing the sounds we hear in each word. Call one word at a time, stretching each sound. Say the word slowly; write a letter for each sound you hear.*

Conclusion

Ask: *What did we learn today?* We taught the letter **g** makes the sound /g/ We wrote words using the letter **g.** What pictures/words will help you remember the sound /g/ and the letter **g**?

✔ Formative Assessment

If the student completes each task correctly, proceed to the next skill in the sequence. If not, refer to suggested Intervention 2.

Did the student...?	Intervention 2
Identify the name of the letter?	• Use physical rhythmic movements as the letter name is repeated. March while chanting the letter name. Move arms up and down. Sway from side to side.
Identify the sound of the letter?	• Use alliteration, chants that repeat the sound several times then a word that begins with the sound. Example: /g/ /g/ /g/ **gear.**
Produce the sound of the letter?	• Use mirrors to show movement of mouth, tongue, and teeth as the sound is produced. Use hand over mouth to explore movement of air as the sound is produced.
Recognize the beginning sound?	• Use Elkonin boxes – student moves a token into first box as the beginning sound of the word is said.
Write the letter?	• Write the letter, have students trace it. Create letter with clay. • Discuss letter features (lines, shape). Trace over letter with multiple colors.
Know the name of pictures?	• Tell students the name of pictures, have students repeat them aloud. • Discuss word and use each word in context.

Identify and Name Initial Consonant Dd RF.K.3a

CCSS: RF.K.3
Know and apply grade-level phonics and word analysis skills in decoding words both in isolation and in text
a. Demonstrate basic knowledge of one-to-one letter-sound correspondences by producing the primary sounds or many of the most frequent sounds for each consonant.

Lesson Objectives

- Identify and name the letter **Dd**
- Produce the sound of letter **Dd**
  Relate the sound /**d**/ to the letter **d**
- Recognize initial sound d in words/pictures.

METACOGNITIVE STRATEGY
- Selective auditory attention

ACADEMIC LANGUAGE
- letter name, letter sound, initial sound

Additional Materials
Sound Spelling Card Dd
Blackline Master 84

Pre-Assess
Student's ability to recognize the sound represented by the targeted letter of the alphabet and to identify the letter used to represent the corresponding sound.

Introduce

As students participate in this lesson, they identify the name and sound of the targeted letter, and identify the letter when the sound and name is given orally. They will apply their knowledge by recognizing the **initial** sound of the target letter using pictures.

State Learning Goal

Today we will practice matching the sound and letter d. Display letter card d.

Say: This is capital **D**. This is lowercase **d**.

Teach

Letters represent sounds. We remember the sounds each letter makes. We use letters to write words we say. We use letters to read and write words.

Phonemic Awareness
Show picture of sound/spelling card to review the sound. This is the **d** card.

Say: Listen to this sound: /**d**/. Say it with me: /**d**/. Now say it on your own: /**d**/.

Sound-Spelling Correspondence
Show the letter.

Say: *The way we write the sound /**d**/ is with the letter **d**.*

Say: *The letter d makes the sound /**d**/.*

Say: *What is the name of the letter? **d** What sound does the letter make? /**d**/*

Model
Use BLM 84, Row 1.

Say: *We will look at each picture. Say its name. If we hear the sound of **d** at the beginning of the word, we will circle the picture. If we do not hear the sound /**d**/ at the beginning, we will cross out the picture.*

Say: *What do you see in the first picture? **drum**. Do you hear the sound /**d**/ at the beginning of the word **drum**? Circle the picture. If you do not hear the sound /**d**/ at the beginning of the word, then cross out the picture.*

Practice

Use BLM 84, Row 2.

Say: Look *at the second picture.* **Say** *its name.* **Write** *the letter.*

Say: *What do you see in the picture?* **desk** *Do you hear the sound* **/d/** *at the beginning of the word goat?* **Write** *the letter* **d.**

Apply
Blend Words

Use BLM 84, Row 3.

Say: *Look at each letter and listen to the sound as I read:* **/d/u/k/.** *Your turn:* **/d/uuu/kkk/.**

Say: *Now we are going to blend the sounds together by stretching them out as we read them.* Point to each letter in a sweeping motion left to right: **/ddd/uuu/ ccc/kkk/.** What is the word? **duck.**

Spelling

Use BLM 84, Row 4.

Say: *Now we can practice writing the sounds we hear in each word. Call one word at a time, stretching each sound. Say the word slowly; write a letter for each sound you hear.*

Conclusion

Ask: *What did we learn today? We learned that the letter d makes the sound /d/ We wrote words using the letter d. What pictures/words will help you remember the sound /d/ and the letter d?*

Home Connection

Ask students to practice identifying initial sound **d** and writing the letter **d** with a family member. Have students identify other words that begin with letter **d** with their family.

✔ Formative Assessment

If the student completes each task correctly, proceed to the next skill in the sequence. If not, refer to suggested Intervention 2.

Did the student…?	Intervention 2
Identify the name of the letter?	• Use physical rhythmic movements as the letter name is repeated. March while chanting the letter name. Move arms up and down. Sway from side to side.
Identify the sound of the letter?	• Use alliteration, chants that repeat the sound several times then a word that begins with the sound. Example: **/d/ /d/ /d/ drum**
Produce the sound of the letter?	• Use mirrors to show movement of mouth, tongue, and teeth as the sound is produced. Use hand over mouth to explore movement of air as the sound is produced.
Recognize the beginning sound?	• Use Elkonin boxes – student moves a token into first box as the beginning sound of the word is said.
Write the letter?	• Write the letter, have students trace it. Create letter with clay. • Discuss letter features (lines, shape). Trace over letter with multiple colors.
Know the name of pictures?	• Tell students the name of pictures, have students repeat them aloud. • Discuss word and use each word in context.

Identify and Name Initial Consonant Ww RF.K.3a

CCSS: RF.K.3
Know and apply grade-level phonics and word analysis skills in decoding words both in isolation and in text
a. Demonstrate basic knowledge of one-to-one letter-sound correspondences by producing the primary sounds or many of the most frequent sounds for each consonant.

Lesson Objectives

- Identify and name the letter **Ww**
- Produce the sound of letter **Ww**
  Relate the sound /**w**/ to the letter **w**
- Recognize initial sound **w** in words/ pictures.

METACOGNITIVE STRATEGY
- Selective auditory attention

ACADEMIC LANGUAGE
- letter name, letter sound, initial sound

Additional Materials
Sound Spelling Card Ww
Blackline Master 85

Pre-Assess
Student's ability to recognize the sound represented by the targeted letter of thealphabet and to identify the letter used to represent the corresponding sound.

Introduce

As students participate in this lesson, they identify the name and sound of sound of the targeted letter, and identify the letter when the sound and name are given orally. They will apply their knowledge by recognizing the **initial** sound of the target letter using pictures.

State Learning Goal

Today we will practice matching the sound and letter **w**. Display letter card **w**.

Say: This is capital **W**. This is lowercase **w**

Teach

Letters represent sounds. We remember the sounds each letter makes. We use letters to write words we say. We use letters to read and write words.

Phonemic Awareness
Show picture of sound/spelling card to review the sound. This is the **w** card.

Say: *Listen to this sound: /w/. Say it with me: /w/. Now say it on your own: /w/.*

Sound-Spelling Correspondence

Show the letter.
Say: *The way we write the sound /w/ is with the letter **w**.*

Say: *The letter **w** makes the sound /w/.*

Say: *What is the name of the letter? **w** What sound does the letter make? /w/*

Model

Use BLM 85, Row 1.

Say: *We will look at each picture. Say its name. If we hear the sound of **w** at the beginning of the word, we will circle the picture. If we do not hear the sound /w/ at the beginning, we will cross out the picture.*

Say: *What do you see in the first picture? **wind.** Do you hear the sound /w/ at the beginning of the word **wind**? Circle the picture. If you do not hear the sound /w/ at the beginning of the word, then cross out the picture.*

Practice

Use BLM 85, Row 2.

Say: Look *at the second picture.* **Say** *its name.* **Write** *the letter.* **Say:** *What do you see in the picture?* **well.** *Do you hear the sound /***w***/ at the beginning of the word* **well?** **Write** *the letter* **w.**

Apply
Blend Words

Use BLM 85, Row 3.

Say: *Look at each letter and listen to the sound as I read:* **/w//a//s//h/.** *Your turn:* **/w//a//s//h/.** **Say:** *Now we are doing to blend the sounds together by stretching them out as we read them.* Point to each letter in a sweeping motion left to right: **/www/aaa/sh/.** *What is the word?* **wash**

Spelling

Use BLM 85, Row 4.

Say: *Now we can practice writing the sounds we hear in each word. Call one word at a time, stretching each sound. Say the word slowly; write a letter for each sound you hear.*

Conclusion

Ask: *What did we learn today? We learned that the letter* **w** *makes the sound /***w***/ We wrote words using the letter* **d.** *What pictures/words will help you remember the sound /***w***/ and the letter* **w***?*

Home Connection

Ask students to practice identifying initial sound **w** and writing the letter **w** with a family member. Have students identify other words that begin with letter **w** with their family.

✔ Formative Assessment

If the student completes each task correctly, proceed to the next skill in the sequence. If not, refer to suggested Intervention 2.

Did the student...?	Intervention 2
Identify the name of the letter?	• Use physical rhythmic movements as the letter name is repeated. March while chanting the letter name. Move arms up and down. Sway from side to side.
Identify the sound of the letter?	• Use alliteration, chants that repeat the sound several times then a word that begins with the sound. Example: /w/ /w/ /w/ **wind.**
Produce the sound of the letter?	• Use mirrors to show movement of mouth, tongue, and teeth as the sound is produced. Use hand over mouth to explore movement of air as the sound is produced.
Recognize the beginning sound?	• Use Elkonin boxes – student moves a token into first box as the beginning sound of the word is said.
Write the letter?	• Write the letter, have students trace it. Create letter with clay. • Discuss letter features (lines, shape). Trace over letter with multiple colors.
Know the name of pictures?	• Tell students the name of pictures, have students repeat them aloud. • Discuss word and use each word in context.

Identify and Name Initial Consonant Ll RF.K.3a

CCSS: RF.K.3
Know and apply grade-level phonics and word analysis skills in decoding words both in isolation and in text
a. Demonstrate basic knowledge of one-to-one letter-sound correspondences by producing the primary sounds or many of the most frequent sounds for each consonant.

Lesson Objectives

- Identify and name the letter **Ll**
- Produce the sound of letter **Ll**
- Relate the sound /l/ to the letter **l**
- Recognize initial sound l in words/pictures.

METACOGNITIVE STRATEGY
- Selective auditory attention

ACADEMIC LANGUAGE
- letter name, letter sound, initial sound

Additional Materials
Sound Spelling Card Ll
Blackline Master 86

Pre-Assess
Student's ability to recognize the sound represented by the targeted letter of the alphabet and to identify the letter used to represent the corresponding sound.

Introduce

As students participate in this lesson, they identify the name and sound of the targeted letter, and identify the letter when the sound and name are given orally. They will apply their knowledge by recognizing the **initial** sound of the target letter using pictures.

State Learning Goal

Today we will practice matching the sound and letter l. Display letter card **l**.

Say: This is capital **L**. This is lowercase **l**.

Teach

Letters represent sounds. We remember the sounds each letter makes. We use letters to write words we say. We use letters to read and write words.

Phonemic Awareness

Show picture of sound/spelling card to review the sound. This is the l card.

Say: Listen to this sound: /l/. Say it with me: /l/. Now say it on your own: /l/.

Sound-Spelling Correspondence

Show the letter.
Say: *The way we write the sound /l/ is with the letter* **l**.

Say: *The letter l makes the sound /l/.*

Say: *What is the name of the letter?* **l** *What sound does the letter make?* /l/

Model

Use BLM 85, Row 1.

Say: *We will look at each picture. Say its name. If we hear the sound of l at the beginning of the word, we will circle the picture. If we do not hear the sound /l/ at the beginning, we will cross out the picture.*

Say: *What do you see in the first picture?* **loop.** *Do you hear the sound /l/ at the beginning of the word* **loop***? Circle the picture. If you do not hear the sound /l/ at the beginning of the word, then cross out the picture.*

Practice

Use BLM 86, Row 2.

Say: **Look** *at the third picture.* **Say** *its name.* **Write** *the letter.* **Say:** *What do you see in the picture?* **laugh.** *Do you hear the sound /l/ at the beginning of the word laugh?* **Write** *the letter* **l.**

Apply
Blend Words

Use BLM 85, Row 3.

Say: *Look at each letter and listen to the sound as I read:* **/l/a/m/b/.** *Your turn:* **/l/a/m/b/.** **Say:** *Now we are going to blend the sounds together by stretching them out as we read them.* **Point** *to each letter in a sweeping motion left to right: /* **lll/aaa/mmm/.** *What is the word?* **lamb.**

Spelling

Use BLM 86, Row 4.

Say: *Now we can practice writing the sounds we hear in each word. Call one word at a time, stretching each sound. Say the word slowly; write a letter for each sound you hear.*

Conclusion

Ask: *What did we learn today?* We learned that the letter **l** makes the sound /l/. We wrote words using the letter **l.** What pictures/words will help you remember the sound /l/ and the letter **l?**

Home Connection

Ask students to practice identifying initial sound l and writing the letter **l** with a family member. Have students identify other words that begin with letter **l** with their family.

✔ Formative Assessment

If the student completes each task correctly, proceed to the next skill in the sequence. If not, refer to suggested Intervention 2.

Did the student...?	Intervention 2
Identify the name of the letter?	• Use physical rhythmic movements as the letter name is repeated. March while chanting the letter name. Move arms up and down. Sway from side to side.
Identify the sound of the letter?	• Use alliteration, chants that repeat the sound several times then a word that begins with the sound. Example: /l/ /l/ /l/ **loop**
Produce the sound of the letter?	• Use mirrors to show movement of mouth, tongue, and teeth as the sound is produced. Use hand over mouth to explore movement of air as the sound is produced.
Recognize the beginning sound?	• Use Elkonin boxes – student moves a token into first box as the beginning sound of the word is said.
Write the letter?	• Write the letter, have students trace it. Create letter with clay. • Discuss letter features (lines, shape). Trace over letter with multiple colors.
Know the name of pictures?	• Tell students the name of pictures, have students repeat them aloud. • Discuss word and use each word in context.

Identify and Name Initial Consonant Jj RF.K.3a

CCSS: RF.K.3
Know and apply grade-level phonics and word analysis skills in decoding words both in isolation and in text
a. Demonstrate basic knowledge of one-to-one letter-sound correspondences by producing the primary sounds or many of the most frequent sounds for each consonant.

Lesson Objectives

- Identify and name the letter **Jj.**
- Produce the sound of letter **Jj.**
- Relate the sound /**j**/ to the letter **Ij**
- Recognize initial sound /**j**/ in words/pictures.

METACOGNITIVE STRATEGY
- Selective auditory attention

ACADEMIC LANGUAGE
- letter name, letter sound, initial sound

Additional Materials
Sound Spelling Card Jj
Blackline Master 87

Pre-Assess
Student's ability to recognize the sound represented by the targeted letter of the alphabet and to identify the letter used to represent the corresponding sound.

Introduce

As students participate in this lesson, they identify the name and sound of the targeted letter, and identify the letter when the sound and name are given orally. They will apply their knowledge by recognizing the **initial** sound of the target letter using pictures.

State Learning Goal

Today we will practice matching the sound and letter J. Display letter card J.

Say: This is capital **J**. This is lowercase **j**.

Teach

Letters represent sounds. We remember the sounds each letter makes. We use letters to write words we say. We use letters to read and write words.

Phonemic Awareness
Show picture of sound/spelling card to review the sound. This is the j card.

Say: Listen to this sound /**j**/. Say it with me: **j**. Now say it on your own: **j**.

Sound-Spelling Correspondence
Show the letter.

Say: *The way we write the sound* /**j**/ *is with the letter* **j**.

Say: *The letter* **j** *makes the sound* /**j**/.

Say: *What is the name of the letter?* **j** *What sound does the letter make?* /**j**/

Model

Use BLM 87, Row 1.

Say: *We will look at each picture. Say its name. If we hear the sound of j at the beginning of the word, we will circle the picture. If we do not hear the sound* /**j**/ *at the beginning, we will cross out the picture.*

Say: *What do you see in the first picture? jail. Do you hear the sound* /**j**/ *at the beginning of the word jail? Circle the picture of the jail. If you do not hear the sound* /**j**/ *at the beginning of the word, then cross out the picture.*

Practice

Use BLM 87, Row 2.

Say: Look *at the picture.* **Say** *its name.* **Write** *the letter.*
Say: *What do you see in the second picture?* **jeans.** *Do you hear the sound* /ĭ/ *at the beginning of the word* **jeans? Write** *the letter* **j.**

Apply
Blend Words

Use BLM 87, Row 3.

Say: *Look at each letter and listen to the sound as I read:* /ĭ/ /a/ /r/. *Your turn:* /ĭ/ /a/ /r/.
Say: *Now we are going to blend the sounds together by stretching them out as we read them.* Point to each letter in a sweeping motion left to right: /ĭ/aaa/rrr/. *What is the word?* **jar.**

Spelling

Use BLM 87, Row 4.

Say: *Now we can practice writing the sounds we hear in each word. Call one word at a time, stretching each sound. Say the word slowly; write a letter for each sound you hear.*

Conclusion

Ask: *What did we learn today?* We taught the letter **j** makes the sound /ĭ/. We wrote words using the letter **j.** What pictures/words will help you remember the sound /ĭ/ and the letter **j**?

Home Connection

Ask students to practice identifying initial sound /ĭ/ and writing the letter j with a family member. Have students identify other words that begin with letter **j** with their family.

✓ Formative Assessment

If the student completes each task correctly, proceed to the next skill in the sequence. If not, refer to suggested Intervention 2.

Did the student…?	Intervention 2
Identify the name of the letter?	• Use physical rhythmic movements as the letter name is repeated. March while chanting the letter name. Move arms up and down. Sway from side to side.
Identify the sound of the letter?	• Use alliteration, chants that repeat the sound several times then a word that begins with the sound. **Example:** /ĭ/ /ĭ/ /ĭ/ **jab.**
Produce the sound of the letter?	• Use mirrors to show movement of mouth, tongue, and teeth as the sound is produced. Use hand over mouth to explore movement of air as the sound is produced.
Recognize the beginning sound?	• Use Elkonin boxes – student moves a token into first box as the beginning sound of the word is said.
Write the letter?	• Write the letter, have students trace it. Create letter with clay. • Discuss letter features (lines, shape). Trace over letter with multiple colors.
Know the name of pictures?	• Tell students the name of pictures, have students repeat them aloud. • Discuss word and use each word in context.

Identify and Name Initial Consonant Kk RF.K.3a

CCSS: RF.K.3
Know and apply grade-level phonics and word analysis skills in decoding words both in isolation and in text
a. Demonstrate basic knowledge of one-to-one letter-sound correspondences by producing the primary sounds or many of the most frequent sounds for each consonant.

Lesson Objectives

- Identify and name the letter **Kk**
- Produce the sound of letter **Kk.**
- Relate the sound /**k**/ to the letter **k**
- Recognize initial sound /**k**/ in words/pictures.

METACOGNITIVE STRATEGY
- Selective auditory attention

ACADEMIC LANGUAGE
- letter name, letter sound, initial sound

Additional Materials
Sound Spelling Card Kk
Blackline Master 88

Pre-Assess
Student's ability to recognize the sound represented by the targeted letter of the alphabet and to identify the letter used to represent the corresponding sound.

Introduce

As students participate in this lesson, they identify the name and sound of the targeted letter, and identify the letter when the sound and name are given orally. They will apply their knowledge by recognizing the **initial** sound of the target letter using pictures.

State Learning Goal

Today we will practice matching the sound and letter k. Display letter k.

Say: This is capital **K**. This is lowercase **k**.

Teach

Letters represent sounds. We remember the sounds each letter makes. We use letters to write words we say. We use letters to read and write words. .

Phonemic Awareness
Show picture of sound/spelling card to review the sound. This is the k card.

Say: *Listen to this sound* /**k**/. *Say it with me:* **k**. *Now say it on your own:* **k**.

Sound-Spelling Correspondence
Show the letter.

Say: *The way we write the sound* /**k**/ *is with the letter* **k**.

Say: *The letter k makes the sound* /**k**/.

Say: *What is the name of the letter?* **k**. *What sound does the letter make?* /**k**/

Model

Use BLM 88, Row 1.

Say: *We will look at each picture. Say its name. If we hear the sound of k at the beginning of the word, we will circle the picture. If we do not hear the sound* /**k**/ *at the beginning, we will cross out the picture.*

Say: *What do you see in the first picture? A* **kilt**. *Do you hear the sound* /**k**/ *at the beginning of the word* **kilt**? *Circle the picture of the* **kilt**. *If you do not hear the sound* /**k**/ *at the beginning of the word, then cross out the picture.*

Practice

Use BLM 88, Row 2.

Say: Look at the picture. **Say** its name. **Write** the letter.
Say: What do you see in the second picture? **koala.** Do you hear the sound /k/ at the beginning of the word **koala? Write** the letter **k.**

Apply
Blend Words

Use BLM 88, Row 3.

Say: Look at each letter and listen to the sound as I read: /k/ /i/ /t/. Your turn: /k/ /i/ /t/. **Say:** Now we are going to blend the sounds together by stretching them out as we read them. Point to each letter in a sweeping motion left to right /k/iii/ tttt/. What is the word? **kite**

Spelling

Use BLM 88, Row 4.

Say: Now we can practice writing the sounds we hear in each word. Call one word at a time, stretching each sound. Say the word slowly; write a letter for each sound you hear.

Conclusion

Ask: What did we learn today? We taught the letter k makes the sound /k/. We wrote words using the letter k. What pictures/words will help you remember the sound /**k**/ and the letter **k**?

Home Connection

Ask students to practice identifying initial sound /k/ and writing the letter **k** with a family member. Have students identify other words that begin with letter **k** with their family.

✔ Formative Assessment

If the student completes each task correctly, proceed to the next skill in the sequence. If not, refer to suggested Intervention 2.

Did the student...?	Intervention 2
Identify the name of the letter?	• Use physical rhythmic movements as the letter name is repeated. March while chanting the letter name. Move arms up and down. Sway from side to side.
Identify the sound of the letter?	• Use alliteration, chants that repeat the sound several times then a word that begins with the sound. Example: /k/ /k/ /k/ kit
Produce the sound of the letter?	• Use mirrors to show movement of mouth, tongue, and teeth as the sound is produced. Use hand over mouth to explore movement of air as the sound is produced.
Recognize the beginning sound?	• Use Elkonin boxes – student moves a token into first box as the beginning sound of the word is said.
Write the letter?	• Write the letter, have students trace it. Create letter with clay. • Discuss letter features (lines, shape). Trace over letter with multiple colors.
Know name of pictures?	• Tell students the name of pictures, have students repeat them aloud. • Discuss word and use each word in context.

Identify and Name Initial Consonant Yy RF.K.3a

CCSS: RF.K.3
Know and apply grade-level phonics and word analysis skills in decoding words both in isolation and in text
a. Demonstrate basic knowledge of one-to-one letter-sound correspondences by producing the primary sounds or many of the most frequent sounds for each consonant.

Lesson Objectives

- Identify and name the letter **Yy**.
- Produce the sound of letter **Yy**.
- Relate the sounds /y/ to the letter **y**.
- Recognize initial sound /y/ in words/pictures.

METACOGNITIVE STRATEGY
- Selective auditory attention

ACADEMIC LANGUAGE
- letter name, letter sound, initial sound

Additional Materials
Sound Spelling Card Yy
Blackline Master 89

Pre-Assess
Student's ability to recognize the sound represented by the targeted letter of the alphabet and to identify the letter used to represent the corresponding sound.

Introduce

As students participate in this lesson, they identify the name and sound of the targeted letter, and identify the letter when the sound and name are given orally. They will apply their knowledge by recognizing the **initial** sound of the target letter using pictures.

State Learning Goal

Today we will practice matching the sound and letter **Y**. Display letter card **Y**.

Say: This is capital **Y**. This is lowercase **y**.

Teach

Letters represent sounds. We remember the sounds each letter makes. We use letters to write words we say. We use letters to read and write words.

Phonemic Awareness

Show picture of sound/spelling card to review the sound. This is the **y** card.
Say: *Listen to this sound /y/. Say it with me:* **y**. *Now say it on your own:* **y**.

Sound-Spelling Correspondence

Show the letter.

Say: *The way we write the sound /y/ is with the letter* **y**.

Say: *The letter* **y** *makes the sound /y/.*

Say: *What is the name of the letter?* **y**. *What sound does the letter make?* /y/

Model

Use BLM 89, # 1.

Say: *We will look at each picture. Say its name. If we hear the sound of y at the beginning of the word, we will circle the picture. If we do not hear the sound /y/ at the beginning, we will cross out the picture.*

Say: *What do you see in the first picture?* **Year.** *Do you hear the sound /y/ at the beginning of the word* **year**? *Circle the picture. If you do not hear the sound /y/ at the beginning of the word, then cross out the picture.*

Practice

Use BLM 89, # 2.

Say: Look *at the second picture.* **Say** *its name.* **Write** *the letter.*

Say: *What do you see in the second picture? A* **yolk.** *Do you hear the sound /y/ at the beginning of the word* **yolk?** **Write t***he letter* **y.**

Apply
Blend Words

Use BLM 89, # 3.

Say: *Look at each letter and listen to the sound as I read: /y/ /a/ /w/ /n/. Your turn: /y/ /a/ /w/ /n/.* **Say:** *Now we are going to blend the sounds together by stretching them out as we read them.* **Point to each letter in a sweeping motion** left to right: **/y/aaa/www/nnn/.** *What is the word?* **yawn.**

Spelling

Use BLM 89, #4.

Say: *Now we can practice writing the sounds we hear in each word. Call one word at a time, stretching each sound. Say the word slowly; write a letter for each sound you hear.*

Conclusion

Ask: *What did we learn today?* We taught the letter **y** makes the sound /y/. We wrote words using the letter **y**. What pictures/words will help you remember the sound /y/ and the letter **y**?

Home Connection

Ask students to practice identifying initial sound /y/ and writing the letter y with a family member. Have students identify other words that begin with letter **y** with their family.

✔ Formative Assessment

If the student completes each task correctly, proceed to the next skill in the sequence. If not, refer to suggested Intervention 2.

Did the student…?	Intervention 2
Identify the name of the letter?	• Use physical rhythmic movements as the letter name is repeated. March while chanting the letter name. Move arms up and down. Sway from side to side.
Identify the sound of the letter?	• Use alliteration, chants that repeat the sound several times then a word that begins with the sound. **Example:** /y/ /y/ /y/ **yet**
Produce the sound of the letter?	• Use mirrors to show movement of mouth, tongue, and teeth as the sound is produced. Use hand over mouth to explore movement of air as the sound is produced.
Recognize the beginning sound?	• Use Elkonin boxes – student moves a token into first box as the beginning sound of the word is said.
Write the letter?	• Write the letter, have students trace it. Create letter with clay. • Discuss letter features (lines, shape). Trace over letter with multiple colors.
Know the name of pictures?	• Tell students the name of pictures, have students repeat them aloud. • Discuss word and use each word in context.

Identify and Name Initial Consonant Vv RF.K.3a

Introduce

As students participate in this lesson, they identify the name and sound of the targeted letter, and identify the letter when the sound and name are given orally. They will apply their knowledge by recognizing the **initial** sound of the target letter using pictures.

State Learning Goal

Today we will practice matching the sound and letter **v**. Display letter card **v**.

Say: *This is capital* **V**. *This is lowercase* **v**

Teach

Letters represent sounds. We remember the sounds each letter makes. We use letters to write words we say. We use letters to read and write words.

Phonemic Awareness

Show picture of sound/spelling card to review the sound. This is the v card.
Say: Listen to this sound /**v**/. Say it with me: **v**. Now say it on your own: **v**.

Sound-Spelling Correspondence

Show the letter.

Say: *The way we write the sound* /**v**/ *is with the letter* **v**.

Say: *The letter* **v** *makes the sound* /**v**/.

Say: *What is the name of the letter?* **v**. *What sound does the letter make?* /**v**/

Model

Use BLM 90, # 1.

Say: *We will look at each picture. Say its name. If we hear the sound of* **v** *at the beginning of the word, we will circle the picture. If we do not hear the sound* /**v**/ *at the beginning, we will cross out the picture.*

Say: *What do you see in the first picture?* **view**. *Do you hear the sound* /**v**/ *at the beginning of the word* **view**? *Circle the picture of* **view**. *If you do not hear the sound* /**v**/ *at the beginning of the word, then cross out the picture.*

CCSS: RF.K.3
Know and apply grade-level phonics and word analysis skills in decoding words both in isolation and in text
a. Demonstrate basic knowledge of one-to-one letter-sound correspondences by producing the primary sounds or many of the most frequent sounds for each consonant.

Lesson Objectives

- Identify and name the letter **Vv.**
- Produce the sound of letter **Vv.**
- Relate the sounds /**v**/ to the letter **v**.
- Recognize initial sound /**v**/ in words/pictures.

METACOGNITIVE STRATEGY
- Selective auditory attention

ACADEMIC LANGUAGE
- letter name, letter sound, initial sound

Additional Materials
Sound Spelling Card Vv
Blackline Master 90

Pre-Assess
Student's ability to recognize the sound represented by the targeted letter of thealphabet and to identify the letter used to represent the corresponding sound.

Practice
Use BLM 90, # 2

Say: Look *at the second picture.* **Say** *its name.* **Write** *the letter.*

Say: *What do you see in the picture?* **vine.** *Do you hear the sound /v/ at the beginning of the word* **vine? Write** *the letter* **v.**

Apply
Blend Words
Use BLM 90, # 3.

Say: *Look at each letter and listen to the sound as I read: /v/ /ai/ /l/. Your turn: /v/ /ai/ /l/.* **Say:** *Now we are going to blend the sounds together by stretching them out as we read them.* Point to each letter in a sweeping motion left to right: */v/aaa/lll/. What is the word?* **veil.**

Spelling
Use BLM 90, #4.

Say: *Now we can practice writing the sounds we hear in each word. Call one word at a time, stretching each sound. Say the word slowly; write a letter for each sound you hear.*

Conclusion
Ask: *What did we learn today?* We taught the letter v makes the sound /v/. We wrote words using the letter **v.** What pictures/words will help you remember the sound /v/ and the letter **v**?

Home Connection
Ask students to practice identifying initial sound /v/ and writing the letter **v** with a family member. Have students identify other words that begin with letter **v** with their family.

✔ Formative Assessment

If the student completes each task correctly, proceed to the next skill in the sequence. If not, refer to suggested Intervention 2.

Did the student…?	Intervention 2
Identify the name of the letter?	• Use physical rhythmic movements as the letter name is repeated. March while chanting the letter name. Move arms up and down. Sway from side to side.
Identify the sound of the letter?	• Use alliteration, chants that repeat the sound several times then a word that begins with the sound. **Example:** /v/ /v/ /v/ **vet.**
Produce the sound of the letter?	• Use mirrors to show movement of mouth, tongue, and teeth as the sound is produced. Use hand over mouth to explore movement of air as the sound is produced.
Recognize the beginning sound?	• Use Elkonin boxes – student moves a token into first box as the beginning sound of the word is said.
Write the letter?	• Write the letter, have students trace it. Create letter with clay. • Discuss letter features (lines, shape). Trace over letter with multiple colors.
Know the name of pictures?	• Tell students the name of pictures, have students repeat them aloud. • Discuss word and use each word in context.

Identify and Name Initial Consonant Qq RF.K.3a

CCSS: RF.K.3
Know and apply grade-level phonics and word analysis skills in decoding words both in isolation and in text
a. Demonstrate basic knowledge of one-to-one letter-sound correspondences by producing the primary sounds or many of the most frequent sounds for each consonant.

Lesson Objectives

- Identify and name the letter **Qq**.
- Produce the sound of letter **Qq**.
- Relate the sounds /**kw**/ to the letter **q**.
- Recognize initial sounds /**kw**/ in words/pictures.

METACOGNITIVE STRATEGY
- Selective auditory attention

ACADEMIC LANGUAGE
- letter name, letter sound, initial sound

Additional Materials
Sound Spelling Card Qq
Blackline Master 91

Pre-Assess
Student's ability to recognize the sound represented by the targeted letter of the alphabet and to identify the letter used to represent the corresponding sound.

Introduce

As students participate in this lesson, they identify the name and sound of the targeted letter, and identify the letter when the sound and name are given orally. They will apply their knowledge by recognizing the initial sound of the target letter using pictures.

State Learning Goal

Today we will practice matching the sound and letter **Q**. Display letter card **Q**. **Say:** This is capital **Q**. This is lowercase **q**.

Teach

Letters represent sounds. We remember the sounds each letter makes. We use letters to write words we say. We use letters to read and write words.

Phonemic Awareness

Show picture of sound/spelling card to review the sound. This is the q card. **Say:** Listen to this sound /**kw**/. Say it with me: /**kw**/. Now say it on your own: /**kw**/.

Sound-Spelling Correspondence

Show the letter.
Say: *The way we write the sound /**kw**/ is with the letter **q**.*

Say: *The letter q makes the sound /**kw**/.*

Say: *What is the name of the letter?* **q**. *What sound does the letter make?* /**kw**/

Model

Use BLM 91, # 1.

Say: *We will look at each picture. Say its name. If we hear the sound of **q** at the beginning of the word, we will circle the picture. If we do not hear the sound /**kw**/ at the beginning, we will cross out the picture.*

Say: *What do you see in the first picture?* **quail**. *Do you hear the sound /**kw**/ at the beginning of the word quail? Circle the picture of the quail. If you do not hear the sound /**kw**/ at the beginning of the word, then cross out the picture*

Practice

Use BLM 91, # 2.

Say: Look at the second picture. **Say** its name. **Write** the letter.
Say: What do you see in the picture? **Quarter.** Do you hear the sound /**kw**/ at the beginning of the word **quarter? Write** the letter **q.**

Apply

Blend Words

Use BLM 91, # 3.

Say: Look at each letter and listen to the sound as I read: /**kw**/ /**i**/ /**e**/ /**t**/. **Your turn: /kw/ /i/ /e/ /t/. Say:** Now we are going to blend the sounds together by stretching them out as we read them. Point to each letter in a sweeping motion left to right: /**kw**/ /**iii**/ /**eee**/ /**ttt**/. What is the word? **Quiet.**

Spelling

Use BLM 91, #4.

Say: Now we can practice writing the sounds we hear in each word. Call one word at a time, stretching each sound. Say the word slowly; write a letter for each sound you hear.

Conclusion

Ask: What did we learn today? We taught the letter q makes the sound /**kw**/. We wrote words using the letter q. What pictures/words will help you remember the sound /**kw**/ and the letter **q**?

✓ Formative Assessment

If the student completes each task correctly, proceed to the next skill in the sequence. If not, refer to suggested Intervention 2.

Did the student…?	Intervention 2
Identify the name of the letter?	• Use physical rhythmic movements as the letter name is repeated. March while chanting the letter name. Move arms up and down. Sway from side to side.
Identify the sound of the letter?	• Use alliteration, chants that repeat the sound several times then a word that begins with the sound. **Example: /q/ /q/ /q/ quite**
Produce the sound of the letter?	• Use mirrors to show movement of mouth, tongue, and teeth as the sound is produced. Use hand over mouth to explore movement of air as the sound is produced.
Recognize the beginning sound?	• Use Elkonin boxes – student moves a token into first box as the beginning sound of the word is said.
Write the letter?	• Write the letter, have students trace it. Create letter with clay. • Discuss letter features (lines, shape). Trace over letter with multiple colors.
Know the name of pictures?	• Tell students the name of pictures, have students repeat them aloud. • Discuss word and use each word in context.

Identify and Name Initial Consonant Zz RF.K.3a

CCSS: RF.K.3
Know and apply grade-level phonics and word analysis skills in decoding words both in isolation and in text
a. Demonstrate basic knowledge of one-to-one letter-sound correspondences by producing the primary sounds or many of the most frequent sounds for each consonant.

.

Lesson Objectives

- Identify and name the letter **Zz**.
- Produce the sound of letter **Zz**.
- Relate the sounds /**z**/ to the letter **z**.
- Recognize initial sound /**z**/ in words/pictures.

METACOGNITIVE STRATEGY
- Selective auditory attention

ACADEMIC LANGUAGE
- letter name, letter sound, initial sound

Additional Materials
Sound Spelling Card Z
Blackline Master 92

Pre-Assess
Student's ability to recognize the sound represented by the targeted letter of the alphabet and to identify the letter used to represent the corresponding sound.

Introduce

As students participate in this lesson, they identify the name and sound of the targeted letter, and identify the letter when the sound and name are given orally. They will apply their knowledge by recognizing the initial sound of the target letter using pictures.

State Learning Goal

Today we will practice matching the sound and letter **Z**. Display letter card **Z**.
Say: *This is capital Z. This is lowercase z.*

Teach

Letters represent sounds. We remember the sounds each letter makes. We use letters to write words we say. We use letters to read and write words.

Phonemic Awareness

Show picture of sound/spelling card to review the sound. This is the **z** card.
Say: *Listen to this sound /z/. Say it with me: /z/. Now say it on your own: /z/.*

Sound-Spelling Correspondence

Show the letter.
Say: *The way we write the sound /z/ is with the letter **z**.*

Say: *The letter z makes the sound /z/.*

Say: *What is the name of the letter?* **z**. *What sound does the letter make?* /z/

Model

Use BLM 92, # 1.

Say: *We will look at each picture. Say its name. If we hear the sound of **z** at the beginning of the word, we will circle the picture. If we do not hear the sound /z/ at the beginning, we will cross out the picture.*

Say: *What do you see in the first picture?* **zero**. *Do you hear the sound /z/ at the beginning of the word **zero**? Circle the picture showing the word zero. If you do not hear the sound /z/ at the beginning of the word, then cross out the picture.*

Practice

Use BLM 92, # 2.

Say: Look *at the first picture.* **Say** *its name.* **Write** *the letter.* **Say:** *What do you see in the picture?* **zebra.** *Do you hear the sound /z/ at the beginning of the word* **zebra? Write** *the letter* **z.**

Apply
Blend Words

Use BLM 92, # 3.

Say: *Look at each letter and listen to the sound as I read: /z/ /i/ /p/ /e/ /r/. Your turn: /z/ /i/ /p/ /e/ /r/.*

Say: *Now we are going to blend the sounds together by stretching them out as we read them.* Point to each letter in a sweeping motion left to right: /z/iii/ppp/ er/ *What is the word?* **zipper.**

Spelling

Use BLM 92, #4.

Say: *Now we can practice writing the sounds we hear in each word. Call one word at a time, stretching each sound. Say the word slowly; write a letter for each sound you hear*

Conclusion

Ask: *What did we learn today?* We taught the letter **z** makes the sound /z/. We wrote words using the letter **z**. *What pictures/words will help you remember the sound /z/ and the letter* **z?**

✔ Formative Assessment

If the student completes each task correctly, proceed to the next skill in the sequence. If not, refer to suggested Intervention 2.

Did the student...?	Intervention 2
Identify the name of the letter?	• Use physical rhythmic movements as the letter name is repeated. March while chanting the letter name. Move arms up and down. Sway from side to side.
Identify the sound of the letter?	• Use alliteration, chants that repeat the sound several times then a word that begins with the sound. Example: /z/ /z/ /z/ zing
Produce the sound of the letter?	• Use mirrors to show movement of mouth, tongue, and teeth as the sound is produced. Use hand over mouth to explore movement of air as the sound is produced.
Recognize the beginning sound?	• Use Elkonin boxes – student moves a token into first box as the beginning sound of the word is said.
Write the letter?	• Write the letter, have students trace it. Create letter with clay. • Discuss letter features (lines, shape). Trace over letter with multiple colors.
Know the name of pictures?	• Tell students the name of pictures, have students repeat them aloud. • Discuss word and use each word in context.

Identify and Name Final Consonant m RF.K.3a

CCSS: RF.K.3
Know and apply grade-level phonics and word analysis skills in decoding words both in isolation and in text
a. Demonstrate basic knowledge of one-to-one letter-sound correspondences by producing the primary sounds or many of the most frequent sounds for each consonant.

Lesson Objectives

- Identify and name the letter **m**
- Produce the sound of letter **m**
- Relate the sound /**m**/ to the letter **m**
- Recognize final sound **m** in words/pictures

METACOGNITIVE STRATEGY
- Selective auditory attention, imagery, auditory representation

ACADEMIC LANGUAGE
- letter name, letter sound, initial sound, final sound, ending sound

Additional Materials
Sound Spelling Card Mm
Blackline Master 93

Pre-Assess
Student's ability to recognize the sound represented by the targeted letter of the alphabet and to identify the letter used to represent the corresponding sound in final position.

Introduce

As students participate in this lesson, they identify the name and sound of the targeted letter, and identify the letter when the sound and name are given orally. Students will apply their knowledge by recognizing the **final**, or **ending**, sound of the target letter using pictures.

State Learning Goal

Today we will practice listening to the sound /**m**/ that the letter **m** makes at the **end** of words.

Teach

Letters represent sounds. We remember the sounds each letter makes. We use letters to write words we say. We use letters to read and write words.

Phonemic Awareness
Show picture of sound/spelling card to review the sound. **Say:** Listen to this sound /**m**/. Say it with me: **m**. Say it on your own: **m**.

Sound-Spelling Correspondence
Show the letter.
Say: *The way we write the sound. /**m**/ is with the letters **m**.*
Say: *The letters **m** make the sound /**m**/.*
Say: *What is the name of the letters? **m** What sound do the letters make? /**m**/*

Model
Use BLM 93, # 1.

Say: *We will look at each picture. Say its name. If we hear the sounds of m at the end of the word, we will circle the picture. If we do not hear the sound /m/ at the end, we cross out the picture.*

Say: *What do you see in the first picture? **team** Do you hear the sound /m/ at the end of the word **team**? Circle the picture. If you do not hear the sound /m/ at the end of the word, then cross out the picture.*

Practice

Use BLM 93, # 2.

Say: Look at the first picture. **Say** its name. **Write** the letter. **Say:** What is the picture? **steam.** Do you hear the sound /**m**/ at the end of the word steam? **Write** the letter **m.**

Apply

Blend Words

Use BLM 93, # 3.

Say: Look at each letter and listen to the sound as I read. /**s**/ /**w**/ /**ĭ**/ /**m**/. Your turn: /**s**/ /**w**/ /**ĭ**/ /**m**/.

Say: Now we are going to blend the sounds together by stretching them out as we read them. Point to each letter in a sweeping motion left to right: /**s**/**www**/**iii**/ **mmm**/. What is the word? **swim**.

Spelling

Use BLM 93, # 4.

Say: Now we can practice writing the sounds we hear in each word. Call one word at a time, stretching each sound. Say the word slowly; write a letter for each sound you hear.

Conclusion

Ask: What did we learn today? We learned that the letter **m** make the sound /**m**/. We wrote words using the letters **m** at the end. What pictures/words will help you remember the sound /**m**/ and the letter **m** at the end of a word?

Home Connection

Encourage students to practice identifying **final** sound /**m**/ and writing the letter m with a family member. Encourage students to identify other words that **end** with letter **m** with their family.

✔ Formative Assessment

If the student completes each task correctly, proceed to the next skill in the sequence. If not, refer to suggested Intervention 2.

Did the student…?	Intervention 2
Identify the name of the letter?	• Use physical rhythmic movements as the letter name is repeated. March while chanting the letter name. Move arms up and down. Sway from side to side.
Identify the sound of the letter?	• Say words with the target sound in final position, emphasizing the sound. **Example: bummmm**
Produce the sound of the letter?	• Use mirrors to show movement of mouth, tongue, teeth as the sound is produced. Use hand over mouth to explore movement of air as the sound is produced.
Recognize the beginning sound?	• Use Elkonin boxes – student moves a token into the last box as the **final** sound of the word is said.
Write the letter?	• Write the letter, have students trace it. Create the letter with clay. • Discuss letter features (lines, shape). Trace over the letter with multiple colors.
Know the name of pictures?	• Tell students the name of pictures, have students repeat them aloud. Discuss word and use each word in context.

Identify and Name Final Consonant t RF.K.3a

CCSS: RF.K.3
Know and apply grade-level phonics and word analysis skills in decoding words both in isolation and in text
a. Demonstrate basic knowledge of one-to-one letter-sound correspondences by producing the primary sounds or many of the most frequent sounds for each consonant.

Lesson Objectives

- Identify and name the letter **t**
- Produce the sound of letter **t**
- Relate the sound /**t**/ to the letter **t**
- Recognize final sound **t** in words/pictures

METACOGNITIVE STRATEGY
- Selective auditory attention, imagery, auditory representation

ACADEMIC LANGUAGE
- letter name, letter sound, initial sound, final sound, ending sound

Additional Materials
Sound Spelling Card Tt
Blackline Master 94

Pre-Assess
Student's ability to recognize the sound represented by the targeted letter of the alphabet and to identify the letter used to represent the corresponding sound in final position.

Introduce

As students participate in this lesson, they identify the name and sound of the targeted letter, and identify the letter when the sound and name are given orally. Students will apply their knowledge by recognizing the **final**, or **ending**, sound of the target letter using pictures.

State Learning Goal

Today we will practice listening to the sound /**t**/ that the letter **t** makes at the end of words.

Teach

Letters represent sounds. We remember the sounds each letter makes. We use letters to write words we say. We use letters to read and write words.

Phonemic Awareness

Show picture of sound/spelling card to review the sound. **Say:** Listen to this sound /**t**/. Say it with me: **t**. Say it on your own: **t**.

Sound-Spelling Correspondence

Show the letter.
Say: *The way we write the sound. /**t**/ is with the letter **t**.*

Say: *The letter **t** makes the sound /**t**/.*

Say: *What is the name of the letter?* **t** *What sound does the letter make?* /**t**/

Model

Use BLM 94, # 1.

Say: *We will look at each picture. Say its name. If we hear the sound of **t** at the end of the word, we will circle the picture. If we do not hear the sound /**t**/ at the end, we will cross out the picture.*

Say: *What do you see in the first picture?* **feet** *Do you hear the sound /**t**/ at the end of the word* **feet**? *Circle the letter **t**. If you do not hear the sound /**t**/ at the end of the word, then cross out the letter **t**.*

Practice

Use BLM 94, # 2.

Say: *Look at the first picture. Say its name. Write the letter.*

Say: *What is the picture? root Do you hear the sound /t/ at the end of the word root? Write the letter t.*

Apply
Blend Words

Use BLM 94, # 3.

Say: *Look at each letter and listen to the sound as I read.* / **c** / / **oa** / / **t**/. *Your turn:* /**c**/ / **oa** / / **t** /

Say: Now we are going to blend the sounds together by stretching them out as we read them. Point to each letter in a sweeping motion left to right: / **c** / **oooaaa** / **ttt** /. *What is the word?* **coat**

Spelling

Use BLM 94, # 4.

Say: *Now we can practice writing the sounds we hear in each word. Call one word at a time, stretching each sound. Say the word slowly; write a letter for each sound you hear.*

Conclusion

Ask: *What did we learn today?* We learned that the letter **t** makes the sound /**t**/. We wrote words using the letter **t** at the end. What pictures/words will help you remember the sound /**t**/ and the letter **t** at the end of a word?

Home Connection

Encourage students to practice identifying **final** sound /t/ and writing the letter t with a family member. Encourage students to identify other words that **end** with letter **t** with their family.

✔ Formative Assessment

If the student completes each task correctly, proceed to the next skill in the sequence. If not, refer to suggested Intervention 2.

Did the student…?	Intervention 2
Identify the name of the letter?	• Use physical rhythmic movements as the letter name is repeated. March while chanting the letter name. Move arms up and down. Sway from side to side.
Identify the sound of the letter?	• Say words with the target sound in final position by repeating the words three times. **Example: cat, cat, cat**
Produce the sound of the letter?	• Use mirrors to show movement of mouth, tongue, teeth as the sound is produced. Use hand over mouth to explore movement of air as the sound is produced.
Recognize the **final** sound?	• Use Elkonin boxes – student moves a token into the last box as the **final** sound of the word is said.
Write the letter?	• Write the letter, have students trace it. Create the letter with clay. • Discuss letter features (lines, shape). Trace over the letter with multiple colors.
Know the name of pictures?	• Tell students the name of pictures, have students repeat them aloud. Discuss word and use each word in context.

Identify and Name Final Consonant n RF.K.3a

CCSS: RF.K.3
Know and apply grade-level phonics and word analysis skills in decoding words both in isolation and in text
a. Demonstrate basic knowledge of one-to-one letter-sound correspondences by producing the primary sounds or many of the most frequent sounds for each consonant.

Lesson Objectives

- Identify and name the letter **n**
- Produce the sound of letter **n**
- Relate the sound /**n**/ to the letter **n**
- Recognize final sound **n** in words/ pictures

METACOGNITIVE STRATEGY
- Selective auditory attention, imagery, auditory representation

ACADEMIC LANGUAGE
- letter name, letter sound, initial sound, final sound, ending sound

Additional Materials
Sound Spelling Card Nn
Blackline Master 95

Pre-Assess
Student's ability to recognize the sound represented by the targeted letter of the alphabet and to identify the letter used to represent the corresponding sound in final position.

Introduce

As students participate in this lesson, they identify the name and sound of the targeted letter, and identify the letter when the sound and name are given orally. Students will apply their knowledge by recognizing the **final**, or **ending**, sound of the target letter using pictures.

State Learning Goal

Today we will practice listening to the sound /**n**/ that the letter **n** makes at the **end** of words.

Teach

Letters represent sounds. We remember the sounds each letter makes. We use letters to write words we say. We use letters to read and write words.

Phonemic Awareness

Show picture of sound/spelling card to review the sound.

Say: *Listen to this sound /**n**/. Say it with me:* **n**. *Say it on your own:* **n**.

Sound-Spelling Correspondence

Show the letter.
Say: *The way we write the sound. /**n**/ is with the letter* **n**.

Say: *The letter* **n** *makes the sound /**n**/.*

Say: *What is the name of the letter?* **n** *What sound does the letter make?* /**n**/

Model

Use BLM 95, #1.

Say: *We will look at each picture. Say its name. If we hear the sound of* **n** *at the end of the word, we will circle the picture. If we do not hear the sound /**n**/ at the end, we cross out the picture.*

Say: *What do you see in the first picture?* **barn** *Do you hear the sound /**n**/ at the end of the word* **barn**? *Circle the picture. If you do not hear the sound /**n**/ at the end of the word, then cross out the picture.*

Practice

Use BLM 95, #2.

Say: Look *at the second picture.* **Say** *its name.* **Write** *the letter.*

Say: *What is the picture? Do you hear the sound /n/ at the end of the word* **corn***? Write the letter* **n***.*

Apply

Blend Words

Use BLM 95, #3.

Say: *Look at each letter and listen to the sound as I read. /d/ /o/ /w/ /n/. Your turn: /d/ /o/ /w/ /n/.*

Say: *Now we are going to blend the sounds together by stretching them out as we read them.* Point to each letter in a sweeping motion left to right: */d/oooo/* **www/nnn** */. What is the word?* **down***.*

Spelling

Use BLM 95, #4.

Say: *Now we can practice writing the sounds we hear in each word. Call one word at a time, stretching each sound. Say the word slowly; write a letter for each sound you hear.*

Conclusion

Ask: *What did we learn today?* We learned that the letter **n** makes the sound /n/. We wrote words using the letter **n** at the end. What pictures/words will help you remember the sound /n/ and the letter **n** at the end of a word?

Home Connection

Encourage students to practice identifying **final** sound /n/ and writing the letter **n** with a family member. Encourage students to identify other words that **end** with letter **n** with their family.

✔ Formative Assessment

If the student completes each task correctly, proceed to the next skill in the sequence. If not, refer to suggested Intervention 2.

Did the student...?	Intervention 2
Identify the name of the letter?	• Use physical rhythmic movements as the letter name is repeated. March while chanting the letter name. Move arms up and down. Sway from side to side.
Identify the sound of the letter?	• Say words with the target sound in final position, emphasizing the sound. **Example: bunnnn.**
Produce the sound of the letter?	• Use mirrors to show movement of mouth, tongue, teeth as the sound is produced. Use hand over mouth to explore movement of air as the sound is produced.
Recognize the **final** sound?	• Use Elkonin boxes – student moves a token into the **last** box as the **final** sound of the word is said.
Write the letter?	• Write the letter, have students trace it. Create the letter with clay. • Discuss letter features (lines, shape). Trace over the letter with multiple colors.
Know the name of pictures?	• Tell students the name of pictures, have students repeat them aloud. Discuss word and use each word in context.

Identify and Name Final Consonant p RF.K.3a

CCSS: RF.K.3
Know and apply grade-level phonics and word analysis skills in decoding words both in isolation and in text.
a. Demonstrate basic knowledge of one-to-one letter-sound correspondences by producing the primary sounds or many of the most frequent sounds for each consonant.

Lesson Objectives

- Identify and name the letter **p**
- Produce the sound of letter **p**
- Relate the sound /**p**/ to the letter **p**
- Recognize final sound **p** in words/pictures

METACOGNITIVE STRATEGY
- Selective auditory attention, imagery, auditory representation

ACADEMIC LANGUAGE
- letter name, letter sound, initial sound, final sound, ending sound

Additional Materials
Sound Spelling Card Pp
Blackline Master 96

Pre-Assess
Student's ability to recognize the sound represented by the targeted letter of the alphabet and to identify the letter used to represent the corresponding sound in final position.

Introduce

As students participate in this lesson, they identify the name and sound of the targeted letter, and identify the letter when the sound and name are given orally. Students will apply their knowledge by recognizing the **final**, or **ending**, sound of the target letter using pictures.

State Learning Goal

Today we will practice listening to the sound /**p**/ that the letter **p** makes at the **end** of words.

Teach

Letters represent sounds. We remember the sounds each letter makes. We use letters to write words we say. We use letters to read and write words.

Phonemic Awareness
Show picture of sound/spelling card to review the sound.

Say: *Listen to this sound /**p**/. Say it with me:* **p**. *Say it on your own:* **p**.

Sound-Spelling Correspondence

Show the letter.
Say: *The way we write the sound. /**p**/ is with the letter* **p**.

Say: *The letter* **p** *makes the sound /**p**/.*

Say: *What is the name of the letter?* **p** *What sound does the letter make?* /**p**/

Model
Use BLM 96, # 1.

Say: *We will look at each picture. Say its name. If we hear the sound of* **p** *at the end of the word, we will circle the picture. If we do not hear the sound /**p**/ at the end, we cross out the picture.*

Say: *What do you see in the first picture?* **soap** *Do you hear the sound /**n**/ at the end of the word soap? Circle the picture. If you do not hear the sound /**p**/ at the end of the word, then cross out the picture.*

Practice

Use BLM 96, #2.

Say: Look *at the second picture.* **Say** *its name.* **Write** *the letter.* **Say: What is the picture?** *Do you hear the sound* **/p/** *at the end of the word* **sleep? Write** *the letter* **p.**

Apply

Blend Words

Use BLM 96, #3.

Say: *Look at each letter and listen to the sound as I read.* **/sh/ /eee/ /p/. Your turn: /sh/ /eee/ /p/**

Say: *Now we are going to blend the sounds together by stretching them out as we read them.* Point to each letter in a sweeping motion left to right: **/sh/eee/ppp/.** *What is the word?* **sheep.**

Spelling

Use BLM 96, #4.

Say: *Now we can practice writing the sounds we hear in each word. Call one word at a time, stretching each sound. Say the word slowly; write a letter for each sound you hear.*

Conclusion

Ask: *What did we learn today?* We learned that the letter **p** makes the sound **/p/**. We wrote words using the letter **p** at the end. What pictures/words will help you remember the sound **/p/** and the letter **p** at the end of a word?

Home Connection

Encourage students to practice identifying **final** sound **/p/** and writing the letter **p** with a family member. Encourage students to identify other words that **end** with letter **p** with their family.

✔ Formative Assessment

If the student completes each task correctly, proceed to the next skill in the sequence. If not, refer to suggested Intervention 2.

Did the student…?	Intervention 2
Identify the name of the letter?	• Use physical rhythmic movements as the letter name is repeated. March while chanting the letter name. Move arms up and down. Sway from side to side.
Identify the sound of the letter?	• Say words with the target sound in final position by repeating the words three times. **Example: cap, cap, cap.**
Produce the sound of the letter?	• Use mirrors to show movement of mouth, tongue, teeth as the sound is produced. Use hand over mouth to explore movement of air as the sound is produced.
Recognize the **final** sound?	• Use Elkonin boxes – student moves a token into the **last** box as the **final** sound of the word is said.
Write the letter?	• Write the letter, have students trace it. Create the letter with clay. • Discuss letter features (lines, shape). Trace over the letter with multiple colors.
Know the name of pictures?	• Tell students the name of pictures, have students repeat them aloud. Discuss word and use each word in context.

Identify and Name Final Consonant b RF.K.3a

CCSS: RF.K.3
Know and apply grade-level phonics and word analysis skills in decoding words both in isolation and in text
a. Demonstrate basic knowledge of one-to-one letter-sound correspondences by producing the primary sounds or many of the most frequent sounds for each consonant.

Lesson Objectives

- Identify and name the letter **b**
- Produce the sound of letter **b**
- Relate the sound /**b**/ to the letter **b**
- Recognize final sound **b** in words/pictures

METACOGNITIVE STRATEGY
- Selective auditory attention, imagery, auditory representation

ACADEMIC LANGUAGE
- letter name, letter sound, initial sound, final sound, ending sound

Additional Materials
Sound Spelling Card Bb
Blackline Master 97

Pre-Assess
Student's ability to recognize the sound represented by the targeted letter of the alphabet and to identify the letter used to represent the corresponding sound in final position.

Introduce

As students participate in this lesson, they identify the name and sound of the targeted letter, and identify the letter when the sound and name are given orally. Students will apply their knowledge by recognizing the **final**, or **ending**, sound of the target letter using pictures.

State Learning Goal

Today we will practice listening to the sound /**b**/ that the letter **b** makes at the **end** of words.

Teach

Letters represent sounds. We remember the sounds each letter makes. We use letters to write words we say. We use letters to read and write words.

Phonemic Awareness
Show picture of sound/spelling card to review the sound.
Say: Listen to this sound /**b**/. Say it with me: **b**. Say it on your own: **b**.

Sound-Spelling Correspondence
Show the letter.

Say: *The way we write the sound. /**b**/ is with the letter* **b.**

Say: *The letter* **b** *makes the sound* /**b**/.

Say: *What is the name of the letter?* **b** *What sound does the letter make?* /**b**/

Model

Use BLM 97, # 1.

Say: *We will look at each picture. Say its name. If we hear the sound of* **b** *at the end of the word, we will circle the picture. If we do not hear the sound* /**b**/ *at the end, we cross out the picture.*

Say: *What do you see in the first picture?* **scrub** *Do you hear the sound* /**b**/ *at the end of the word* **scrub**? *Circle the picture. If you do not hear the sound* /**b**/ *at the end of the word, then cross out the picture.*

Practice

Use BLM 97, # 2.

Say: Look at the second picture. **Say** its name. **Write** the letter. **Say:** What is the picture? Do you hear the sound **/b/** at the end of the word **shrub? Write** the letter **b.**

Apply

Blend Words

Use BLM 97, #3.

Say: *Look at each letter and listen to the sound as I read.* /t/ /u/ /b/. *Your turn:* /t/ /u/ /b/

Say: *Now we are going to blend the sounds together by stretching them out as we read them.* Point to each letter in a sweeping motion left to right: /ttt/**uuuu**/bbb/. *What is the word?* **tub.**

Spelling

Use BLM 97, #4.

Say: *Now we can practice writing the sounds we hear in each word. Call one word at a time, stretching each sound. Say the word slowly; write a letter for each sound you hear.*

Conclusion

Ask: *What did we learn today?* We learned that the letter **b** makes the sound /b/. We wrote words using the letter **b** at the end. What pictures/words will help you remember the sound /b/ and the letter **b** at the end of a word?

Home Connection
Encourage students to practice identifying **final** sound /b/ and writing the letter **b** with a family member. Encourage students to identify other words that **end** with letter **b** with their family.

✔ Formative Assessment

If the student completes each task correctly, proceed to the next skill in the sequence. If not, refer to suggested Intervention 2.

Did the student…?	Intervention 2
Identify the name of the letter?	• Use physical rhythmic movements as the letter name is repeated. March while chanting the letter name. Move arms up and down. Sway from side to side.
Identify the sound of the letter?	• Say words with the target sound in final position by repeating the words three times. **Example: cab, cab, cab**
Produce the sound of the letter?	• Use mirrors to show movement of mouth, tongue, teeth as the sound is produced. Use hand over mouth to explore movement of air as the sound is produced.
Recognize the **final** sound?	• Use Elkonin boxes – student moves a token into the last box as the **final** sound of the word is said.
Write the letter?	• Write the letter, have students trace it. Create the letter with clay. • Discuss letter features (lines, shape). Trace over the letter with multiple colors.
Know the name of pictures?	• Tell students the name of pictures, have students repeat them aloud. Discuss word and use each word in context.

Identify and Name Final Consonant g RF.K.3a

CCSS: RF.K.3
Know and apply grade-level phonics and word analysis skills in decoding words both in isolation and in text
a. Demonstrate basic knowledge of one-to-one letter-sound correspondences by producing the primary sounds or many of the most frequent sounds for each consonant

Lesson Objectives

- Identify and name the letter **g**
- Produce the sound of letter **g**
- Relate the sound /**g**/ to the letter **g**
- Recognize final sound **g** in words/pictures

METACOGNITIVE STRATEGY
- Selective auditory attention, imagery, auditory representation

ACADEMIC LANGUAGE
- letter name, letter sound, initial sound, final sound, ending sound

Additional Materials
Sound Spelling Card Gg
Blackline Master 98

Pre-Assess
Student's ability to recognize the sound represented by the targeted letter of the alphabet and to identify the letter used to represent the corresponding sound in final position.

Introduce

As students participate in this lesson, they identify the name and sound of the targeted letter, and identify the letter when the sound and name are given orally. Students will apply their knowledge by recognizing the **final,** or **ending,** sound of the target letter using pictures.

State Learning Goal

Today we will practice listening to the sound /**g**/ that the letter **g** makes at the **end** of words.

Teach

Letters represent sounds. We remember the sounds each letter makes. We use letters to write words we say. We use letters to read and write words.

Phonemic Awareness
Show picture of sound/spelling card to review the sound.
Say: *Listen to this sound /g/. Say it with me:* **g.** *Say it on your own:* **g.**

Sound-Spelling Correspondence
Show the letter.

Say: *The way we write the sound. /g/ is with the letter* **g.**

Say: *The letter* **g** *makes the sound /g/.*

Say: *What is the name of the letter?* **g** *What sound does the letter make? /g/*

Model

Use BLM 98, # 1.

Say: *We will look at each picture. Say its name. If we hear the sound of* **g** *at the end of the word, we will circle the picture. If we do not hear the sound /g/ at the end, we cross out the picture.*

Say: *What do you see in the first picture?* **wig** *Do you hear the sound /g/ at the end of the word* **wig***? Circle the picture. If you do not hear the sound /g/ at the end of the word, then cross out the picture.*

Practice

Use BLM 98, # 2.

Say: Look *at the second picture.* **Say** *its name.* **Write** *the letter.*

Say: *What is the picture? Do you hear the sound* **/g/** *at the end of the word* **egg**? *Write the letter* **g.**

Apply

Blend Words

Use BLM 98, #3.

Say: *Look at each letter and listen to the sound as I read.* **/b/ /u/ /g/.** *Your turn:* **/b/ /u/ /g/.**

Say: *Now we are going to blend the sounds together by stretching them out as we read them.* Point to each letter in a sweeping motion left to right: **/b/uuu/ggg/.** *What is the word?* **bug.**

Spelling

Use BLM 98, #4.

Say: *Now we can practice writing the sounds we hear in each word. Call one word at a time, stretching each sound. Say the word slowly; write a letter for each sound you hear.*

Conclusion

Ask: *What did we learn today?* We learned that the letter **g** makes the sound **/g/.** We wrote words using the letter **g** at the end. What pictures/words will help you remember the sound **/g/** and the letter **g** at the end of a word?

Use BLM 98, # 2.

Home Connection

Encourage students to practice identifying **final** sound **/g/** and writing the letter **g** with a family member. Encourage students to identify other words that **end** with letter **g** with their family.

✔ Formative Assessment

If the student completes each task correctly, proceed to the next skill in the sequence. If not, refer to suggested Intervention 2.

Did the student…?	Intervention 2
Identify the name of the letter?	• Use physical rhythmic movements as the letter name is repeated. March while chanting the letter name. Move arms up and down. Sway from side to side.
Identify the sound of the letter?	• Say words with the target sound in final position by repeating the words three times. Example: bag, bag, bag.
Produce the sound of the letter?	• Use mirrors to show movement of mouth, tongue, teeth as the sound is produced. Use hand over mouth to explore movement of air as the sound is produced.
Recognize the **final** sound?	• Use Elkonin boxes – student moves a token into the **last** box as the **final** sound of the word is said.
Write the letter?	• Write the letter, have students trace it. Create the letter with clay. • Discuss letter features (lines, shape). Trace over the letter with multiple colors.
Know the name of pictures?	• Tell students the name of pictures, have students repeat them aloud. Discuss word and use each word in context.

Identify and Name Final Consonant d RF.K.3a

CCSS: RF.K.3
Know and apply grade-level phonics and word analysis skills in decoding words both in isolation and in text.
a. Demonstrate basic knowledge of one-to-one letter-sound correspondences by producing the primary sounds or many of the most frequent sounds for each consonant.

Lesson Objectives

- Identify and name the letter **d**
- Produce the sound of letter **d**
- Relate the sound /**d**/ to the letter **d**
- Recognize final sound **d** in words/ pictures

METACOGNITIVE STRATEGY
- Selective auditory attention, imagery, auditory representation

ACADEMIC LANGUAGE
- letter name, letter sound, initial sound, final sound, ending sound

Additional Materials
Sound Spelling Card Dd
Blackline Master 99

Pre-Assess
Student's ability to recognize the sound represented by the targeted letter of the alphabet and to identify the letter used to represent the corresponding sound in final position.

Introduce

As students participate in this lesson, they identify the name and sound of the targeted letter, and identify the letter when the sound and name are given orally. Students will apply their knowledge by recognizing the **final**, or **ending**, sound of the target letter using pictures.

State Learning Goal

Today we will practice listening to the sound /**d**/ that the letter **d** makes at the **end** of words.

Teach

Letters represent sounds. We remember the sounds each letter makes. We use letters to write words we say. We use letters to read and write words.

Phonemic Awareness
Show picture of sound/spelling card to review the sound.
Say: Listen to this sound /**d**/. Say it with me: **d**. Say it on your own: **d**.

Sound-Spelling Correspondence

Show the letter.
Say: *The way we write the sound. /**d**/ is with the letter* **d**.

Say: *The letter d makes the sound /**d**/.*

Say: *What is the name of the letter?* **d** *What sound does the letter make?* /**d**/

Model
Use BLM 99, # 1.

Say: *We will look at each picture. Say its name. If we hear the sound of* **d** *at the end of the word, we will circle the picture. If we do not hear the sound /**d**/ at the end, we cross out the picture.*

Say: *What do you see in the first picture?* **food** *Do you hear the sound /**d**/ at the end of the word* **food**? *Circle the picture. If you do not hear the sound /**d**/ at the end of the word, then cross out the picture.*

Practice

Use BLM 99, # 2.

Say: Look at the second picture. **Say** its name. **Write** the letter.

Say: What is the picture? Do you hear the sound /**d**/ at the end of the word **head**? **Write** the letter **d**.

Apply

Blend Words

Use BLM 99, #3.

Say: Look at each letter and listen to the sound as I read. /**t**/ /**oa**/ /**d**/. Your turn: /**t**/ /**oa**/ /**d**/

Say: Now we are going to blend the sounds together by stretching them out as we read them. Point to each letter in a sweeping motion left to right: /**t/oooaaa/ ddd**/. What is the word? **toad**.

Spelling

Use BLM 99, #4.

Say: Now we can practice writing the sounds we hear in each word. Call one word at a time, stretching each sound. Say the word slowly; write a letter for each sound you hear.

Conclusion

Ask: What did we learn today? We learned that the letter **d** makes the sound /**d**/. We wrote words using the letter **d** at the end. What pictures/words will help you remember the sound /**d**/ and the letter **d** at the end of a word?

Home Connection
Encourage students to practice identifying **final** sound /**d**/ and writing the letter **d** with a family member. Encourage students to identify other words that **end** with letter **d** with their family.

✓ Formative Assessment

If the student completes each task correctly, proceed to the next skill in the sequence. If not, refer to suggested Intervention 2.

Did the student...?	Intervention 2
Identify the name of the letter?	• Use physical rhythmic movements as the letter name is repeated. March while chanting the letter name. Move arms up and down. Sway from side to side.
Identify the sound of the letter?	• Say words with the target sound in final position by repeating the words three times. **Example: dad, dad, dad**
Produce the sound of the letter?	• Use mirrors to show movement of mouth, tongue, teeth as the sound is produced. Use hand over mouth to explore movement of air as the sound is produced.
Recognize the **final** sound?	• Use Elkonin boxes – student moves a token into the **last** box as the **final** sound of the word is said.
Write the letter?	• Write the letter, have students trace it. Create the letter with clay. • Discuss letter features (lines, shape). Trace over the letter with multiple colors.
Know the name of pictures?	• Tell students the name of pictures, have students repeat them aloud. Discuss word and use each word in context.

Identify and Name Final Consonant x RF.K.3a

CCSS: RF.K.3
Know and apply grade-level phonics and word analysis skills in decoding words both in isolation and in text
a. Demonstrate basic knowledge of one-to-one letter-sound correspondences by producing the primary sounds or many of the most frequent sounds for each consonant.

Lesson Objectives

- Identify and name the letter **x**
- Produce the sound of letter **x**
- Relate the sound /**x**/ to the letter **x**
- Recognize final sound **x** in words/pictures

METACOGNITIVE STRATEGY
- Selective auditory attention, imagery, auditory representation

ACADEMIC LANGUAGE
- letter name, letter sound, initial sound, final sound, ending sound

Additional Materials
Sound Spelling Card Xx
Blackline Master 100

Pre-Assess
Student's ability to recognize the sound represented by the targeted letter of the alphabet and to identify the letter used to represent the corresponding sound in final position.

Introduce

As students participate in this lesson, they identify the name and sound of the targeted letter, and identify the letter when the sound and name are given orally. Students will apply their knowledge by recognizing the **final**, or **ending**, sound of the target letter using pictures.

State Learning Goal

Today we will practice listening to the sound /**x**/ that the letter **x** makes at the end of words.

Teach

Letters represent sounds. We remember the sounds each letter makes. We use letters to write words we say. We use letters to read and write words.

Phonemic Awareness

Show picture of sound/spelling card to review the sound.
Say: Listen to this sound /**x**/. Say it with me: **x**. Say it on your own: **x**.

Sound-Spelling Correspondence

Show the letter.
Say: *The way we write the sound. /**x**/ is with the letter* **x.**

Say: *The letter* **x** *makes the sound /**x**/.*

Say: *What is the name of the letter?* **x** *What sound does the letter make? /**x**/*

Model

Use BLM 100, # 1.

Say: *We will look at each picture. Say its name. If we hear the sound of* **x** *at the end of the word, we will circle the picture. If we do not hear the sound /**x**/ at the end, we will cross out the picture.*

Say: *What do you see in the first picture?* **a box** *Do you hear the sound /**x**/ at the end of the word* **box**? *Circle the picture. If you do not hear the sound /**x**/ at the end of the word, then cross out the picture.*

Practice

Use BLM 100, # 2.

Say: Look *at the second picture.* **Say** *its name.* **Write** *the letter.*

Say: *What is the picture? Do you hear the sound /x/ at the end of the word* **sax***?* **Write** *the letter* **x.**

Apply
Blend Words

Use BLM 100, #3.

Say: *Look at each letter and listen to the sound as I read. /p/ /o/ /x/. Your turn:* /**p**/ /**o**/ /**x**/

Say: *Now we are going to blend the sounds together by stretching them out as we read them.* Point to each letter in a sweeping motion left to right: /**p**/**ooo**/**xxx**/. *What is the word?* **pox.**

Spelling

Use BLM 100, #4.

Say: *Now we can practice writing the sounds we hear in each word. Call one word at a time, stretching each sound. Say the word slowly; write a letter for each sound you hear.*

Conclusion

Ask: *What did we learn today?* We learned that the letter **x** makes the sound /x/. We wrote words using the letter **x** at the end. What pictures/words will help you remember the sound /x/ and the letter **x** at the end of a word?

Home Connection

Encourage students to practice identifying **final** sound /x/ and writing the letter **x** with a family member. Encourage students to identify other words that **end** with letter **x** with their family.

✔ Formative Assessment

If the student completes each task correctly, proceed to the next skill in the sequence. If not, refer to suggested Intervention 2.

Did the student...?	Intervention 2
Identify the name of the letter?	• Use physical rhythmic movements as the letter name is repeated. March while chanting the letter name. Move arms up and down. Sway from side to side.
Identify the sound of the letter?	• Say words with the target sound in final position by repeating the words three times. **Example: fix, fix, fix**
Produce the sound of the letter?	• Use mirrors to show movement of mouth, tongue, teeth as the sound is produced. Use hand over mouth to explore movement of air as the sound is produced.
Recognize the **final** sound?	• Use Elkonin boxes – student moves a token into the last box as the **final** sound of the word is said.
Write the letter?	• Write the letter, have students trace it. Create the letter with clay. • Discuss letter features (lines, shape). Trace over the letter with multiple colors.
Know the name of pictures?	• Tell students the name of pictures, have students repeat them aloud. Discuss word and use each word in context.

Identify and Name Initial Short Vowel a RF.K.3b

CCSS: RF.K.3
Know and apply grade-level phonics and word analysis skills in decoding words both in isolation and in text.
b. Associate the long and short sounds with common spellings (graphemes) for the five major vowels.

Lesson Objectives

- Identify and name the letter **a**
- Produce the sound of letter **a**
- Relate the sound /**a**/ to the letter **a**
- Recognize **initial short vowel** sound **a** in words/pictures

METACOGNITIVE STRATEGY
- Selective auditory attention, imagery, auditory representation

ACADEMIC LANGUAGE
- letter name, letter sound, initial sound, vowel, short vowel sound, long vowel sound

Additional Materials
Sound Spelling Card Aa
Blackline Master 101

Pre-Assess
Student's ability to recognize the sound represented by the target letter of the alphabetand to identify the letter used to represent the corresponding sound.

Introduce

As students participate in this lesson, they identify the name and sound of the target letter, and identify the letter when the sound and name are given orally. Students will apply their knowledge by recognizing the **short** sound of the target letter using pictures.

State Learning Goal

The letter **a** is a vowel. It has two sounds. The long sound /**a**/ and the short sound /**a**/. Today we will listen to the short sound of the letter a at the beginning of words.

Teach

Letters represent sounds. We remember the sounds each letter makes. We use letters to write words we say. We use letters to read and write words. The letter **a** is a vowel. It has a long sound /**a**/ and a short sound /**a**/.

Phonemic Awareness

Show picture of sound/spelling card to review sound.
Say: *Listen to this sound:* /**a**/. *Say it with me:* **a**. *Say it on your own:* **a**.

Sound-Spelling Correspondence

Show the letter.
Say: *The way we write the sound* /**a**/ *is with the letter* **a.**

Say: *The letter* a *makes the sound* /**a**/**.**

Say: *What is the name of the letter?* **a** *What sound does the letter make?* /**a**/

Model

Use BLM 101, # 1.

Say: *We will look at each picture. Say its name. If we hear the sound of* **a** *at the beginning of the word, we will circle the picture. If we do not hear the sound* /**a**/ *at the beginning, we will cross out the picture.*

Say: *What is the picture?* **arch** *Do you hear the sound* /**a**/ *at the beginning of* **arch***? If you do not hear the sound* /**a**/ *at the beginning of the word, then cross out the picture.*

Practice

Use BLM 101, # 2.

Say: Look *at the picture.* **Say** *its name.* **Write** *the letter.*

Say: *What is the picture?* **actor** *Do you hear the sound /a/ at the beginning of the word* **actor**? *Then* **write** *the letter* **a**.

Apply

Blend Words

Use BLM 101, #3.

Say: *Look at each letter and listen to the sound as I read:* **/a/ /r/ /m/ /e/.** *Your turn:* **/a/ /r/ /m/ /e/**

Say: *Now we are going to blend the sounds together by stretching them out as we read them.* Point to each letter in a sweeping motion left to right: **/aaaa/rrrr/ mmm/eeee/.** *What is the word?* **army.**

Spelling

Use BLM 101, #4.

Say: *Now we can practice writing the sounds we hear in each word. Call one word at a time, stretching each sound. Say the word slowly; write a letter for each sound you hear.*

Conclusion

Ask: *What did we learn today?* We learned that the letter a makes the sound /a/ at the beginning of some words. What pictures/words will help you remember the sound /a/ and the letter **a**?

Home Connection

Encourage students to practice identifying initial short vowel sound **a** and writing the letter **a** with a family member. Encourage students to identify other words that begin with the short vowel sound **a** with their family.

✔ Formative Assessment

If the student completes each task correctly, proceed to the next skill in the sequence. If not, refer to suggested intervention 2.

Did the student…?	Intervention 2
Identify the name of the letter?	• Use physical rhythmic movements as the letter name is repeated. March while chanting the letter name. Move arms up and down. Sway from side to side.
Identify the sound of the letter?	• Use alliteration, chants that repeat the sound several times then a word that begins with the sound. **Example:** /a/ /a/ /a/ arch
Produce the sound of the letter?	• Use mirrors to show movement of mouth, tongue, teeth as the sound is produced. • Use hand over mouth to explore movement of air as the sound is produced.
Recognize the **final** sound?	• Use Elkonin boxes – student moves a token into first box as the beginning sound of the word is said.
Write the letter?	• Write the letter, have students trace it. Create letter with clay. • Discuss letter features (lines, shape). Trace over letter with multiple colors.
Know the name of pictures?	• Tell students the name of pictures, have student repeat it aloud. • Discuss meaning of word. Use word in context.

Identify and Name Initial Short Vowel i RF.K.3b

CCSS: RF.K.3
Know and apply grade-level phonics and word analysis skills in decoding words both in isolation and in text.
b. Associate the long and short sounds with common spellings (graphemes) for the five major vowels.

Lesson Objectives

- Identify and name the letter **i**
- Produce the sound of letter **i**
- Relate the sound /i/ to the letter **i**
- Recognize **initial short vowel** sound **i** in words/pictures

METACOGNITIVE STRATEGY
- Selective auditory attention, imagery, auditory representation

ACADEMIC LANGUAGE
- letter name, letter sound, initial sound, vowel, short vowel sound, long vowel sound

Additional Materials
Sound Spelling Card Ii
Blackline Master 102

Pre-Assess
Student's ability to recognize the sound represented by the target letter of the alphabetand to identify the letter used to represent the corresponding sound.

Introduce

As students participate in this lesson, they identify the name and sound of the target letter, and identify the letter when the sound and name are given orally. Students will apply their knowledge by recognizing the short sound of the target letter using pictures.

State Learning Goal

The letter **i** is a vowel. It has two sounds. The long sound /i/ and the short sound /i/. Today we will listen to the short sound of the letter **i** at the beginning of words.

Teach

Letters represent sounds. We remember the sounds each letter makes. We use letters to write words we say. We use letters to read and write words. The letter i is a vowel. It has a long sound /i/ and a short sound /i/.

Phonemic Awareness

Show picture of sound/spelling card to review sound.
Say: Listen to this sound: /i/. Say it with me: **i**. Say it on your own: **i**.

Sound-Spelling Correspondence

Show the letter.
Say: *The way we write the sound /i/ is with the letter* **i**.

Say: *The letter a makes the sound /i/.*

Say: *What is the name of the letter?* **i** *What sound does the letter make?* /i/

Model

Use BLM 102, #1.

Say: *We will look at each picture. Say its name. If we hear the sound of* **i** *at the beginning of the word, we will circle the picture. If we do not hear the sound /i/ at the beginning, we cross out the picture.*

Say: *What is the picture?* **ink** *Do you hear the sound /i/ at the beginning of* **ink**? *If you do not hear the sound /i/ at the beginning of the word, then cross out the picture.*

Practice

Use BLM 102, # 2.

Say: *Look at the picture. Say its name. Write the letter.*

Say: *What is the picture? inch Do you hear the sound /ĭ/ at the beginning of the word inch? Then write the letter i.*

Apply

Blend Words

Use BLM 102, #3.

Say: *Look at each letter and listen to the sound as I read: /ĭ/ /t/ /ch/.*

Your turn: /ĭ/ /t/ /ch/.

Say: *Now we are going to blend the sounds together by stretching them out as we read them. Point to each letter in a sweeping motion left to right: /iiii/ttt/ch/. What is the word?* **itch**.

Spelling

Use BLM 102, #4.

Say: *Now we can practice writing the sounds we hear in each word. Call one word at a time, stretching each sound. Say the word slowly; write a letter for each sound you hear.*

Conclusion

Ask: *What did we learn today?* We learned that the letter **i** makes the sound /ĭ/ at the beginning of some words. What pictures/words will help you remember the sound **/i/** and the letter **i**?

Home Connection

Encourage students to practice identifying initial short vowel sound i and writing the letter **i** with a family member. Encourage students to identify other words that begin with the short vowel sound **i** with their family.

✔ Formative Assessment

If the student completes each task correctly, proceed to the next skill in the sequence. If not, refer to suggested intervention 2.

Did the student...?	Intervention 2
Identify the name of the letter?	• Use physical rhythmic movements as the letter name is repeated. March while chanting the letter name. Move arms up and down. Sway from side to side.
Identify the sound of the letter?	• Use alliteration, chants that repeat the sound several times then a word that begins with the sound. **Example:** /i/ /i/ /i/ **image**
Produce the sound of the letter?	• Use mirrors to show movement of mouth, tongue, teeth as the sound is produced. • Use hand over mouth to explore movement of air as the sound is produced.
Recognize the **final** sound?	• Use Elkonin boxes – student moves a token into first box as the beginning sound of the word is said.
Write the letter?	• Write the letter, have students trace it. Create letter with clay. • Discuss letter features (lines, shape). Trace over letter with multiple colors.
Know the name of pictures?	• Tell students the name of pictures, have student repeat it aloud. • Discuss meaning of word. Use word in context.

Identify and Name Initial Short Vowel o RF.K.3b

CCSS: RF.K.3
Know and apply grade-level phonics and word analysis skills in decoding words both in isolation and in text.
b. Associate the long and short sounds with common spellings (graphemes) for the five major vowels.

Lesson Objectives

- Identify and name the letter **o**
- Produce the sound of letter **o**
- Relate the sound /**o**/ to the letter **o**
- Recognize **initial short vowel** sound **o** in words/pictures

METACOGNITIVE STRATEGY
- Selective auditory attention, imagery, auditory representation

ACADEMIC LANGUAGE
- letter name, letter sound, initial sound, vowel, short vowel sound, long vowel sound

Additional Materials
Sound Spelling Card Oo
Blackline Master 103

Pre-Assess
Student's ability to recognize the sound represented by the target letter of the alphabet and to identify the letter used to represent the corresponding sound.

Introduce

As students participate in this lesson, they identify the name and sound of the target letter, and identify the letter when the sound and name are given orally. Students will apply their knowledge by recognizing the **short** sound of the target letter using pictures.

State Learning Goal

The letter **o** is a vowel. It has two sounds. The long sound /**o**/ and the short sound /**o**/. Today we will listen to the short sound of the letter **o** at the beginning of words.

Teach

Letters represent sounds. We remember the sounds each letter makes. We use letters to write words we say. We use letters to read and write words. The letter o is a vowel. It has a long sound /**o**/ and a short sound /**o**/.

Phonemic Awareness

Show picture of sound/spelling card to review sound.
Say: *Listen to this sound:* /**o**/. *Say it with me:* **o**. *Say it on your own*: **o**.

Sound-Spelling Correspondence

Show the letter.
Say: *The way we write the sound* /**o**/ *is with the letter* **o**.

Say: *The letter a makes the sound* /**o**/.

Say: *What is the name of the letter?* **o** *What sound does the letter make?* /**o**/

Model

Use BLM 103, #1.

Say: *We will look at each picture. Say its name. If we hear the sound of o at the beginning of the word, we will circle the picture. If we do not hear the sound /**o**/ at the beginning, we will cross out the picture.*

Say: *What is the picture?* **olive** *Do you hear the sound /**o**/ at the beginning of* **olive**? *If you do not hear the sound /**o**/ at the beginning of the word, then cross out the picture.*

Practice

Use BLM 103, # 2.

Say: **Look** *at the picture*. **Say** *its name*. **Write** *the letter*.

Say: *What is the picture?* **onion** *Do you hear the sound* /**o**/ *at the beginning of the word* **onion***? Then write the letter* **o***.*

Apply

Blend Words

Use BLM 103, #3.

Say: *Look at each letter and listen to the sound as I read:* /**o**/ /**k**/ /**t**/ /**a**/ /**g**/ /**o**/ /**n**/. *Your turn* /**o**/ /**k**/ /**t**/ /**a**/ /**g**/ /**o**/ /**n**/.

Say: *Now we are going to blend the sounds together by stretching them out as we read them.* Point to each letter in a sweeping motion left to right: /**oooo/kkk/ttt/ aaa/ggg/ooo/nnn**/. What is the word? **octagon**.

Spelling

Use BLM 103, #4.

Say: *Now we can practice writing the sounds we hear in each word. Call one word at a time, stretching each sound. Say the word slowly; write a letter for each sound you hear.*

Conclusion

Ask: *What did we learn today?* We learned that the letter a makes the sound /**o**/ at the beginning of some words. What pictures/words will help you remember the sound /**o**/ and the letter **o**?

Home Connection

Encourage students to practice identifying initial short vowel sound **o** and writing the letter **o** with a family member. Encourage students to identify other words that begin with the short vowel sound o with their family.

✔ Formative Assessment

If the student completes each task correctly, proceed to the next skill in the sequence. If not, refer to suggested intervention 2.

Did the student...?	Intervention 2
Identify the name of the letter?	• Use physical rhythmic movements as the letter name is repeated. March while chanting the letter name. Move arms up and down. Sway from side to side.
Identify the sound of the letter?	• Use alliteration, chants that repeat the sound several times then a word that begins with the sound. **Example:** /**o**/ /**o**/ /**o**/ **olive**
Produce the sound of the letter?	• Use mirrors to show movement of mouth, tongue, teeth as the sound is produced. • Use hand over mouth to explore movement of air as the sound is produced.
Recognize the beginning sound?	• Use Elkonin boxes – student moves a token into first box as the beginning sound of the word is said.
Write the letter?	• Write the letter, have students trace it. Create letter with clay. • Discuss letter features (lines, shape). Trace over letter with multiple colors.
Know the name of pictures?	• Tell students the name of pictures, have student repeat it aloud. • Discuss meaning of word. Use word in context.

Identify and Name Initial Short Vowel u RF.K.3b

CCSS: RF.K.3
Know and apply grade-level phonics and word analysis skills in decoding words both in isolation and in text.
b. Associate the long and short sounds with common spellings (graphemes) for the five major vowels.
.

Lesson Objectives

- Identify and name the letter **u**
- Produce the sound of letter **u**
- Relate the sound /**u**/ to the letter **u**
- Recognize **initial short vowel** sound **u** in words/pictures

METACOGNITIVE STRATEGY
- Selective auditory attention, imagery, auditory representation

ACADEMIC LANGUAGE
- letter name, letter sound, initial sound, vowel, short vowel sound, long vowel sound

Additional Materials
Sound Spelling Card Uu
Blackline Master 104

Pre-Assess
Student's ability to recognize the sound represented by the target letter of the alphabet and to identify the letter used to represent the corresponding sound.

Introduce

As students participate in this lesson, they identify the name and sound of the target letter, and identify the letter when the sound and name are given orally. Students will apply their knowledge by recognizing the short sound of the target letter using pictures.

State Learning Goal

The letter **u** is a vowel. It has two sounds. The long sound /**u**/ and the short sound /**u**/. Today we will listen to the short sound of the letter **u** at the beginning of words.

Teach

Letters represent sounds. We remember the sounds each letter makes. We use letters to write words we say. We use letters to read and write words. The letter **u** is a vowel. It has a long sound /**u**/ and a short sound /**u**/.

Phonemic Awareness
Show picture of sound/spelling card to review sound.
Say: *Listen to this sound:* /**u**/. *Say it with me:* **u**. *Say it on your own*: **u**.

Sound-Spelling Correspondence

Show the letter.
Say: *The way we write the sound* /**u**/ *is with the letter* **u**.

Say: *The letter a makes the sound* /**u**/.

Say: *What is the name of the letter?* **u** *What sound does the letter make?* /**u**/

Model

Use BLM 104, #1.

Say: *We will look at each picture. Say its name. If we hear the sound of* **u** *at the beginning of the word, we will circle the picture. If we do not hear the sound* /**u**/ *at the beginning, we cross out the picture.*

Say: *What is the picture?* **up** *Do you hear the sound* /**u**/ *at the beginning of* **up**? *If you do not hear the sound* /**u**/ *at the beginning of the word, then cross out the picture.*

Practice

Use BLM 104, # 2.

Say: Look *at the picture.* **Say** *its name.* **Write** *the letter.*

Say: *What is the picture?* **umbrella** *Do you hear the sound /**u**/ at the beginning of the word* **umbrella**? *Then* **write** *the letter* **u**.

Apply
Blend Words

Use BLM 104, #3.

Say: *Look at each letter and listen to the sound as I read: /**u**/ /**n**/ /**p**/ /**a**/ /**k**/. Your turn: /**u**/ /**n**/ /**p**/ /**a**/ /**k**/.*

Say: *Now we are going to blend the sounds together by stretching them out as we read them. Point to each letter in a sweeping motion left to right: /uuuu/nnnn/ ppp/aaa/kkk/. What is the word?* unpack

Spelling

Use BLM 104, #4.

Say: *Now we can practice writing the sounds we hear in each word. Call one word at a time, stretching each sound. Say the word slowly; write a letter for each sound you hear.*

Conclusion

Ask: *What did we learn today?* We learned that the letter a makes the sound /**u**/ at the beginning of some words. What pictures/words will help you remember the sound /**u**/ and the letter **u**?

Home Connection

Encourage students to practice identifying initial short vowel sound **u** and writing the letter **u** with a family member. Encourage students to identify other words that begin with the short vowel sound u with their family.

✔ Formative Assessment

If the student completes each task correctly, proceed to the next skill in the sequence. If not, refer to suggested intervention 2.

Did the student…?	Intervention 2
Identify the name of the letter?	• Use physical rhythmic movements as the letter name is repeated. March while chanting the letter name. Move arms up and down. Sway from side to side.
Identify the sound of the letter?	• Use alliteration, chants that repeat the sound several times then a word that begins with the sound. **Example:** /u/ /u/ /u/ **uncle**
Produce the sound of the letter?	• Use mirrors to show movement of mouth, tongue, teeth as the sound is produced. Use hand over mouth to explore movement of air as the sound is produced.
Recognize the beginning sound?	• Use Elkonin boxes – student moves a token into first box as the beginning sound of the word is said.
Write the letter?	• Write the letter, have students trace it. Create letter with clay. • Discuss letter features (lines, shape). Trace over letter with multiple colors.
Know the name of pictures?	• Tell students the name of pictures, have student repeat it aloud. • Discuss meaning of word. Use word in context.

Identify and Name Initial Short Vowel e RF.K.3b

CCSS: RF.K.3
Know and apply grade-level phonics and word analysis skills in decoding words both in isolation and in text.
b. Associate the long and short sounds with common spellings (graphemes) for the five major vowels.

Lesson Objectives

- Identify and name the letter **e**
- Produce the sound of letter **e**
- Relate the sound /**e**/ to the letter **e**
- Recognize **initial short vowel** sound e in words/pictures

METACOGNITIVE STRATEGY
- Selective auditory attention, imagery, auditory representation

ACADEMIC LANGUAGE
- letter name, letter sound, initial sound, vowel, short vowel sound, long vowel sound

Additional Materials
Sound Spelling Card Ee
Blackline Master 105

Pre-Assess
Student's ability to recognize the sound represented by the target letter of the alphabet and to identify the letter used to represent the corresponding sound.

Introduce

As students participate in this lesson, they identify the name and sound of the target letter, and identify the letter when the sound and name are given orally. Students will apply their knowledge by recognizing the **short** sound of the target letter using pictures.

State Learning Goal

The letter **e** is a vowel. It has two sounds. The long sound /**e**/ and the short sound /**e**/. Today we will listen to the short sound of the letter **e** at the beginning of words.

Teach

Letters represent sounds. We remember the sounds each letter makes. We use letters to write words we say. We use letters to read and write words. The letter e is a vowel. It has a long sound /**e**/ and a short sound /**e**/.

Phonemic Awareness

Show picture of sound/spelling card to review sound.
Say: Listen to this sound: /**e**/. Say it with me: **e**. Say it on your own: **e**.

Sound-Spelling Correspondence

Show the letter.
Say: *The way we write the sound* /**e**/ *is with the letter* **e.**

Say: *The letter a makes the sound* /**e**/*.*

Say: *What is the name of the letter?* **e** *What sound does the letter make?* /**e**/

Model

Use BLM 105, #1.

Say: *We will look at each picture. Say its name. If we hear the sound of* **e** *at the beginning of the word, we will circle the picture. If we do not hear the sound* /**e**/ *at the beginning, we will cross out the picture.*

Say: *What is the picture?* **edge** *Do you hear the sound* /**e**/ *at the beginning of* **edge***? If you do not hear the sound* /**e**/ *at the beginning of the word, then cross out the picture.*

Practice

Use BLM 105, # 2.

Say: Look *at the picture.* **Say** *its name.* **Write** *the letter.*

Say: *What is the picture?* **eraser** *Do you hear the sound* /**e**/ *at the beginning of the word* **eraser**? *Then write the letter* **e**.

Apply

Blend Words

Use BLM 105, #3.

Say: *Look at each letter and listen to the sound as I read:* /**e**/ /**m**/ /**p**/ /**t**/ /**e**/.

Your turn: /**e**/ /**m**/ /**p**/ /**t**/ /**e**/.

Say: *Now we are going to blend the sounds together by stretching them out as we read them.* Point to each letter in a sweeping motion left to right: /**eeee**/**mmm**/ **ppp**/**ttt**/**eeee**/. What is the word? **empty.**

Spelling

Use BLM 105, #4.

Say: *Now we can practice writing the sounds we hear in each word. Call one word at a time, stretching each sound. Say the word slowly; write a letter for each sound you hear.*

Conclusion

Ask: *What did we learn today?* We learned that the letter **e** makes the sound /**e**/ at the beginning of some words. What pictures/words will help you remember the sound /**e**/ and the letter **e**?

Home Connection

Encourage students to practice identifying initial short vowel sound **e** and writing the letter **e** with a family member. Encourage students to identify other words that begin with the short vowel sound **e** with their family.

✔ Formative Assessment

If the student completes each task correctly, proceed to the next skill in the sequence. If not, refer to suggested intervention 2.

Did the student…?	Intervention 2
Identify the name of the letter?	• Use physical rhythmic movements as the letter name is repeated. March while chanting the letter name. Move arms up and down. Sway from side to side.
Identify the sound of the letter?	• Use alliteration, chants that repeat the sound several times then a word that begins with the sound. **Example:** /**e**/ /**e**/ /**e**/ **edge**
Produce the sound of the letter?	• Use mirrors to show movement of mouth, tongue, teeth as the sound is produced. Use hand over mouth to explore movement of air as the sound is produced.
Recognize the beginning sound?	• Use Elkonin boxes – student moves a token into first box as the beginning sound of the word is said.
Write the letter?	• Write the letter, have students trace it. Create letter with clay. • Discuss letter features (lines, shape). Trace over letter with multiple colors.
Know the name of pictures?	• Tell students the name of pictures, have student repeat it aloud. • Discuss meaning of word. Use word in context.

Identify and Name Medial Short Vowel a RF.K.3b

CCSS: RF.K.3
Know and apply grade-level phonics and word analysis skills in decoding words both in isolation and in text.
b. Associate the long and short sounds with common spellings (graphemes) for the five major vowels.

Lesson Objectives

- Identify and name the letter **a**
- Produce the sound of letter **a**
- Relate the sound /**a**/ to the letter **a**
- Recognize **medial short vowel** sound **a** in words/pictures

METACOGNITIVE STRATEGY
- Selective auditory attention, imagery, auditory representation

ACADEMIC LANGUAGE
- letter name, letter sound, vowel, short sound, medial sound, middle

Additional Materials
Sound Spelling Card Aa
Blackline Master 106

Pre-Assess
Student's ability to recognize the sound represented by the target letter of the alphabet and to identify the letter used to represent the corresponding sound.

Introduce

As students participate in this lesson, they identify the name and sound of the target letter, and identify the letter when the sound and name are given orally. Students will apply their knowledge by recognizing the short sound of the target letter using pictures.

State Learning Goal

The letter **a** is a vowel. It has two sounds. The long sound /**a**/ and the short sound /**a**/. Today we will listen to the short vowel sound of the letter **a** in the **middle** of words.

Teach

Letters represent sounds. We remember the sounds each letter makes. We use letters to write words we say. We use letters to read and write words. The letter a is a vowel. It has a long sound /**a**/ and a short sound /**a**/.

Phonemic Awareness

Show picture of sound/spelling card **to review the short sound of a.**
Say: Listen to this sound /**a**/. Say it with me: aaaa. Say it on your own: aaaa.

Sound-Spelling Correspondence

Show the letter.
Say: *The way we write the sound /**a**/ is with the letter* **a.**

Say: *The letter* **a** *makes the* **short sound /a/.**

Say: *What is the name of the letter?* **a** *What is the short sound the letter* **a** *makes?*/**a**/

Model

Use BLM 106, #1.

Say: *Look at each picture. Say its name. Listen for the short sound of /**a**/ in the* **middle.**

Say: *Do you hear the sound /**a**/ in the* **middle** *of the word* **chart***? If we hear the sound of* **a** *in the middle of the word, we will circle the picture. If we do not hear the sound /**a**/ in the middle, we will cross out the picture.*

Practice

Use BLM 106, # 2.

Say: Look at the picture. **Say** its name. **Write** the letter.

Say: *What is the picture?* **flash** *Do you hear the sound* /a/ *in the* **middle** *of the word* **flash**? *Then write the letter* **a**.

Apply
Blend Words

Use BLM 106, #3.

Say: *Look at each letter and listen to the sound as I read.* /gl/ /a/ /ss/. *Your turn:* /gl/ /a/ /ss/.

Say: *Now we are going to blend the sounds together by stretching them out as we read them.* Point to each letter in a sweeping motion left to right: /gl//aaa//sss/. *What is the word?* **glass**.

Spelling

Use BLM 106, #4.

Say: *Now we can practice writing the sounds we hear in each word. Call one word at a time, stretching each sound. Say the word slowly; write a letter for each sound you hear.*

Conclusion

Ask: *What did we learn today?* We learned that the letter **a** makes the sound /a/ in the middle of some words. What pictures/words will help you remember the sound /a/ and the letter **a**?

Home Connection

Encourage students to practice identifying the medial short vowel sound and writing the letter **a** with a family member. Encourage students to identify other words that have a medial short **a** vowel sound with their family.

✔ Formative Assessment

If the student completes each task correctly, proceed to the next skill in the sequence. If not, refer suggested Intervention 2.

Did the student...?	Intervention 2
Identify the name of the letter?	• Use physical rhythmic movements as the letter name is repeated. March while chanting the letter name. Move arms up and down. Sway from side to side.
Identify the sound of the letter?	• Use alliteration, chants that repeat the sound several times then a word that contains the sound. **Example:** /a/ /a/ /a/ **bag**
Produce the sound of the letter?	• Use mirrors to show movement of mouth, tongue, teeth as the sound is produced. Use hand over mouth to explore movement of air as the sound is produced.
Recognize the beginning sound?	• Use Elkonin boxes – student moves a token into first box as the beginning sound of the word is said.
Write the letter?	• Write the letter, have students trace it. Create letter with clay. • Discuss letter features (lines, shape). Trace over letter with multiple colors.
Know the name of pictures?	• Tell students the name of pictures, have student repeat it aloud. • Discuss meaning of word. Use word in context.

Identify and Name Medial Short Vowel i RF.K.3b

CCSS: RF.K.3
Know and apply grade-level phonics and word analysis skills in decoding words both in isolation and in text.
b. Associate the long and short sounds with common spellings (graphemes) for the five major vowels.

Lesson Objectives

- Identify and name the letter **i**
- Produce the sound of letter **i**
- Relate the sound /**i**/ to the letter **i**
- Recognize **medial short vowel** sound **i** in words/pictures

METACOGNITIVE STRATEGY
- Selective auditory attention, imagery, auditory representation

ACADEMIC LANGUAGE
- letter name, letter sound, vowel, short sound, medial sound, middle

Additional Materials
Sound Spelling Card Ii
Blackline Master 107

Pre-Assess
Student's ability to recognize the sound represented by the target letter of the alphabet and to identify the letter used to represent the corresponding sound.

Introduce

As students participate in this lesson, they identify the name and sound of sound of the target letter, and identify the letter when the sound and name are given orally. Students will apply their knowledge by recognizing the short sound of target letter using pictures.

State Learning Goal

The letter **i** is a vowel. It has two sounds. The long /**i**/ sound and the short /**i**/ sound. Today we will listen to the short vowel sound of the letter **i** in the **middle** of words.

Teach

Letters represent sounds. We remember the sounds each letter makes. We use letters to write words we say. We use letters to read and write words. The letter **i** is a vowel. It has a long /**i**/ sound and a short /**i**/ sound.

Phonemic Awareness
Show picture of sound/spelling card **to review the short sound of i.**
Say: *Listen to this /i/ sound. Say it with me: iii. Say it on your own: iii.*

Sound-Spelling Correspondence

Show the letter.
Say: *The way we write the sound /**i**/ is with the letter* **i.**

Say: *The letter* **i** *makes the* **short /i/ sound.**

Say: *What is the name of the letter?* **i** *What is the short sound the letter* **i** *makes?* /i/

Model

Use BLM 107, #1.

Say: *Look at each picture. Say its name. Listen for the short sound of /i/ in the* **middle.**

Say: *Do you hear the sound /i/ in the* **middle** *of the word* **sip**? *If we hear the sound of* **i** *in the middle of the word, we will circle the picture. If we do not hear the sound /i/ in the middle, we will cross out the picture.*

Practice

Use BLM 107, # 2.

Say: **Look** *at the picture.* **Say** *its name.* **Write** *the letter.*

Say: *What is the* picture? **chimp** *Do you hear the sound* /**i**/ *in the* **middle** *of the word* **chimp**? *Then write the letter* **i**.

Apply
Blend Words

Use BLM 107, #3.

Say: *Look at each letter and listen to the sound as I read.* /**t**/ /**w**/ /**i**/ /**n**/ /**s**/. *Your turn:* /**t**/ /**w**/ /**i**/ /**n**/ /**s**/.

Say: *Now we are going to blend the sounds together by stretching them out as we read them.* Point to each letter in a sweeping motion left to right: /**t**/**www**/**iii**/ **nnn**/**s**/. *What is the* word? **twins**.

Spelling

Use BLM 107, #4.

Say: *Now we can practice writing the sounds we hear in each word. Call one word at a time, stretching each sound. Say the word slowly; write a letter for each sound you hear.*

Conclusion

Ask: *What did we learn today?* We learned that the letter i makes the sound /i/ in the middle of some words. What pictures/words will help you remember the sound /**i**/ and the letter **i**?

Home Connection
Encourage students to practice identifying the medial short vowel sound and writing the letter **i** with a family member. Encourage students to identify other words that have a medial short **i** vowel sound with their family.

✔ Formative Assessment

If the student completes each task correctly, proceed to the next skill in the sequence. If not, refer suggested Intervention 2.

Did the student...?	Intervention 2
Identify the name of the letter?	• Use physical rhythmic movements as the letter name is repeated. March while chanting the letter name. Move arms up and down. Sway from side to side.
Identify the sound of the letter?	• Use alliteration, chants that repeat the sound several times then a word that contains the sound. **Example:** /i/ /i/ /i/ **lit**
Produce the sound of the letter?	• Use mirrors to show movement of mouth, tongue, teeth as the sound is produced. • Use hand over mouth to explore movement of air as the sound is produced.
Recognize the beginning sound?	• Use Elkonin boxes – student moves a token into first box as the beginning sound of the word is said.
Write the letter?	• Write the letter, have students trace it. Create letter with clay. • Discuss letter features (lines, shape). Trace over letter with multiple colors.
Know the name of pictures?	• Tell students the name of pictures, have student repeat it aloud. • Discuss meaning of word. Use word in context.

Identify and Name Medial Short Vowel o RF.K.3b

CCSS: RF.K.3
Know and apply grade-level phonics and word analysis skills in decoding words both in isolation and in text.
b. Associate the long and short sounds with common spellings (graphemes) for the five major vowels.

Lesson Objectives

- Identify and name the letter **o**
- Produce the sound of letter **o**
- Relate the sound /**o**/ to the letter **o**
- Recognize **medial short vowel** sound **o** in words/pictures

METACOGNITIVE STRATEGY
- Selective auditory attention, imagery, auditory representation

ACADEMIC LANGUAGE
- letter name, letter sound, vowel, short sound, medial sound, middle

Additional Materials
Sound Spelling Card Oo
Blackline Master 108

Pre-Assess
Student's ability to recognize the sound represented by the target letter of the alphabet and to identify the letter used to represent the corresponding sound.

Introduce

As students participate in this lesson, they identify the name and sound of the target letter, and identify the letter when the sound and name are given orally. Students will apply their knowledge by recognizing the short sound of the target letter using pictures.

State Learning Goal

The letter **o** is a vowel. It has two sounds. The long sound /**o**/ and the short sound /**o**/. Today we will listen to the short vowel sound of the letter **o** in the **middle** of words.

Teach

Letters represent sounds. We remember the sounds each letter makes. We use letters to write words we say. We use letters to read and write words. The letter o is a vowel. It has a long sound /o/ and a short sound /o/.

Phonemic Awareness
Show picture of sound/spelling card **to review the short sound of o.**
Say: Listen to this sound /**o**/. Say it with me: **ooo**. Say it on your own: **ooo**.

Sound-Spelling Correspondence

Show the letter.
Say: *The way we write the sound /**o**/ is with the letter* **o.**

Say: *The letter* **o** *makes the* **short** /**o**/ *sound.*

Say: *What is the name of the letter?* **o** *What is the short sound the letter* **o** *makes?* /**o**/

Model
Use BLM 108, #1.

Say: *Look at each picture. Say its name. Listen for the* **short sound** *of /**o**/ in the* **middle.**

Say: *Do you hear the sound /**o**/ in the middle of the word* **floss**? *If we hear the sound of* **o** *in the middle of the word, we will circle the picture* **floss***. If we do not hear the sound /**o**/ in the middle, we will cross out the picture.*

Practice

Use BLM 108, # 2.

Say: Look *at the picture.* **Say** *its name.* **Write** *the letter.*

Say: *What is the* picture? **clock** *Do you hear the sound* **/o/** *in the* **middle** *of the word* **clock**? Then **write** the letter **o**.

Apply
Blend Words
Use BLM 108, #3.

Say: Look at each letter and listen to the sound as I read. **/s/ /o/ /ck/.** Your turn: **/s/ /o/ /ck/.**

Say: *Now we are going to blend the sounds together by stretching them out as we read them.* Point to each letter in a sweeping motion left to right: **/s/ooo/ccckkk/.** What is the word? **sock.**

Spelling

Use BLM 108, #4.

Say: *Now we can practice writing the sounds we hear in each word. Call one word at a time, stretching each sound. Say the word slowly; write a letter for each sound you hear*

Conclusion

Ask: *What did we learn today?* We learned that the letter **o** makes the sound **/o/** in the middle of some words. What pictures/words will help you remember the sound **/o/** and the letter **o**?

Home Connection

Encourage students to practice identifying the medial short vowel sound and writing the letter **o** with a family member. Encourage students to identify other words that have a medial short **o** vowel sound with their family.

✔ Formative Assessment

If the student completes each task correctly, proceed to the next skill in the sequence. If not, refer suggested Intervention 2.

Did the student...?	Intervention 2
Identify the name of the letter?	• Use physical rhythmic movements as the letter name is repeated. March while chanting the letter name. Move arms up and down. Sway from side to side.
Identify the sound of the letter?	• Use alliteration, chants that repeat the sound several times then a word that contains the sound. **Example: /o/ /o/ /o/ pot**
Produce the sound of the letter?	• Use mirrors to show movement of mouth, tongue, teeth as the sound is produced. • Use hand over mouth to explore movement of air as the sound is produced.
Recognize the beginning sound?	• Use Elkonin boxes – student moves a token into first box as the beginning sound of the word is said.
Write the letter?	• Write the letter, have students trace it. Create letter with clay. • Discuss letter features (lines, shape). Trace over letter with multiple colors.
Know the name of pictures?	• Tell students the name of pictures, have student repeat it aloud. • Discuss meaning of word. Use word in context.

Identify and Name Medial Short Vowel u RF.K.3b

CCSS: RF.K.3
Know and apply grade-level phonics and word analysis skills in decoding words both in isolation and in text.
b. Associate the long and short sounds with common spellings (graphemes) for the five major vowels.

Lesson Objectives

- Identify and name the letter **u**.
- Produce the sound of letter **u**.
- Relate the sound /**u**/ to the letter **u**.
- Recognize **medial short vowel** sound **u** in words/pictures.

METACOGNITIVE STRATEGY
- Selective auditory attention, imagery, auditory representation

ACADEMIC LANGUAGE
- letter name, letter sound, vowel, short sound, medial sound, middle

Additional Materials
Sound Spelling Card Uu
Blackline Master 109

Pre-Assess
Student's ability to recognize the sound represented by the target letter of the alphabet and to identify the letter used to represent the corresponding sound.

Introduce

As students participate in this lesson, they identify the name and sound of the target letter, and identify the letter when the sound and name are given orally. Students will apply their knowledge by recognizing the short sound of the target letter using pictures.

State Learning Goal

The letter **u** is a vowel. It has two sounds. The long sound /**u**/ and the short sound /**u**/. Today we will listen to the short vowel sound of the letter **u** in the middle of words.

Teach

Letters represent sounds. We remember the sounds each letter makes. We use letters to write words we say. We use letters to read and write words. The letter **u** is a vowel. It has a long sound /**u**/ and a short sound /**u**/.

Phonemic Awareness
Show picture of sound/spelling card **to review the short sound of u.**
Say: Listen to this sound /**u**/. Say it with me: **uuu.** Say it on your own: **uuu.**

Sound-Spelling Correspondence

Show the letter.
Say: *The way we write the sound /**u**/ is with the letter* **u.**

Say: *The letter* **u** *makes the* **short /u/** *sound.*

Say: *What is the name of the letter?* **u** *What is the short sound the letter* **u** *makes?* /**u**/

Model
Use BLM 109, #1

Say: *Look at each picture. Say its name.* **Listen for the short sound of /u/ in the middle.**

Say: *Do you hear the sound /**u**/ in the* **middle** *of the word plug? If we hear the sound of* **u** *in the middle of the word, we will circle the picture* **plug**. *If we do not hear the sound /**u**/ in the middle, we will cross out the picture.*

Practice

Use BLM 109, # 2

Say: Look at the picture. **Say** its name. **Write** the letter.

Say: What is the picture? **drums** Do you hear the sound /**u**/ in the **middle** of the word **drums**? Then **write** the letter **u**.

Apply
Blend Words

Use BLM 109, #3

Say: *Look at each letter and listen to the sound as I read.* /b/ /r/ /u/ /sh/. **Your turn:** /b/ /r/ /u/ /sh/.

Say: *Now we are going to blend the sounds together by stretching them out as we read them.* Point to each letter in a sweeping motion left to right: */b/r/uuu/ sssshhh/. What is t*he word? **brush.**

Spelling

Use BLM 109, #4

Say: *Now we can practice writing the sounds we hear in each word. Call one word at a time, stretching each sound. Say the word slowly; write a letter for each sound you hear.*

Conclusion

What did we learn today? We learned that the letter **u** makes the sound /**u**/ in the middle of some words. What pictures/words will help you remember the sound /**u**/ and the letter **u**?

Home Connection

Encourage students to practice identifying the medial short vowel sound and writing the letter **u** with a family member. Encourage students to identify other words that have a medial short **u** vowel sound with their family.

✔ Formative Assessment

If the student completes each task correctly, proceed to the next skill in the sequence. If not, refer suggested Intervention 2.

Did the student…?	Intervention 2
Identify the name of the letter?	• Use physical rhythmic movements as the letter name is repeated. March while chanting the letter name. Move arms up and down. Sway from side to side.
Identify the sound of the letter?	• Use alliteration, chants that repeat the sound several times then a word that contains the sound. **Example: /u/ /u/ /u/ rut**
Produce the sound of the letter?	• Use mirrors to show movement of mouth, tongue, teeth as the sound is produced. • Use hand over mouth to explore movement of air as the sound is produced.
Recognize the beginning sound?	• Use Elkonin boxes – student moves a token into first box as the beginning sound of the word is said.
Write the letter?	• Write the letter, have students trace it. Create letter with clay. • Discuss letter features (lines, shape). Trace over letter with multiple colors.
Know the name of pictures?	• Tell students the name of pictures, have student repeat it aloud. • Discuss meaning of word. Use word in context.

Identify and Name Medial Short Vowel e RF.K.3b

CCSS: RF.K.3
Know and apply grade-level phonics and word analysis skills in decoding words both in isolation and in text.
b. Associate the long and short sounds with common spellings (graphemes) for the five major vowels.

Lesson Objectives

- Identify and name the letter **e**
- Produce the sound of letter **e**
- Relate the sound /**e**/ to the letter **e**
- Recognize **medial short vowel** sound **e** in words/pictures

METACOGNITIVE STRATEGY
- Selective auditory attention, imagery, auditory representation

ACADEMIC LANGUAGE
- letter name, letter sound, vowel, short sound, medial sound, middle

Additional Materials
Sound Spelling Card Ee
Blackline Master 110

Pre-Assess
Student's ability to recognize the sound represented by the target letter of the alphabet and to identify the letter used to represent the corresponding sound.

Introduce

As students participate in this lesson, they identify the name and sound of the target letter, and identify the letter when the sound and name are given orally. Students will apply their knowledge by recognizing the short sound of the target letter using pictures.

State Learning Goal

The letter **e** is a vowel. It has two sounds. The long sound /**e**/ and the short sound /**e**/. Today we will listen to the short vowel sound of the letter **e** in the **middle** of words.

Teach

Letters represent sounds. We remember the sounds each letter makes. We use letters to write words we say. We use letters to read and write words. The letter e is a vowel. It has a long sound /**e**/ and a short sound /**e**/.

Phonemic Awareness
Show picture of sound/spelling card **to review the short sound of e.**
Say: Listen to this sound /**e**/. Say it with me: **eee.** Say it on your own: **eee.**

Sound-Spelling Correspondence

Show the letter.
Say: *The way we write the sound /**e**/ is with the letter* **e.**

Say: *The letter* **e** *makes the* **short sound /e/.**

Say: *What is the name of the letter?* **e** *What is the short sound the letter* **e** *makes?* /**e**/

Model
Use BLM 110, #1

Say: *Look at each picture. Say its name. Listen for the* **short sound** *of /**e**/ in the* **middle.**

Say: *Do you hear the sound /**e**/ in the* **middle** *of the word* **cent**? *If we hear the sound of e in the middle of the word, we will circle the picture* **cent***. If we do not hear the sound /**e**/ in the middle, we will cross out the picture.*

Practice

Use BLM 110, # 2

Say: Look at the picture. **Say** its name. **Write** the letter.

Say: What is the picture? **blend** Do you hear the sound /**e**/ in the **middle** of the word **blend**? Then **write** the letter **e**.

Apply
Blend Words

Use BLM 110, #3

Say: Look at each letter and listen to the sound as I read. /**s**/ /**e**/ /**v**/ /**e**/ /**n**/. Your turn: /**s**/ /**e**/ /**v**/ /**e**/ /**n**/.

Say: Now we are going to blend the sounds together by stretching them out as we read them. Point to each letter in a sweeping motion left to right /s/eee/vvv/eee/nnn/. What is the word? seven.

Spelling

Use BLM 110, #4

Say: Now we can practice writing the sounds we hear in each word. Call one word at a time, stretching each sound. Say the word slowly; write a letter for each sound you hear.

Conclusion

Ask: What did we learn today? We learned that the letter **e** makes the sound /**e**/ in the middle of some words. What pictures/words will help you remember the sound /**e**/ and the letter **e**?

Home Connection

Encourage students to practice identifying the medial short vowel sound and writing the letter **e** with a family member. Encourage students to identify other words that have a medial short **e** vowel sound with their family.

✔ Formative Assessment

If the student completes each task correctly, proceed to the next skill in the sequence. If not, refer suggested Intervention 2.

Did the student...?	Intervention 2
Identify the name of the letter?	• Use physical rhythmic movements as the letter name is repeated. March while chanting the letter name. Move arms up and down. Sway from side to side.
Identify the sound of the letter?	• Use alliteration, chants that repeat the sound several times then a word that contains the sound. **Example:** /e/ /e/ /e/ **eleven**
Produce the sound of the letter?	• Use mirrors to show movement of mouth, tongue, teeth as the sound is produced. • Use hand over mouth to explore movement of air as the sound is produced.
Recognize the beginning sound?	• Use Elkonin boxes – student moves a token into first box as the beginning sound of the word is said.
Write the letter?	• Write the letter, have students trace it. Create letter with clay. • Discuss letter features (lines, shape). Trace over letter with multiple colors.
Know the name of pictures?	• Tell students the name of pictures, have student repeat it aloud. • Discuss meaning of word. Use word in context.

Recognize Long Vowel Sound (CVCe) Pattern with Long a RF.K.3b

CCSS: RF.K.3
Know and apply grade-level phonics and word analysis skills in decoding words both in isolation and in text.
b. Associate the long sounds with common spellings (graphemes) for the five major vowels.

Lesson Objectives

- Identify and name the letter a
- Produce the sound of letter a
- Relate the sound /a/ to the letter a
- Recognize long vowel sound a in words/pictures
- Recognize long vowel sound (CVCe) pattern with long a

METACOGNITIVE STRATEGY
- Selective auditory attention, imagery, auditory representation

ACADEMIC LANGUAGE
- letter name, letter sound, vowel, long vowel sound, silent e, pattern

Additional Materials
Sound Spelling Card Aa
Blackline Master 111

Pre-Assess
Student's ability to recognize the **short vowel sound** represented by the target letter of the alphabet and to identify the letter used to represent the corresponding sound. Ability to **pronounce the long vowel** sound.

Introduce

As students participate in this lesson, they identify the name and sound of the target letter, and identify the letter when the sound and name are given orally. Students will apply their knowledge by recognizing the initial sound of the target letter using pictures.

State Learning Goal

Today we will learn to read words with the long sound of vowel **a**. We are going to learn that when we put the **vowel e** at the **end** of some words, the **first vowel** in the word **make its long sound** and the **vowel e** remains silent.

Teach

Letters represent sounds. We remember the sounds each letter makes. We use letters to write words we say. We use letters to read and write words. The letter a is a vowel. It has a long sound /a/ and a short sound /a/. We are going to learn words that have the long sound of vowel a.

Phonemic Awareness

Show picture of sound/spelling card **to review long sound of a.**
Say: *Listen to this sound /āāā/. Say it with me: /āāā/. Say it on your own: /āāā/.*

Say: *This is the long sound of vowel **a**. It sounds like it is saying its name: /āāā/, say it again /āāā/.*

Sound-Spelling Correspondence

Write the word amaze on the board. Point out the vowel a at the beginning of the word and the vowel e at the end.

Say: *Say when you see vowel **e** at the end of a 4 letter word, the **e** is silent and the first vowel makes its long sound.*

Say: *Look at the word **amaze.** Point: Does it have a vowel **e** at the end? Point: Then vowel āāā says its name.*

Say: *Read it with me **amaze.** Repeat with words **brace, cable,** and **fable.***

Model

Use BLM 111, #1.

Say: *Look at each picture. Say its name. Listen for the long sound of a. Does it have vowel e at the end?*

Say: *Do you hear the long sound of a? If so, circle the picture. If it does not, cross out the picture.*

Practice

Use BLM 111, # 2

Say: *Look at the picture. Say its name. cable. Listen for the long sound of a. Does it have vowel e at the end?*

Say: *Do you hear the long sound of a? Put a long line over vowel a and cross out vowel e. It is silent.*

Apply
Blend Words

Use BLM 111, #3

Say: *Look at each letter and listen to the long sound of vowel a as I read brace. Your turn: brace.*

Say: *Now we are going to blend the sounds together by stretching them out as we read them.*

Point to each letter in a sweeping motion left to right ***/bbb/rrr/aaa/ccc/.*** *What is the word? brace.*

Spelling

Use BLM 111, #4

Say: *Now we can practice writing the sounds we hear in each word. Call one word at a time, stretching each sound. Say the word slowly; write a letter for each sound you hear.*

Conclusion

Ask: *What did we learn today?* We learned that the vowel **a** makes the long sound /āāā/, when vowel **e** is at the end. What pictures/words will help you remember the long sound /ā/ with the silent **e** at the end?

Home Connection

Encourage students to practice identifying the medial short vowel sound and writing the letter **e** with a family member. Encourage students to identify other words that have a medial short **e** vowel sound with their family.

✔ Formative Assessment

If the student completes each task correctly, proceed to the next skill in the sequence. If not, refer suggested Intervention 2.

Did the student…?	Intervention 2
Identify the name of the letter?	• Use physical rhythmic movements as the letter name is repeated. March while chanting the letter name. Move arms up and down. Sway from side to side.
Identify the sound of the letter?	• Use chants that repeat the sound several times then a word that includes the sound. **Example:** /a/ /a/ /a/ cage.
Produce the sound of the letter?	• Use mirrors to show movement of mouth, tongue, teeth as the sound is produced. Use hand over mouth to explore movement of air as the sound is produced. .
Recognize the CVCe pattern?	• Arrange a list of common same vowel CVCe words vertically, point out pattern
Know the name of pictures?	• Tell students the name of pictures, have student repeat it aloud. • Discuss meaning of word. Use word in context.

©2017 Benchmark Education Company, LLC   **Benchmark Advance** • Intervention • Phonics and Word Recognition • Grade 3   **223**

Recognize Long Vowel Sound (CVCe) Pattern with Long o RF.K.3b

CCSS: RF.K.3
Know and apply grade-level phonics and word analysis skills in decoding words both in isolation and in text.
b. Associate the long sounds with common spellings (graphemes) for the five major vowels.

Lesson Objectives

- Identify and name the letter **o**
- Produce the sound of letter **o**
- Relate the sound /**o**/ to the letter **o**
- Recognize long vowel sound **o** in words/pictures
- Recognize long vowel sound (CVCe) pattern with long **o**

METACOGNITIVE STRATEGY
- Selective auditory attention, imagery, auditory representation

ACADEMIC LANGUAGE
- letter name, letter sound, vowel, long vowel sound, silent e, pattern

Additional Materials
Sound Spelling Card Oo
Blackline Master 112

Pre-Assess
Student's ability to recognize the **short vowel sound** represented by the target letter of the alphabet and to identify the letter used to represent the corresponding sound. Ability to **pronounce the long vowel** sound.

Introduce

As students participate in this lesson, they identify the name and sound of the target letter, and identify the letter when the sound and name are given orally. Students will apply their knowledge by recognizing the initial sound of the target letter using pictures.

State Learning Goal

Today we will learn to read words with the long sound of vowel **o**. We are going to learn that when we put the **vowel e** at the **end** of some words, the **first vowel** in the word **make its long sound** and the **vowel e** remains silent.

Teach

Letters represent sounds. We remember the sounds each letter makes. We use letters to write words we say. We use letters to read and write words. The letter **o** is a vowel. It has a long sound /ō/ and a short sound /o/. We are going to learn words that have the long sound of vowel **o**.

Phonemic Awareness

Show picture of sound/spelling card to review long sound of **o**.
Say: *Listen to this sound /ōōō/. Say it with me: /ōōō/. Say it on your own: /ōōō/.*

Say: *This is the long sound of vowel **o**. It sounds like it is saying its name: /ōōō/, say it again /ooo/.*

Sound-Spelling Correspondence

Write the word **phone** on the board. Point out the vowel **o** at the beginning of the word and the vowel **e** at the end.
Say: *Say when you see vowel **e** at the end of a 4 letter word, the **e** is silent and the first vowel makes its long sound.*

Say: *Look at the word **phone**. Point: Does it have a vowel **e** at the end?*

Point: Then vowel **ooo** says its name.

Say: *Read it with me **phone**. Repeat with words **slope, smoke, stove**.*

Model
Use BLM 112, #1.

Say: *Look at each picture. Say its name. Listen for the long sound of /**o**/. Does it have vowel **e** at the end?*

Say: *Do you hear the long sound of **o** in phone? If so, circle the picture of the phone. If not, cross out the picture.*

Practice

Use BLM 112, # 2

Say: *Look at the picture. Say its name. Listen for the long sound of* **o**. *Does it have vowel* **e** *at the end?*

Say: *Do you hear the long sound /ō/ in smoke? Put a line long line over vowel* **o** *and cross out vowel* **e**. *It is silent.*

Apply

Blend Words

Use BLM 112, #3

Say: *Look at each letter and listen to the long sound of vowel* **a** *as I read* **slope**. *Your turn:* **slope**.

Say: *Now we are going to blend the sounds together by stretching them out as we read them.*

Point to each letter in a sweeping motion left to right /bbb/rrr/aaa/ccc/. What is the word? **slope**.

Spelling

Use BLM 112, #4

Say: *Now we can practice writing the sounds we hear in each word. Call one word at a time, stretching each sound. Say the word slowly; write a letter for each sound you hear.*

Conclusion

Ask: *What did we learn today?* We learned that the vowel **o** makes the long sound /ōōō/, when vowel **e** is at the end. What pictures/words will help you remember the long sound /ō/ with the silent **e** at the end?

Home Connection

Encourage students to practice identifying the long **o** sound and writing the letter **o** with a family member. Encourage students to identify other words that have a medial **o** sound with their long **o** family.

✔ Formative Assessment

If the student completes each task correctly, proceed to the next skill in the sequence. If not, refer suggested Intervention 2.

Did the student…?	Intervention 2
Identify the name of the letter?	• Use physical rhythmic movements as the letter name is repeated. March while chanting the letter name. Move arms up and down. Sway from side to side.
Identify the sound of the letter?	• Use chants that repeat the sound several times then a word that includes the sound. **Example:** /o/ /o/ /o/ **hope**.
Produce the sound of the letter?	• Use mirrors to show movement of mouth, tongue, teeth as the sound is produced. Use hand over mouth to explore movement of air as the sound is produced. .
Recognize the CVCe pattern?	• Arrange a list of common same vowel CVCe words vertically, point out pattern
Know the name of pictures?	• Tell students the name of pictures, have student repeat it aloud. • Discuss meaning of word. Use word in context.

Recognize Long Vowel Sound (CVCe) Pattern with Long i RF.K.3b, c

CCSS: RF.K.3
Know and apply grade-level phonics and word analysis skills in decoding words both in isolation and in text.
b. Associate the long sounds with common spellings (graphemes) for the five major vowels.

Lesson Objectives

- Identify and name the letter **i**
- Produce the sound of letter **i**
- Relate the sound /i/ to the letter **i**
- Recognize long vowel sound **i** in words/pictures
- Recognize long vowel sound (CVCe) pattern with long **i**

METACOGNITIVE STRATEGY
- Selective auditory attention, imagery, auditory representation

ACADEMIC LANGUAGE
- letter name, letter sound, vowel, long vowel sound, silent e, pattern

Additional Materials
Sound Spelling Card Ii
Blackline Master 113

Pre-Assess
Student's ability to recognize the **short vowel sound** represented by the target letter of the alphabet and to identify the letter used to represent the corresponding sound. Ability to **pronounce the long vowel** sound.

Introduce

As students participate in this lesson, they identify the name and sound of the target letter, and identify the letter when the sound and name are given orally. Students will apply their knowledge by recognizing the initial sound of the target letter using pictures.

State Learning Goal

Today we will learn to read words with the long sound of vowel i. We are going to learn that when we put the **vowel e** at the **end** of some words, the **first vowel** in the word **make its long sound** and the **vowel e** remains silent.

Teach

Letters represent sounds. We remember the sounds each letter makes. We use letters to write words we say. We use letters to read and write words. The letter **i** is a vowel. It has a long sound /i/ and a short sound /i/. We are going to learn words that have the long sound of vowel **i**.

Phonemic Awareness

Show picture of sound/spelling card to review long sound of **i**.
Say: *Listen to this sound /ī/. Say it with me: /ī/. Say it on your own: / ī /.*
Say: *This is the long sound of vowel **i**. It sounds like it is saying its name: /ī/, say it again /ī/.*

Sound-Spelling Correspondence

Write the word **chime** on the board. Point out the vowel **i** at the beginning of the word and the vowel **e** at the end.
Say: *Say when you see vowel e at the end of a 4 letter word, the **e** is silent and the first vowel makes its long sound.*
Say: *Look at the word **chime**. Point: Does it have a vowel **e** at the end? Point: Then vowel **i** says its name.*
Say: *Read it with me **chime**. Repeat with words **grime**, **shine**, **mice**.*

Model

Use BLM 113, #1.

Say: *Look at each picture. Say its name. Listen for the long sound of /i/. Does it have vowel **e** at the end?*
Say: *Do you hear the long sound of /i/ in chime? If so, circle the picture. If not, cross out the picture.*

Practice

Use BLM 113, # 2

Say: *Look at the picture. Say its name. Listen for the long sound of* **i**. *Does it have vowel* **e** *at the end?*

Say: *Do you hear the long sound of* **i** *in shine? Put a line long line over vowel* **i** *and cross out vowel* **e**. *It is silent.*

Apply
Blend Words

Use BLM 41, #3

Say: *Look at each letter and listen to the long sound of vowel* **i** *as I read* **grime**. *Your turn:* **grime**.

Say: *Now we are going to blend the sounds together by stretching them out as we read them.*

Point to each letter in a sweeping motion left to right /**ggg**/**rrr**/**iii**/**mmm**/. *What is the word?* **grime**.

Spelling

Use BLM 113, #4

Say: *Now we can practice writing the sounds we hear in each word. Call one word at a time, stretching each sound.*

Say: *Say the word slowly; write a letter for each sound you hear.*

Conclusion

Ask: *What did we learn today?* We learned that the vowel **i** makes the long sound /iii/, when vowel **e** is at the end. What pictures/words will help you remember the long sound /**i**/ with the silent **e** at the end?

Home Connection

Encourage students to practice identifying the long vowel sound **i** in CVCe words with a family member.

✔ Formative Assessment

If the student completes each task correctly, proceed to the next skill in the sequence. If not, refer to suggested Intervention 2.

Did the student...?	Intervention 2
Identify the name of the letter?	• Use physical rhythmic movements as the letter name is repeated. March while chanting the letter name. Move arms up and down. Sway from side to side.
Identify the sound of the letter?	• Use chants that repeat the sound several times then a word that includes the sound. **Example:** /i/ /i/ /i/ **bike**.
Produce the sound of the letter?	• Use mirrors to show movement of mouth, tongue, teeth as the sound is produced. Use hand over mouth to explore movement of air as the sound is produced.
Recognize the CVCe pattern?	• Arrange a list of common same vowel CVCe words vertically, point out pattern.
Know the name of pictures?	• Tell students the name of pictures, have student repeat it aloud. • Discuss meaning of word. Use word in context.

Recognize Long Vowel Sound (CVCe) Pattern with Long u RF.K.3b

CCSS: RF.K.3
Know and apply grade-level phonics and word analysis skills in decoding words both in isolation and in text.
b. Associate the long sounds with common spellings (graphemes) for the five major vowels.

Lesson Objectives

- Identify and name the letter **u**
- Produce the sound of letter **u**
- Relate the sound /**u**/ to the letter u
- Recognize long vowel sound **u** in words/pictures
- Recognize long vowel sound (CVCe) pattern with long **u**

METACOGNITIVE STRATEGY
- Selective auditory attention, imagery, auditory representation

ACADEMIC LANGUAGE
- letter name, letter sound, vowel, long vowel sound, silent e, pattern

Additional Materials
Sound Spelling Card Uu
Blackline Master 114

Pre-Assess
Student's ability to recognize the **short vowel sound** represented by the target letter of the alphabet and to identify the letter used to represent the corresponding sound. Ability to **pronounce the long vowel** sound.

Introduce

As students participate in this lesson, they identify the name and sound of the target letter, and identify the letter when the sound and name are given orally. Students will apply their knowledge by recognizing the initial sound of the target letter using pictures.

State Learning Goal

Today we will learn to read words with the long sound of vowel i. We are going to learn that when we put the **vowel e** at the **end** of some words, the **first vowel** in the word **make its long sound** and the **vowel e** remains silent.

Teach

Letters represent sounds. We remember the sounds each letter makes. We use letters to write words we say. We use letters to read and write words. The letter u is a vowel. It has a long sound /u/ and a short sound /u/. We are going to learn words that have the long sound of vowel u.

Phonemic Awareness

Show picture of sound/spelling card to review long sound of **u**.
Say: Listen to this sound /ūūū/. Say it with me: /ūūū/. Say it on your own: /ūūū/.
Say: This is the long sound of vowel **u**. It sounds like it is saying its name: /ūūū/, say it again /ūūū/.

Sound-Spelling Correspondence

Write the word **amuse** on the board. Point out the vowel **u** at the beginning of the word and the vowel **e** at the end.
Say: Say when you see vowel **e** at the end of a 4 letter word, the **e** is silent and the first vowel makes its long sound.
Say: Look at the word **amuse**. Point: Does it have a vowel **e** at the end? Point: Then vowel **u** says its name.
Say: Read it with me **amuse**. Repeat with words **cubes, prune, argue.**

Model

Use BLM 114, #1.

Say: Look at each picture. Say its name. Listen for the long sound of /**u**/. Does it have vowel **e** at the end?

Say: Do you hear the long sound of /ū/ in **statue**? If so, circle the picture. If not, cross out the picture.

Practice

Use BLM 114, # 2

Say: Look at the picture. Say its name. Listen for the long sound /ū/. Does it have vowel **e** at the end?

Say: Do you hear the long sound of **u** in argue? Put a line long line over vowel **u** and cross out vowel **e**. It is silent.

Apply
Blend Words

Use BLM 114, #3

Say: Look at each letter and listen to the long sound of vowel **u** as I read **e**. Your turn: **cubes**.
Say: Now we are going to blend the sounds together by stretching them out as we read them.
Point to each letter in a sweeping motion left to right **/k/ūūū/bbb/zzz/**. What is the word? **cubes**.

Spelling

Use BLM 114, #4

Say: *Now we can practice writing the sounds we hear in each word. Call one word at a time, stretching each sound.*
Say: *Say the word slowly; write a letter for each sound you hear.*

Conclusion

Ask: *What did we learn today?* We learned that the vowel **u** makes the long sound /ūūū/, when vowel **e** is at the end. What pictures/words will help you remember the long sound /ū/ with the silent **e** at the end?

Home Connection
Encourage students to practice identifying long vowel sound **u** in CVCe words with a family member.

✔ Formative Assessment

If the student completes each task correctly, proceed to the next skill in the sequence. If not, refer to suggested Intervention 2.

Did the student…?	Intervention 2
Identify the name of the letter?	• Use physical rhythmic movements as the letter name is repeated. March while chanting the letter name. Move arms up and down. Sway from side to side.
Identify the sound of the letter?	• Use chants that repeat the sound several times then a word that includes the sound. **Example:** /u/ /u/ /u/ cube.
Produce the sound of the letter?	• Use mirrors to show movement of mouth, tongue, teeth as the sound is produced. Use hand over mouth to explore movement of air as the sound is produced.
Recognize the CVCe pattern?	• Arrange a list of common same vowel CVCe words vertically, point out pattern.
Know the name of pictures?	• Tell students the name of pictures, have student repeat it aloud. • Discuss meaning of word. Use word in context.

Recognize Long Vowel Sound (CVCe) Pattern with Long e RF.K.3b

CCSS: RF.K.3
Know and apply grade-level phonics and word analysis skills in decoding words both in isolation and in text.
b. Associate the long sounds with common spellings (graphemes) for the five major vowels.

Lesson Objectives

- Identify and name the letter **Ee**
- Produce the sound of letter **e**
- Relate the sound /**e**/ to the letter **e**
- Recognize long vowel sound **e** in words/pictures
- Recognize long vowel sound (CVCe) pattern with long **e**

METACOGNITIVE STRATEGY
- Selective auditory attention, imagery, auditory representation

ACADEMIC LANGUAGE
- letter name, letter sound, vowel, long vowel sound, silent e, pattern

Additional Materials
Sound Spelling Card Ee
Blackline Master 115

Pre-Assess
Student's ability to recognize the **short vowel sound** represented by the target letter of the alphabet and to identify the letter used to represent the corresponding sound. Ability to **pronounce the long vowel** sound.

Introduce

As students participate in this lesson, they identify the name and sound of the target letter, and identify the letter when the sound and name are given orally. Students will apply their knowledge by recognizing the initial sound of the target letter using pictures.

State Learning Goal

Today we will learn to read words with the long sound of vowel e. We are going to learn that when we put the **vowel e** at the **end** of some words, the **first vowel** in the word **make its long sound** and the **vowel e** remains silent.

Teach

Letters represent sounds. We remember the sounds each letter makes. We use letters to write words we say. We use letters to read and write words. The letter **e** is a vowel. It has a long sound /ē/ and a short sound /e/. We are going to learn words that have the long sound of vowel **e**.

Phonemic Awareness

Show picture of sound/spelling card to review long sound of **e**.
Say: Listen to this sound /ēēē/. Say it with me: /ēēē/. Say it on your own: /ēēē/.
Say: This is the long sound of vowel **e**. It sounds like it is saying its name: /ēēē/, say it again /ēēē/.

Sound-Spelling Correspondence

Write the word **grease** on the board. Point out the vowel **e** at the beginning of the word and the vowel **e** at the end.
Say: Say when you see vowel **e** at the end of a 4 letter word, the **e** is silent and the first vowel makes its long sound.
Say: Look at the word **freeze**. Point: Does it have a vowel **e** at the end? Point: Then vowel **eee** says its name.
Say: Read it with me **freeze**. Repeat with words **cheese** and **geese**.

Model

Use BLM 115, #1.

Say: Look at each picture. Say its name. Listen for the long sound of /**e**/. Does it have vowel **e** at the end?

Say: Do you hear the long sound of /ē/ in **weave**? If so, circle the picture. If not, cross out the picture.

Practice

Use BLM 115, # 2

Say: Look at the picture. Say its name. Listen for the long sound of **e**. Does it have vowel **e** at the end?

Say: Do you hear the long sound /ē/ in **cheese**? Put a line long line over vowel **e** and cross out vowel **e**. It is silent.

Apply–Blend Words

Use BLM 115, #3

Say: Look at each letter and listen to the long sound of vowel **e** as I read **e**. Your turn: **sneeze**.
Say: Now we are going to blend the sounds together by stretching them out as we read them.
Point to each letter in a sweeping motion left to right /**sn**/ēēē/**zzz**. What is the word? **sneeze**.

Spelling

Use BLM 115, #4

Say: *Now we can practice writing the sounds we hear in each word. Call one word at a time, stretching each sound.*
Say: *Say the word slowly; write a letter for each sound you hear.*

Conclusion

What did we learn today? We learned that the vowel **e** makes the long sound /ē/, when vowel **e** is at the end. What pictures/words will help you remember the long sound /ē/ with the silent **e** at the end?

Home Connection
Encourage students to practice identifying long vowel sound **e** in CVCe words with a family member.

✔ Formative Assessment

If the student completes each task correctly, proceed to the next skill in the sequence. If not, refer to suggested Intervention 2.

Did the student…?	Intervention 2
Identify the name of the letter?	• Use physical rhythmic movements as the letter name is repeated. March while chanting the letter name. Move arms up and down. Sway from side to side.
Identify the sound of the letter?	• Use chants that repeat the sound several times then a word that includes the sound. **Example:** /e/ /e/ /e/ **bee**.
Produce the sound of the letter?	• Use mirrors to show movement of mouth, tongue, teeth as the sound is produced. Use hand over mouth to explore movement of air as the sound is produced.
Recognize the CVCe pattern?	• Arrange a list of common same vowel CVCe words vertically, point out pattern.
Know the name of pictures?	• Tell students the name of pictures, have student repeat it aloud. • Discuss meaning of word. Use word in context.

Differentiate between long and short vowel a RF.K.3b

CCSS: RF.K.3
Know and apply grade-level phonics and word analysis skills in decoding words both in isolation and in text.
b. Associate the long sounds with common spellings (graphemes) for the five major vowels.

Lesson Objectives

- Recognize short vowel sounds in pictures/words
- Recognize long vowel sound in pictures/words
- Differentiate between long and short vowel sounds

METACOGNITIVE STRATEGY
- Selective auditory attention, imagery, auditory representation

ACADEMIC LANGUAGE
- letter sound, vowel, long vowel sound

Additional Materials
Sound Spelling Card Aa
Blackline Master 116

Pre-Assess
Student's ability to recognize the **short vowel sound** and long vowel sound represented by each vowel. Ability to **distinguish** and orally **pronounce the short and long vowel** sound of each vowel.

Introduce

As students participate in this lesson, they identify the name and the long and short sound of the targeted vowel, and identify the letter when the sound and name are given orally. Students will apply their knowledge by distinguishing between long and short vowel sounds in pictures/words.

State Learning Goal

Today we will read words with short vowel sounds and long sound of vowel **a**. We are going to practice reading short vowel words that have the letter pattern CCVC and adding the silent e at the end to create the letter pattern CCVCe so that the **first vowel** in the word **make its long sound** and the **vowel e** remains silent.

Teach

Letters represent sounds. We remember the sounds each letter makes. We use letters to write words we say. We use letters to read and write words. Each vowel has a **short sound and a long sound**.

Phonemic Awareness

Show sound/spelling cards **to review the short and long sound of each vowel.**

Say: This is a picture of a **lamp**. It represents the short sound of vowel **a**.

Say: Listen to the sound of short vowel /**a**/ Say it with me: /**a**/. Say it on your own: /**a**/.

Say: This is a picture of a **plate**. It represents the long sound of vowel **a**.

Say: This is the long sound of vowel **a**. It sounds like it is saying its name: /ā/, say it again /ā/.

Sound-Spelling Correspondence

Write the word **clam** on the board. Point out the vowel **a**. Point out the pattern CCVC.
Say: Look at the word **clam**. Read each sound. /**c**/ /**l**/ /**a**/ /**m**/. The vowel says its short sound. What is the word? **clam**
Say: Look at the word **blame**. Point: Does it have a vowel **e** at the end? Point: Then, vowel **a** says its name.
Say: Read each sound: /**b**/ /**l**/ /ā/ /**m**/. The **e** at the end is silent. It does not make a sound. What is the word? **blame**.

Model
Use BLM 116, #1.

Say: Look at the word **blast**. The vowel is in the middle. It is a short sound. Read each sound. /**b**/ /**l**/ /**a**/ /**s**/ /**t**/.

Say: Look at the word **paste**. Point: Does it have a vowel **e** at the end? Point: Then, vowel **a** says its name. Read each sound: /**p**/ /**a**/ /**s**/ /**t**/ . The **e** at the end is silent. It does not make a sound.

Say: Circle word(s) with the short **a** sound like **blast**. Draw a box around word(s) with the long **a** sound like **paste**.

Practice
Use BLM 116, # 2

Say: Look at the word **grass.** The vowel is in the middle. Read each sound. /g/ /r/ /a/ /s/. What is the word? **grass.**

Say: Look at the word place. Does it have a vowel **e** at the end? Then, vowel **a** says its name. Read each sound: **/p/ /l/ /ā/ /s/.** The **e** at the end is silent. It does not make a sound. What is the word? **place.**

Say: Write the letter **a** on the line for word(s) with a short a sound like grass. Cross out the letter **e** at the end of word(s) with a long a sound like **place.**

Apply
Blend Words
Use BLM 116, #3

Say: Look at each word. Think: Does it have a silent **e** at the end? Will the first vowel say its name? Look again. Is the vowel in the middle? Will the vowel say its short sound?
Say: Now we are going to blend the sounds together by stretching them out as we read them. Point to each letter in a sweeping motion left to right **/s/ppp/lll/aaa// sh/.** What is the word? **splash.**

Spelling

Use BLM 116, #4
Say: *Now we can practice writing the sounds we hear in each word. Call one word at a time, stretching each sound. Say the word slowly. Listen for the short or long vowel sound of vowel **a**. Do not forget the silent **e** at the end if you hear the vowel say its name.*

Conclusion

Ask: *What did we learn today?* We learned that the vowel **a** makes a short sound when it is in between two consonants. It makes the long sound /ā/, when vowel **e** is at the end. What pictures/words will help you remember the long sound /ā/ with the silent **e** at the end? What pictures or words will help you remember the short sound of vowel **a**?

Home Connection
Encourage students to practice identifying short vowel sound of **a** in CCVC words and the long sound of **a** in CCVCe words with a family member.

✔ Formative Assessment

If the student completes each task correctly, proceed to the next skill in the sequence. If not, refer to suggested Intervention 2.

Did the student…?	Intervention 2
Identify the name of the letter?	• Use physical rhythmic movements as the letter name is repeated. March while chanting the letter name. Move arms up and down. Sway from side to side
Identify the sound of the letter?	• Use chants that repeat the sound several times then a word that includes the sound. **Example:** /a/ /a/ /a/ **bald** and / // // / **brake.**
Produce the sound of the letter?	• Use mirrors to show movement of mouth, tongue, teeth as the sound is produced. Use hand over mouth to explore movement of air as the sound is produced.
Recognize the CVCe pattern?	• Arrange a list of common same vowel CVCe words vertically, point out pattern.
Know the name of pictures?	• Tell students the name of pictures, have student repeat it aloud. • Discuss meaning of word. Use word in context.

Differentiate between long and short vowel i RF.K.3b, c

CCSS: RF.K.3
Know and apply grade-level phonics and word analysis skills in decoding words both in isolation and in text.
b. Associate the long sounds with common spellings (graphemes) for the five major vowels.

Lesson Objectives

- Recognize short vowel sounds in pictures/words
- Recognize long vowel sound in pictures/words
- Differentiate between long and short vowel sounds

METACOGNITIVE STRATEGY
- Selective auditory attention, imagery, auditory representation

ACADEMIC LANGUAGE
- letter sound, vowel, long vowel sound

Additional Materials
Sound Spelling Card I
Blackline Master 117

Pre-Assess
Student's ability to recognize the **short vowel sound** and long vowel sound represented by each vowel. Ability to **distinguish** and orally **pronounce the short and long vowel** sound of each vowel.

Introduce

As students participate in this lesson, they identify the name and the long and short sound of sound of the targeted vowel, and identify the letter when the sound and name are given orally. Students will apply their knowledge by distinguishing between long and short vowel sounds in pictures/words.

State Learning Goal

Today we will read words with short vowel sounds and long sound of vowel **i**. We are going to practice reading short vowel words that have the letter pattern CVC and adding the silent e at the end to create the letter pattern CVCe so that the **first vowel** in the word **make its long sound** and the **vowel e** remains silent.

Teach

Letters represent sounds. We remember the sounds each letter makes. We use letters to write words we say. We use letters to read and write words. Each vowel has a **short sound and a long sound.**

Phonemic Awareness

Show sound/spelling cards **to review the short and long sound of each vowel.**
Say: This is a picture of a **swing**. It represents the short sound of vowel **i**.
Say: Listen to the sound of short vowel /**i**/ Say it with me: / **i**/. Say it on your own: / **i**/.
Say: This is a picture of a **bride.** It represents the long sound of vowel **i**.
Say: This is the long sound of vowel **i**. It sounds like it is saying its name: /ī/, say it again /ī/.

Sound-Spelling Correspondence

Write the word **skill** on the board. Point out the vowel **i**. Point out the pattern CCVCC.
Say: Look at the word **skill**. Read each sound. /**s**//**k**/ /**i**/ /**l**/ /**l**/. The vowel says its short sound. What is the word? **skill**. **Say:** Look at the word **shine**. Point: Does it have a vowel **e** at the end? Point: Then, vowel **i** says its name. **Say:** Read each sound: /**sh**/ /ī/ /**n**/ . The **e** at the end is silent. It does not make a sound. What is the word? **shine.**

Model

Use BLM 117, #1.

Say: Look at the word **fifth**. The vowel is in the middle. It says its short sound. Read each sound. /**f**/ /**i**/ /**f**/ /**th**/.
Say: Look at the word **while**. Point: Does it have a vowel **e** at the end? Point: Then, vowel i says its name. Read each sound: /**hw**/ /ī/ /**l**/. The **e** at the end is silent. It does not make a sound.
Say: Circle word(s) with the short **i** sound like **fifth**. Draw a box around word(s) with the long **i** sound like **while.**

Practice

Use BLM 117, # 2

Say: Look at the word **stink**. The vowel is in the middle. Read each sound. /s/ /t/ /i/ /n/ /k/. What is the word? **stink**.

Say: Look at the word **prime**. Does it have a vowel **e** at the end? Then, vowel i says its name. Read each sound: /p/ /r/ /i/ /m/ . The **e** at the end is silent. It does not make a sound. What is the word? **prime**.

Say: Write the letter **i** on the line for word(s) with a short i sound like **stink**. Cross out the letter e at the end of word(s) with a long **i** sound like **prime**.

Apply
Blend Words

Use BLM 117, #3

Say: Look at each word. Think: Does it have a silent **e** at the end? Will the first vowel say its name? Look again. Is the vowel in the middle? Will the vowel say its short sound?

Say: Now we are going to blend the sounds together by stretching them out as we read them. Point to each letter in a sweeping motion left to right /th/rrr/ī/vvv/. What is the word? **thrive**.

Spelling

Use BLM 117, #4

Say: *Now we can practice writing the sounds we hear in each word. Call one word at a time, stretching each sound. Say the word slowly. Listen for the short or long vowel sound of vowel* **i***. Do not forget the silent* **e** *at the end if you hear the vowel say its name.*

Conclusion

Ask: *What did we learn today?* We learned that the vowel **i** makes a short sound when it is in between two consonants. It makes the long sound /ī/, when vowel **e** is at the end. What pictures/words will help you remember the long sound /ī/ with the silent **e** at the end? What pictures or words will help you remember the short sound of vowel **i**?

Home Connection

Encourage students to practice identifying short vowel sound of **i** in CVC words and the long sound of **i** in CVCe words with a family member.

✔ Formative Assessment

If the student completes each task correctly, proceed to the next skill in the sequence. If not, refer to suggested Intervention 2.

Did the student…?	Intervention 2
Identify the name of the letter?	• Use physical rhythmic movements as the letter name is repeated. March while chanting the letter name. Move arms up and down. Sway from side to side.
Identify the sound of the letter?	• Use chants that repeat the sound several times then a word that includes the sound. **Example:** /sl/ /sl/ /sl/ **slink** and /sl/ /sl/ /sl/ **slime**
Produce the sound of the letter?	• Use mirrors to show movement of mouth, tongue, teeth as the sound is produced. Use hand over mouth to explore movement of air as the sound is produced.
Recognize the CVCe pattern?	• Arrange a list of common same vowel CVCe words vertically, point out pattern.
Know the name of pictures?	• Tell students the name of pictures, have student repeat it aloud. • Discuss meaning of word. Use word in context.

Differentiate between long and short vowel O RF.K.3b

Introduce

As students participate in this lesson, they identify the name and the long and short sound of the targeted vowel, and identify the letter when the sound and name are given orally. Students will apply their knowledge by distinguishing between long and short vowel sounds in pictures/words.

State Learning Goal

Today we will read words with short vowel sounds and long sound of vowel **o**. We are going to practice reading short vowel words that have the letter pattern CVC and adding the silent e at the end to create the letter pattern CVCe so that the **first vowel** in the word make its long sound and the **vowel e** remains silent.

Teach

Letters represent sounds. We remember the sounds each letter makes. We use letters to write words we say. We use letters to read and write words. Each vowel has a **short sound and a long sound**.

Phonemic Awareness

Show sound/spelling cards **to review the short and long sound of each vowel.**

Say: This is a picture of a **clock**. It represents the short sound of vowel **o**. Listen to the sound of short vowel /o/ Say it with me: /o/. Say it on your own: /**o**/. This is a picture of a **phone**. It represents the long sound of vowel **o**. This is the long sound of vowel **o**. It sounds like it is saying its name: /ō/, say it again /ō/.

Sound-Spelling Correspondence

Write the word **crop** on the board. Point out the vowel **o**. Point out the pattern CCVC.
Say: Look at the word **crop**. Read each sound. /c/ /r/ /o/ /p/. The vowel says its short sound. What is the word? **crop**.
Say: Look at the word **chose**. Point: Does it have a vowel **e** at the end? Point: Then, vowel **o** says its name.
Say: Read each sound: /ch/ /ō/ /z/ . The **e** at the end is silent. It does not make a sound. What is the word? **chose**.

Model

Use BLM 118, #1.

Say: Look at the word **flop**. The vowel is in the middle. It says its short sound. Read each sound. /f/ /l/ /o/ /p/.
Say: Look at the word **slope**. Point: Does it have a vowel **e** at the end? Point: Then, vowel **o** says its name. Read each sound: /s/ /l/ /ō/ /p/ . The **e** at the end is silent. It does not make a sound.
Say: Circle word(s) with the short **o** sound like **flop**. Draw a box around word(s) with the long **o** sound like **slope**.

CCSS: RF.K.3
Know and apply grade-level phonics and word analysis skills in decoding words both in isolation and in text.
b. Associate the long sounds with common spellings (graphemes) for the five major vowels.

Lesson Objectives

- Recognize short vowel sounds in pictures/words
- Recognize long vowel sound in pictures/words
- Differentiate between long and short vowel sounds

METACOGNITIVE STRATEGY
- Selective auditory attention, imagery, auditory representation

ACADEMIC LANGUAGE
- letter sound, vowel, long vowel sound

Additional Materials
Sound Spelling Card Oo
Blackline Master 118

Pre-Assess
Student's ability to recognize the **short vowel sound** and long vowel sound represented by each vowel. Ability to **distinguish** and orally **pronounce the short and long vowel** sound of each vowel.

Practice

Use BLM 118, # 2

Say: Look at the word **moth**. The vowel is in the middle. Read each sound. /**m**/ /**o**/ /**th**/. What is the word? **moth**.

Say: Look at the word **grove**. Does it have a vowel **e** at the end? Then, vowel **o** says its name. Read each sound: /**g**/ /**r**/ /**ō**/ /**v**/. The **e** at the end is silent. It does not make a sound. What is the word? **grove**.

Say: Write the letter **o** on the line for word(s) with a short **o** sound like **moth**. Cross out the letter **e** at the end of word(s) with a long **o** sound like **grove**.

Apply

Blend Words

Say: Look at each word. Think: Does it have a silent **e** at the end? Will the first vowel say its name? Look again, is the vowel in the middle? Will the vowel say its short sound?

Say: Now we are going to blend the sounds together by stretching them out as we read them. Point to each letter in a sweeping motion left to right /**th**/**rrr**/**ōōō**/**nnn**/. What is the word? **throne**.

Spelling

Use BLM 118, #4

Say: *Now we can practice writing the sounds we hear in each word. Call one word at a time, stretching each sound. Say the word slowly. Listen for the short or long vowel sound of vowel* **o**. *Do not forget the silent* **e** *at the end if you hear the vowel say its name.*

Conclusion

Ask: *What did we learn today?* We learned that the vowel o makes a short sound when it is in between two consonants. It makes the long sound /ō/, when vowel **e** is at the end. What pictures/words will help you remember the long sound /ō/ with the silent **e** at the end? What pictures or words will help you remember the short sound of vowel **o**?

Home Connection

Encourage students to practice identifying short vowel sound of **o** in CVC words and the long sound of **o** in CVCe words with a family member.

✔ Formative Assessment

If the student completes each task correctly, proceed to the next skill in the sequence. If not, refer to suggested Intervention 2.

Did the student…?	Intervention 2
Identify the name of the letter?	• Use physical rhythmic movements as the letter name is repeated. March while chanting the letter name. Move arms up and down. Sway from side to side.
Identify the sound of the letter?	• Use chants that repeat the sound several times then a word that includes the sound. **Example:** / / / / / / **short** and / / / / / / **shore**
Produce the sound of the letter?	• Use mirrors to show movement of mouth, tongue, teeth as the sound is produced. Use hand over mouth to explore movement of air as the sound is produced.
Recognize the CVCe pattern?	• Arrange a list of common same vowel CVCe words vertically, point out pattern..
Know the name of pictures?	• Tell students the name of pictures, have student repeat it aloud. • Discuss meaning of word. Use word in context.

Differentiate between long and short vowel U RF.K.3b

CCSS: RF.K.3
Know and apply grade-level phonics and word analysis skills in decoding words both in isolation and in text.
b. Associate the long sounds with common spellings (graphemes) for the five major vowels.

Lesson Objectives

- Recognize short vowel sounds in pictures/words
- Recognize long vowel sound in pictures/words
- Differentiate between long and short vowel sounds

METACOGNITIVE STRATEGY
- Selective auditory attention, imagery, auditory representation

ACADEMIC LANGUAGE
- letter sound, vowel, long vowel sound

Additional Materials
Sound Spelling Card U
Blackline Master 119

Pre-Assess
Student's ability to recognize the **short vowel sound** and long vowel sound represented by each vowel. Ability to **distinguish** and orally **pronounce the short and long vowel** sound of each vowel.

Introduce

As students participate in this lesson, they identify the name and the long and short sound of the targeted vowel, and identify the letter when the sound and name are given orally. Students will apply their knowledge by distinguishing between long and short vowel sounds in pictures/words.

State Learning Goal

Today we will read words with short vowel sounds and long sound of vowel **u**. We are going to practice reading short vowel words that have the letter pattern CCVC and adding the silent e at the end to create the letter pattern CCVCe so that the **first vowel** in the word **make its long sound** and the **vowel e** remains silent.

Teach

Letters represent sounds. We remember the sounds each letter makes. We use letters to write words we say. We use letters to read and write words. Each vowel has a **short sound and a long sound**.

Phonemic Awareness

Show sound/spelling cards to review the short and long sound of each vowel.
Say: This is a picture of a truck. It represents the short sound of vowel u. Listen to the sound of short vowel /u/ Say it with me: /u/. Say it on your own: /u/. This is a picture of juice. It represents the long sound of vowel **u**. This is the long sound of vowel **u**.

Sound-Spelling Correspondence

Write the word **trunk** on the board. Point out the vowel **u**. Point out the pattern CCVCC.

Say: Look at the word **trunk**. Read each sound. /t/ /r/ /u/ /n/ /k/. The vowel says its short sound. What is the word? **trunk**.

Say: Look at the word **truce**. Point: Does it have a vowel **e** at the end? Point: Then, vowel **u** says its name.

Say: Read each sound: /t/ /r/ /ū/ /c/. The **e** at the end is silent. It does not make a sound. What is the word? **truce.**

Model

Use BLM 119, #1.

Say: Look at the word **crust**. The vowel is in the middle. It says its short sound. Read each sound. /k/ /r/ /u/ /s/ /t/.
Say: Look at the word **crude**. **Point:** Does it have a vowel **e** at the end? **Point:** Then, vowel **u** says its name. Read each sound: /k/ /r/ /ū/ /d/. The **e** at the end is silent. It does not make a sound.
Say: Circle word(s) with the short **u** sound like **crust**. Draw a box around word(s) with the long **u** sound like **crude.**

Practice

Use BLM 119, # 2

Say: Look at the word **crumb**. The vowel is in the middle. Read each sound. /**k**/ /**r**/ /**u**/ /**m**/. What is the word? **crumb**.

Say: Look at the word **bugle**. Does it have a vowel **e** at the end? Then, vowel **u** says its name. Read each sound: /**b**/ /**ū**/ /**g**/ /**l**/. The **e** at the end is silent. It does not make a sound. What is the word? **bugle**.

Say: Write the letter **u** on the line for word(s) with a short **u** sound like **crumb**. Cross out the letter e at the end of word(s) with a long **u** sound like **bugle**.

Apply

Blend Words

Use BLM 119, #3.

Say: Look at each word. Think: Does it have a silent **e** at the end? Will the first vowel say its name? Look again, is the vowel in the middle? Will the vowel say its short sound?

Say: Now we are going to blend the sounds together by stretching them out as we read them. Point to each letter in a sweeping motion left to right /**bbb**/**rrr**/**ūūū**/**ttt**/. What is the word? **brute**.

Spelling

Use BLM 119, #4

Say: *Now we can practice writing the sounds we hear in each word. Call one word at a time, stretching each sound. Say the word slowly. Listen for the short or long vowel sound of vowel **u**. Do not forget the silent **e** at the end if you hear the vowel say its name.*

Conclusion

Ask: *What did we learn today?* We learned that the vowel **u** makes a short sound when it is in between two consonants. It makes the long sound /ū/, when vowel **e** is at the end. What pictures/words will help you remember the long sound /ū/ with the silent **e** at the end? What pictures or words will help you remember the short sound of vowel **u**?

Home Connection

Encourage students to practice identifying short vowel sound of **u** in CVC words and the long sound of **u** in CVCe words with a family member.

✔ Formative Assessment

If the student completes each task correctly, proceed to the next skill in the sequence. If not, refer to suggested Intervention 2.

Did the student...?	Intervention 2
Identify the name of the letter?	• Use physical rhythmic movements as the letter name is repeated. March while chanting the letter name. Move arms up and down. Sway from side to side.
Identify the sound of the letter?	• Use chants that repeat the sound several times then a word that includes the sound. **Example:** / / / / / / **bust** and / / / / / / **brute**
Produce the sound of the letter?	• Use mirrors to show movement of mouth, tongue, teeth as the sound is produced. Use hand over mouth to explore movement of air as the sound is produced.
Recognize the CVCe pattern?	• Arrange a list of common same vowel CVCe words vertically, point out pattern.
Know the name of pictures?	• Tell students the name of pictures, have student repeat it aloud. • Discuss meaning of word. Use word in context.

Name _____   **Date** _____

1. MODEL

_____   _____   _____

2. PRACTICE

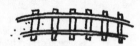      

_____   _____   _____

3. APPLY - BLEND WORDS

day   **raindrops**   **hay**

→   →

4. SPELLING

_____

_____

_____

Name _____ **Date** _____

1. MODEL

_____ _____ _____

2. PRACTICE

_____ _____ _____

3. APPLY - BLEND WORDS

boat   **toe**   **row**

→   →   →

4. SPELLING

_____

_____

_____

Name _____ **Date** _____

1. MODEL

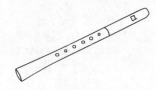 

_____ _____

2. PRACTICE

_____ _____

3. APPLY - BLEND WORDS

chew suit fuse

→ → →

4. SPELLING

_____

_____

Name _____ **Date** _____

1. MODEL

 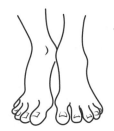 

_____   _____   _____

2. PRACTICE

 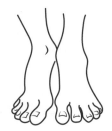 

_____   _____   _____

3. APPLY - BLEND WORDS

 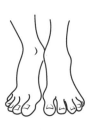 

dream   **feet**   **yield**

→   →   →

4. SPELLING

_____

_____

_____

Name _____ **Date** _____

1. MODEL

_____   _____   _____

2. PRACTICE

_____   _____   _____

3. APPLY - BLEND WORDS

cry → high → bicycle →

4. SPELLING

_____

_____

_____

Name _____   **Date** _____

1. MODEL

_____   _____   _____

2. PRACTICE

_____   _____   _____

3. APPLY - BLEND WORDS

yarn   **park**   **barn**

→   →   →

4. SPELLING

_____

_____

Name _____   Date _____

1. MODEL

_____   _____   _____

2. PRACTICE

_____   _____   _____

3. APPLY - BLEND WORDS

turn   **herd**   **dirt**

→   →   →

4. SPELLING

_____

_____

_____

Name _____ **Date** _____

1. MODEL

  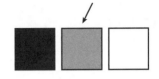

_____ _____ _____

2. PRACTICE

  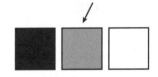

_____ _____ _____

3. APPLY - BLEND WORDS

butter **trumpet** **pencil**

⟶ ⟶ ⟶

4. SPELLING

_____

_____

_____

Name _____ **Date** _____

Directions: Add the suffix ing-. Then write the new word.

1. MODEL

 sing   sing_____

 teach   teach_____

2. PRACTICE

 collect   collect_____

 paint   paint_____

3. APPLY-BLEND WORDS

act

→

actor

→

Name _____ Date _____

1. MODEL

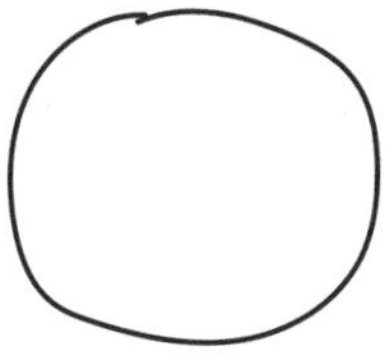

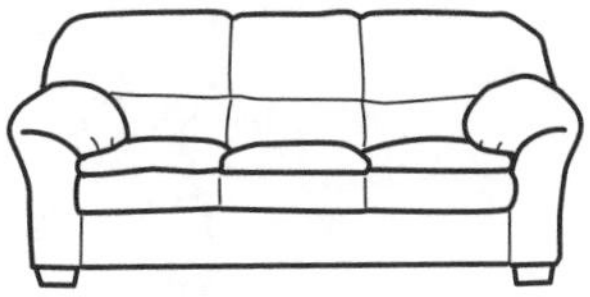

2. PRACTICE

3. APPLY - BLEND WORDS

turtle

→

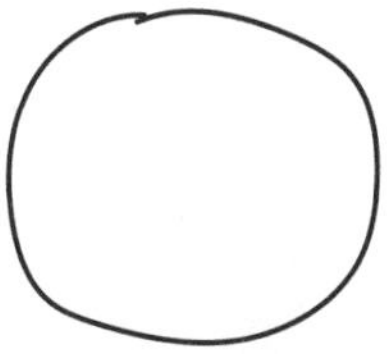

circle

→

middle

→

4. SPELLING

_____

_____

_____

Name _____ **Date** _____

1. MODEL

2. PRACTICE

_____ _____

3. APPLY – BLEND WORDS

play

→

playing

→

played

→

Name _____ **Date** _____

1. MODEL

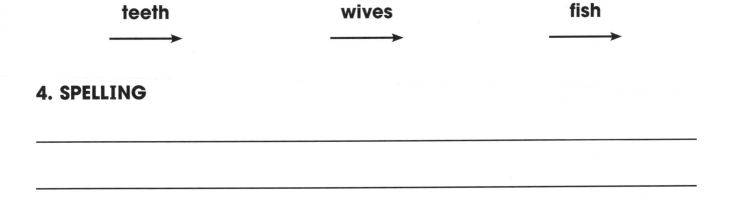

_____   _____   _____

2. PRACTICE

_____   _____   _____

3. APPLY - BLEND WORDS

teeth →   wives →   fish →

4. SPELLING

_____

_____

_____

Name _____ **Date** _____

1. MODEL

2. PRACTICE

_____ _____ _____

3. APPLY - BLEND WORDS

 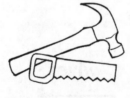 

book **tools** **noon**

→ → →

4. SPELLING

_____

_____

_____

Name _____ **Date** _____

1. MODEL

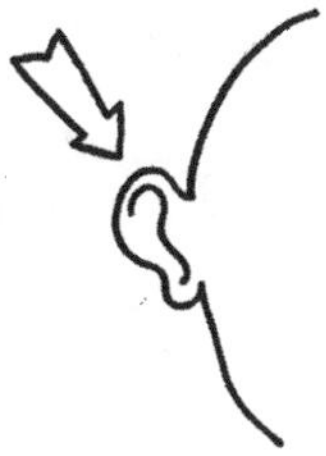

2. PRACTICE

_____ _____ _____

3. APPLY – BLEND WORDS

mouse

→

town

→

4. SPELLING

_____

_____

_____

Name _____ **Date** _____

1. MODEL

2. PRACTICE

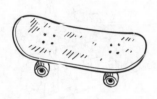  

_____ _____ _____

3. APPLY - BLEND WORDS

horse   storm   skateboard

→   →   →

4. SPELLING

_____

_____

_____

Name _____   Date _____

1. MODEL

A

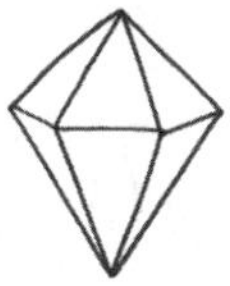

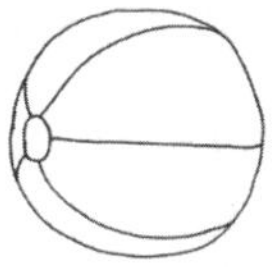

B

2. PRACTICE

A

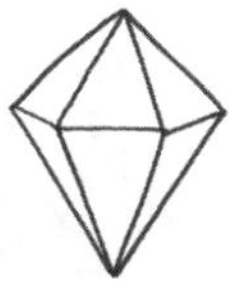

_____   _____   _____

B

_____   _____   _____

3. APPLY - BLEND WORDS

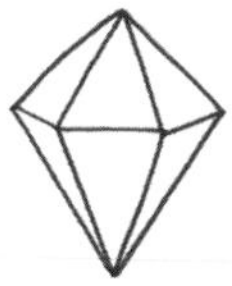

gem
→

magic
→

cell
→

face
→

4. SPELLING

_____

_____

_____

Benchmark Advance • Intervention • Phonics and Word Recognition • Grade 3   **255**

Name _____ Date _____

1. MODEL

2. PRACTICE

_____   _____

3. APPLY - BLEND WORDS

oil   joy

→   →

4. SPELLING

_____

_____

_____

Name _____ **Date** _____

Directions: Add the suffixes *–ful*, *–less*.

MODEL

1. care   careful   care   careless

PRACTICE

2. faith   faith_____   flaw   flaw_____

3. fright   fright_____   home   home_____

4. mercy   merci_____   mercy   merci_____

APPLY

5. sorrow   sorrow_____   defense   defense_____

6. plenty   plenti_____   power   power_____

7. power   power_____   motion   motion_____

Name _____ **Date** _____

Directions: Add the prefix *un–*.

MODEL

1. lock   _____lock

PRACTICE

2. able   _____able

3. aware   _____aware

APPLY

4. available   _____available

5. tie   _____tie

6. tie   untie   available   unavailable

   ⟶   ⟶

Name _____ **Date** _____

Directions: Add prefixes *de–*, *dis–*. Then write the new word.

MODEL

1. belief   _____belief   _____

PRACTICE

2. ice   _____ice   _____

3. form   _____form   _____

4. code   _____code   _____

APPLY

5. like   _____like   _____

6. own   _____own   _____

7. connect   _____connect   _____

Name _____ Date _____

MODEL

Directions: Underline the suffix.

1. sensible   **detachable**   **removable**

PRACTICE

Directions: Underline the suffix.

2. comical   **horrible**   **terrible**

3. visible   **incredible**

APPLY

Directions: Add the suffix.

4. accept   **suggest_____**

5. access   **renew_____**   **detach_____**

Write your own word with the suffix *–ible* or *–able*. _____

Name _____ **Date** _____

Directions: Add the prefix *re–*. Then write the new word.

MODEL

1. name   _____name   _____

PRACTICE

2. fresh   _____fresh   _____

3. write   _____write   _____

4. visit   _____visit   _____

APPLY

5. state   _____state   _____

6. load   _____load   _____

7. inform   _____inform   _____

Name _____ **Date** _____

Directions: Add the prefix *mis–*. Then write the new word.

MODEL

1. treat   _____treat   _____

PRACTICE

2. dial   _____dial   _____

3. fire   _____fire   _____

4. print   _____print   _____

APPLY

5. handle   _____handle   _____

6. direct   _____direct   _____

7. grade   _____grade   _____

Name _____ **Date** _____

Directions: Add the prefixes *trans–*, *inter–*. Then write the new word.

MODEL

   1. state   _____state   _____

PRACTICE

   2. port   _____port   _____

   3. action   _____action   _____

   4. Pacific   _____Pacific   _____

APPLY

   5. faith   _____faith   _____

   6. office   _____office   _____

   7. city   _____city   _____

Name _____ Date _____

Directions: Add the suffixes *-ment*, *-tion.* Then write the new word.

MODEL

1. adopt   adopt_____   _____

PRACTICE

2. develop   develop_____   _____

3. except   except_____   _____

4. object   object_____   _____

APPLY

5. announce   announce_____   _____

6. arrange   arrange_____   _____

7. move   move_____   _____

Name _____ Date _____

Directions: Add the suffixes *-ous*, *-eous*, *-ious*. Then write the new word.

MODEL

1. joy   joy_____   _____

PRACTICE

2. mystery   myster_____   _____

3. ceremony   ceremon_____   _____

4. glory   glor_____   _____

APPLY

5. advantage   advantag_____   _____

6. gas   gas_____   _____

7. courtesy   courte_____   _____

Name _____ **Date** _____

Directions: Add the suffixes *-ive*, *-ative*, *-itive*. Then write the new word.

MODEL

1. protect   protect_____   _____

PRACTICE

2. add   add_____   _____

3. define   defin_____   _____

4. compete   compet_____   _____

APPLY

5. imagine   imagin_____   _____

6. compare   compar_____   _____

7. cure   cure_____   _____

Name _____   **Date** _____

Directions: Add the suffixes *–ology, –graphic, –graphy.* Then write the new word.

MODEL

1. geo   geo_____   _____

PRACTICE

2. bio   bio_____   _____

3. photo   photo_____   _____

4. video   video_____   _____

APPLY

5. planet   planet_____   _____

6. ocean   ocean_____   _____

7. criminal   crimin_____   _____

Name _____ **Date** _____

Directions: Add the suffixes *-phobia*, *-scope*. Then write the new word.

MODEL

1. tele   tele_____   _____

PRACTICE

2. aqua   aqua_____   _____

3. claustra   claustra_____   _____

4. arachna   arachna_____   _____

APPLY

5. night   night_____   _____

6. stetho   stetho_____   _____

7. peri   peri_____   _____

Name _____ Date _____

Directions: Add the suffixes *-ory, -ist*. Then write the new word.

MODEL

1. guitar   guitar_____   _____

PRACTICE

2. direct   direct_____   _____

3. explore   explora_____   _____

4. labor   laborat_____   _____

APPLY

5. piano   pian_____   _____

6. cartoon   cartoon_____   _____

7. style   styl_____   _____

Name _____ Date _____

Directions: Add the suffixes *-ate*, *-fy*. Then write the new word.

MODEL

1. beauty   beauti_____   _____

PRACTICE

2. accent   accentu_____   _____

3. alter   altern_____   _____

4. circle   circul_____   _____

APPLY

5. simple   simpli_____   _____

6. glory   glori_____   _____

7. pure   puri_____   _____

Name _____ **Date** _____

1. MODEL

2. PRACTICE

 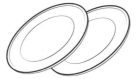

_____ _____

3. APPLY - BLEND WORDS

keys

benches

→

→

4. SPELLING

_____

_____

_____

Name _____ **Date** _____

1. MODEL

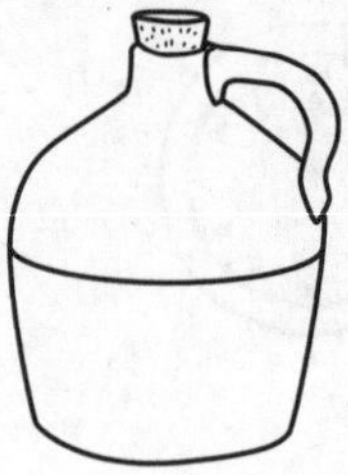

_____   _____

2. PRACTICE

_____   _____

3. APPLY – BLEND WORDS

view
→

future
→

juice
→

4. SPELLING

_____

_____

_____

Name _____ **Date** _____

1. MODEL

_____ _____ _____

2. PRACTICE

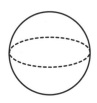  

_____ _____ _____

3. APPLY - BLEND WORDS

 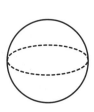 

spear **sphere** **cheers**

→ → →

4. SPELLING

_____

_____

_____

Name _____   Date _____

1. MODEL

_____   _____   _____

2. PRACTICE

_____   _____   _____

3. APPLY - BLEND WORDS

hair   **share**   **square**

→   →   →

4. SPELLING

_____

_____

_____

Name _____ **Date** _____

1. MODEL

scoop   stop   bruise

2. PRACTICE

spoon   screw   bruise

3. APPLY - BLEND WORDS

   stoop   newt   bruise

   →   →   →

4. SPELLING

_____

_____

_____

Name _____ **Date** _____

MODEL

1. grab   grabbed   grabbing

2. change   changed   changing

3. PRACTICE

      grabbed   changing   changed

_____   _____   _____

4. APPLY - BLEND WORDS

      grabbing   grabbed   changed

      ——→   ——→   ——→

5. SPELLING

_____

_____

_____

Name _____ **Date** _____

1. MODEL

scare   juice   mess

_____   _____   _____

2. PRACTICE

busy   merry   quick

_____   _____   _____

3. APPLY - BLEND WORDS

greedily   hungrily   totally

$\longrightarrow$ $\longrightarrow$ $\longrightarrow$

4. SPELLING

_____

_____

_____

Name _____ **Date** _____

1. MODEL

elf   moose   leaf

_____   _____   _____

2. PRACTICE

women   leaves   geese

_____   _____   _____

3. APPLY – BLEND WORDS

lives   children   wolves

⟶   ⟶   ⟶

4. SPELLING

_____

_____

_____

Name _____ **Date** _____

1. MODEL

2. PRACTICE

_____ _____ _____

3. APPLY - BLEND WORDS

shell   **grass**   **cliff**

→   →   →

4. SPELLING

_____

_____

_____

Name _____ **Date** _____

1. MODEL

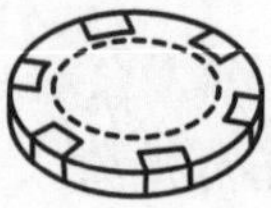

2. PRACTICE

_____ _____ _____

3. APPLY - BLEND WORDS

slip →

plant →

black →

4. SPELLING

_____

_____

_____

Name _____ **Date** _____

1. MODEL

2. PRACTICE

   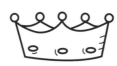   

_____ _____ _____

3. APPLY - BLEND WORDS

crown ⟶   **frown** ⟶   **bright** ⟶

4. SPELLING

_____

_____

_____

Name _____ **Date** _____

1. MODEL

2. PRACTICE

_____ _____ _____

3. APPLY - BLEND WORDS

blast **stump** **snail**

→ → →

4. SPELLING

_____

_____

Name _____ **Date** _____

MODEL

1.

2.

3.

4. PRACTICE

_____ _____ _____

5. APPLY - BLEND WORDS

stamp
→

round
→

peppermint
→

6. SPELLING

_____

_____

_____

Name _____ **Date** _____

MODEL

1.

2.

3.

4. PRACTICE

_____ | _____ | _____

5. APPLY - BLEND WORDS

track

→

stitch

→

chick

→

6. SPELLING

_____

_____

_____

Name _____ **Date** _____

1. MODEL

2. PRACTICE

_____ _____ _____

3. APPLY - BLEND WORDS

brush **shirt** **clash**

→ → →

4. SPELLING

_____

_____

_____

Name _____ **Date** _____

MODEL

1.

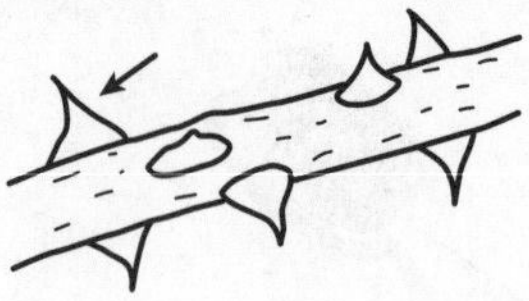

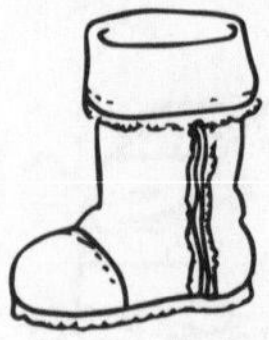

2.

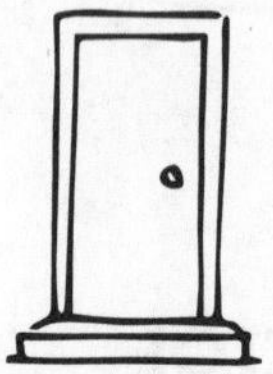

3. PRACTICE

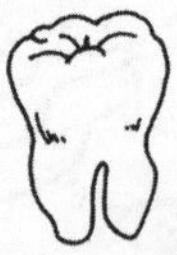

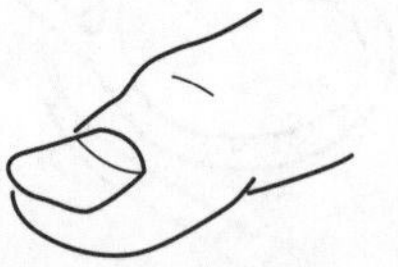

_____ _____ _____

4. APPLY - BLEND WORDS

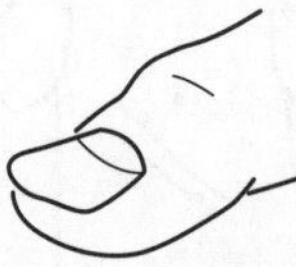

wheat

→

thumb

→

month

→

5. SPELLING

_____

_____

_____

Name _____ Date _____

MODEL

1. climbs

2. climbing

3. climbed

4. PRACTICE

climbs   climbing   climbed

_____   _____   _____

5. APPLY - BLEND WORDS

climbing   climbs   climbed
⟶   ⟶   ⟶

6. SPELLING

_____

_____

_____

Name _____ **Date** _____

MODEL

1.

2.

3. PRACTICE

4. APPLY – BLEND WORDS

dark **darker** **darkest**

5. SPELLING

_____

_____

_____

Name _____ **Date** _____

1. MODEL

pumpkin
→

happy
→

hamster
→

2. PRACTICE

dentist
→

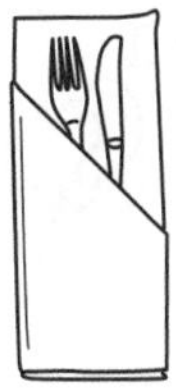

napkin
→

pumpkin
→

_____ _____ _____

3. APPLY - BLEND WORDS

napkin
→

hamster
→

dentist
→

4. SPELLING

_____

_____

_____

Name _____ **Date** _____

1. MODEL

A

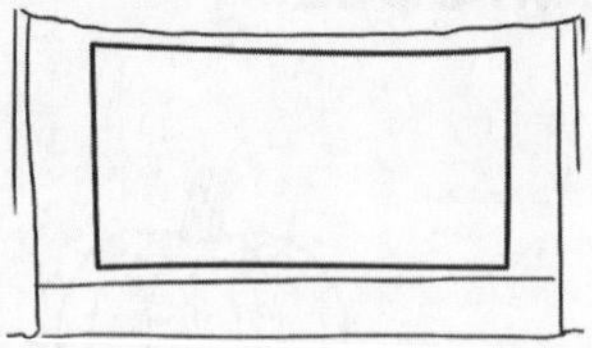

B

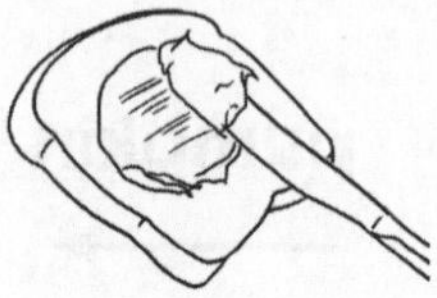

C

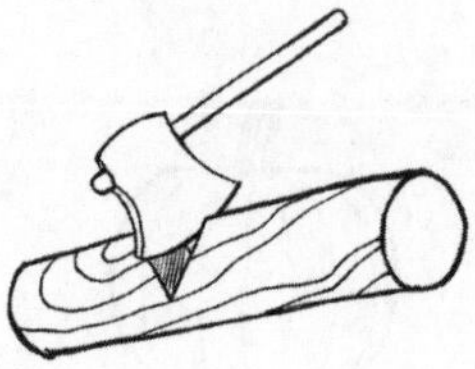

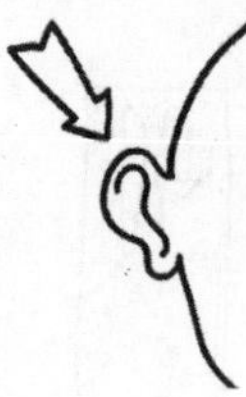

2. PRACTICE

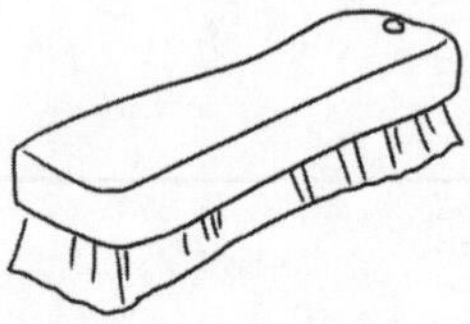

_____ _____ _____ _____

3. APPLY

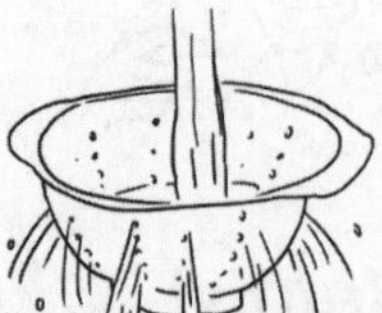

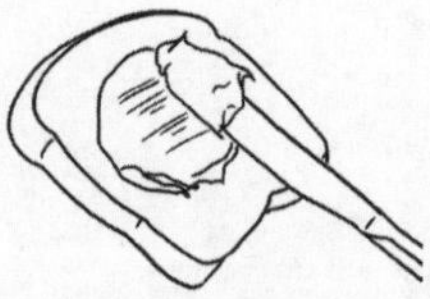

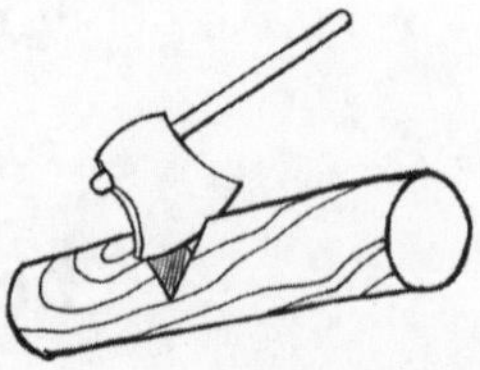

4. SPELLING

_____

_____

_____

Name _____ **Date** _____

1. MODEL

A

B

2. PRACTICE

A

_____ _____ _____

B

_____ _____ _____

3. APPLY

4. SPELLING

_____ _____ _____ _____

Name _____ **Date** _____

1. MODEL

2. PRACTICE

_____ _____

3. APPLY – BLEND WORDS

scale   sale

→   →

4. SPELLING

_____

_____

Name _____ **Date** _____

1. MODEL

2. PRACTICE

 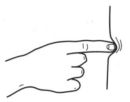

_____ _____

3. APPLY - BLEND WORDS

 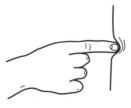

lone **poke**

→ →

4. SPELLING

_____

_____

Name _____ **Date** _____

1. MODEL

2. PRACTICE

_____ _____

3. APPLY - BLEND WORDS

slide   Nile

→   →

4. SPELLING

_____

_____

_____

Name _____ Date _____

1. MODEL

2. PRACTICE

_____   _____

3. APPLY - BLEND WORDS

flute   **glue**

$\longrightarrow$ $\longrightarrow$

4. SPELLING

_____

_____

_____

Name _____ Date _____

1. MODEL

2. PRACTICE

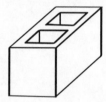  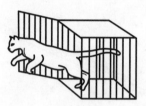

_____ _____ _____

3. APPLY - BLEND WORDS

athlete   **cascade**   **extreme**   **ignore**

4. SPELLING

_____

_____

_____

Name _____ **Date** _____

1. MODEL

2. PRACTICE

_____ _____ _____

3. APPLY - BLEND WORDS

chain **braid** **train**

→ → →

4. SPELLING

_____

_____

_____

Name _____ **Date** _____

1. MODEL

2. PRACTICE

_____ _____ _____

3. APPLY - BLEND WORDS

float **grown** **cloak**

→ → →

4. SPELLING

_____

_____

Name _____ **Date** _____

1. MODEL

2. PRACTICE

_____ _____ _____

3. APPLY - BLEND WORDS

chief **wheel** **bleach**

→ → →

4. SPELLING

_____

_____

_____

Name _____ Date _____

1. MODEL

2. PRACTICE

_____ _____ _____

3. APPLY - BLEND WORDS

light   **grind**   **night**

→   →   →

4. SPELLING

_____

_____

_____

Name _____ **Date** _____

1. MODEL

3      

2. PRACTICE

3      

_____   _____   _____

3. APPLY - BLEND WORDS

3      

three   **pie**   **frozen**

→   →   →

4. SPELLING

_____

_____

_____

Name _____ **Date** _____

1. MODEL

2. PRACTICE

_____ _____ _____

3. APPLY - BLEND WORDS

farmer   **garden**   **shark**

→   →   →

4. SPELLING

_____

_____

_____

Name _____ **Date** _____

1. MODEL

2. PRACTICE

_____ _____ _____

3. APPLY - BLEND WORDS

horn **sword** **cord**

→ → →

4. SPELLING

_____

_____

_____

Name _____ **Date** _____

1. MODEL

2. PRACTICE

_____ _____ _____

3. APPLY - BLEND WORDS

skirt **surf** **fern**

→ → →

4. SPELLING

_____

_____

_____

Name _____ **Date** _____

1. MODEL

_____ _____ _____ _____

2. PRACTICE

_____ _____

3. APPLY - BLEND WORDS

mouse **town**

⟶ ⟶

4. SPELLING

_____

_____

_____

Benchmark Advance • Intervention • Phonics and Word Recognition • Grade 3 **305**

Name _____ **Date** _____

1. MODEL

_____   _____   _____

2. PRACTICE

_____   _____

3. APPLY - BLEND WORDS

oil   joy

→   →

4. SPELLING

_____

_____

_____

Name _____ **Date** _____

1. MODEL

Grl_ea129_cat

2. PRACTICE

_____ _____ _____

3. APPLY - BLEND WORDS

cook → **tools** →

4. SPELLING

_____

_____

_____

Name _____ **Date** _____

MODEL

1.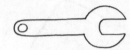

2.

3.

4. PRACTICE

_____ _____ _____

5. APPLY - BLEND WORDS

knot **gnaws** **wreath**

→ → →

6. SPELLING

_____

_____

_____

Name _____   Date _____

1. MODEL

A

crawl 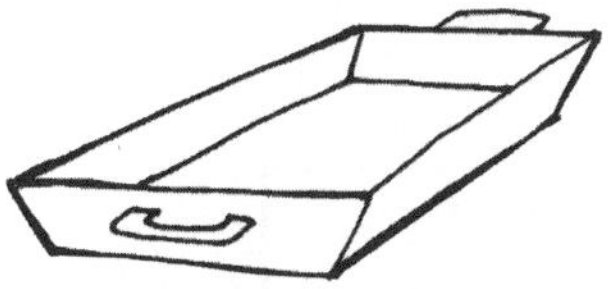   tray    straw

B

saucer    faucet    teapot

C

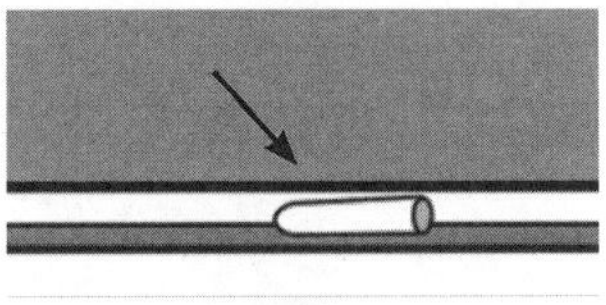

chalk    stove    stalk

2. PRACTICE

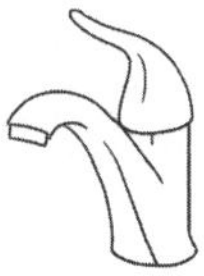

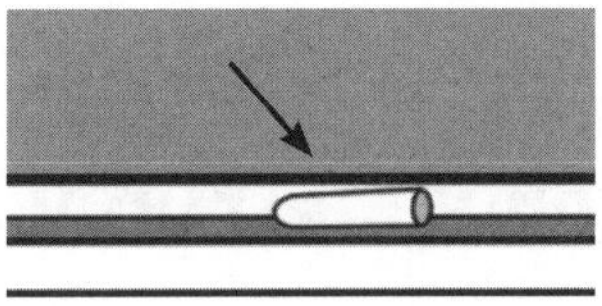

_____   _____   _____

3. APPLY – BLEND WORDS

distraught  →   saucer  →   straw →

4. SPELLING

_____

_____

_____

Name _____ Date _____

1. MODEL

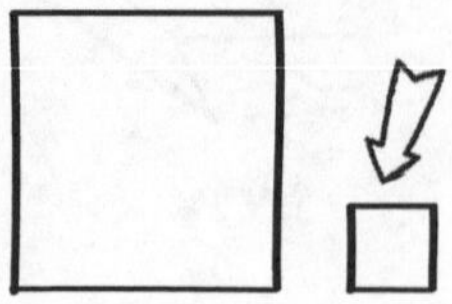

2. PRACTICE

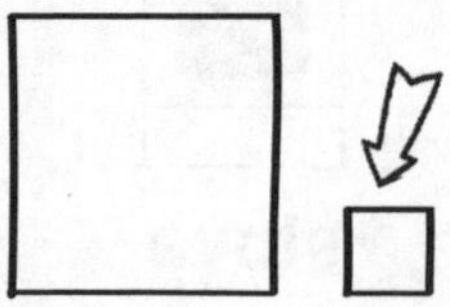

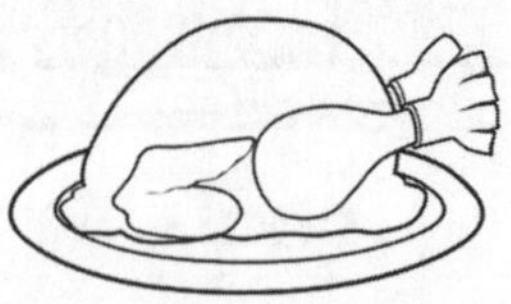

_____ _____ _____

3. APPLY - BLEND WORDS

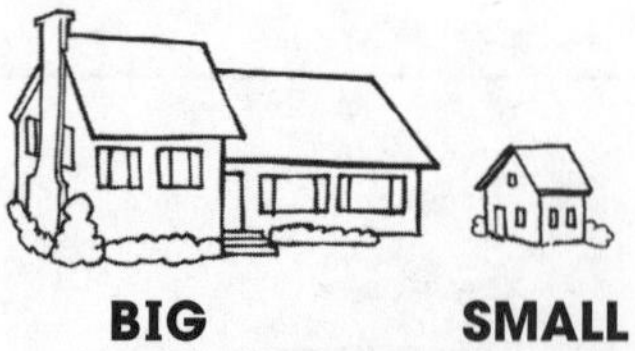

BIG   **SMALL**

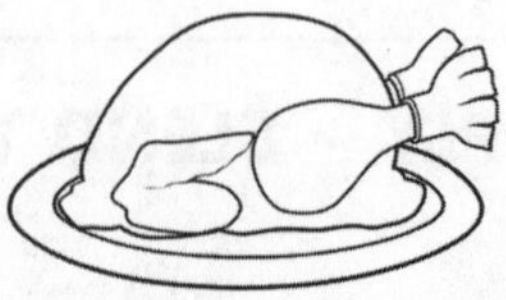

family   **tiny**   **turkey**

→   →   →

4. SPELLING

_____

_____

_____

Name _____ **Date** _____

1. MODEL

2. PRACTICE

_____   _____   _____

3. APPLY - BLEND WORDS

needle   **pickle**   **candle**

→   →   →

4. SPELLING

_____

_____

_____

Benchmark Advance • Intervention • Phonics and Word Recognition • Grade 3   **311**

Name _____ **Date** _____

1. MODEL

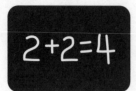  

2. PRACTICE

_____ _____ _____

3. APPLY - BLEND WORDS

math →   **meat** →   **mash** →

4. SPELLING

_____

_____

Name _____ Date _____

1. MODEL

2. PRACTICE

_____ _____ _____

3. APPLY - BLEND WORDS

star **stairs** **store**

⟶ ⟶ ⟶

4. SPELLING

_____

_____

_____

Name _____ **Date** _____

1. MODEL

2. PRACTICE

_____ _____ _____

3. APPLY - BLEND WORDS

  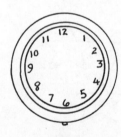

test   turkey   time

→   →   →

4. SPELLING

_____

_____

Name _____ **Date** _____

1. MODEL

2. PRACTICE

_____ _____ _____

3. APPLY - BLEND WORDS

nail **noon** **neat**

⟶ ⟶ ⟶

4. SPELLING

_____

_____

_____

Name _____   Date _____

1. MODEL

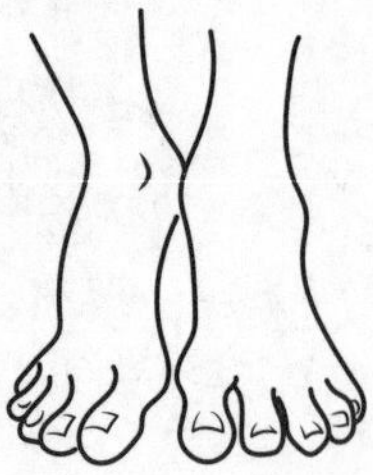

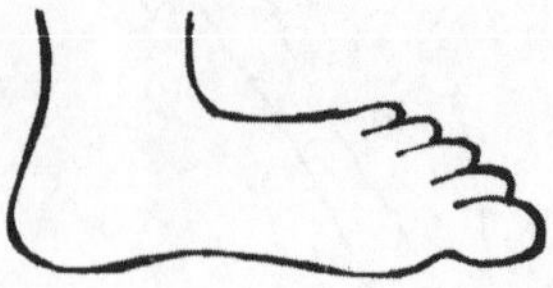

2. PRACTICE

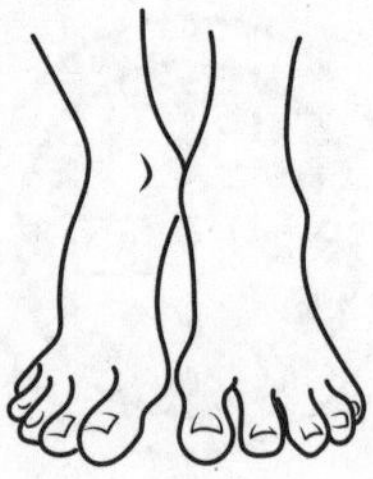

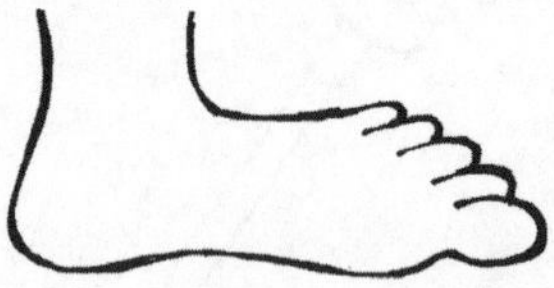

_____   _____   _____

3. APPLY - BLEND WORDS

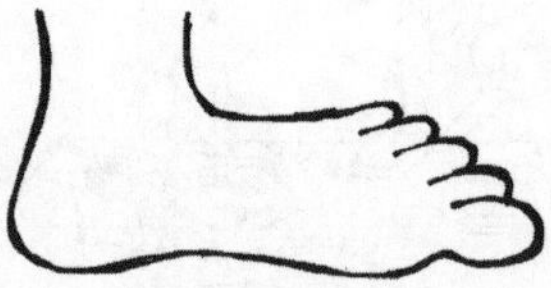

foot

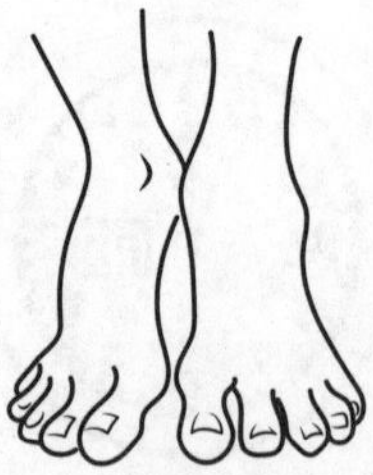

→

feet

→

fruit

→

4. SPELLING

_____

_____

_____

Name _____ **Date** _____

1. MODEL

2. PRACTICE

_____ _____ _____

3. APPLY - BLEND WORDS

peek →   pail →   plow →

4. SPELLING

_____

_____

_____

Name _____ **Date** _____

1. MODEL

2. PRACTICE

_____   _____   _____

3. APPLY - BLEND WORDS

cook **cloud** **coat**

→ → →

4. SPELLING

_____

_____

_____

Name _____ **Date** _____

1. MODEL

2. PRACTICE

_____ _____ _____

3. APPLY - BLEND WORDS

house   heel   hair

⟶   ⟶   ⟶

4. SPELLING

_____

_____

_____

Name _____ **Date** _____

1. MODEL

2. PRACTICE

_____ _____ _____

3. APPLY - BLEND WORDS

beaver **beetle** **book**

→ → →

4. SPELLING

_____

_____

_____

Name _____ **Date** _____

1. MODEL

2. PRACTICE

_____ _____ _____

3. APPLY - BLEND WORDS

rain   **roof**   **ram**

→   →   →

4. SPELLING

_____

_____

_____

Name _____   Date _____

1. MODEL

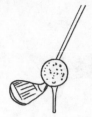      

2. PRACTICE

_____   _____   _____

3. APPLY - BLEND WORDS

gear   **goat**   **grass**

→   →   →

4. SPELLING

_____

_____

_____

Name _____ **Date** _____

1. MODEL

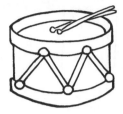   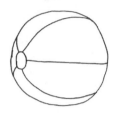

2. PRACTICE

_____ _____ _____

3. APPLY - BLEND WORDS

drum   **desk**   **duck**

⟶   ⟶   ⟶

4. SPELLING

_____

_____

_____

Name _____ **Date** _____

1. MODEL

  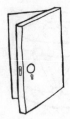

2. PRACTICE

  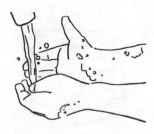

_____ _____ _____

3. APPLY - BLEND WORDS

  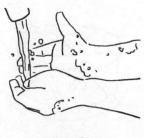

wind **well** **wash**

→ → →

4. SPELLING

_____

_____

_____

Name _____ **Date** _____

1. MODEL

2. PRACTICE

_____ _____ _____

3. APPLY - BLEND WORDS

loop → **lamb** → **laugh** →

4. SPELLING

_____

_____

_____

Name _____ **Date** _____

1. MODEL

2. PRACTICE

_____   _____   _____

3. APPLY - BLEND WORDS

jail   **jeans**   **jar**

→   →   →

4. SPELLING

_____

_____

_____

Name _____ **Date** _____

1. MODEL

2. PRACTICE

_____   _____   _____

3. APPLY – BLEND WORDS

kilt   **koala**   **kite**

$\longrightarrow$ $\longrightarrow$ $\longrightarrow$

4. SPELLING

_____

_____

_____

Name _____ **Date** _____

1. MODEL

2. PRACTICE

_____ _____ _____

3. APPLY - BLEND WORDS

math   **yolk**   **yawn**

→   →   →

4. SPELLING

_____

_____

Name _____ **Date** _____

1. MODEL

2. PRACTICE

_____ _____ _____

3. APPLY - BLEND WORDS

view **vine** **veil**

→ → →

4. SPELLING

_____

_____

_____

Name _____ **Date** _____

1. MODEL

2. PRACTICE

_____ _____ _____

3. APPLY - BLEND WORDS

quiet   quarter   quail

→   →   →

4. SPELLING

_____

_____

_____

Name _____ **Date** _____

1. MODEL

2. PRACTICE

  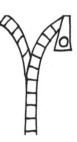

_____   _____   _____

3. APPLY - BLEND WORDS

zipper   **zero**   **zebra**

→   →   →

4. SPELLING

_____

_____

_____

Name _____ **Date** _____

1. MODEL

2. PRACTICE

_____ _____ _____

3. APPLY - BLEND WORDS

swim   team   steam

→   →   →

4. SPELLING

_____

_____

Name _____ **Date** _____

1. MODEL

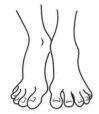  

2. PRACTICE

 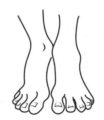 

_____ _____ _____

3. APPLY - BLEND WORDS

 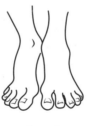 

coat   **feet**   **root**

→   →   →

4. SPELLING

_____

_____

_____

Name _____ Date _____

1. MODEL

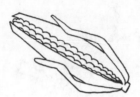

2. PRACTICE

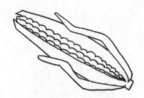
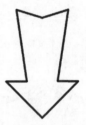

_____   _____   _____

3. APPLY - BLEND WORDS

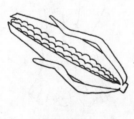

barn   **corn**   **down**

→   →   →

4. SPELLING

_____

_____

_____

Name _____ **Date** _____

1. MODEL

2. PRACTICE

_____ _____ _____

3. APPLY - BLEND WORDS

soap ⟶   **sleep** ⟶   **sheep** ⟶

4. SPELLING

_____

_____

_____

Name _____ **Date** _____

1. MODEL

2. PRACTICE

      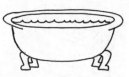

_____   _____   _____

3. APPLY - BLEND WORDS

      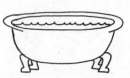

scrub   **shrub**   **tub**

→   →   →

4. SPELLING

_____

_____

Name _____ **Date** _____

1. MODEL

2. PRACTICE

_____ _____ _____

3. APPLY - BLEND WORDS

wig **egg** **bug**

→ → →

4. SPELLING

_____

_____

_____

Name _____ **Date** _____

1. MODEL

2. PRACTICE

_____ _____ _____

3. APPLY - BLEND WORDS

food **head** **toad**

→ → →

4. SPELLING

_____

_____

Name _____ **Date** _____

1. MODEL

2. PRACTICE

_____ _____ _____

3. APPLY - BLEND WORDS

box **sax** **pox**

→ → →

4. SPELLING

_____

_____

_____

Name _____ **Date** _____

1. MODEL

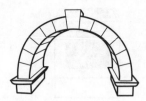      

2. PRACTICE

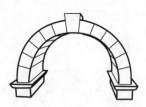      

_____   _____   _____

3. APPLY – BLEND WORDS

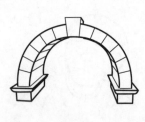      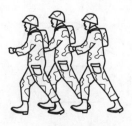

arch   **actor**   **army**

→   →   →

4. SPELLING

_____

_____

_____

Name _____ **Date** _____

1. MODEL

   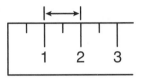

2. PRACTICE

   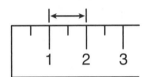

_____ _____ _____

3. APPLY - BLEND WORDS

   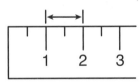

image   **inch**   **itch**

→   →   →

4. SPELLING

_____

_____

_____

Name _____ **Date** _____

1. MODEL

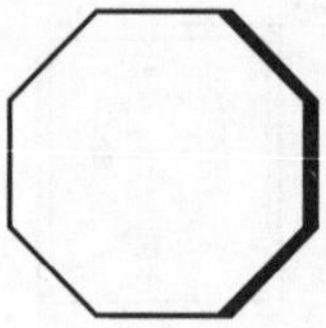

2. PRACTICE

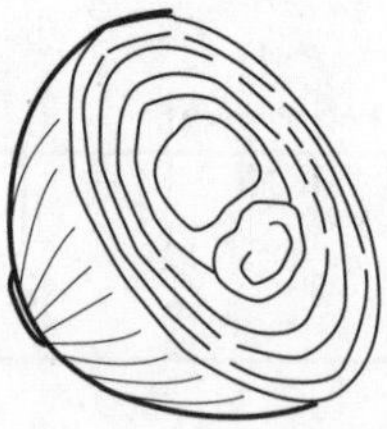

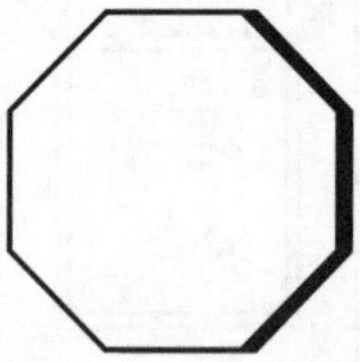

_____ _____ _____

3. APPLY - BLEND WORDS

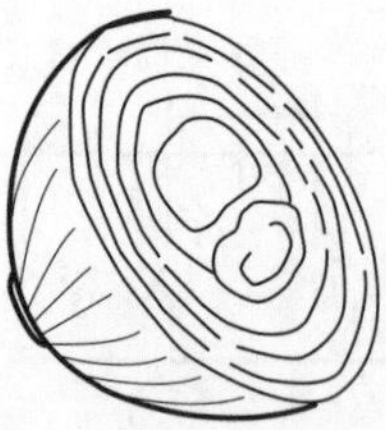

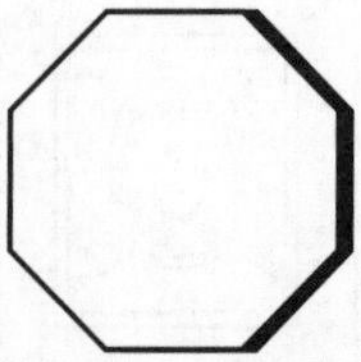

olive **onion** **octagon**

→ → →

4. SPELLING

_____

_____

Name _____ Date _____

1. MODEL

2. PRACTICE

 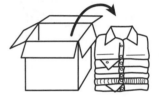

_____ _____ _____

3. APPLY - BLEND WORDS

  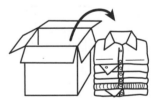

unicorn **unbrella** **unpack**

→ → →

4. SPELLING

_____

_____

_____

Name _____ **Date** _____

1. MODEL

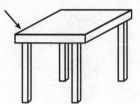 

2. PRACTICE

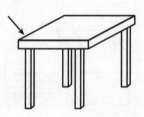  

_____ _____ _____

3. APPLY - BLEND WORDS

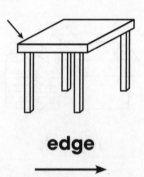  

edge   eraser   empty

→   →   →

4. SPELLING

_____

_____

_____

Name _____ Date _____

1. MODEL

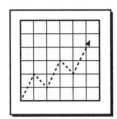      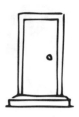

2. PRACTICE

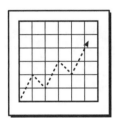   

_____   _____   _____

3. APPLY - BLEND WORDS

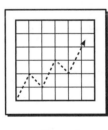   

chart   **flash**   **glass**

⟶   ⟶   ⟶

4. SPELLING

_____

_____

_____

Name _____ **Date** _____

1. MODEL

2. PRACTICE

_____ _____ _____

3. APPLY - BLEND WORDS

drink chimp twins

→ → →

4. SPELLING

_____

_____

_____

Name _____ **Date** _____

1. MODEL

2. PRACTICE

_____ _____ _____

3. APPLY - BLEND WORDS

floss   clock   sock

$\longrightarrow$ $\longrightarrow$ $\longrightarrow$

4. SPELLING

_____

_____

_____

Name _____ **Date** _____

1. MODEL

2. PRACTICE

_____ _____ _____

3. APPLY – BLEND WORDS

plug   **drums**   **brush**

→   →   →

4. SPELLING

_____

_____

Name _____ **Date** _____

1. MODEL

2. PRACTICE

      **7**

_____ _____ _____

3. APPLY - BLEND WORDS

      **7**

cent   **blend**   **seven**

⟶   ⟶   ⟶

4. SPELLING

_____

_____

_____

Name _____ **Date** _____

1. MODEL

amaze

mask

2. PRACTICE

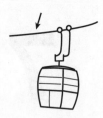

cable

fable

3. APPLY - BLEND WORDS

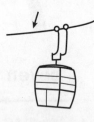

cable

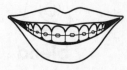

braces

4. SPELLING

_____

_____

Name _____ **Date** _____

1. MODEL

phone

baby

2. PRACTICE

smoke

stove

3. APPLY - BLEND WORDS

slope

→

rope

→

4. SPELLING

_____

_____

_____

Name _____ **Date** _____

1. MODEL

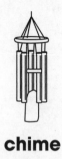

chime

gift

2. PRACTICE

shine

mice

3. APPLY - BLEND WORDS

grime

→

dime

→

4. SPELLING

_____

_____

Name _____ **Date** _____

1. MODEL

statue

worm

2. PRACTICE

argue

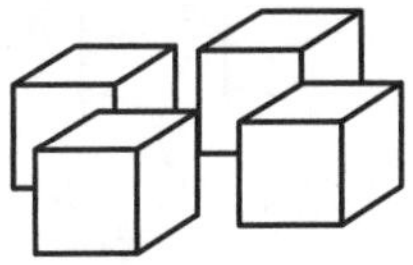

cubes

3. APPLY - BLEND WORDS

argue

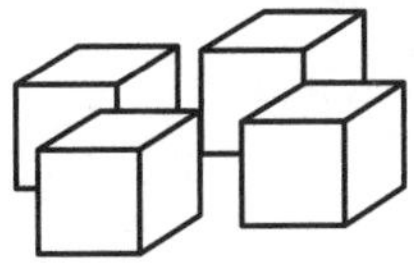

→

cubes

→

4. SPELLING

_____

_____

_____

Name _____ **Date** _____

1. MODEL

weave

lemon

2. PRACTICE

cheese

geese

3. APPLY - BLEND WORDS

cheese

→

sneeze

→

4. SPELLING

_____

_____

_____

Name _____ Date _____

1. MODEL

blast   paste   track

2. PRACTICE

grass   trash   place

_____   _____   _____

3. APPLY

splash   whale   grape
⟶   ⟶   ⟶

4. SPELLING

_____

_____

_____

Name _____ **Date** _____

1. MODEL

| fifth | while | stick | tribe |

2. PRACTICE

| stink | prime | brink | write |

_____ _____ _____ _____

3. APPLY

thrive →   drink →   prize →   trick →

4. SPELLING

_____

_____

_____

Name _____ Date _____

1. MODEL

flop   slope   prop   store

2. PRACTICE

moth   grove   smock   stroke

_____   _____   _____   _____

3. APPLY

throne   stock   stole   flock

⟶   ⟶   ⟶   ⟶

4. SPELLING

_____

_____

_____

Name _____ Date _____

1. MODEL

crust   crude   stuck   cruise

2. PRACTICE

crumb   bugle   thumb   bruise

_____ _____ _____ _____

3. APPLY

brute   chunk   stuff   fluke

→   →   →   →

4. SPELLING

_____

_____

_____